HISTORY, RELIGION, AND ANTISEMITISM

▲

GAVIN I. LANGMUIR

UNIVERSITY OF CALIFORNIA PRESS
BERKELEY   LOS ANGELES   OXFORD

University of California Press
Berkeley and Los Angeles, California

University of California Press
Oxford, England

Copyright © 1990 by
The Regents of the University of California

Library of Congress Cataloging-in-Publication Data
Langmuir, Gavin I.
    History, religion, and antisemitism / Gavin I. Langmuir.
        p.   cm.
    Includes bibliographical references.
    ISBN 0-520-06141-1
    ISBN 0-520-07728-8 (ppb.)
    1. Religion—Study and teaching. 2. Historiography.
    3. Religion—Historiography.   4. Antisemitism.
    5. Christianity and antisemitism.   I. Title.
    BL41.L376   1990
    291'.07—dc20   89-78166
                                                         CIP

Printed in the United States of America

1   2   3   4   5   6   7   8   9

HISTORY,
RELIGION,
AND
ANTISEMITISM

CEl

University of California, Los Angeles

320 – 328

Contents

Contents

Preface

This is a book by a historian and addressed primarily to his fellow historians about something we all do one way or another. Whether or not historians focus on religious events, they write about—or pass over—religious phenomena. How they do so has changed from generation to generation and varied from historian to historian in each generation. Yet there has been remarkably little discussion about how historians should describe and explain religious phenomena, no obvious book to which one could turn. That relative silence contrasts markedly with the debates among sociologists, anthropologists, and social psychologists for whom religion and how to treat it has long been a central issue. Consequently, when I tried to decide for myself how I as a historian should discuss religious phenomena, I had to look closely at the approaches to religion in other disciplines.

For scholars in those disciplines, my summarizations of some of the most influential conceptions of religion in their fields and of the debates about them will be old hat. But I had to indicate my debt to them and also to make clear where I agreed or disagreed with them and why. Moreover, I could not assume that every historian would be familiar with the works I discussed. Yet if scholars in other disciplines may find much of what I have to say in chapters 4 to 6 all too familiar, I hope they will forgive my trespasses and find the reactions of a historian of some interest for their own work.

What made me ask how historians should discuss religion in their professional work was my work on the formation of antise-

mitism. It is impossible to write about the history of antisemitism—a subject on which the need for objectivity is peculiarly
obvious—without discussing religion, for religion is linked with
antisemitism, Genesis with genocide. No more than one can deny
a relation between Jews and Judaism can one ignore the historical
connection between Judaism, Christianity, and the intense hostility manifested against Jews in Europe in the nineteenth and
twentieth centuries. While there may be sharp disagreement
about the nature of the connections, few who have studied the
question seriously would now deny that there are connections. The
problem for the historian is not whether religion and antisemitism
were linked, but how. And to answer that question, the historian
has to take a professional stand on the much broader problem of
religion. How, and how far, can historians, as objective scholars
rather than as adherents of a religion or as denigrators of religion,
determine what are religious phenomena and describe and explain
them rationally and empirically?

The connections between the writing of history and conceptions
of religion pose a basic problem of historical method, for how
historians write about past human actions is inextricably influenced by the way they presently conceive of religion. The problem is vast and the range of data relevant to it almost limitless.
I have only scratched the surface. My approach has been nar-
rowed by my concern with the considerations that seemed most
relevant to the particular historical problem that preoccupied me,
the problem of antisemitism. That focus has its advantages, however. Attitudes toward Jews illustrate the problems involved in
historical discussions of religion in peculiarly acute and concrete
form, and my focus on them enabled me to restrict the issue to
somewhat manageable proportions. Even then my reach has ex-
ceeded my grasp, but I hope my efforts will encourage others to
pursue the problem further.

Many people made this book possible. A grant from the Pew
Foundation gave me time free to write. Stanley Holwitz, Shirley
Warren, and Nicholas Goodhue of the University of California
Press patiently provided invaluable encouragement and practical
help, and Mary L. Lombardi produced the index. My colleagues
at Stanford University, Arnold Eisen, George Fredrickson, Hes-
ter Gelber, and James Sheehan made various highly helpful sug-

gestions and criticisms. One anonymous reader for the Press deserves to be singled out for reading my manuscript with unusual care and making constructive suggestions that improved it greatly. To all of them my warm thanks. I would also like to thank Tavistock Publications, Ltd., London, for permission to quote passages by Clifford Geertz that first appeared in their publication, *Anthropological Approaches to the Study of Religion*, ed. M. Banton (London, 1966).

It is impossible, or course, to thank all the people to whom I and this book are indebted. Inevitably, when one deals with phenomena as enduring and massive as religion and antisemitism, the citations of particular works only acknowledge a small part of the author's debts. I have certainly been influenced by, and paraphrased unconsciously, many more books, teachers, and colleagues than I have cited in my notes. Thus I have not cited Frank Underhill or Crane Brinton, both now dead, though their gift of intelligent irreverence surely encouraged me to examine received ideas with a skeptical eye. Nor have I cited David M. Potter whose subtle mind and deep ethics influenced all who had the good fortune to know him. It is even more impossible to acknowledge all those who have influenced my thinking and enriched me by their lives, not their books. My gratitude to them can only be represented here by my thanks to Hugh W. Watson and to one other person who has helped me immeasurably by being herself, my wife Nelee (née Rainès-Lambé), to whom this book is dedicated.

Part One

Religion as a Problem for Historians

Chapter One

The Problem

Religion poses a problem for historians. Whether or not all human beings are religious, so many have been that historians of every place and period have to deal, directly or indirectly, with human conduct of the kind customarily categorized as religious. As historians strive to reconstruct and explain past human actions, they cannot help making many explicit or implicit assertions about religions and religious conduct. But how do they or how should they do so? Although religious scholars may base their work on their own religious beliefs, objective historians are not supposed either to base their work on religious beliefs or to assert the validity or invalidity of beliefs that are not susceptible of empirical verification. The usual solution, if we leave Marxist and other professedly reductionist historians aside, has been to bracket the problem, that is, to describe religions and religious conduct in the past without taking a position on their fundamental source, nature, or validity. But can historians in the present make assertions about religion in the past that do not depend on their own conception of religion?

For one enduring school of historiography, the positivist tradition that goes back to Ranke, there was no problem. Objective historians only report or record, so far as the evidence permits, what people in the past did and thought about what they were doing. When describing past religious activity, historians should repress their own convictions and content themselves with paraphrasing the language and concepts of the people they are studying. By describing what religion was thought to be then without

3

taking any position of their own on the problem of what it really was or is, historians can preserve their impartiality, leaving it up to their readers to interpret the historical record as they wish.

I will argue that, in fact, all historians infuse their descriptions of religious activity with their own interpretation and that historians who discuss past religious activity should indicate explicitly how they themselves understand or interpret "religious" phenomena. The neo-Rankian or positivist solution is no more satisfactory for dealing with religious conduct in the past than it is for dealing with any other aspect of history. Although positivistic history was a great advance, its claims of objectivity were considerably exaggerated. However impressive and apparently impartial the positivist depiction of the past, its web of magisterial, apparently impersonal, descriptive assertions camouflaged modern, often personal, interpretations of the human condition. It soon became apparent to historians with different outlooks that obvious biases were embedded in what purported to be purely objective accounts of the past. Faith in history without interpretation was further undermined at a more theoretical level as sociologists of knowledge and anthropologists demonstrated the extent to which human understanding was culturally conditioned. More recently, insights gained from semiotic and hermeneutic analyses and the work of people such as Michel Foucault, Hans-Georg Gadamer, and Hayden White, whatever one may think of their more extreme theses, have made the limitations of the positivist approach even more obvious.

We are now aware that the history historians write is not a transcript or recreation of the past as it was as a whole or of any entire section of it. What historians produce as history is a selective series of related verbal assertions about some aspects of some past human actions. Although those assertions must be verifiably based on evidence about the past, they are inspired by present interests, connected to one another according to present preconceptions or explicit hypotheses about the human condition, and worded so as to be meaningful to readers in the present, who understand their existence very differently from people in the past—and often very differently from any particular historian.

For these and other reasons, few, if any, historians would now support the more extreme claims of positivist history.[1] Most historians now formulate their problems and organize and frame their descriptions and analyses quite consciously according to their own conceptions of human and historical processes, conceptions they know were unknown to the people they study. To take an example relevant to antisemitism, the way the role of blacks or Jews in history is now described depends explicitly on assumptions very different from those of previous centuries. Similarly, it would be difficult to find a historian who described economic thought and activity in the past without introducing his or her own ideas and relying on recent economic theories or concepts. The same could be said of political or social history.

Yet if most historians are now very aware that they are advancing their own interpretations of human conduct in the past, that awareness is often muted when it comes to discussion of religions or religious activities, for three main reasons. In the first place, because religions express profound values, they are more like poetry or art than science, politics, or other pragmatic activities; and however much historians may have abandoned the positivist dream, most still pursue its ideal of objectivity or value-neutrality. Hence, although they may use highly rhetorical language, laden with connotations of value, in an effort to represent the drama of past beliefs to people in the present, they feel constrained to avoid making explanatory judgments of their own about religious activity. In the second place, historians do not want to offend their many readers who belong to religions. And in the third place, historians do not have their own professional conception of religion. They have few conceptual tools of their

---

1. Marc Bloch, *Métier d'historien* (Paris, 1952), p. 26: "But the moment we no longer resign ourselves to enregistering purely and simply the assertions of our [historical] witnesses, from the moment that we intend to force them to speak, even against their will—a questionnaire is more necessary than ever. That, indeed, is the first necessity of any well-conducted historical research. . . . Never, in any science, has passive observation been at all fruitful—supposing, moreover, that it is possible. . . . Indeed, let us not delude ourselves. It happens, doubtless, that the questionnaire remains purely instinctive. It is there nonetheless. Without the worker being conscious of it, its items are dictated by the affirmations and negations that his prior experiences have obscurely inscribed in his brain, by tradition, and by common sense, that is, all too often, by common prejudices."

own to determine what is a religion or whether some conduct is or is not religious. They therefore rely heavily on the beliefs of the people they study to make the decision for them.

When it comes to political, economic, or social activities, historians have a fund of modern, more or less technical, concepts and terms developed by political scientists, economists, sociologists, psychologists, anthropologists, demographers, and others, as well as by historians themselves, that enable them to categorize types of human action and to describe and analyze those activities in their own language without making value judgments—other than pragmatic judgments—about them. When it comes to describing religious activities, however, historians typically fall back on the solution of the positivist school. Typically, they do not specify the criteria they use to define "religion"or "religious" or make explicit why they distinguish some conduct in the past as religious and other conduct as something else. Instead, they rely almost exclusively for their categorization and explication of religious thought and action on the terminology and concepts of those they are studying and of customary religious thought in the present. They explain religious activity primarily by descriptions, intended to arouse comprehending empathy in the reader, of the beliefs or thoughts of the historical actors—albeit those descriptions are often accompanied by authorial asides about the political or psychological effect of such religious thinking.

Of course, historians do borrow language or concepts from other disciplines when discussing religion so that their language is somewhat different from that of religious believers. Thanks to Max Weber, Ernst Troeltsch, and others, they speak in a technical sense of charisma, churches, denominations, sects, secularization, religious pluralism, and the like. And they may refer to religious positions as conservative or liberal or as worldly or unworldly or to individuals as once-born or twice-born. But they rarely make clear what they themselves think religion itself is. Instead, they follow common usage, which frees them from problems of precision.

"Religion" and its cognate terms seem self-evidently meaningful because they are so deeply embedded and widely used in everyday language. But their meaning is loose and heavily influenced by traditional—and conflicting—religious preconceptions. Their ambiguity makes them blunt tools for rational analysis of empirical phenomena, and their freight of traditional connotations makes it easy to load apparently neutral discussions with concealed convictions, whether for or against traditional religions or religion as such. As scholars in other disciplines have realized, common usage obfuscates objective analysis of a major dimension of human action. In anthropology, sociology, and, to a lesser extent, psychology, "religion" has become a technical term of scholarship, even though there are great debates about how it should be defined and analyzed.[2] I believe historians would do well to follow suit and lay their cards on the table equally openly.

In saying this, I am not arguing that historians should not try to the best of their ability to convey to people in the present what people in the past said, believed, thought, and felt and how that was connected with what they did. What I am questioning is the way they often use such descriptions of belief implicitly or explicitly as satisfactory explanations of past actions. I am questioning the way in which historians often use, acceptingly or dismissively, what people then thought and believed as their own and their only way of categorizing and explaining why those people acted as they did.[3] When historians do so, I would argue, they infuse present thought with the understandings—or misunderstandings—of the past. Of this there are few better examples than the way non-Jewish historians of the late nineteenth and early twentieth centuries described and explained past hatred of Jews.[4]

Because recent radical changes in most non-Jews' attitudes toward Jews have made previous explanations of hatred of Jews seem so false, the dangers of this technique of explanation are obvious when we look at old explanations of hatred of Jews. They are much less apparent, however, when historians are dealing with widely shared beliefs of the period studied that are still held, albeit with significant modifications, by many people, including many historians, in the present. They are less apparent—especially in the case of religious beliefs that historians cannot verify empirically—because the apparent continuity of the beliefs con-

2. See below, chap. 4.
3. For further discussion, see below, chap. 3.
4. See "Majority History and Postbiblical Jews," in my *Toward a Definition of Antisemitism*, chap. 2.

ceals the difference between present and past understanding of
the human condition in general and makes the conduct connected
with those beliefs seem self-explanatory. Not only do such beliefs
seem immediately comprehensible because we grew up surrounded by them, but we all know people who explain their actions by those beliefs; and we do not pronounce them fools. It
therefore seems as natural to use such beliefs to explain why people in the past acted as they did as to use them to explain the
action of our contemporaries.

In my case, I was raised in an atheistic family that nonetheless
went to church (the Canadian version of the Church of England)
at Easter and Christmas and utilized religious ceremonies for rites
of passage; and as a boy I earned pocket money by singing in the
choir. I became familiar with many Christian beliefs and much
Christian ceremony and literature—and with some biblical Judaism and Jewish history, in however distorted a form. Although
I never became a believer in the divinity of Jesus of Nazareth,
by the time I emerged from adolescence, that transmission of
Christian history and beliefs, reinforced by Bach and Handel, had
influenced my conception of history and humanity to a considerable extent, although it would be hard to say how and how much.
That I later became a medieval historian had, however, nothing
to do with any interest in religion; my interest in political thought
and institutions played the major role. Nonetheless, as a medievalist, I now had to deal with a period in which religions were
highly influential. At least at a superficial level, that posed few
problems. My earlier religious indoctrination made much of what
I encountered seem immediately understandable; and although I
had to learn about many features of medieval religion that were
unfamiliar, what I already knew made them seem easily accessible.

In graduate school, I apprenticed as a historian, acquiring
knowledge of historiographic practice and the application of informed and disciplined common sense. And for much of my ca-
reer, I was content to follow the habits of my predecessors and
masters and use the customary language that other historians used
when talking about medieval religious thoughts and actions. In
other words, I used medieval terminology and concepts to categorize and describe religious phenomena, for they made sense to

me even though I did not think as medieval people did. I did not believe what they believed, but that was what they believed. Hence, whenever I wrote about something connected with religion, their understanding of religion served as my explanation of the influence of religion on their conduct.

It was only after I had begun to study the formation of antisemitism, and had to deal directly with religion and religious conflict, that I began to wonder whether my previous approach to religion was an evasion. What medieval Jews and Christians believed could not be my own historical explanation of their conduct toward each other, for what they believed provided two radically different explanations of human conduct. Not only did those explanations conflict, but, whether personally or as a professional historian, I could not accept either of them. And once alerted to the problem, I recognized that the same problem arose in dealing with people who professed the same religion but disagreed on specific issues. Whose categorization of what was "religious" and what was not could I accept? Or could I accept either? For example, should I consider that massacres of Jews by medieval self-professed Christians were religious acts?

If some people believed that their massacre of Jews was a religious act, then by customary historiographic criteria their actions were a part of their religion. And if that was the case, then those actions were something that I, as a historian, could describe but should not try to explain empirically and would have to bracket. Alternately, like some historians,[5] I could avoid the whole issue if I treated the religious language of the killers as hypocritical, mere camouflage, and gave some normal empirical explanation of their actions in terms such as the distribution of scarce goods, greed, violence, and hatred of outgroups. Or, after noting that some medieval people believed such massacres to be religious acts, while others, including church officials, condemned them as against their religion, I could protect the good name of Catholicism or religion by accepting the judgment of those officials as if it were my own.[6] None of those solutions seemed acceptable. My

5. See "The Transformation of Anti-Judaism," in *Toward a Definition of Antisemitism*, chap. 4.

6. A related and more general form of this approach is the way some his-

analysis of the formation of antisemitism was unlikely to advance
if I had to bracket what caused people to massacre Jews, giving
no other explanation than their own beliefs about Jews. It was
also clear that the religious language of most of those who mas-
sacred Jews in 1096 was not camouflage. And to decide the issue
by relying on the judgment of church officials was simply to take
the side of Catholicism. The question of what was or was not
religion or religious seemed unavoidable.

The same fundamental problem arose in connection with a very
different issue. Several historians, perhaps most notably Hannah
Arendt, have distinguished sharply between the older hatred of
Jews as religious and the modern hatred as secular (or racial).[7]
But what was the difference in kind between Catholicism and
Nazism or between Christianity and the Aryan mythology? On
what basis had people decided that Nazism, like Communism,
was only a surrogate religion, whereas Catholicism or Calvinism
were genuine religions? Consideration of Nazism, moreover, reinforced my initial doubts about using descriptions of people's beliefs to explain their actions. I knew that I could not use what
the Nazis believed as my own explanation of Nazi conduct toward
Jews, for the falsity of their beliefs about race was manifest. But
if so, why should I accept the beliefs of medieval Catholics or
Jews as a satisfactory explanation of the conduct of Catholics toward Jews? Even if I could not say they were false in the sense
that I knew the Aryan racial beliefs were false, neither could I
know they were true.[8] And I knew that Jews did not believe them.
Whichever way I faced, I encountered dilemmas that forced me
to reexamine how, as a historian, I should discuss religious phenomena.

---

torians have treated some beliefs as religious while dismissing other very similar
ones as superstitions. See Keith Thomas, *Religion and the Decline of Magic*
(New York, 1971), pp. 625-628, 663-668.

7. Hannah Arendt, *The Origins of Totalitarianism*, 2d ed. (New York, 1958),
Part One. A much more sophisticated version of the same distinction is main-
tained by Jacob Katz, *From Prejudice to Destruction: Anti-Semitism, 1700-1933*
(Cambridge, Mass., 1980). The same position has been taken very recently in
an unpublished thesis presented to the University of Paris for the Doctorat ès
Lettres et Sciences Humaines: Yves Chevalier, "Le Juif, bouc émissaire" (1986).

8. The problem of explanation by the beliefs of the actors is discussed at
length in chap. 3.

Partly to resolve that uncertainty, and as a counterpart to a course I had developed on the formation of antisemitism, I developed a course on the Christianization of Europe. If the course was intended to teach students about a major aspect of medieval history, I also wanted to use it as an opportunity to look more closely at Christianization in order to understand why Christian attitudes toward Jews changed markedly in the course of the Middle Ages. Beyond that, I wanted to see if I could analyze Christianization as objectively and neutrally as historians, at least some of them, analyzed the development of Communism. That, after all, was the way I was supposed to teach. The ideal of neutrality in a nondenominational university and the presence in the course of students of various traditional religions, as well as those with none, made it imperative that any explanations I gave should not be those of any particular religion. Now had I been giving a course on, say, the development of medieval monasticism, I would not have felt that to be a problem; I and the students could have simply assumed that I was talking about something within Catholicism that was based on its beliefs, thereby bracketing the problem of what Catholicism was. As it was, however, the very title of the course made the fundamental problem inescapable. My lectures could not simply repeat what some medieval people believed about themselves, for my selective reporting would merely conceal the preconceptions that had determined my choices. But how could I analyze almost the whole range of medieval religious developments without relying on the concepts of Catholicism or some other religion to define the phenomena?

What was "Christianization"? If the students could agree that the newly baptized Celts and Germans of the fifth and sixth centuries were certainly religious—although some thought them merely superstitious—many students, each with his or her own conception of Christianity, doubted that they were really Christian. We solved that problem neutrally by agreeing to count as a Christian anyone who believed in some way that Jesus of Nazareth was supernatural. But did Christianization then mean no more than the spread of that belief? Or did it mean the implementation of that belief, the development of an embracing pattern of thought and conduct based on it? Was there some standard we could use to judge the degree of Christianization? Did Christianization occur as people's thought and conduct came to correspond more and more closely to some highly worked out expression of the consequences of that belief, for example, that of the church fathers, the theologians of the thirteenth century, or the present authorities of the Roman Catholic church? But that criterion raised the same problem, for they were all Catholics. What of the highly developed practices and norms of the Orthodox or Protestant churches? And what of people in the Middle Ages who rejected the authority of the Catholic church? The obvious neutral solution, and my original intention, was to say that we would analyze how people came to believe in Christ, and how the religious conduct of people who believed in Christ changed, without trying to judge how "Christian" they were. But how could we do that without first agreeing on what we, as objective students of history in the present, understood by "religious"?

Those questions raised another issue. Although the Roman Catholic religion became so dominant in Europe during the Middle Ages that it is easy when restricting one's attention to medieval Europe to think of it as Christianity, there have manifestly been a multitude of Christian religions (autonomous churches, denominations, and sects). But if each of them was a religion, then what was Christianity? As a term, it might be used to refer to the whole array of Christian religions, but then it could not itself be the name of a religion—an issue of some significance for the analysis of relations between Christianity and Judaism. Moreover, if Christianity is thought of as an all-embracing term that refers to everything dependent on belief in Christ, then what of the Christianity of individuals? Individuals within each Christian religion have expressed their personal belief in Christ in a variety of complex and often very different and conflicting ways that were not commanded by the religion they professed; indeed, some of the ways they expressed their faith were often disapproved by the authorities of their religion. Could some conduct then be Christian and part of Christianity but not the expression of a Christian religion?[9]

All of these specific questions pointed to the fundamental problem. If the purpose of the course was to examine objectively the

9. The issue is discussed in chaps. 7 and 10.

development of religious conduct as distinguished from other forms of conduct, what criteria or language could I use—and propose to the students—to distinguish what was religious, categorize its different manifestations, and relate them to one another and to whatever else was going on? Clearly, something had to be done, for one thing was obvious: my students, some of considerable historical sophistication, and I—and the books they were to read—shared no common language to do so. Nor had most of the students any familiarity with anthropological, sociological, and psychological scholarship on religion. Worse than that, although I had my own ideas about how to discuss religious phenomena, I found that I had not thought them through sufficiently to be able to express them clearly and convey them to my students. I could not provide a clear definition of religion that enabled me to define Christianity and categorize its manifestations, including Catholicism, objectively.

There was the problem. As a historian who dealt with the Middle Ages and was working on the formation of antisemitism, I could not avoid lecturing and writing at length about religious phenomena. But I had not been trained to analyze religious phenomena; I had only been given the models of discourse provided by the habits of other historians. Of course, like most historians, I had read outside my discipline. Because of my work on antisemitism, I had read fairly widely in sociology and been influenced by Max Weber, Karl Mannheim, Gordon W. Allport, Robert K. Merton, Gerhard Lenski, and Peter Berger, among others. I had dabbled in anthropology and been influenced by Bronislaw Malinowski and Clifford Geertz. I was also broadly familiar with the Freudian position on religion and had read some works in the history of religion. I was not, however, trained in those disciplines and had never sat down to think systematically about how their treatment of religion had affected or should influence my historian's treatment of it. But now, because of the problems I had encountered, I felt compelled to make clear, at least to myself, what I meant when I spoke of "religion."

Why did I want to distinguish some conduct as "religious" while assigning other conduct to different categories, and why did I distinguish as I did between different types of religious action? Unless I could express those distinctions in reasonably unambiguous language that referred reasonably clearly to empirical data, I could not resolve the problems I faced or construct a relatively logical, empirically based hypothesis about the formation of antisemitism. Something had to be done. Initially, before I realized the depth of my problem, I only wanted to clarify the meaning I assigned to some key terms in order to use them consistently when I taught or wrote, and to alert my audience that I was departing from customary usage. Indeed, that remains my major purpose. But, as I attempted to do so and turned for help to other disciplines, I found myself drawn ever deeper into a lively debate about the proper way to define or conceive religion. I was also fascinated to discover that hostility between Jews and Christians might be important for differences in the fundamental presuppositions with which scholars of religion and sociologists approached the study of religion.[10]

What started as a little mental housecleaning became ever more complicated. To keep track of my thoughts and reexamine them, I had to work them out in writing. Then, since I found that my position was diverging more and more from customary historical usage, I decided to write an essay on my approach to religion to serve as a forewarning introduction about my terminology for a collection of my essays on antisemitism.[11] But the essay took on a life of its own and expanded until it reached the proportions of a book.

For a mere medieval historian, especially one who had not even specialized in religious history, to publish a book on religion in general seemed highly presumptuous, not to say dangerously rash. What emboldened me to proceed was my knowledge that, however incompetent I might be to pronounce on so vast a subject, I would only be doing explicitly and in general what most historians do all the time through their work in detail. Whether

10. Robert N. Bellah, "Christianity and Symbolic Realism," with comments by James T. Burtchaell, Samuel K. Klausner, Benjamin Nelson, and a reply by Bellah, *Journal for the Scientific Study of Religion* 9 (1970): 89-115.

11. "No original assertion can be made, I think, by simply drawing on the cards readily available in the language pack that is in use. The pack has been dealt too often, and all simple statements in it have been made many times before. Hence a new contribution to a topic is possible only by re-designing a pack so as to make a new statement possible in it" (Ernest Gellner, *Nations and Nationalism* [Ithaca, N.Y., 1983], p. 137).

explicitly or, more usually, implicitly, they take a stand about the nature of religion.[12] And since the way I conceived of religion necessarily underlay my historical essays on antisemitism, was central to my hypotheses about the nature of antisemitism, and diverged markedly from customary usage, I wanted to make my interpretation explicit. Moreover, I had long felt that what was needed for a better understanding of antisemitism was not more details about hostility toward Jews but a rethinking of the problem. This book, then, is my effort to rethink a major aspect of that problem as broadly and deeply as I could.

Because of the limitations of time and my knowledge, the result is highly schematic and only draws eclectically on relevant scholarship and data. But most historians are no better off. What this book proposes, then, is no more than one medieval historian's effort to solve a problem he could not avoid. Its limitations will be obvious to all who specialize in the study of religion. Although, as will be apparent, I fully intend my analysis to apply to religious phenomena in general, I am respectably knowledgeable only about the history of the West since the fall of the Roman Empire and am most at home in the Middle Ages. Consequently, most of my examples are drawn from that period and area, to the neglect of a mountain of other obviously relevant data. Yet even if my arguments only hold there and not, for example, for China, they may still advance my primary goal, the understanding of a primarily Western phenomenon, antisemitism. A further obvious limitation is my inadequate knowledge and use of scholarship from other disciplines. I am very aware that many assertions made in a single sentence are highly debatable, often naive, and could be the subject of a book, that the selective citations of scholarship in many of my notes could be expanded into small bibliographies, and that I have skipped lightly over, or completely avoided, many highly important issues.

My excuse is obvious. Publications on religion are endless; debates about details and generalizations also. To support my in-

12. It is not surprising but nonetheless remarkable that Harry Ritter, *Dictionary of Concepts in History* (Westport, Conn., 1986) has entries for alienation, capitalism, civilization, culture, nationalism, process, understanding, and value judgment, among many other terms, but no entry for religion, faith, or spirituality.

terpretation properly, I would have had to specialize in the study
of religion from an early age. Yet had I chosen that different path,
I might never have asked the questions that led me to make this
argument, for my questioning derives from investigation of what
non-Jews have done to Jews, not from the study of polytheism,
Buddhism, Judaism, Christianity, and Islam, or even of Nazi ideology. This book is not an examination of religion in all its aspects
or an attempt to explain the ultimate mysteries of the cosmos. It
is concerned with religious phenomena only insofar as they can
be discussed rationally and empirically. And if it is not a treatise
about religion, neither is it a philosophical treatise. To the extent
that I have referred to philosophical matters I have done so only
to indicate where I stand, and I have left metaphysics and the
philosophy of religion entirely aside, not because I deny their
importance but because they are not immediately relevant to the
historian's problem.

What I am addressing is a practical problem of historical
method, one that historians cannot avoid, one they must deal with
even though they cannot resolve all the philosophical issues involved in the position they take. How can historians explain past
religious phenomena without pronouncing on matters beyond
their competence? What thoughts and actions should historians
consider "religious"; to what extent can they explain them rationally and empirically; and how should they do so?

Yet if these broad questions are the first agenda of this book,
what led me to ask them was a very different question about
concrete and historically undeniable events, and my discussion of
religion will use that horrifying question as a focus. Why did non-
Jews from the Middle Ages to the present kill millions of almost
defenseless Jews? Any answer to that question raises the issue of
religion; and most answers over the last hundred years have relied
explicitly or tacitly on Christian or Jewish religious beliefs. Even
today, most discussions of the problem are thought of as debates
or dialogues between Christians and Jews, between people divided by their religions or religious backgrounds.

Once the theological dimensions of much of the debate over the
causes of antisemitism have been recognized, the general problem
facing historians who seek to be objective becomes obvious: how
can we analyze religious phenomena without relying on theology?

Unless we face that general problem of historical method squarely, it will be difficult to achieve a more objective understanding of the formation of antisemitism. This book is one effort to confront it.

After a chapter that emphasizes the historiographical problem by examining the debate over the formation of antisemitism in greater depth, the remaining chapters of Part I of the book will be devoted to an examination of the broad methodological problems religion poses for historians. Part II will present proposals about how to resolve them. I intend these proposals to apply broadly and hope that historians who deal with matters other than antisemitism may find them useful. But if they do no more than provoke discussion, they may contribute to our common pursuit. Then, since my own particular goal is to advance knowledge about antisemitism, Part III will illustrate my proposals by presenting their implications for an explanation of antisemitism.

Chapter Two

An Extreme Example

Perhaps nowhere is the conflict between—or intermingling of—religious belief and historical objectivity more evident than in historiography about the treatment of Jews. And that for obvious reasons. Any historian who discusses Jews and reactions to them must accept, modify, or reject various assumptions about "religion" that are embedded in the common language historians use. Not only has the identification of humans as Jews been dependent on religion, Judaic religions, but Christianity has been one of the most powerful components in the formation of Western culture,[1] and almost from the outset one of its features has been hostility toward Jews. That hostility became very intense in the so-called Middle Ages, the period in which many of the fundamental characteristics of modern European society and culture were formed. In the following centuries, Christians were generally hostile to Jews and often intensely so where Jews were still present. It was not until the late nineteenth or early twentieth century that several prominent Christians began to speak against such hostility, and it was not until the revelation of what an anti-Christian, Hitler, and his followers had done that many Christians became concerned to purge Christianity of that hostility.

Any analysis of the formation of antisemitism therefore immediately confronts the prior, deeply rooted, and very difficult problem inescapably involved in writing about Jews and Chris-

---

1. Since our dating assumes the centrality of Jesus' birth, it even structures our sense of historical time.

tians in languages that have been profoundly influenced by Judaism and Christianity. To complicate matters further, these are the languages of societies in which many are still believers, and much of the present discussion of antisemitism is carried on by Jews and by Christians for whom the extent to which Christianity was responsible for Hitler's Final Solution is a burning question.

The problem is obvious. We cannot discuss antisemitism without referring to adherents of Judaism and Christianity, to "Jews" and "Christians" who practiced "religions" that proclaimed the existence of "God." But Jews cannot agree as to who is a Jew; Christians cannot agree as to what is true Christianity; historians or social scientists when acting professionally can say nothing about the existence of God; and social scientists cannot even agree on a definition of "religion." And one result, as we shall see, is wide disagreement about when antisemitism first appeared. How can a historian who seeks objectivity about antisemitism use current terminology to analyze such phenomena?

Most of the early attempts to understand antisemitism objectively were carried out by Christians whose primary concern was the extent of Christian responsibility for contemporary antisemitism. That Christianity bore some responsibility was indisputable. Almost from the beginning, professed Christians had displayed hostility against Jews, and throughout the centuries Christian thinkers had provided a reasoned theological explanation of their distinctive hostility. In the late nineteenth century, however, some Christians, influenced partly by the new interest in objective history and more immediately by the new, frequently anti-Christian, racial theories, made a serious effort to reach an objective empirical explanation of that hostility.

Horribly misguided as the pseudoscientific efforts of the racial theorists may have been, they forced those who disagreed with them to look for more objective—and morally acceptable—explanations for the centuries-old hostility that Wilhelm Marr, Houston Stewart Chamberlain, Alfred Rosenberg, Hitler, and many faceless others were explaining pseudoscientifically and unchristianly by the Aryan myth. With the field thus open, and in a period in which historical scholarship had advanced greatly in competence and objectivity, many very different kinds of explanations were proposed by historians and somewhat later by sociologists and psychologists. But almost from the outset, one old explanation, which had been taken for granted until the Aryan mythologists' confusion of philology and bad biology had distracted attention from it, reclaimed attention: Christianity.

For Jews, that explanation was natural. The oldest and most obvious difference between Jews and non-Jews had been their religion; religion had remained central for most Jews' sense of their social identity; and for centuries Jews had been surrounded by Christians, many of whom had attacked Jews with intense hatred. As Jews looked over their past, religion seemed the central thread of their history, and wrong faith—or irreligion—the obvious explanation of the hostility against them. That assumption was reflected in Jewish scholarship. When Jewish historiography was reborn in the nineteenth century, it was written for Jews, about Jews, and by Jews who had relatively little understanding of the history of the surrounding non-Jewish culture.[2] Not surprisingly, therefore, its most influential pioneer, Heinrich Graetz, and many other Jewish historians who were deeply influenced by him, found in Christian "fanaticism" a ready and sufficient explanation of the anti-Jewish conduct of the majority.

It had long been equally natural for non-Jews to explain their hostility against Jews after Jesus of Nazareth in religious terms. Since antiquity, Christians who hated Jews had explained, justified, or rationalized their hatred most explicitly by their Christian beliefs. Indeed, no radically different explanation of the roots of hostility against Jews could be put forward by non-Jews in Europe until it became possible to be only nominally Christian or to reject Christianity openly. And although religious pluralism brought increased toleration in the seventeenth century, even of Jews in some areas such as England and Holland, it was not until the eighteenth century that some devotees of a new deity, Reason, provided a new explanation of hostility against Jews: religion itself. They condemned traditional religions as irrational superstitions; they explained hostility against Jews as a result of the superstitions on both sides; and they believed that it would

2. See "Tradition, History, and Prejudice," in *Toward a Definition of Antisemitism*, chap. 2.

disappear once such irrationality had been eradicated on both sides.

Their optimism was badly misplaced. Despite the movement toward legal and social emancipation of Jews in the nineteenth century, or partly because of it, and despite the increased assimilation and the "modernization" of Judaism represented by the movement for *Wissenschaft des Judentums*, the last quarter of the nineteenth century was marked by a sharp increase in hostility toward Jews. Some of that hostility came from Christians who felt threatened by modernizing forces and secularization and reacted, as during the Dreyfus case, by reemphasizing their Christianity and becoming more hostile toward Jews. But far more significant was the hostility explicitly based on racist theories that implicitly or explictly rejected most traditional Christian beliefs. At the same time, however, some Christians, a very few, were reacting in just the opposite way and opposing hostility toward Jews. Although they were influenced by the ideas of the Enlightenment and more recent liberal ideas, and were therefore alienated by intolerance, they were not against religion; indeed, their objection to current attitudes toward Jews was based on their religious convictions. What particularly bothered them was that Christians had treated Jews in a way that defiled what they considered true Christianity.

As a Christian, the author is one of those who believe that the spirit of intolerance is repugnant to Christianity; and nothing seems to him less in conformity with the gospel than racial hatred. Wars of races or wars of classes, the jealousies of the crowd cannot cover themselves with the robe of Christ. Aryans or Semites, it is not by the proscription of others that the salvation of peoples ought to be won.

So wrote Anatole Leroy Beaulieu in the introduction to *Israël chez les nations*,[3] the first profound analysis of hatred of Jews. He went on to argue that the peculiar hatred of Jews arose from the fact that three powerful kinds of hostility which were normally dispersed were concentrated at one and the same time on Jews: the hostility engendered by a war of religion, by a conflict of culture or nationality, and by class struggle. He held that antisemitism as a body of ideas was essentially simplistic and appealed

3. (Paris, 1893), p.i.

to the masses for just that reason. He noted perceptively that antisemites credited the tiny number of Jews with being more powerful than all other peoples. And he argued that what gave antisemitism its powerful appeal was that it absolved those who believed it from evil and located the root of the evils that beset them in an external virus. He was also well aware of the impact on Jews, beginning in the Middle Ages, of what we would now call the self-fulfilling prophecy.

It was a brilliant and perceptive book. But if the desire to absolve his Christianity of responsibility was one motive behind Beaulieu's pioneering analysis of hostility against Jews, he certainly was not attracted by Judaism. Jews had characteristics he did not like; and although he attributed them largely to the conduct forced on Jews by medieval and modern intolerance and ghettoization, he found a more fundamental cause in the servitude of Jews to the laws of Judaism. Obedience to those laws he saw as both the cause and the effect of Jewish sequestration and the tribal spirit of Jews.[4] Thus, theological considerations were not absent from Beaulieu's analysis; they had only been overlaid by his emphasis on other factors at work and been avoided by the assertion that intolerance was alien to Christianity—if not to Judaism. And given his analysis of antisemitism, it is ironic that Beaulieu not only asserted that the new self-labeled antisemitism was not Christian, Catholic, or French but also argued that it was an evil virus that came from outside, from assertive Germany and backward Russia. He was, as he himself proclaimed, both a Catholic and a Frenchman, in other words a Christian nationalist who externalized evil in his own way.

The issue of intolerance was central in another early analysis and condemnation of antisemitism. Although favorable to religion, Count Coudenhove-Kalergi was an antisemite as a young man; and when he started to work on *Das Wesen des Antisemitismus*,[5] he expected to confirm his attitude but came instead to a very different conclusion in the book published in 1901. After an ironic critique of the new racial theories, he declared that the essence of antisemitism was simply fanatical religious hatred. He attrib-

4. Ibid., pp. 141, 145-146, 152.
5. (Vienna, 1901).

uted that fanaticism to religious bigotry and found its origin in the promulgation of Torah under Esra. That bigotry provoked opposition even from the tolerant Greco-Roman polytheists who, because they were not bigoted, reacted with·anti-Judaism but not antisemitism. Antisemitism was only born when Christianity and Islam appeared, took over the intolerant fanaticism of Judaism, and turned it back on Jews. Coudenhove-Kalergi thus condemned religious intolerance as a violation of what he considered genuine religious principles and attributed its origin to the Jews.

A more sophisticated form of the thesis that racial theories were false and antisemitism the fruit of religious intolerance was propounded after World War I by Matthias Mieses, a Jew.[6] Like Coudenhove-Kalergi, he saw confessional separatism as the basic and enduring cause of antisemitism—and of any secondary differences between Jews and non-Jews. But he argued that the hatred engendered by confessional intolerance became peculiarly intense only when directed against a minority that professed a different religion from that of the majority. The intensity of the hostility against Jews was the result of their long dispersion and existence as a religious minority within Christian society, and the new racial antisemitism was but a masked extension of that hatred.

Even before the rise of Nazism, however, but particularly after the revelation of what Hitler had done to Jews, religious intolerance no longer seemed a very convincing explanation of hostility against Jews. What seemed more apparent was that there had been two antithetical kinds of hostility. Since the hostility of earlier centuries had been explicitly justified by religious beliefs, while the antisemites' hostility in the nineteenth and twentieth centuries purported explicitly to be scientific and nonreligious, many scholars since the late nineteenth century have sharply distinguished the two kinds of hostility: anti-Judaism and antisemitism.

One of the first to contrast anti-Judaism and antisemitism was Bernard Lazare, a Jew and staunch defender of Dreyfus who nonetheless disliked the characteristic conduct of Jews throughout history. He announced in 1893 that Judaism was the root cause

6. *Der Ursprung des Judenhasses* (Vienna, 1923).

of all hostility against the Jews, and prophesied—or hoped—that it would be the first religion to disappear. Lazare believed that hostility against Jews had been basically religious until the nineteenth century, when anti-Judaism was subordinated to antisemitism, that is, to a reasoned hostility that had primarily economic and social causes.[7] But perhaps the most unqualified assertion of this temporal division was made by Hannah Arendt. In 1951, she inveighed against the doctrine of an "eternal antisemitism," distinguished between the old religious "Jew-hatred" and modern anti-Christian antisemitism, and regarded them as fundamentally different in nature and causation.[8] But assertion is not argument. She had not examined the earlier Jew-hatred at all closely and did not begin to face the problem of possible connections between it and what came later. She analyzed the modification of hostility against Jews after 1800, but not the hostility that was modified. Luther does not even figure in her index!

This line of argument, which disculpates Christianity from the worst persecution by drawing a sharp line between a religious period of European civilization and a period in which religion was not responsible for major events, should have been welcomed by Christians, and doubtless was by many. But others, while agreeing that nineteenth- and twentieth-century antisemitism was not Christian, remained convinced—precisely because they were much more familiar with the history of Christianity—that the hostility rationalized by the racists had much older and deeper roots. Moreover, scholars who were religious believers were unwilling to admit that Europe had passed from a religious era to a secular one.

Already around 1900, the works of Beaulieu, Coudenhove-Kalergi, and Mieses indicated that liberal Christians and Jews might ally to protect both religions—or religion as such—against the menace of the new "secularism." With the rise of Communism and Nazism, of explicit ideological hostility against both Christianity and Judaism, the need for such an alliance became even more obvious. But for an alliance to be realized, some conciliatory

7. *L'antisémitisme: Son histoire et ses causes* (Paris, 1893), pp. 95, 123, 207; see also Emil J. Long, *2,000 Years: A History of Anti-Semitism* (New York, 1953), p. 110, for a similar distinction.
8. *The Origins of Totalitarianism* (New York, 1958), p. 7 and passim.

answer had to be found to the fundamental question underlying those earlier works: was antisemitism a consequence of Jewish and/or Christian beliefs or did it have different roots? As might be expected from those concerned to protect the good name of religion, different roots were found. In 1938, with all the prestige he had acquired by his neo-Thomism, Jacques Maritain argued that hatred of Jews and of Christians sprang from the same source: a refusal to accept the burden of the absolute truths and commandments of the Bible.[9] And in 1940, a prominent Jewish scholar, Maurice Samuel, proclaimed that antisemitism was a reaction against Christianity by worshipers of force, a masked attack on Christ the Jew which expressed the concealed hatred of the constraints imposed by belief in Christ and Christianity.[10]

Hatred of Jews was becoming ungodly for some Christians, a remarkable inversion. But Christians who sought to disculpate Christianity had somehow to deal with the inescapable fact that many outstanding and indisputable Christians throughout the centuries had condemned Judaism and enforced harsh measures on its adherents. The solution of the dilemma was a predictable syllogism: intolerance and antisemitism are bad; right religious faith is eternally good; therefore, whatever Christians have done that might be classified as antisemitism was not done out of genuine faith. This implied two possible stands: that any aversion to "the Jews" was unchristian, or that one—tolerant—kind of aversion (anti-Judaism) was Christian and another (antisemitism) was not.

The first and more radical solution had already been propounded in 1934 by James Parkes in his great pioneering reexamination of the development of Christian attitudes toward Jews from the beginnings to the ninth century.[11] Parkes argued, like Coudenhove-Kalergi and, most recently, J. N. Sevenster,[12] that pagan hostility against Jews in the classical world was a thoroughly understandable reaction of tolerant polytheists to real characteristics imprinted on Jews by their own religion. With the advent of Christianity, however, a new hostility that had nothing to do with the older enmities appeared. The root cause of that hostility,

9. *Les Juifs parmi les nations* (Paris, 1938).
10. *The Great Hatred* (London, 1943).
11. *The Conflict of the Church and the Synagogue* (London, 1934).
12. *The Roots of Pagan Anti-Semitism in the Ancient World* (Leiden, 1975).

Parkes argued, was theological conceptions that were already apparent in Paul's failure to do justice to the Law and in elements of the fourth Gospel, conceptions that were further developed in the first three centuries.[13] These conceptions sought to validate Christianity and refute Jewish and pagan criticisms by preempting Jewish Scripture, distorting its meaning, and proclaiming the supersession of Judaism. Almost inevitably they incited hatred against Jews. And as Parkes traced the elaboration of those misconceptions and their impact on Jewish status after the church had acquired political power, he had no trouble in demonstrating conclusively that some of the most famous Christian saints, theologians, and churchmen had expressed hatred of Jews and Judaism and sought to ensure their degradation. Then, with his knowledge of the impact of Christianity on later history and his prescient horror at what he saw in his own day, only one conclusion seemed to follow.

And if on this ground, so carefully prepared, modern antisemites have reared a structure of racial and economic propaganda, the final responsibility still rests with those who prepared the soil, created the deformation of the people, and so made these ineptitudes credible.[14]

The conclusion that antisemitism was indeed a necessary consequence of Christianity would seem to follow. But since Parkes was a Christian and had been moved to condemn antisemitism by his own beliefs, he believed he could demonstrate that hatred of Judaism and Jews was no part of the genuine Christian message. It had been early and enduringly infused into Christian doctrine from wrong but understandable human motives as misguided Christians had defended themselves against Jewish and pagan criticisms of their faith. Hence, for Parkes, the hatred of the Jews and Judaism that had marked Christians for nearly two millennia was not an expression of true Christianity but a very ancient deformation that had to be eliminated.

However admirable Parkes's plea, there is an unresolved tension in his arguments. Whatever his faith, his explicit argument was historical. While he may have felt as a Christian that hatred

13. *The Conflict of the Church and the Synagogue*, pp. 57, 82-84.
14. Ibid., p. 376. An almost identical judgment was made by Jules Isaac, *Genèse de l'antisémitisme* (Paris, 1956), pp. 17-18.

of Jews was not Christian, it was as a historian that he sought to demonstrate that it was not present in the initial message or among the first Christians. Yet, as he had demonstrated so convincingly, hostility against Jews had been a manifest characteristic of historical Christianity almost from the outset. If the nature of Christianity could be decided by historical arguments, then hatred of Jews was manifestly one of its earliest, most obvious, and enduring characteristics.

The problem with Parkes's arguments is that he could provide no empirical criterion whereby others without his faith could distinguish between genuine Christian faith and historical Christianity. On the basis of his own faith, he had decided that many passages in the canonical New Testament could not be an expression of genuine Christianity, but that was a criterion no objective historian could accept, and one many Christians would not accept. As for his historical argument, it was one few historians could accept. It attributed to Jesus' original "good news" empirically verifiable characteristics that no other teaching known to historians has had. For Parkes to discern by purely historical methods what was genuine Christianity and what were later deviations, the original announcement of Christian belief would have to have been so clear, complete, and far-sighted—and to have been so accurately recorded and authentically preserved—that anyone, whether Christian or not, would have been able to recognize any deviation from it.

Had that been the case, the good news would have to have been so complete that anyone thereafter would know exactly how to conform to Jesus' message even though he or she was confronting very different conditions from those at the time of Jesus. There could be no unforeseen problems of interpretation and no unforeseen consequences of the spread and institutionalization of Jesus' message. But the New Testament does not provide such a guide, as the countless debates over its meaning demonstrate, nor did the world come to an end in Jesus' generation, nor did most Jews accept the Christian message. Almost from the outset, Christians had to face unenvisaged situations without clear guidance. After Jesus, Christian beliefs were developed and elaborated in complex and conflicting intellectual and institutional ways that no one could have predicted in his lifetime. Parkes's assumption—

that anti-Judaism was not inherent in belief in Jesus and his message—thus rested on an act of faith that he could not and did not
substantiate by historical analysis of the original teaching and its
consequences.

The responsibility Christianity bore for antisemitism was therefore still very much in question. In 1955 another professed Christian, Fadiey Lovsky, developed a different disculpation of Christian faith by insisting on the contrast between anti-Judaism and
antisemitism. His fundamental premise was theological but not
original. Following Maritain, he held that although the term was
new, "antisemitism" itself was "perhaps one of the simplest and
most instinctive manifestations of the revolt of man against God"
and had existed ever since "God" had elected Israel.[15] It followed
that the reaction of pagan polytheists against the Jewish refusal
to tolerate other gods or eat at the table of others was a revolt
against "God" and therefore "antisemitism." Hence Lovsky could
and did lump together all obvious hostility against the Jews of the
pagan Egyptians, Greeks, and Romans as "antisemitism."[16] For,
as J. N. Sevenster has demonstrated anew, the only characteristics
that set Jews apart from others in the pagan world of antiquity
and aroused particular hostility were those dictated by their religion.[17]

Yet if "antisemitism" was basically a revolt against "God," it
should have followed that Christians who had had Lovsky's faith
in "God" could not have been "antisemites." Unfortunately, most
Christians apparently either were not logical or did not fully trust
their god, for as Lovsky fully acknowledged, excellent Christians—doctors of theology and men whose lives were otherwise
edifying, to say nothing of ordinary Christians—"had allowed antisemitism to disfigure Christian charity, faith, and hope."[18] How,
he asked, could that be possible?

Since Lovsky argued explicitly from religious premises, his answer was necessarily different from that of Parkes, whose explicit

15. *Antisémitisme et mystère d'Israël* (Paris, 1955), p. 21. This is stated in
somewhat vaguer terms in his more recent book *L'antisémitisme chrétien* (Paris,
1970), pp. 11, 50-51.
16. *Antisémitisme et mystère d'Israël*, pp. 44-100.
17. Above, n. 12.
18. *Antisémitisme et mystère d'Israël*, p. 114.

argument was purely historical. Parkes had avoided theological issues and stressed the unfortunate consequences of the institutional conflict between the evolving Church and the Synagogue.[19] He had thereby minimized the conflict of faith and was able to argue that what his faith led him to consider a deformation had sprung, not from Christ, but from the secular human passions of institutional politics. Lovsky could not use that clean distinction since he believed that Christian faith had been fundamentally opposed to Judaism from the beginning. Anti-Judaism was innate and inherent in Christianity.[20]

For Lovsky, as for almost all other Christians, Christian belief was opposed to Judaism since Christ on the status of Jesus of Nazareth.[21] Christianity originated in the faith that Jesus was the Christ, the Messiah, Son of God, or God. Hence, Jews who did not become Christian and denied that foundation stone were in at least partial revolt against God. Conflict was therefore inescapable since Christians had to reject such disbelief. Inescapable also were many of the other reactions that Parkes had so ably described as understandable in terms of merely human and not too admirable motives. But theologically, Lovsky asserted, Christians must deny that Judaism, as it had existed before Christ and now existed outside of the Christian movement, was the highest truth. Christians have to be anti-Judaic in the sense that they refuse the alternative of Judaism.

In Lovsky's eyes, however, that necessary Christian anti-Judaism was not intolerant; it did not necessitate aversion toward or hatred of Jews as persons. To think that it did was to refuse "the elementary distinction between the sin and the sinner."[22] But if that distinction is easy to draw verbally and has been a commonplace in Christian homiletics, it is difficult to make empirically, for "sin" is observable only as an action or disposition of real humans, and what Lovsky describes here as "sin" was central in the sense of identity and conduct of Jews. To that extent, Lovsky seems to devalue Jews as people who cannot be considered to be as good as Christians unless they change their ideas and

---

19. *The Conflict of the Church and the Synagogue*, pp. 33, 37.
20. *Antisémitisme et mystère d'Israël*, pp. 103-104.
21. Ibid., pp. 103, 144.
22. Ibid., p. 20.

actions fundamentally. At best, his distinction only serves to differentiate degrees of hostility rather than to discriminate between different kinds of hostility; and it does not explain how to draw the line. Indeed, even after he had drawn that "elementary" distinction, Lovsky himself declared that "antisemitism is always a degradation and an extension of anti-Judaism."[23]

Lovsky's distinction between "anti-Judaism" and "antisemitism" thus seems only a question of degree. And when he went on to discuss the growth of hostility against Jews among Christians, he was forced, like Parkes, to recognize how much it owed to motives peculiar to Christians. And he called that increased hostility antisemitism. He acknowledged that as early as the second century, because of the refusal of Jews to accept the Christian message, because of Christian jealousy of the prestige of Judaism and its ability to attract proselytes, and because of the "exaggerated" desire to differentiate the Church from the Synagogue, the Church came increasingly to regard Jews as the worst enemy and developed a rich *theological* antisemitism.[24] Thus, although Lovsky had defined antisemitism as a revolt against God, he maintained that when antisemitism was manifested by Christians under stress, it was not a revolt against God but simply an emotional intensification of a necessary corollary of their faith in God. It would therefore seem to follow that, for Lovsky, the antisemitism of Christians sprang directly from their Christian anti-Judaism.

To avoid that unwanted conclusion, Lovsky added other arguments that seemed to locate the source of "antisemitism" outside of Christianity. In the first place, ignorance. Initially, Christian anti-Judaism had been based on an understanding of Judaism and involved an aversion to non-Christian Jews solely because of their persistent denial of Christ's divinity. In the course of the first centuries, however, converts to Christianity were increasingly non-Jews who were ignorant of Judaism and thought of Jews as fundamentally alien. Confronted with the Judaic denial of their Christ, these converts therefore displayed a profound emotional and doctrinal antipathy toward Jews and Judaism.[25]

23. Ibid., p. 20.
24. Ibid., pp. 65, 160, 162, 175, 192.
25. Ibid., pp. 139-141, 159.

In the second place, positive error. These non-Jewish converts did not, Lovsky argued, come to Christianity with a clean slate. They had grown up amidst pagan "antisemitism" and brought with them into Christianity some of the attitudes of that revolt against "God."[26] To sustain that assertion, however, Lovsky had to demonstrate that some of the hostile statements by Christians about Jews were not distinctively Christian but clearly pagan assertions. His argument at this point is remarkably weak, starting with his untenable assertion that the medieval Christian charge of ritual murder came from pagan antiquity.[27] Yet even Lovsky did not claim that pagan antisemitism was the foundation of Christian antisemitism, for he believed that this infusion of pagan "antisemitism" only affected Christian ideas significantly in the third century, hence after the appearance of what he recognized as distinctively Christian antisemitism.

The contention that antisemitism appeared *before* Christianity and was introduced into it from outside has such a bearing on the relation of Christianity to antisemitism that it deserves further attention. In the most important work to date on the attitudes of Christians toward Jews between 135 and 425, a non-Jew, Marcel Simon, acknowledged that the foundation of "Christian antisemitism" was the anger aroused by the refusal of Jews to accept Christ's divinity, their responsibility for his death, and their persecution of Christians.[28] Simon notes that, for obvious reasons and in direct contrast with pagan hostility, Christians did not condemn Judaic exclusivism or the practices of Judaism before Christ. Nor did Christians object, like pagans, to the Jewish condemnation of images or the prohibition of work on the Sabbath or accuse Jews of worshiping an ass. He also notes that the attack on Jewish sexual morality, so frequent in Christian rhetoric as a corollary of Christian asceticism, is almost totally absent in pagan works.[29] And since he knew that pagans had rarely destroyed synagogues, whereas Christian mobs led by clerics did so frequently by the end of the fourth century, he considered that a specifically Chris-

26. Ibid., p. 160.
27. Cf. my "Thomas of Monmouth: Detector of Ritual Murder,"in *Toward a Definition of Antisemitism*, chap. 9.
28. *Verus Israël*, 2d ed. (Paris, 1964), p. 246.
29. Ibid., pp. 215-216, 252-253.

tian reaction.[30] He also demonstrated admirably that the most famous Christian virulence against Jews in the period, the homilies
of John Chrysostom of 388, were anything but pagan in origin;
their metaphoric language was drawn from the Bible.[31]

When it [the invective] is not gross and gratuitous insult, it consists in
the application to the present situation, in isolation from their context
and the particular and momentary circumstances which gave them their
sense, of fragments of prophetic diatribes.[32]

For all those reasons, as well as his awareness that there was
still much respect for Jews among the mass of Christians, Simon
concluded that,

if one takes into account all the information and indices we possess, one
can affirm that the official anti-Judaism was counterbalanced among the
people, and sometimes among certain elements of the clergy, by an
equally strong philo-Judaism. Or rather, it is in this popular philo-Judaism that the true explanation of Christian antisemitism can be found.
The latter seems, in the last analysis, a defensive reaction of the orthodox
hierarchy against the Jewish danger, the Jewish evil.[33]

The most typically pagan accusations were thus absent, and the
central accusations and reactions were distinctively Christian,
based on Christian sources and convictions and advanced most
vigorously, not by a mass of imperfectly Christianized pagan converts, but by the clergy. It would therefore seem hard to deny
that the core and mass of Christian hostility against Jews, which
Simon calls antisemitism, was fundamentally and distinctively
Christian. But strangely enough, despite all the evidence he had
advanced that Christian antisemitism was distinctively Christian,
Simon nonetheless asserted that almost all the old pagan accusations were taken over by the Christians,[34] even though neither
he nor Jean Juster, whom he cited, had provided much evidence
in support of the contention. On the one hand, almost all of the
limited fund of harsh epithets such as "plague of the universe"

30. Ibid., p. 265.
31. Ibid., p. 257.
32. Ibid., p. 259. See also Robert L. Wilken, *John Chrysostom and the Jews*
(Berkeley, Los Angeles, London, 1984).
33. *Verus Israël*, p. 272.
34. Ibid., p. 247.

that Juster found applied to Jews were of the kind available in the common language of any period to apply to people one disliked thoroughly, and they were, of course, used by both pagans and Christians.[35] On the other hand, it is very hard to find Christians repeating any pagan condemnations of specific, allegedly distinctive Jewish conduct. The only example of such a distinctive condemnation that Simon gives, the accusation of ritual murder, is one that he has to acknowledge was used by pagans against Christians but not by Christians against Jews until the Middle Ages.

The argument is very weak and seems even weaker when further considerations are taken into account. Pagans applied most of the epithets they used against Jews to Christians. Genuine conversion to Christian beliefs therefore involved a transvaluation that made pagan hostility toward Jews irrelevant; and most of Simon's evidence comes not from lukewarm converts but from Christian leaders. It should also be noted that whereas many pagan Greco-Romans thoroughly disliked Jews, they were also fundamentally ignorant of the principles of Judaism, and their sense of identity depended in no way on Judaism. By contrast, Christians learned about pre-Pharisaic Judaism from the Old Testament; their sense of identity depended heavily on Judaic beliefs and practices; and they had developed, as pagans never had, an integrated doctrine about Jews and Judaism to justify their hostility to Jews. Simon's emphasis on the infusion of pagan antisemitism thus seems more the reflection of an unshakable belief in an eternal antisemitism than a conclusion warranted by the evidence. In any case, what the bulk of the evidence does make clear, as Simon himself recognizes, is that what he calls Christian antisemitism was purely Christian in origin, was propounded most clearly by leading Christian thinkers and officials, and became a recognized part of church doctrine.

Despite the weakness of Simon's argument and Lovsky's use of it, an argument very similar to Lovsky's and with equally fuzzy distinctions between anti-Judaism and antisemitism was put forward by Edward Flannery in 1965. Thus Flannery stated that

35. See Jean Juster, *Les Juifs dans l'Empire romain*, 2 vols. (Paris, 1914; reprint, New York, 1965), 1:45, n. 1.

Greco-Roman hostility to Jews was anti-Judaic but not theological, since it was a reaction to Jewish intolerance; and he calls this pagan anti-Judaism *antisemitism*.[36] He does not, however, call Christian anti-Judaism antisemitism and justifies that discrimination by the assertion that Christian anti-Judaism—which is essential to the Christological dogmas of the Church—is the rejection of Judaism as a way of salvation, not of the Jews as a people.[37] He declares it difficult to categorize most Christian writings and actions of the first three centuries as antisemitism[38] and argues that antisemitism was introduced into Christianity by pagan converts who brought it with them, by Christian "distortions of Christian teachings and hermeneutics," and by "zeal" as pastors defended their flocks against Judaizing tendencies.[39] In other words, opposition to the beliefs and consequent conduct of Jews is both anti-Judaism and antisemitism if manifested by those who believe in "gods"—or by the godless—but is only anti-Judaism if not too zealously manifested by believers who profess faith in Flannery's God.[40]

Apologetics is an art, not a science, and such arguments could only convince Christians eager to dissociate their Christianity from the recent horrors. Lovsky and Flannery's distinction between anti-Judaism and antisemitism rests so obviously on theological premises and is so unsupported by evidence that no scholar who sought empirical objectivity could be satisfied by it. And ironically, if their work failed to provide any objective criterion to distinguish anti-Judaism from antisemitism, it did make even more obvious how early and deeply anti-Judaism had marked Christianity. Far from settling the issue, the work of these apologists pointed to the need for a more radical solution.

It should be noted, however, that Lovsky and Flannery had agreed with Parkes rather than Arendt. They acknowledged that the hostility of historical Christianity had prepared the way for

36. Edward H. Flannery, *The Anguish of the Jews*, 1st ed. (New York, 1965), p. 23.

37. Ibid., pp. 43, 60.

38. Ibid., p. 43.

39. Ibid., pp. 61-63.

40. In his second edition (New York, 1985), pp. 23, 46, 62-65, Flannery has admitted a closer connection between Christian anti-Judaism and what he calls antisemitism.

the self-labeled, explicitly antireligious antisemitism of the nineteenth and twentieth centuries. Indeed, it was because those scholars could not avoid that conviction that they had focused their efforts of absolution on early Christianity. And if their work made recognition of the responsibility of Christianity even harder to avoid, that recognition was made even more unavoidable by the work of non-Christian scholars such as Jules Isaac, who addressed the problem of Christian responsibility directly,[41] and of historians such as Léon Poliakov, who focused, not on Christianity, but on the detailed history of hostility toward Jews through the centuries. Their work made the importance of historic Christian hostility as a necessary, though not sufficient, cause of modern antisemitism ever clearer.[42] The inadequacy of Lovsky's defense of Christianity was therefore soon apparent to some Christians who were concerned to eliminate hostility against Jews from Christianity but refused to reject rational empirical analysis in order to protect their faith.

The radical approach of these recent scholars has concentrated on the origins of Christianity but approached the problem in a very different way. Perhaps Christians through the centuries had not simply been wrong about proper attitudes toward Jews but had been wrong about Jews because their Christology had been wrong! The reexamination of Christian history forced by Hitler had finally reached Christ.

Under the impact of the holocaust that destroyed six million Jews, some Christian theologians have been ready to submit Christianity to a radical ideological critique. They have been willing to face the possibility that the anti-Jewish trends in Christianity are not simply peripheral and accidental, but woven into the core of the message.[43]

What is here described as a possibility had, of course, been a platitudinous truth for innumerable Christians—and Jews—for centuries, as Parkes, Isaac, Lovsky, Flannery, and others had

---

41. In addition to the work cited above, n. 14, see *Jésus et Israël* (Paris, 1948).

42. Léon Poliakov, *Histoire de l'antisémitisme*, 4 vols. (Paris, 1956-1977), vol. 1, *Du Christ aux Juifs de cour*; vol. 2, *De Mahomet aux marranes*; vol. 3, *De Voltaire à Wagner*; vol. 4, *L'Europe suicidaire*.

43. Gregory Baum, Introduction to Rosemary Ruether, *Faith and Fratricide* (New York, 1979), p. 5.

demonstrated. Only in the nineteenth and twentieth centuries, when Christians who valued tolerance, such as Beaulieu and Parkes, had sought to disculpate the Christian faith, had those "anti-Jewish trends" been set aside as alien to Christianity and centuries of Christian judgment thereby set aside as unchristian. Yet their efforts and those of other scholars had served only to make the intolerance of historic Christianity morally manifest to Christians as it never had been before; and the failure of their attempts to distinguish that intolerance from true Christianity had made it increasingly difficult to avoid the fundamental issue any longer. If many might have been willing to avoid the challenge, Rosemary Ruether made it impossible by formulating it in terms too explicit to be disregarded.

The wheat and the tares have grown together from the beginning, and so it may seem impossible to pull up the weed without uprooting the Christian faith as well. Yet as long as Christology and anti-Judaism intertwine, one cannot be safe from a repetition of this history in new form.[44]

Although Reuther was fully aware of the differences between Christian anti-Judaism and racial antisemitism,[45] she was sure that modern antisemitism would have been impossible without the deep-rooted attitudes developed during the earlier centuries when Europe saw itself as "Christendom," and she was convinced that Christian anti-Judaism was largely responsible for those attitudes.[46] The most substantial parts of her book are therefore devoted to locating the origin of Christian anti-Judaism and arguing, not a theological reinterpretation that could distinguish it from antisemitism, but a Christology that would eliminate it from Christian faith.

When the first Christians had an unverifiable experience that convinced them that Jesus was indeed the Messiah, and that his return and the end of the world were imminent, they were, Ruether argues, but one of several Jewish messianic sects. They sought like other such sects to convince Israel that the time was at hand, and like other such sects they were opposed by the ex-

44. *Faith and Fratricide*, p. 226.
45. Ibid., p. 224.
46. Ibid., pp. 183-225.

isting authorities and particularly by the Pharisees. But at some time prior to Paul's writings and before the influx of gentiles, some Christians or "the Church" reacted with "an alienated and angry Jewish sectarianism" and sought to legitimate their revelation in Jewish terms by making faith in Jesus a new and exclusive principle of salvation.[47]

As might have been expected from her Christianity and condemnation of anti-Judaism, Ruether finds no anti-Judaism "in the teachings of Jesus himself." "He neither regarded himself as the messiah, nor called for his followers to regard the Law as superseded by a New Covenant."[48] "More likely, he saw himself as a messianic prophet calling Israel to repentance in the light of an imminent advent of a messianic figure which he called 'Son of Man.' "[49] But after his death and their experience of his resurrection, some of his followers conceived him to be the Messiah. Then, because Christ had not returned and the world had not ended in the way they had anticipated, and because the majority of Jews who did not believe had not thereby been dramatically proven wrong, Christians developed their own peculiar interpretation of Jewish Scripture to demonstrate that their Christ really was the Messiah predicted by Scripture, an intepretation that relied very heavily on some parts of Isaiah and deemphasized or rejected other elements of Scripture long considered essential by Jews.

Already in the first decade after Jesus' death, the Petrine section of the Christian movement had made faith in Messiah Jesus a new principle of salvation and "relativized the Mosaic covenant to a mere predictive status."[50] By the second decade, the more radical Pauline element had made faith in the Christian conception of the Messiah, and acceptance of the Christian interpretation of Scripture which validated it, the sole path to salvation. Paul also turned the prophetic distinction between circumcision of the heart and of the flesh into a dualistic opposition, and did the same with the difference between the faith of Abraham and the Cov-

---

47. Ibid., pp. 78, 94.
48. Reuther, "The *Faith and Fratricide* Discussion," in *Antisemitism and the Foundations of Christianity*, ed. Alan T. Davies (New York, 1979), p. 235.
49. Ibid., p. 236.
50. *Faith and Fratricide*, p. 83.

enant and Law of Moses.[51] Whatever element of Scripture was not required by his interpretation, or was in conflict with it, he rejected or reinterpreted. Thereby the way of salvation was opened to non-Jews who rejected most of the precepts of Judaism that the first Christians had accepted. And very soon thereafter, an increasingly gentile Church angrily denounced "the Jews" and consigned them to eternal damnation.

This summary inevitably ignores the details and nuances of Ruether's argument and distorts her position, but it is accurate in indicating that she depicts Christian anti-Judaism as the result of the way Jews who were Christians developed their Christology in the first two decades after Jesus' death in reaction to the de-layed second coming and end of the world, and in reaction to the consequent disbelief and opposition of most Jews. It would then seem to follow that anti-Judaism can be found in every writing in the New Testament and thus is inseparable from faith in Christ. But Ruether does not want to accept that judgment and concludes with a theological argument to enable people to be Christian with-out being anti-Judaic.

Briefly and imprecisely, the argument is that Christians have mistaken dialectical relations—judgment and promise, particular-ism and universalism, letter and spirit, history and eschatology—for irreconcilable opposites, for basic dualisms of evil and good that distinguish Jews from Christians. Consequently, Christians have been able to proclaim their own monopoly of the good—despite their own unfulfilled promise, despite the particularism of their universal salvation, despite their devotion to their own legalism and letter, and despite their long involvement in the compromises of history. Ruether then argues to the contrary that, although these antitheses are indeed central in the dynamics of religious history, they are not dualisms that separate Christianity from Judaism; they are dialectical relations operating within both Judaism and Christianity and characteristic also of relations be-tween them.

What led Christians into their error, according to Ruether, is that they historicized the eschatological event by locating the ul-timate crisis of human existence within history and declaring that

51. Ibid., pp. 97-99.

evil had been conquered once and for all by the Messiah Jesus.[52] "This clearly has not taken place, nor has Christianity appropriated its message in a way that has been a very convincing means to this 'end.' "[53] Christians should not attribute "an absolute finality to the heightened expectations surrounding the life and death of Jesus." Instead, they should empathize with the way the idea of a messianic advent first appeared to Christians and thereby discover a historical Jesus, "a faithful Jew within the Mosaic covenant, who did not set out to replace Judaism by another religion, but who lived in lively expectation of the coming of God's Kingdom and judged society in its light."[54] The "Resurrection experience" of the first believers is to be understood as a paradigm for the dynamics of reexperiencing the hope of death and resurrection, but not as the final accomplishment of that hope. Moreover, that experience must be relativized, recognized to be a paradigm only for Christians who accept it as such. Christians must not condemn others who find a different paradigm more compelling because of their own history.[55]

Both the historical and theological sections of Ruether's book lead to the same conclusion, that Christian anti-Judaism was not intended by Jesus but can be traced back to the Christology developed within ten years of his death by Christians, many of whom had known Jesus. Needless to say, this representation of Jesus as a messianic prophet rather than the Messiah through whom salvation comes to all has provoked opposition and criticism.[56] Equally obvious, it would be foolhardy for anyone not deeply versed in the history of the period and New Testament hermeneutics to assay the outcome. The same is true of recent efforts to demonstrate that when Paul said that the Law had come to an end, he meant it for gentile converts to Christianity, not for Jews, that he did not believe that that God had abandoned Jews who remained faithful to the Law.[57] Fortunately, it is not

---

52. Ibid., p. 247.
53. Ibid., p. 248.
54. Ibid., pp. 248-249.
55. Ibid., p. 250.
56. E.g., the essays in *Antisemitism and the Foundations of Christianity*.
57. E.g., Krister Stendahl, *Paul among Jews and Gentiles* (Philadelphia, 1976); John G. Gager, *The Origins of Anti-Semitism* (New York, 1983); Lloyd Gaston, *Paul and Torah* (Vancouver, 1987).

necessary for our present purposes to traverse these minefields. All that matters is the fact that it now takes remarkably fine readings and subtle arguments—and perhaps faith—to argue that Christian anti-Judaism did not appear as early as the Christian belief that Jesus was the turning point in history and that faith in him was necessary for salvation. On that point Lovsky remains convincing.

Contrary to the desires of those who have elaborated them, the arguments of Ruether, Stendahl, Gager, and others only make it more impossible now to argue cogently that anti-Judaism has not been inherent in Christianity from the beginning—whatever the future may hold—and that Christianity did not prepare the ground for antisemitism in the nineteenth and twentieth centuries. Their arguments may defend Christian faith after Hitler by changing it; they cannot change its past. And insofar as their arguments are historical rather than theological, I think they are on the wrong track.

The problem with their arguments, even for those who seek to defend their Christian faith, is that they try to disconnect Jesus and genuine Christianity from anti-Judaism but fail to demonstrate that differentiation in an empirically convincing way. They might be better served by an argument that accepted what Parkes and other Christian scholars have demonstrated ever more convincingly. They might accept that the historical corollary of the emergence of Christian faith and the continuation of Judaic faith was Christian anti-Judaism, a rejection of Judaism that has varied in intensity but has been accompanied for nearly two thousand years by a hostility toward Jews on the part of Christians that was often extreme and prepared the way for antisemitism. If that position were accepted, the crucial problem would then be to distinguish anti-Judaism from antisemitism, to demonstrate that although Christian beliefs prepared the way for antisemitism, they were not themselves *the* cause of antisemitism.

Necessary causes are not sufficient causes. Judaism was necessary for there to be Jews, Jews for there to be Jesus of Nazareth, Christ for there to be Christian beliefs, Christian beliefs for there to be Christians, Jews and Christians for there to be Christian anti-Judaism, and Christian anti-Judaism for there to be antisemitism. But that does not mean either that Judaism is *the* cause of antisemitism or that Christianity is—or both. Much more is needed to explain the evolution of Judaism, the splits within it, the development of Christianity in all its diversity, and the appearance of modern self-labeled antisemitism, that peculiar combination of inheritances from Christianity, ideas from philology and biology, nationalistic passions, and economic misunderstanding.

It is one thing to understand Christian anti-Judaism as one necessary cause or condition of modern antisemitism and quite another to say that antisemitism was the result of faith in the divinity of Jesus of Nazareth and appeared with that faith. The differences in the nature of the hostility and in chronology are too obvious. The problem—both for Christians and for objective scholars—is to find a way of distinguishing reactions against Jews that were direct or unavoidable consequences of belief in Christ from the hatred of antisemites without taking a theological position or denying the connections between them. For both Christians and non-Christians who seek to be objective, the crucial questions are: how does antisemitism differ in nature from anti-Judaic hostility; did a distinctively Christian antisemitism appear; and if so, when did it appear and why?

To ask these questions, however, is to raise a more fundamental problem: what are Judaism and Christianity? More generally, what do we mean when we speak of a religion and of religious conduct? The scholars discussed in this chapter had a ready answer because of their religious faith; historians who seek to be neutral are denied that solution and must find their own. If we use only the methods available to objective historians, what shall we categorize as religious and what not? Are religions what their adherents say they are? To solve that problem, however, we first have to face a more general problem of historical method: can historians accept the beliefs of people in the past as a sufficient explanation of their actions?

Chapter Three

Rationalization and Explanation

Can objective historians in the present accept that a religion is what its believers have said it is, and can they explain the believers' conduct by their beliefs? Formulated more generally, we confront a more basic question that has long bedeviled critical philosophy of history. It is also relevant to descriptions and explanations of religion in other disciplines. There have been many efforts to define religion in other disciplines, some of which will be discussed in the three following chapters. But, similar in this to the practice of historians, most of those scholarly definitions incorporate beliefs of the adherents of traditional religions, particularly belief in "God," as their own principal criterion for religion. However concealed by modern generalizing language—for example, "belief in a superior, supra-empirical being"—these scholars make the content of such beliefs a necessary criterion of their own definition of religion and, hence, of their own explanations of the conduct of religious believers.

But can we accept other people's explanations of their actions as our own best description and explanation of their actions? Most people happily avoid the question most of the time, and it does not affect the natural sciences, since few of their practitioners attribute free will to the objects they study. It does, however, affect any effort to explain the thought of the scientists themselves, for it haunts any discipline that attempts to provide verifiable explanations of human actions. And it so crucial for any

42

explanation of religious action or antisemitism that we must look at it closely. For most people, the answer is obvious. When I gave my course on the Christianization of Europe, many students simply took for granted that a description of what people in the past believed was the best explanation of why they acted as they did.

The approach of many historians, if more sophisticated, has been little different, especially when dealing with religious beliefs. Yet if this approach is persuasive when applied to beliefs whose existence we take for granted because they are part of our cultural inheritance and resemble some of our own beliefs, it seems highly unconvincing when applied to people with whom we refuse to identify because we judge their conduct immoral or the beliefs with which they justified it demonstrably false or simply undemonstrable. To say that Jewish avoidance of certain kinds of contact with non-Jews or the hostility of many Christians to Jews was caused by the beliefs those human beings had about a god—or that Nazi hatred of Jews was caused by their beliefs about Aryan blood—may be accurate as a partial description of part of *their* conduct, of the thoughts that accompanied their actions. And their explanation may be a sufficient explanation for those who believe—in mutually contradictory ways—that such unobservable entities exist and act as asserted, and who want to protect their beliefs from further analysis. But, as Sydney Ahlstrom declared in 1969, religious history "no longer enjoys any rights of sanctuary."[1] For the professionally neutral and agnostic historian who cannot observe Christ or Aryan blood and cannot therefore explain anything by their action, such beliefs are not a sufficient explanation. What they have to explain so far as possible—a caveat I want to emphasize heavily—is why those people believed as they did so that they acted as they did.

But that is just what historians who bracket religious topics fail to do. When historians describe what the adherents of a religion believed and did in the believers' terms and refuse to describe and explain them in their own professional terms, the only ex-

1. Sydney E. Ahlstrom, "The Problem of the History of Religion in America," *Church History* 57, Supplement (1988): 136. This is a reprint of an address first made in 1969 and first published in *Church History* 39 (1970): 224-235.

planation they present is the beliefs of the historical actors. They thereby imply that those beliefs are the only possible historical explanation of what those people did, and that no other or further explanation is now possible. Of course, historians who adhere to the same religion may find the explanation satisfactory because they share those beliefs and are disinclined to explain them in other terms. But historians who do not share those beliefs, or who set them aside when acting professionally, cannot accept the explanations of the historical actors as satisfactory because they cannot use the premises on which they rest. They know that the beliefs underlying such explanations are not universally accepted as premises for rational empirical explanations. They therefore have to use more universally accepted premises to provide their own, often very different, explanation of why those people believed and did what they did. And they should make them explicit, for if they do not, they avoid part of their responsibility as objective scholars.

If explanation by the beliefs of the historical actors often seems plausible when historians are describing people with common beliefs, its problems become apparent when we attempt to explain the actions of people who held conflicting beliefs. If, in discussing the religious hostility between Christians and Jews in the Middle Ages, one used only the thoughts of Christians to explain the conduct of Christians and Jews, it would be a tacit adherence to the faith of one side. And what is sauce for the goose should be sauce for the gander. Judaic thoughts about Christians should be an equally good explanation of Jewish and Christian conduct. The error is so obvious that professional historians have long abandoned explicit reliance on such one-sided ethnocentric descriptions and explanations. But to explain the mutual hostility by the religious thoughts on both sides (as many scholars have) is no better. If neither set of explanations is empirically verifiable, to use both together as the best objective explanation only compounds error and involves self-contradiction.

Since Jews and Christians had mutually incompatible ideas about their own conduct and that of their opponents, a scholar cannot assert that both sets of ideas taken together somehow add up to an integrated explanation of the interaction of those human beings. To do so is tantamount to asserting that Jews acted as they did because of the covenant of the one God with them, and that Christians acted as they did because Christ was truly divine and saved those who believed in him. The obvious self-contradiction can, of course, be avoided if the historian only asserts that Christians and Jews were mutually hostile because of their different ideas about existence. But the fact of difference explains little. The very broad and not universally valid generalization that people with different ideas about central issues will be hostile to one another throws little light on the specific causes of the mutual hostility. Indeed, the historian's problem of explanation arises because of the existence of a third viewpoint: her or his own knowledge and beliefs about existence. If difference in belief caused the hostility, then the historian's task is to explain, so far as that is empirically possible, why that difference had developed, why each group had come to believe and act as it did. And that explanation must be based not on the beliefs of Jews and Christians but on premises that are acceptable to all professional historians in the present, regardless of differences in their other beliefs.

What cries out for historical explanation is why both sides believed as they did and rationalized their conduct and hostility as they did. And since historians are not supposed to take sides or engage in self-contradiction, they must seek an explanation of the mutual aversion that is based on premises or a faith independent of, or more universal than, the distinctive beliefs of Jews and Christians, whether it be another substantive faith such as Buddhism, nationalism, Marxism, or Freudianism—or the methodological faith of rational empiricism. But since reliance on one substantive faith is suspect for obvious reasons, that leaves rational empiricism as the only possible solution.

Of course, to believe that rational and empirical thinking is necessary to reduce error in historical research and inform moral or political decisions is not something that can be decided by rational methods. It seems an act of faith or moral decision; and when emphasized, it resembles a religious commitment. All who accept its constraints or present paradigm, regardless of their differences in personal background, concerns, and other beliefs, must accept what is revealed by its methods and cannot presently be denied by its own methods; and scholars who do not accept those constraints will be damned as biased ideologues. But the use of rational empirical thinking is not an act of faith or moral decision in the usual sense. It is something we can no more abandon than our trust in our bodily processes, for it is a universal human characteristic.

When I speak of "rational empirical thinking," I will be using the term very broadly to denote the kind of thinking, whether primitive and pretheoretical or highly developed, that has enabled human beings to develop tools and demonstrate their efficacy by results in principle observable and repeatable by anyone else. In however simple and pretheoretical form, and however limited its use, rational empirical thinking is necessary for survival and is present even in the most primitive human societies, as Lévi-Strauss has insisted.[2] In its most developed form, it has produced the knowledge of science, physiology, psychology, economics, and so forth that enabled human beings to get to the moon. If we value that capacity, we will apply it to the thoughts and actions of believing Jews, Christians, and Moslems and the relations between them. And when we do so, we will be compelled to try to describe and explain them not simply according to the conflicting ideas of Judaism, Christianity, or Islam but also, so far as possible, in present rational empirical terms that have at least some present claim to universality. And the same applies to religious phenomena in general.

If historians categorize Judaism and Christianity as instances of the same kind of basic human activity, as "religion," despite the obvious differences in the beliefs and actions of Jews and Christians, they should recognize that they themselves are deciding what they mean by religion. Unless they are writing as believers, historians cannot use the beliefs of Judaic or Christian religions to determine what they mean by religion. They must decide for themselves. At least, they must have a provisional conception that distinguishes thoughts and conduct that are "religious" from those that are not. As—among other things—rational empiricists, historians can accept the reality of belief as a human characteristic and as one causal link in human actions (with all that that implies

2. Claude Lévi-Strauss, *La pensée sauvage* (Paris, 1962), pp. 3-21.

for indeterminacy). They can observe, classify, and compare the particular beliefs of particular humans. They can describe beliefs, recognize agreement and conflict between sets of beliefs, and analyze how they correlate with cooperation and friction between humans. But if they purport to be objective, they cannot accept beliefs about entities they cannot observe as an adequate characterization or explanation of that conduct.

When people make assertions that state without self-contradiction that certain relatively unambiguously denoted entities can be empirically observed, and observed to be related in reasonably precise, frequent, or enduring ways, there can be rational empirical discussion, and agreement may be reached on whether those assertions are commonly acceptable. But assertions of belief that refer to entities that cannot presently be detected by common observation cannot be judged true. Nor, indeed, can such assertions of belief be judged false unless they are self-contradictory or entail subordinate propositions that can be demonstrated false by empirical observation. Beliefs that assert the existence of undetectable entities such as hobgoblins, connect them with other observable entities and are constitutive of some human action, may be data for rational empirical analysis, but they cannot be a rational empirical explanation of the existence of those beliefs, of the actions of the believers, or of any aversion that others may have had toward people who believed in hobgoblins.

Many historians, however, do use the thoughts or beliefs of the people they study as a sufficient explanation of their actions and accept their definition of religion. Moreover, several philosophers of history, from Vico forward, have asserted that historians must and should use that form of explanation. According to R. G. Collingwood, the thoughts of historical actors are not simply one way of explaining their actions; they are the ultimately satisfactory explanation.[3] The best known recent supporter of that position, William Dray, does not go quite as far. He acknowledges that some kinds of historical explanation are (as Hempel argued they all should be)[4] similar to scientific explanations in that they subsume

3. *The Idea of History* (Oxford, 1951), esp. pp. 282-302.
4. Carl G. Hempel, "The Function of General Laws in History," in *Theories of History*, ed. Patrick Gardiner (Glencoe, Ill., 1959), pp. 344-356.

actions under laws or, in the case of history, under well-warranted generalizations. But Dray argues that there is another type of explanation, which he distinguishes carefully from the covering-law model and calls "rational" explanations. He means by that, not the rationality of the historians, but the rational calculations of the agent, the historical actor(s). "And it is by eliciting some such calculation that we explain the [agent's] action."[5] "The general belief that people act for sufficient reason does not arise out of definite pieces of evidence in particular cases; it is a *standing* presumption which requires contrary evidence in a particular case to defeat" it—for example, manifest irrationality.[6] It is the frequent reliance of historians on this kind of explanation, Dray believes, that makes history closer to literature than to social science; and he asserts that explanation by the reasons of the actor is a "perfectly adequate" kind of explanation.[7] The same position has recently been reasserted by Ian G. Barbour.[8]

At first sight, the position seems thoroughly understandable and acceptable, especially when it relies on universal rational empirical knowledge, however pretheoretical. If I have good evidence that someone in the past was hungry, found some meat, cooked it, and ate it, I can at least partially understand what the person did. Since I assume that the normal physical laws or biological needs were working properly, I have what seems an obviously adequate explanation of his or her action—unless I am a vegetarian. Indeed, my ability to understand the words in a historical document rests on this kind of simple commonality of knowledge. If I read *castrum* on a piece of parchment, it is meaningful to me because I can translate it as "castle" and picture a castle, not simply because I have seen some medieval castles (albeit altered and restored) but also because the language of the period links "castle" with words used to refer to very concrete things familiar then and now (such as stone, mound, family, war-

5. *Laws and Explanation in History* (Oxford, 1957), pp. 123-124.
6. Ibid., p. 137. We should note here that Dray only distinguishes between rational and irrational thoughts. He makes no allowance for the nonrational thoughts that play so vast a role in all human action. See below, chap. 8, for a discussion of nonrational thinking.
7. Ibid., pp. 139, 142.
8. *Issues in Science and Religion* (New York, 1971), p. 200.

rior, food, wall, chamber, and the like) in a way that enables me to have some idea of what they denoted by *castrum*.

Our ability to understand people in the past depends heavily on our conviction that one way in which both we and people then used words was to refer to specific, very concrete, external objects that both we and they could perceive, even though our perceptions of those objects is somewhat different, and even though we normally relate them to each other in very different ways, and relate them to things or ideas medieval people never thought of. Hence, if I read that someone decided to besiege a castle because he wanted it for himself, and that he did so and captured it, not only can I picture in some measure what went on physically but, because I assume that my mind and his worked similarly, at least in certain basic ways, I can partly understand why it happened. Our historical assertions do depend importantly upon our assurance that we have some limited access to the thoughts of people in the past that gives us some understanding, some explanation, of their actions.

What makes the position that the thoughts of the historical actors are an adequate explanation of conduct so attractive is that it seems to correspond to so much of our understanding of everyday life, including our explanations of our own conduct. Nonetheless, and even though I have long been a devotee of Collingwood, I find the position untenable. I cannot accept it because it makes the beliefs that historical agents themselves give as explanations for, or justifications of, their actions my explanation, and I know that I do not understand existence as they did. *Their* explanation of those actions cannot be *mine*. Or, more correctly, whatever they and I may have in common as human beings, whatever commonalities of experience we may share (and they may be many), my total explanation of their actions cannot be the same as theirs. Since I live in a different mental world, I inescapably connect their thoughts with many thoughts they never had.

The word "explanation" here can cause trouble because there are many kinds of explanation, or, more correctly, we accept different kinds of explanations in different contexts, depending on what we are looking for and what we already know. What is sufficient as an immediate explanation of a particular action in a highly familiar context may not be what we want when we are curious about an action distant in time and space. In other words, historical explanation is very different from our immediate explanation of some everyday occurrence in a highly familiar context.[9]

The kind of explanation I need when I ask my wife of many years why she just did something is very different from the kind of explanation that would satisfy my curiosity about why Oliver Cromwell did something. Whereas, for my immediate purposes, all I may need to explain why my wife did what she did may be her assertion of her intention, my historical explanation of Cromwell's action will be very different because I can take so little for granted about the person or the period. I must broaden my perspective greatly and take into consideration a much wider set of conditions, including thoughts, with which, save as a historian, I am unfamiliar. Indeed, when I know that someone intended to do something and did it in a period with which I am thoroughly unfamiliar, their action and explanation for it may be practically meaningless to me until I can connect it with conduct with which I am familiar. Before I have a satisfying explanation of their action, I need to know what they thought and believed and be able to explain those thoughts in my own terms. Thus, what count as satisfying explanations will differ from person to person and will vary depending on the person's purpose and perspective. Explanations will also differ depending on whether we focus on the knowledge or on the beliefs of the people whose actions we seek to explain.

When we discuss knowledge and beliefs, we need to avoid the ambiguities lurking in the expressions "I know" and "I believe." "I believe" can indicate either a firm conviction based on faith or a high degree of incertitude because of inadequate knowledge; "I know" can indicate either consciousness of highly reliable rational empirical knowledge or a conviction that is not derived from empirical knowledge but is maintained as firmly as—or more firmly than—the most widely substantiated empirical knowledge. We often recognize that our knowledge about some matter is very

9. This is a problem that I think Searle failed to take sufficiently into account in his discussion of explanation of action by the actor's intention in his Reith lectures: John Searle, *Minds, Brains and Science* (Cambridge, Mass., 1984), pp. 57-61.

uncertain or incomplete and indicate our uncertainty by saying "I believe that" rather than "I know that." "Believe" here does not indicate profound certitude but rather that we are uncertain of our knowledge about the matter. "I believe it is going to rain" indicates a tentative hypothesis based on prior experience, whereas "I know it is going to rain" is a confident prediction based on what we feel is highly reliable knowledge. Yet if I say, "I know that my Redeemer liveth and that He shall stand at the latter day upon the earth," "know" here refers to a sense of ample certitude that does not derive from rational empirical knowledge but expresses faith.

As I am using it, "know" here means rational empirical assertions, however pretheoretical, that can be convincingly inferred by rational analysis of observable evidence and can be modified by the discovery of new evidence—in brief, knowledge of varying degrees of certainty. By "belief " I mean assurances we cannot obtain through the exercise of our rational empirical capacities, the faith that guides our use of those capacities.

When we explain our own actions or those of other people, we do so in two very different ways: by regarding them as implementations of knowledge or as expressions of belief. On the one hand, we may explain that people did various things because they knew, more or less reliably, that if they—or anyone else—used these means, certain consequences that anyone could observe would follow. Thus, if we know that someone pierced another with a spear or bayonet to the heart, we can confidently assume, insanity aside, that they were trying to kill the person and acted as they did because they knew, as we do, that people pierced to the heart die. Explanations of this sort rely on the fact that, although we have highly sophisticated scientific knowledge, we and people in very different cultures share a wide range of pretheoretical rational empirical knowledge. In other words, once we know what practical goals people are seeking to achieve, we can partially explain why they acted as they did by our commonality of understanding, by the basic rational empirical knowledge we share. On the other hand, we may find that many actions cannot be satisfactorily explained by such widely shared knowledge. They cannot be explained without reference to the person's beliefs, and because those beliefs may differ radically from ours, they pose the further problem of explaining why those persons believed as they did.

If we know that a woman pierced a waxen image of someone with pins, we can assume fairly confidently that she wished that person ill—the metaphor is obvious. But we cannot say that she knew the person would die; generals throughout history have not stuck pins in thousands of images of their enemies. To explain why this person acted as she did, we have to refer to her beliefs and those prevalent in her society and then try to explain why she held those beliefs. As with the person who used a spear, the goal is the same, to harm someone, but the means employed to achieve the goal, the person's actions, are radically different. One relies on some pretheoretical rational empirical knowledge common to people of different faiths throughout history; the other expresses a belief about the nature of unseen forces that many people throughout history, including ourselves, do not have.

Now one could imagine much more complicated examples. Thus, if we knew that Abraham intended to kill his beloved only son, we might be able to explain why he planned to kill him in that particular way by his—and our—knowledge of how humans or animals can be killed. But we would not feel that a sufficient explanation of his actions. To explain his actions rationally and empirically to our satisfaction, we would also have to know what his intentions were, what beliefs were leading him to use his knowledge in that unusual way. But then we would have to try and explain why he held those beliefs. Even if we knew that he believed that his God had commanded him to commit the deed, we would want to explain why he believed what led him to commit that otherwise inexplicable act. And we could not accept his explanation as sufficient unless we believed, like him, that there was what he called God and that God had acted that way. The same is true of all explanations that seek to explain why people engaged in actions motivated by beliefs that were not common to all humanity. Even if we know that someone killed Jews with a sword, to explain the action satisfactorily we have not only to describe his beliefs about Jews but also to explain why he believed what he did about Jews. And it would have to be an explanation that satisfies us, whether we are Jews or non-Jews.

A further problem is that any explanation of a person's actions by that person's thoughts depends on that person's capacity to explain his or her own actions. Yet we are all aware how limited our own ability to explain our own actions is. We may be aware of, and able immediately to describe, some proximate or precipitating causes of some of our basic actions, but on reflection we recognize that that provides little explanation beyond the overwhelmingly obvious of why we acted as we did, of why we satisfied a need or desire common throughout history in the particular way we did. Hunger—in very different degrees—is common or universal, and we may be sure that people throughout history have eaten "because" they were hungry and thought of food. But my associations with hunger do not lead me to try to assuage my hunger by taking a bow and arrow into the forest to kill a deer— nor make me refuse to assuage it by killing a cow.

If you ask why I ate what I did at a particular time, my immediate explanation, the one closest to my action, will be very simple: I was hungry and ate what I preferred among the foods readily available. But not only is that explanation very simple and incomplete, it also fails to explain why how I ate was different from how people in the past ate—or how contemporaries in other regions or of other religions eat. The very universality of the "truism"[10] robs it of any grip on detailed historical reality save for my reference to the specific food I ate, and that descriptive detail is not an explanation of why I ate—or refused to eat—that specific food, pork, for example. Although such "explanations" may link historical events that we can describe by ascribing motives to the actors, they do not significantly explain historical variation. They do not explain in our terms why what existed then and there existed, how it changed, and how one event led to another.

If, however, with a serious scholarly mien, you ask me why I ate what I did at dinner last night, my thoughts would be very different from those I had had at the time. And here we come to a major difference between immediate and historical explanation. Mention of metabolism might spring to my lips; a discussion of

10. For a discussion of the use of truisms as explanations, see Michael Scriven, "Truisms as the Grounds for Historical Explanations," in *Theories of History*, ed. Gardiner, pp. 443-475.

our household economics and local stores might lead to a reference to Marx; and I might even refer to a fascinating article by Jonathan Z. Smith which, among other things, compares what is established as canonical in a religion with the establishment of regional cuisines.[11] My later explanation as observer of myself would thus be very different from my explanation as actor at the time. In scholarly jargon, my discursive consciousness after the event would be very different from my practical consciousness at the time. It would be different partly because my need had been satisfied, but even more because I would have responded to a question, to a demand for explanation, and tried to connect the event of my eating with anything and everything in my total knowledge of myself and my environment that seemed fairly directly relevant. From that perspective, both my thoughts and my actions at the time I ate would have become objects that I could try to describe, and my memory of them would then seem rather a description of part of my action at the time than a satisfactory explanation of its peculiarities. That is even more obviously the case when we look at the thoughts of historical actors. Even when they are at their most reflective and rational, so far as we can judge, and are themselves trying to explain events, their explanations cannot be ours because our knowledge, our conception of reality, coming after theirs and informed by experiences unknown to them, is—in varying degrees—different from theirs.

What makes explanation by the thoughts of the actors seem convincing to some analytic philosophers of history is that the examples they choose from historians' works are often passages that describe people confronted with particular, fairly immediate, and distinctly practical problems whose resolution demands knowledge, not belief.[12] And as we read such passages, which describe the context, the general dispositions of the actors, and their particular thoughts about practical problems, we can suspend disbelief and imagine ourselves in their shoes—much as in literature. That is, we can temporarily repress our own vision of reality and, in varying degrees, enter their mental world. Our—partial—knowledge of their thoughts then becomes our expla-

11. *Imagining Religion* (Chicago, 1982), pp. 39-41.
12. E.g., Dray, *Laws and Explanation in History*, pp. 122, 153.

nation of their actions. But it can be our explanation only so long as we are willing to suspend our demand for explanation according to our own criteria for explaining human action.

A peculiar feature of Dray's analysis of historical explanation is that it distinguishes between determinism (the covering-law model), free will (the rational calculations of the historical actors), and manifest irrationality. What Dray fails to recognize is that only some of the thought of "rational" people is rational. Explanation by the thought of the historical actors about very practical problems in the past may be convincing when we and they shared the same kind of more or less universal pretheoretical empirical knowledge. It may even have a certain plausibility when beliefs about unobservable objects were part of their explanation, but only so long as we suspend disbelief and "forget" our own normal consciousness of reality. For things look very different when the mental events accompanying a historical action were not simply rational thoughts about concrete objects and observable events but also conscious expressions of beliefs and values—for example, when people prayed to Christ for victory in battle. When dealing with such nonrational thinking in the past, it becomes much harder for us to "forget" our own convictions—partly because our own values are so important for our sense of our own identity. That is even truer when the values of the historical actors were ones we strongly reject. If we apply explanation by the thought of the historical actors to religion and antisemitism and the relation between them, we run into obvious difficulties.

Millions of Jews through history have explained much of their conduct, including their reactions to non-Jews, by their thoughts about "Torah." Millions of Christians have explained their treatment of Jews by their thoughts about "Christ." Moreover, many scholars who claim neutrality have used the Judaic explanation for Jewish conduct and the Christian explanation for Christian conduct. Similarly, Nazi belief in the biologically determined, normative inferiority of Jews not only was the Nazis' explanation for the killing of millions of Jews but has also been used as the explanation of Nazi conduct by non-Nazis. Now granted that those Christians and Nazis explained their actions against Jews to their own satisfaction by their thoughts, does our partial ability to describe their beliefs provide an explanation that fully satisfies us here and now? The answer, I think, is clearly no. In cases such as these, we may gain descriptive knowledge about the nonrational thought of the historical actors and the actions that accompanied them, but their nonrational beliefs cannot be our rational empirical explanation of either their thoughts or their actions.[13]

Human beings rationalize their own conduct and explain the conduct of others according to their rationalization of their own conduct. When an individual seeks to explain his or her own conduct, he or she "steps back" and tries to see himself or herself as another might see him or her. And when numerous people agree on an explanation of some people's conduct, or when an individual accepts other people's explanation of his or her own conduct, that is because they rationalize that kind of conduct in the same way. Conversely, when people understand and explain religion and antisemitism in different ways, that is because of differences in the way they rationalize their own thought and actions.

I start with myself. How do I understand my own actions? Since I am conscious of my actions only as thoughts that pass through my mind, it seems that my explanation of my actions is my thoughts about my own thoughts. But how can I explain thoughts I remember by other thoughts of which I am now conscious? There are many approaches to this problem, including intersubjectivity, set theory, distinctions between the part and the whole, hermeneutical establishment of relations between them, and the distinction between reflexive monitoring of behavior and the rationalization of action.[14]

It would surpass my competence and further exhaust the tolerance of readers concerned primarily with religion or antisemitism to attempt to expound those complex theories, so I shall answer the question I posed myself in as simple and immediate terms as I can. It seems to me that our understanding of our actions as we are doing them is necessarily the thoughts that accompany the actions, our "practical consciousness" or the "reflex-

13. What I mean by nonrational thinking will be discussed at length in chap. 8.

14. For the last two, see Richard J. Bernstein, *Beyond Objectivism and Relativism* (Philadelphia, 1983) and Anthony Giddens, *Central Problems in Social Theory* (Berkeley and Los Angeles, 1979).

ive monitoring of behaviour," to use Giddens's terms.[15] And the more reflexively we act, the less do we think about the thoughts that accompany our actions. Our thoughts become an *explanation* or a "rationalization of action" only when our thinking changes, however briefly, so that we ask ourselves what we are doing or why. When that happens, we scan what is already in our minds and realize that we had conceived ourselves to be in a certain situation and that memories of previous experiences made us feel that we should act that way.

Now the way we frame our question about our conduct and our answer to it—the explanation which we then become conscious of—may depend very heavily on the semiotic network in which we have been socialized, and we may even rely explicitly on complex theories we have learned from others. But the only explanation of how we have been acting that we genuinely accept is the thoughts or ideas that in fact satisfy us. And what satisfies us is not identical with the thoughts of anyone else because we relate those socially available ideas to distinctive personal experiences, many of which we do not presently remember consciously. The way we hold those ideas necessarily differs from the way anyone else does. Our rationalization of what we did or do is so satisfying for us because it harmonizes with our sense of reality. It also expresses our conviction that we are free, an independent variable, if not in all our actions, at least in our explaining of our own actions, for without that conviction we could not choose consciously between competing explanations. Indeed, at the cost of self-contradiction, we can even assert ourselves by choosing to believe that all our conduct is determined in some unknown way.

We explain our actions in the more distant past in the same way. If we ask ourselves some time later why we then acted as we did, our first step is usually to rehearse what we can remember about our action and thought at the time: "I did it because at the time I thought that such and such was the case, wanted this or that, and therefore did what I did." Our conscious memory of what we thought remains our primary conception of it, and our

---

15. *The Constitution of Society* (Berkeley and Los Angeles, 1984), pp. 43-44.

own reasons at the time are our only explanation of why we did what we did—unless we now modify our explanation, as we often do.

We often look back at something we did and doubt that we then understood what we were doing or that we should have acted that way. What we have learned or experienced since makes us criticize what we thought and did then. It is not simply that those past actions had consequences unknowable to us at the time, including the reactions of others to our actions. We may have acquired more information about the world in general, and our general beliefs about our own nature and that of the world around us may have changed. As a result, we may feel that we can look back on our past selves and past actions more objectively as something intimately related to, yet different from, what we are now. And we may conclude that, at the time we did something, we did not understand very well what we were doing and why. We are thus able, to some extent, to look at ourselves as an external observer might. Indeed, we are usually influenced by our knowledge of the reactions of external observers. That increased ability to see ourselves as others see us is normally taken as a sign of maturity, albeit so difficult to achieve that it has been thought a grace from beyond. As Robert Burns put it, "Oh wad some power the giftie gie us to see oursels as others see us," for it is much easier to see others as objects than ourselves. But even then we only accept our own thoughts as explanations of their actions.

When we see another person acting as we would, we see them as different from ourselves but feel no need for an explanation of their action. But when we see another person acting in a way that does not immediately make sense to us, our first reaction is often to ask, "What does he or she think he or she is doing?" If we cannot answer our own question, we feel we cannot understand the person's actions. But if we can discover what the person is thinking, what their rationalization of their action is, we may find that the person thinks much as we do but is in a situation we had not fully perceived or understood. Indeed, we often answer our question, not by asking the person, but by getting a fuller understanding of their situation and inferring their thoughts from the reactions we would have had. At other times, we simply ask the person. Whichever way we reach our answer, if we then feel we would have acted in that situation as they did, if we feel that what they took as good reasons are good reasons for us, our rationalizations agree, and we feel we have a satisfactory explanation of the person's actions.

But we often disagree with other people's ideas; and when we do, we do not accept their thoughts as our explanation of their actions. We may be able, with some effort, to empathize partially with them, even with someone we dislike. And we will not deny that the person's thoughts and actions were causally connected. But their understanding of their actions will not and cannot be *our* explanation. What separates us from them is that their non-rational thought about themselves and their world differs from ours. While we may agree with them on many details, even on all the concrete "facts" of a particular situation, we do not put the facts together in the same way, and we think that certain other facts are relevant to the situation in a way they do not. It is here that the commonsense distinction between "facts" and "beliefs" comes in. In customary if not philosophic parlance, "facts" are assertions that neither we nor other people with different religious, moral, or political beliefs, but with common empirical information and rational methods and theories, can presently deny. By contrast, "beliefs" are deniable assertions about how facts are connected with each other and with other facts.

In the natural sciences, "facts" are dependent on theories, on logical assertions that certain kinds of events observed according to precise rules of observation are related in an unambiguous way or highly reliable statistical pattern. Hence, from the theory and some relevant facts, other facts may be predicted and observed. Facts and theories are thus mutually dependent, even though theories may be underdetermined by the "facts" presented to warrant them and even though the facts may depend on theories that rest on premises. "Beliefs," however, differ from theories in that some of what is presented as fact is not observable and the premises of faith are far from universally accepted, or in that the facts are not related logically according to agreed rules of observation so as to permit the prediction of other observable facts. Consequently, people who do not deny the present facts and theories of science may nonetheless have beliefs, nonrational thoughts, which give a different or further meaning to some of those facts.

Jews, Catholics, and atheists can cooperate fruitfully as scientists while directing their personal lives very differently. In brief, theories with their facts differ from beliefs with their facts in that the former are rigorously constrained by the contemporary rules of logic, relatively unambiguous disciplinary language, and highly developed methods of observation while the latter are not.[16] And since broad historical explanation, however much it may be scientific in sections of its argument, does not comply with such rigorous rules and methods, it depends heavily on the historian's beliefs. In that it resembles our understanding of daily life.

In everyday life, we continually distinguish between facts and beliefs. We may disagree with other persons over the facts, over the concrete context of action, but then find that the disagreement can be resolved by investigation conducted according to mutually agreeable methods. If that proves to be the case, we will accept their explanation of the situation and of their actions because their beliefs do not differ from ours. But if that is not the case, we are forced to realize that they have different beliefs about the way things capable of common observation ought to be related, and we cannot accept their thoughts as our explanation of their actions. In daily life, we are frequently uncertain which is the case but are not particularly impelled to find out. When the issue is important, however, and the differences in the other person's beliefs or conception of rationality obvious, we do not accept their explanation and frequently proceed to use our own ideas about human conduct to try to explain why they think as they do.

Psychiatrists obviously often find themselves in this situation, and so do their clients, who—if we are to believe Foucault, Lacan, and Laing—are equally or more justified. And so do anthropologists, sociologists, and historians. Historians have their own understanding of themselves and their world, and their profession engages them in the examination of traces left by people in the past whose understanding of reality was manifestly very different. What are historians to make of them? Their first and primary task, of course, is to use those traces to establish what

16. I recognize that I am dancing very lightly over serious philosophical questions here. But I am only underlining what still seems to me the undeniable difference between the kind of thinking involved in developing irrigation systems and the kind that leads people to engage in rain dances.

can be inferred with high reliability about what people once did, said, and thought. These, when solidly established, are what are called historical facts. And as a very good historian, J. H. Round, once wrote while damning a colleague,

Men have differed, and will always differ, as to how history should be written; but on one point we are all agreed. The true historian is he, and he only, who, from the evidence before him, can divine the facts. Other qualities are welcome, but this is the essential gift.[17]

The historian takes as fact what he or she has been able to conclude would neither have been denied by the actors in the past nor be rejected by other historians in the present, regardless of their beliefs, who are familiar with the relevant evidence, the fact, for example, that Château Gaillard was captured on a particular day, 6 March 1204, according to our calendar. But since a fact is all but meaningless in isolation, enough such facts must be collected and meaningfully connected in order to describe what happened somewhere. But according to whose meaning? Can the historian explain the actions of people long dead, who cannot argue back, by his or her own beliefs? Here enters the problem of objectivity or conflicting beliefs.

One school of historians, positivist or "factual" historians, thought they could avoid the dilemma. And although the weaknesses of their position are now recognized by most historians, the underlying problem has not been fully resolved. The positivist historians recognized that it might be very hard, even after great technical training, to infer the "facts"—undeniable acts and thoughts of people of some period—from the available evidence. But once enough facts had been found, they believed it was easy to connect them "objectively" because the connections had already been made in the minds of the people at the time. Since those connections were obvious from their language, which could be directly observed in the historical evidence and studied as an object, it seemed that all the historian had to do was to connect his facts as those people had linked their thoughts and actions. All modern bias would then be excluded. Thus Ranke, the father of modern historiography, felt that what he wrote was history as

17. James Horace Round, *Feudal England* (London, 1909), p. 388.

it really happened. The past could be recreated. But as has been realized long since, that objectivity was a magnificent illusion.

In the first place, historians accept as facts only those assertions that are undeniable according to their own understanding of themselves and their world. Hence some of what actors in the past took as facts may not be facts for the later historian—for example, miracles. But even granted that facts about concrete actions can be established, their linkage is equally at the mercy of present understanding. No matter how rigorously historians try to be purely factual and simply describe what people did and thought, they are forced to select and group their facts according to their own understanding—and in response to their own questions—in a way that no one in that period grouped them. Every effort at factual historical synthesis, no matter how limited, is a later interpretation. Even at its most rigorous, it is a selective abridgment, rearrangement, and translation into a present language (with all its different connotations) of but some of the things that some people then did and thought about.

Neither all people at the time nor any single one of them ever knew and linked all the thoughts and acts linked by the historian's presentation. The competing actions and contradictory thoughts the historian reports as historical facts after great labor were indeed known immediately, and without any effort, to the people at the time who did and thought them. But they were known by different people, in different ways, and not by everyone. Moreover, people at the time thought and did many things unknown to or unmentioned by the historian. And since the semiotic network of each of those individuals was slightly different from that of his or her contemporaries, and very different from ours, none of them organized his or her awareness of experiences as historians in the present do. We may publish editions of the writings of people in the past, but their lives were not texts; our syntheses cannot be editions of their various lives, and their thoughts cannot be our explanation of their actions.

Except in very narrowly limited monographic work, if then, few historians now think they can do purely "factual" history. Almost all will frequently connect facts by judgments explicitly based on knowledge, methods, and theories unavailable to the historical actors. Yet the desire to keep attention focused on the past and to seem impersonal and objective often, perhaps typically, ensures that explicit use of later understanding by historians will be scattered piecemeal through their works in order to substantiate particular conclusions, while many fundamental convictions will be left implicit, embedded in the language they use to organize their work as a whole. As a result, even though there may be flaws in some particulars, their work as a whole has an objective ring because it seems safely grounded in the present, widely shared, understanding of reality.

By concealing their own fundamental outlook on major aspects of the human condition which they discuss in their work, historians preserve the appearance of impartiality and objectivity. They leave it to reviewers to detect their obvious particular biases, and to later students of historiography who study their lives, works, and cultural environment as a whole to remove the camouflage and reveal their underlying preconceptions.[18] Of course, knowledge that that will happen does not, and should not, discourage practicing historians. Most would probably say, "Let others reveal my assumptions. I have to get on with the job or there won't be anything for them to interpret. To get anything accomplished, I have to rely on the validity of the present common (or at least educated) understanding of the human condition, except where I know I am in disagreement with it."

One advantage claimed for this way of presenting history is that the task of establishing the significance of the information purveyed by the historian is apparently left up to each reader to determine according to his or her own personal perspective, a laudable recognition of the diversity of outlooks. But in fact, the information elicited from the data by the historian is already selected, organized, and explained according to one perspective, which the historian hopes will be persuasive. A historian I greatly admire once said that historians describe and explain, but they describe a lot more than they explain. I would say rather that they describe and explain equally, but whereas their descriptions are explicit, their explanations and the premises of their expla-

18. For a recent probing analysis of some of the preconceptions of a historian who had strong views about religion, see W. B. Carnochan, *Gibbon's Solitude* (Stanford, 1987).

nations are often tacit, with obvious exceptions such as certain Marxist and religious historians.

Take "religion" and "antisemitism" as denotative or explanatory concepts. While religious historians, theologians, and sociologists often make explicit the meaning they ascribe to those terms and the premises on which those meanings rest, many historians who use the terms do not. Yet who would believe that historians do not have their own conception of the basic nature and causes of the thoughts and actions they cluster under the customary rubrics of "religion" and "antisemitism"? In many cases, of course, they do not have any clear conception of the phenomena thus labeled, only a more or less cohesive set of associations provided by the conventional usage of the terms and their own personal experiences. But that is enough for them to get on with their immediate task. And they can defend that approach by saying that, although they have no clear definitions or explanations of these salient forms of human conduct, that very openness avoids prejudgment, while their detailed work nonetheless provides the material necessary for anyone ill-advised enough to attempt a restrictive definition. They feel that common sense and modesty before the complexity of human action is preferable to conceptual arrogance.

In fact, however, preconceptions pervade the works of historians. Some, those that reviewers will quickly spot, may be personal to the historian or restricted to a particular subgroup of society. Far more difficult to detect are the tacit preconceptions of the general culture in which the historian and his audience were socialized, assumptions embedded in the language that the historian must use when writing history. And it is peculiarly difficult for historians to avoid those preconceptions because they cannot rely on technical terms to convey their reconstruction of past human actions in the round; for the most part, they must use the ordinary language of educated people. To describe aspects of the seamless web of history, they must deploy a large vocabulary in common usage; and if they hope to be praised for writing well, it must flow effectively. The flow of language, however, has impulsions of its own that may carry the historian into channels of thought dredged deep in the past.

Historians cannot rethink every word or analyze every natural turn of phrase; and although some words like "class" have warning signals attached as the result of work in other disciplines, most have never been given any more precise meaning than that supplied by common usage. Unless some particular consideration forces reflection, the historian will use them as they have been generally used—often as they have been used with little change for decades or centuries. And that is especially true of denotations such as "Jews" or "Christians" whose empirical referents have existed for millennia and are still important. But as our dictionaries remind us, these words carry a rich freight of old associations that are difficult to unload. "Jew": "A person of Hebrew *race*; an Israelite"; "any Israelite who adhered to the worship of Jehovah as conducted at Jerusalem"; "Applied to a grasping or extortionate usurer"; "To cheat or overreach." Compare "Christian": "Believing or professing the religion of Christ"; "Pertaining to Christ or Christianity"; "Following the precepts and example of Christ"; "human; civilized, decent respectable."[19]

Those brief definitions condense a multitude of usages from Shakespeare and Marlowe to the present. In the case of "Jew," of course, recent events have forced conscious reconsideration so that many people, if by no means all, now try to avoid such connotations. Yet if most historians now avoid obviously false or misleadingly stereotypical conceptions of Jews, have they reconsidered what they do mean by Jew, Christian, or religion? Theologians have, of course, but have historians? Or do most still discuss religious phenomena and explain them in the traditional language used by the adherents of religions? The fact that historians writing in English typically capitalize "God" while denigrating polytheists by writing of their "gods" is but one indication of the reliance on customary language. When medieval historians speak of the Church instead of the Roman Catholic church, they may only be engaging in a convenient ellipsis, but their language echoes the assumption expressed as dogma by Pope Boniface VIII in 1302: "we are bound to believe and to hold, our faith urging us, that there is one holy Catholic and apostolic church."

These are obvious cases, and most scholars recognize the am-

19. *The Oxford Universal Dictionary*, 3d ed. (Oxford, 1955), italics mine. Note also, only in "Addenda and Corrigenda": "Anti-Semitism": "Theory, action, or practice directed against the Jews."

biguity inherent in the historiographic convention of capitalizing God or speaking of the Church—or of "heretics"—however much the usage may reinforce the predispositions of some historians and many readers. But how many other less concrete turns of phrase that have been consecrated by long usage are a natural part of historical discourse? Since many historians are themselves adherents of religions, they can scarcely avoid many traditional turns of phrase they use in their personal lives. Nor are they likely to seek strenuously for empirical rational explanations of religious beliefs. And many other historians who are not adherents, having paid little attention to religion as such, have no language, no concepts of their own, to analyze religious phenomena and little interest in doing so. Consequently, they are content to fulfill the historian's primary duty and describe or "recreate" religious life in the past simply by paraphrasing the language of the believers they study—a procedure that has the advantage of avoiding controversy. As a result, the only explanation of religious conduct they present seems that supplied by those past believers, although in fact the historians have tacitly remolded those beliefs of the past through selection and emphasis according to their own preconceptions.

Of course, some historians may also surround their historical descriptions of religious activity with rhetorical devices that make the historian's disbelief fairly obvious to the reader, but irony still provides no explanation other than that people in the past were, for some reason, deceived in a way the historian is not. And some historians, Marxists for example, do explain (away) religious beliefs completely and explicitly in their own language as distorted expressions of other human needs which these historians consider more important and have studied intensively. But typically, such historians have never examined religious data at all closely; they have no precise terminology to distinguish religious phenomena from other phenomena; and their explanation often seems something imposed rather than something developed after careful consideration of the data for religion.

If anthropologists, sociologists, and psychologists all have terminology proper to their disciplines with which they discuss religion, so that we are not surprised to hear someone refer to the sociology or psychology of religion, history as a discipline does not. True, there is the subbranch known as the history of religion, and its practitioners certainly debate as to how they should best approach their subject. But although much concerned to establish taxonomies that permit them to type religious actions and compare religions, they typically do not analyze the fundamental questions about the nature of religion debated by anthropologists, sociologists, and psychologists. As for historians who do not specialize in the history of religions, most do not reflect on the terms they use to refer to religious phenomena; they are usually content to rely on the traditional language customary in their particular field of history, which is often that of the religions of the times they study.

Because history is concerned with human action in the round and with all kinds of human actions, and that in detail, historiography has never been constrained by careful definitions and lawlike generalizations, and probably never should or could be. Common sense is often the best, often the only, guide. But events sometimes reveal that common sense, even the sophisticated common sense of the highly educated, has been misleading, sometimes tragically so. When that seems the case, historians may have to abandon it. They may have to reexamine the preconceptions that have infused historiography on certain subjects and make explicit their disagreement with common usage. Such conceptual reexamination requires considerable effort and a lowering of defenses. And it may make the work of historians more readily recognizable for what it is: assertions that are a partial expression of the historians' efforts to frame and understand their own existence.[20] But it may also enlarge their understanding of the past.

In my case, as I studied the formation of antisemitism, I became aware that "commonsense" explanations of antisemitism had long been disastrous, albeit in very different ways, for both Jews and non-Jews, and that the ambiguities and contradictions in the way scholars used the term made conceptual clarification a ne-

20. I shall not attempt to decide whether my position expresses a "narrativist" or "epistemological" philosophy of history, a compromise between them, or something much more philosophically disreputable. On these matters, see F.R. Ankersmit, "The Dilemma of Contemporary Anglo-Saxon Philosophy of History," in *Knowing and Telling History*, ed. F. R. Ankersmit (*History and Theory*, Beiheft 25 [1986]), pp. 1-27.

cessity. The general problem of historical explanation by the thoughts of the actors early concerned me because that was the prevailing explanation of antisemitism. And because of the undeniable connection between religion and antisemitism, it was obvious that any explanation I gave of the formation of antisemitism would depend on how I distinguished what was religious from what was not, and how I explained the conduct of self-professedly religious people. Since historians seemed little concerned about their conceptualization of religion, I turned for help to other disciplines whose practioners dealt explicitly with the problem. But, perhaps because I was a historian, my problems in conceptualizing religion only deepened.

Chapter Four

The Concept of Religion

Few words are so deeply freighted as "religion," and few raise so many questions. If the first is "What is the meaning of life?" others follow rapidly. At the pedestrian level of empirical discourse, some obvious ones arise. Is religion one or several? If the latter, what do they have in common, and why are there so many of them? How did they arise? Why are they so different? What has determined their content and their demographic boundaries? What distinguishes religion or religions from other types of human conduct? Why do particular religions emerge and disappear? Is religion a social phenomenon or a property of individuals? Are all individuals religious? Is religion a delusory form of wishful thinking or a kind of understanding? Is it an unavoidable aspect of human existence or a characteristic of one phase of human history? To all these questions and more, different people will give different answers, but one thing is certain: the answers we give on the empirical level will depend on the way we conceive of our humanity.

Whatever the referent of "religion," the word itself originated on the Mediterranean littoral in antiquity. In the Latin of polytheistic Romans, *religio* was derived from *ligo* or *lego* and more directly from *religo* or *relego*, which had the sense of "to bind, constrain, or tie securely." *Religio* denoted the constraint caused by awareness of a supernatural power that prohibited or impeded certain actions and provoked fear and awe. It also denoted the rituals, ceremonies, and customs by which people expressed obedience to, or scrupulous observance of, the obligations imposed by such a power. The other substantive form, *religiositas*, similarly denoted regard for the divine law. We might therefore say that *religio* primarily indicated recognition of a system of supernatural constraints or obligations (*obligo*, to bind or tie), while *religiositas* denoted action in conformity with those obligations.[1] Because those words, born in pagan Latin culture and used amidst the religious pluralism of the tolerant Roman Empire, were used by Latin Christians in the empire, they became embedded in Catholicism, where *religio* was primarily used in a special sense to indicate monastic life with its peculiarly rigorous restraints or obligations. In the fifteenth century, with the renewed interest in classical literature, its earlier Roman sense came back into currency; and by 1700, after the Catholic monopoly had dissolved, it came to be applied to the beliefs of the competing religious societies into which Europe had been fragmented.[2] It then entered the European vernacular languages and came, by extension, to denote beliefs and conduct that seemed to fulfill the same function for non-Christians.

"Religion" thus came to designate something apparently common to all peoples: their avowal that they were obligated by supernatural powers to act in certain ways. But beyond that vague similarity, the term had no specific content. Religion was only real, observable, and meaningful in its concrete instances, Latin polytheism, Judaism, Catholicism, Lutheranism, and so forth, and that rich meaning was provided by the adherents of each of those religions themselves. "Religion" had no ontological status beyond that of a convenient term to point to an amazing variety of real, but mutually contradictory, sets of beliefs about gods or god and the conduct by which they were expressed.

In the nineteenth century, however, after the intellectual attacks on traditional religions in the eighteenth century, and more directly as a result of the work of Kant, Schleiermacher, Dilthey, Hegel, Marx, Comte, and others, "religion" also became a term in a metalanguage of scholars who sought to discover the truth *about* religion in general rather than the truth *in* particular re-

1. *Oxford Latin Dictionary*, ed. P. G. W. Glare (Oxford, 1982), pp. 1605-1606.
2. John Bossy, *Christianity in the West, 1400-1700* (Oxford, 1985), p. 170.

ligions. Used in this new way, "religion" itself acquired ontological status; it referred to a type of observable human conduct that needed objective analysis in terms other than those of the believers or actors. Where previously scholars had argued for Catholicism, Lutheranism, Calvinism, or Deism, now some thinkers regarded the particular claims of any and all religions with suspicion. Marx's conclusion that religion is the opium of the working class is only the most famous example of this new perspective and the new meaning of religion that it engendered. But it was not until the first third of the twentieth century that a frontal assault on the problem of religion was made by several great thinkers, all of whom had been born about the middle of the nineteenth century and reached maturity later in the century when nationalism was at its height and the term "antisemitism" appeared and spread rapidly.

In 1902, William James (1842-1910) published *The Varieties of Religious Experience*. Max Weber (1864-1920) first published *The Protestant Ethic and the Spirit of Capitalism* in 1904-1905 as articles in a journal, and it was republished in revised form in 1920 as the first in what proved to be the posthumous collection of all his studies of religion. *The Elementary Forms of Religious Life* by Emile Durkheim (1858-1917) appeared in 1912. Rudolph Otto (1869-1937) introduced his novel terminology in *Das Heilige* or *The Idea of the Holy* in 1917. In 1913, Sigmund Freud (1856-1939) published *Totem and Taboo*, following it with "The Future of an Illusion" in 1927 and *Moses and Monotheism* between 1934 and 1938. And in 1935 appeared *La mythologie primitive* of Lucien Lévy-Bruhl (1857-1939).

Beside Judaism, Roman *religio*, Catholicism, Islam, and so forth, and frequently in competition with them, reality was attributed to religion in general, religion in and of itself, a reality dependent on the existence not of supernatural forces or "God" but of observable and comparable human conduct. Yet if religion was no longer viewed as simply the aggregate of what believers in each of the accepted religions said their religion was, what was it? If religion was to be understood as a human activity that could be studied objectively, there had to be some agreement on what was being examined and how it was conceived, some new taxonomy and terminology, some definition other than all the conflicting beliefs and practices that common usage had categorized as religions. Although some scholars—Max Weber, for instance—avoided a formal definition while nonetheless introducing new terminology to analyze and compare well-known religions, others attempted to define religion in their own terms, thereby making their fundamental presuppositions explicit and beginning a debate that has continued to the present.

The most fundamental disagreement has been between those who use nominal, ostensive, operational, or substantive definitions and those who use real, normative, or functional definitions.[3] We might characterize the broad difference by saying that those who use the first kind of definitions incorporate convictions of believers in traditional religions into their definition of religion, while those who use the second kind exclude such convictions and employ concepts derived from their empirical disciplines to define religion.

For brevity's sake, I shall lump nominal, ostensive, operational, and substantive definitions together and refer to them collectively as denotative definitions. Those who use denotative definitions point directly at what have traditionally been considered religions and imply that religion is a distinctive and irreducible phenomenon. They arrive at their definitions through comparative study of what had already been accepted as being "religions"; and—in however general language—they incorporate as a necessary criterion of religion certain beliefs or reactions that the adherents of those religions themselves felt essential, whether belief in powerful supernatural entities or belief in a profound cleavage between the sacred and profane dimensions of life. And they see those beliefs as irreducible, incapable of explanation in other terms. Denotative definitions are therefore restrictive, since what traditionally "religious" people have considered essential must be present for there to be a "religion." They exclude phenomena such as Communism which are often categorized as "surrogate

3. See Melford E. Spiro, "Religion: Problems of Definition and Explanation" (originally published in *Anthropological Approaches to the Study of Religion*, ed. Michael Banton [London, 1966]), in Spiro, *Culture and Human Nature*, ed. Benjamin Kilborne and L. L. Langness (Chicago, 1987), pp. 189-197; Peter L. Berger, *The Sacred Canopy* (New York, 1969), pp. 175-177; Roland Robertson, *The Sociological Interpretation of Religion* (New York, 1970), pp. 36-43.

religions" because, although they seem remarkably similar to a neutral observer, they lack traditional supernatural beliefs.[4]

This definitional stance is likely to appeal to historians, including atheists, for several reasons. Their work emphasizes detailed events circumscribed in time and space. They are concerned with the uniqueness of events and suspicious of overly broad generalizations; and one of their primary tasks is to resurrect and describe past ideas and beliefs regardless of whether they themselves agree with those concepts. Such definitions are also likely to appeal to those who believe in a traditional religion but are attracted by generalization, sociological or otherwise, for these definitions function to generalize yet protect the experiences which adherents of particular historical religions have felt uniquely valuable. They are, moreover, a bulwark against any proposal to view any particular religion as merely a context-bound expression of more fundamental and very different processes.

On the other side in the battle are those who use real, normative, or functional definitions, which I shall refer to collectively as explanatory definitions. Explanatory definitions describe religion as an expression of—or reduce religion to—general and fundamental processes that can be described in nonreligious terms. They specify as criteria elements that are not those that believers in the traditional religions recognize as essential. And the elements they specify are so primary or so general (e.g., ego) that they do not immediately bring traditional "religions" to mind and imply that a much broader range of conduct is religious—for example, "nationalism" as well as Christianity. They also typically assign primary functions to religion (e.g., false consciousness, ego-

4. E.g., Donald Wiebe, *Religion and Truth*, Religion and Reason, vol. 23 (The Hague, 1981), pp. 16-18. The distinction is assumed in a fascinatingly ambiguous fashion by Robert N. Bellah, *Beyond Belief* (New York, 1970), p. 245: "When ordinary reality turns into a nightmare, as it increasingly has in modern society, only some transcendental perspective offers any hope. It is of course impossible to prove Christianity or any religion, but it is impossible to prove cognitively or scientifically any ultimate perspective on human life, including Marxism, rationalism, or any kind of scientism. The adequacy of any ultimate perspective is its ability to transform human experience so that it yields life instead of death." See also Robertson, *The Sociological Interpretation of Religion*, pp. 37-39; and Michael Hill, *A Sociology of Religion* (New York, 1973), pp. 243-245. The validity of this distinction will be criticized at length in chap. 14.

maintenance, or the formation of Self) very different from the expressed intentions of the adherents of particular religions. They tend, moreover, to make distinctions that some believers felt absolute (e.g., awe before the "sacred") into differences of degree.

For those with this approach, religion—like so many other phenomena studied by contemporary science—is something long perceived as important but not heretofore understood by those who experienced it. Hence it is not to be dismissed as merely an illusion or superseded superstition but is something to be understood. The polytheists, Jews, Catholics, Calvinists, and so forth, were indeed doing something conducive to their well-being as they retold their myths, performed their rituals, and propounded their creeds. But they did not know what they were really doing. They had only a very limited understanding of the real function(s) of the rich, diverse, and mutually contradictory tapestries of their diverse religions; and they did not understand how their religiosity was related to and determined by other characteristics of themselves and their environment.

As a very lively debate testifies, there is still little agreement on the meaning of "religion." Although the reliance of denotative definitions on common usage ensures considerable agreement among them, there is still considerable variation, and the disagreement between explanatory definitions is much greater. To make matters worse, although scholars distinguish analytically between denotative and explanatory definitions, they are not as easy to distinguish as my description implies. Though most definitions of religion are basically denotative, many do not fall clearly in one camp or the other. And definitions of both kinds also differ markedly on whether religion is a social phenomenon or something whose core is within individuals.

As Peter Berger—who explicitly favors a denotative definition—noted, one of the most famous sociological definitions combines a denotative and an explanatory definition.[5] Emile Durkheim defined religion as a system of beliefs and practices that distinguished certain things as sacred and made those who ad-

5. *The Sacred Canopy*, p. 176.

hered to that system members of a single moral community.[6] He then assumed that if one studied the most primitive form of religion, one would be looking at the simplest form, in which it would be easiest to detect the fundamental characteristics of the phenomenon. He therefore based his great pioneering study of religion on an intensive analysis of the religion of the aborigines. He concluded from it that when the aborigines were acting religiously they were in effect worshiping the social relations that made their existence and thought possible. From this he generalized that any religion, even the most complex, is "a system of ideas with which the individuals represent to themselves the society of which they are members, and the obscure but intimate relations they have with it."[7] "Religious force is only the sentiment inspired by the group in its members, but projected outside of the consciousnesses that experience them and objectified. To be thus objectified, they are fixed upon some object which thus becomes sacred; but any object might fulfill this function."[8]

Durkheim thus insisted that religion is a social phenomenon; and although he started with a denotative definition, he concluded with an explanatory definition that would not exclude nationalism or Russian Communism as religions. He was able to move from one to the other because he interpreted the attitudes that determined what was "sacred" very differently from those who believed that certain things were sacred. He relativized them, much in the way theologies that insist on "ultimate concerns" have done, so that any peoples who treated some things with much greater respect or awe than others had their own religion. Consequently any society that was not completely anomic would have its religion.

As is evident in Durkheim's denotative definition, one feature that distinguishes denotative from explanatory definitions is that at least one of the necessary component elements or criteria is a characteristic or element that people had already distinguished and consciously attributed only to what had been considered re-

6. *The Elementary Forms of the Religious Life*, trans. Joseph W. Swain (New York, 1965), pp. 52, 62.
7. Ibid., p. 257.
8. Ibid., p. 261.

ligions. Since Western languages used "religion" to refer to the
conduct of people who believed they were related to "gods" or
"God," and since believers referred to them or what directly em-
anated from them as "holy," or "sacred," the two favorite, distinctive terms in denotative definitions of religion are "god" and
"the sacred."[9] But as a recent definition indicates, the difference
between definitions that specify the "sacred" and those that specify a relation with "gods," "superhuman beings," or a "supra-empirical segment of reality" is not that great. For Louis Schneider,
religion is "an apprehension of a sacred imbued with power, a
conceiving of the sacred in such a way that it makes human life
and values meaningful, beliefs and practices relating man to the
sacred."[10] Thus definitions that start from the sacred and those
that start from god(s), when generalized, reach common ground
in a fundamental distinction between a supra-empirical reality
with superhuman power and a humanly or empirically known
reality of natural powers.

   "God(s)" is, of course, usually expressed now by more general
language such as "superhuman beings" with the power to "assist
or to harm man,"[11] because the definer wishes to include instances
such as the beliefs of "primitive" peoples or Buddhism where
there is no explicit "god." From there, it is easy to specify something even less specific: "a distinction between an empirical and
super-empirical, transcendent reality; the affairs of the empirical
being subordinated in significance to the non-empirical";[12] or "the
distinction between an empirical reality and a related and significant supra-empirical segment of reality";[13] or "super-empirical"
ends.[14] The difference between definitions that refer to "God"—
or some more general term for awesome power that transcends
human capacities—and those that specify the "sacred" seems to
be that the former point at the *concepts* of a superior reality in
the minds of the believers, whereas the latter point rather at the

      9. For good discussions of this position see Spiro, *Culture and Human Na-
ture*, pp. 189-220; and Wiebe, *Religion and Truth*, pp. 9-22.
      10. *Sociological Approach to Religion* (New York, 1970), p. 6.
      11. Spiro, *Culture and Human Nature*, p. 195.
      12. Robertson, *The Sociological Interpretation of Religion*, p. 47.
      13. Hill, *A Sociology of Religion*, p. 42.
      14. Bryan Wilson, *Religion in Sociological Perspective* (Oxford, 1982), p. 44.

emotions or *psychological reactions* provoked in the believers when they feel they are in contact with such a reality.

Durkheim used both approaches but concluded that the emotions aroused in individuals by what they considered sacred were the result of their social relations. Religion was a social phenomenon. William James, the pioneer of an empirical psychological approach to religion, took exactly the opposite stand. He saw traditional religions as petrifactions of beliefs that arose from individual experiences; and he hesitated to denote these personal experiences as religion.[15] His individualizing and relativizing of religion had little immediate impact, however. The most famous argument for the importance of psychological reactions was the highly unscientific one made in 1917 by Rudolf Otto in *Das Heilige*. "Instead of studying the *ideas* of God and religion, Otto undertook to analyze the modalities of *the religious experience*."[16]

Otto fully acknowledged that religion could be rational in the sense that belief as contrasted with simple feeling necessitated clear and definite concepts; and he proclaimed that Christianity possessed such concepts "in unique clarity and abundance," which was one sign of its superiority to all other religions.[17] But he argued that, since the purpose of language was to convey concepts, expositions of religious truth in language stressed "the 'rational' attributes of God" but were unable to grasp the deeper essence. What differentiates the nonrational, irrational, or suprarational in religion from rationalism, he argued, is a difference of quality "in the mental attitude and emotional content of the religious life itself, something that makes the religious experience unmistakably unique and specific."[18]

For Otto, "the sacred" is, beyond whatever can be said about it, something ineffable, a living force that cannot be named or expressed in concepts yet is the core of religion. He employed the term "numen" to denote that essential element encountered in the sacred which exceeds any conceptualization of it, and he therefore coined the term "numinous" to denote the state of mind or feeling it induced. He then described the numinous state as a

15. His position will be discussed at greater length below, chap. 9.
16. Mircea Eliade, *The Sacred and the Profane* (New York, 1959), p. 8.
17. Rudolf Otto, *The Idea of the Holy*, 2d ed. (London, 1950), p. 1.
18. Ibid., p. 3.

feeling of dependence far more absolute than anything experienced in any other connnection, so much so that it cannot be compared with anything else and is, for those who have experienced it, a primary and elemental datum of psychic life. To indicate its incomparability, he replaced Schleiermacher's term "absolute dependence" with his own term "creature-consciousness," by which he meant "the emotion of a creature, submerged and overwhelmed by its own nothingness in contrast to that which is supreme above all creatures."[19]

Having thus used words to conceptualize so far as possible the numen and the numinous, Otto went on to describe the encounter that provoked those feelings, the feeling of being in the presence of the *mysterium tremendum*, by which he meant the fascinating, awe-inspiring, unapproachably overpowering energy of the "wholly other" that is beyond our apprehension and comprehension.[20] And although Otto maintained that it is impossible to teach the numinous state or describe in words the encounter with the *mysterium tremendum*, he tried to do so metaphorically in the richest language of romanticism,[21] language so evocative that a late-twentieth-century student penciled in a library copy: "Sounds like intercourse."

Otto's approach to religion was psychological rather than sociological or anthropological. But however valuable his insistence on the nonrational dimension of religion, his psychological approach was different from most later ones because he assumed what he wanted to demonstrate. Although he emphasized the nonrational, he did not try to analyze human mental processes as such but rather depicted in literary language and in his own religious terminology the emotional states of those who had had traditional religious experiences, illustrated them from religious writings, and explained such emotions as the result of contact with the "wholly other." His investigation of psychological processes was thus based on, and restricted by, his assumption of contact with the "wholly other" or *mysterium tremendum*, and he assumed that those who had not had religious experiences had not

19. Ibid., pp. 5-7, 10.
20. Ibid., pp. 12-40.
21. Ibid., especially pp. 12-13.

experienced such emotions.[22] But he did not attempt to explain, in terms acceptable to someone without his faith, why some people had that experience of the *mysterium tremendum* with those emotions while others did not, or why people in other periods or societies expressed their encounter with the numen in such radically different ways. He assumed that his Christianity was the ideal form of religion, and his implicit definition of religion was therefore radically denotative.

The contrast between Otto's psychological approach and that of Freud is obvious. Although Freud, like Otto, emphasized emotional reactions as the core of religion, Freud thought religion a childish delusion stemming from oedipal problems, and he thoroughly disliked Christianity, especially Catholicism. But as his god = father solution indicates, his implicit definition was a denotative one that depended on traditional religious beliefs; and unlike James, he thought of religions as social institutions.[23]

Max Weber never defined religion, but his implicit definition was also clearly denotative since he drew his data from what had long been thought of as the major historical religions; and he apparently simply assumed with Durkheim and Otto that they were all characterized by an explicit distinction between the sacred and the profane. "To the natural uncertainties and resistances of every innovator, religion thus adds powerful impediments of its own. The sacred is the uniquely unalterable."[24] But although his work was sociological, Weber, like Otto, located the core of religion in the individual and treated it as an independent variable.

The external courses of religious behavior are so diverse that an understanding of this behavior can only be achieved from the viewpoint of the subjective experiences, ideas, and purposes of the individuals concerned—in short, from the viewpoint of the religious behavior's "meaning" (*Sinn*).[25]

Where he departed from Otto, of course, was that he then set

22. Ibid., p. 8.
23. Philip Rieff, *Freud: The Mind of the Moralist* (New York, 1961), p. 311, n. q: "Freud always saw religion in an authoritative (i.e., political) mode, and the Roman church, with its highly bureaucratized militancy, was the nearest fit to his theory."
24. Max Weber, *The Sociology of Religion* (Boston, 1964), p. 9.
25. Ibid., p. 1.

out to explain how changes or differences in religious conduct were correlated with changes in social organization. He did so by a comparative study of societies with different religions or societies in different stages of change. As a result, individuals appear primarily as role-players or "ideal types" in a social context that gives them their "meaning," rather than as psychically complex individuals. Yet his emphasis on individual motives, intellectual creativity, prophets, and charismatic individuals demonstrates that for Weber, although the mode of religious expression might be determined by interaction with a particular social situation, the core of religion lay within individuals.

Very different was the work of the scholar who most explicitly argued the quasi-universality of the distinction between the sacred and the profane. Mircea Eliade's perspective was anthropological rather than historical, sociological, or psychological, and he was not concerned to explain why the "sacred" was expressed in such diverse ways. He only sought to argue that the distinction was constant across that variety; and despite his focus on different societies, he too found the seat of religion as an observable phenomenon in the individual. His analysis relied primarily on data drawn from earlier or less complex societies, and he assumed, whether correctly or not, that individuals in each of those societies thought and reacted in the same basic way in religious matters. Consequently, although he might seem to be talking about societies as collectivities, he was really concentrating on what he believed went on in common in the mind and psyche of each member.

It is noticeable that although Eliade gave *The Sacred and the Profane* the subtitle *The Nature of Religion*, what concerned him was *homo religiosus* or "religious man," whom he contrasted with "the non-religious man [who] refuses transcendence,"[26] a being whose existence he does not explain apart from saying that he has been formed by opposing his predecessor, religious man, "by attempting to empty himself of all religion and all trans-human meaning."[27] "Religion" is thus something fundamentally and orig-

26. Mircea Eliade, *The Sacred and the Profane*, trans. Willard R. Trask (New York, 1957), p. 202.
27. Ibid., p. 204.

inally *within* individuals (in a very Jungian way) that transcends history and induces them to distinguish between the elements of their experience they deem sacred and those they deem profane.

The same assumption of a clear distinction between the sacred and the profane appears in very different guise in the empirical study of the psychology of religion that has flourished so greatly in the last thirty years. Perhaps because no single integrating theory now dominates empirical psychology, there has been no attempt to provide an all-embracing intepretation of the phenomenon of religion and little concern with the definition of religion. Instead, psychologists have relied implicitly on the traditional denotative conception of religion. A host of detailed, highly statistical studies have analyzed the relation between some dimensions of accepted religions and diverse psychological conditions and reactions. An example relevant to antisemitism is the series of studies, started by Gordon Allport, that examined the statistical correlation between religion and prejudice and produced the now widely used distinction between intrinsic and extrinsic religiosity.[28]

These studies have relied almost entirely on operational definitions formulated in questionnaires designed to see whether two or more kinds of phenomena—for example, political conservatism and Christian fundamentalism—are positively correlated. Although religion as such is not defined, the conception of religion involved is clearly indicated by the questions posed to the respondents, questions such as whether there is an afterlife, whether prayer is efficacious, whether they believe in God, attend church or synagogue frequently, and so forth. The questions thus define religion denotatively by pointing to beliefs and practices characteristic of traditional, especially Christian, religions.

The centrality of an implicit denotative definition in recent psychological investigations is obvious in a recent survey of the field. Spilka, Hood, and Gorsuch consider defining religion an exercise in futility[29] and favor attribution theory. They define religion

28. See Bernard Spilka, Ralph W. Hood, and Richard L. Gorsuch, *The Psychology of Religion: An Empirical Approach* (Englewood Cliffs, N.J., 1985), pp. 27-28, 44, 270-274; Gordon W. Allport, *The Nature of Prejudice* (Boston, 1954), pp. 444-456.
29. *The Psychology of Religion*, p. 31.

operationally by finding out the probability and frequency with which people make what have traditionally been considered religious attributions such as explaining events by the involvement of God in daily affairs.[30] One could summarize the definition latent in their own approach and that of the bulk of the studies they discuss as: religion is what people in Western civilization have customarily considered religious.[31] And in striking contrast with James, although they speak of the religious experiences of individuals, they consider religion a social phenomenon. "Being religious in our society, or for that matter in any social order, invariably means affiliation with a religious group—a sect, a cult, or a church."[32] Moreover, although the authors do correlate religious thought and conduct and psychological reactions, they make religion impermeable to further investigation by declaring, "Let us recognize that it is *not* the place of psychologists to challenge religious institutions and their theologies."[33]

With the uncertain exception of James, all these conceptions or definitions of religion insist on the criterion of belief in supraempirical entities or of the sense of the sacred. They are denotative definitions because they delimit religion by pointing only to the reactions that believers in traditional religions have consciously expressed and themselves defined as religion. That is true even of Freud's functional conception of religion, or rather his argument that religion impedes proper functioning, because his conception of what was religious was determined by his one-sided knowledge of traditional religions.

These denotative definitions are apparently objective, for they do not assert that superhuman powers exist or proclaim that there are two kinds of reality. They only claim to be discussing what can be empirically observed and discussed: human concepts, beliefs, or emotions. But there are problems about how these definitions formulate the beliefs. The specification of what must be

---

30. Ibid., p. 55.

31. "If one looks at the accumulated literature, one will find that the vast majority of psychological studies of religion have been topically organized by the categories of religion itself, or by religious designations of religious experience" (Paul W. Pruyser, "Where Do We Go from Here? Scenarios for the Psychology of Religion," *Journal for the Scientific Study of Religion* 26 [1987]: 177).

32. *The Psychology of Religion*, p. 255.

33. Ibid., p. 2.

believed for something to count as religion has been made very general so as to take into account all cases that the definers believe intuitively to be religions. But the belief specified—for example, in "superhuman powers"—was not as such a belief "in the minds" of Pharaohs or Pharisees, Mithraists or Moslems, Greeks or Germans, cave dwellers or Christians. Believers in different traditional religions have had very specific beings in mind to whom they gave specific names—Marduk, Ashur, Zeus, Jupiter, Thor, Christ, and the like. The entities thus conceptualized had different qualities and powers, so much so that the entities in which one set of people believed were often conceived as different from, and opposed to, those of neighboring peoples, or that one people would deny that the entities conceived by another people existed. It is only we, looking back and across, who can think of all such entities conceived by humans throughout history as the same, as "superhuman powers" or "supra-empirical realities"—terms that hardly provoke awe in anyone. Such definitions attribute to other people throughout history concepts or beliefs that are in fact concepts or classifications of modern scholars.

The psychological approach through emotions aroused by encounter with "the sacred" encounters the same objection. It attributes to people in the past a modern concept; "sacred" is used in the sense "understood by *Religionswissenschaft* since Rudolph Otto."[34] The psychological approach also confronts another problem. If we have access to what people said or wrote, we can speak fairly precisely about their concepts, including conceptualized beliefs. But it is notoriously much more difficult to assess their psychic states either from such evidence or even from direct observation.

The problem here is not whether millions of people have manifested great awe at certain times and places in the presence of certain people, animals, or things that were connected in their minds with their concepts of entities that we classify as supraempirical. They certainly have. The problem is whether there was as sharp and qualitative a difference as scholars such as Eliade have said between those people's psychic reactions in their religious activities and in all their other "profane" activities. Scholars

34. Berger, *The Sacred Canopy*, p. 177.

such as Otto and Eliade, who have pursued the distinction between the sacred and profane in other people's psyches, have
typically used those peoples' *concepts* about supra-empirical entities to guide their own search for expressions of awe before supra-empirical reality or power. And recent research on the psychological correlates of religion has used those concepts to guide
its search for psychic reactions.

Not surprisingly, these scholars have found intense awe connected with the centers, areas, objects, and activities designated
by traditional religious concepts as foci of contact with supernatural beings or realities. But was awe always aroused equally intensely during all religious conduct? And, since scholars have had
only limited access to the psychic reactions of other people during
intense "profane" experiences, can we say that the emotions
thereby aroused—for example, by Hitler's voice or observation
of the first atomic explosion—were always that clearly different
in quality from those aroused by the "sacred"? Otto certainly felt
that there was such a difference in his own psychic reactions, but
his description of them made one student reader think of his or
her psychic reactions to intercourse. What has been presented by
scholars, especially Christian scholars, as a fundamental psychic
distinction may be a personal psychic reaction they project on
other people.

As for the more recent psychology of religion, the problem is
that it has not developed its conception of religion from the concepts of its own discipline. It relies on customary religious concepts and demonstrates, not too surprisingly, that being religious
in that sense in contemporary Western society is correlated with
various psychological conditions or reactions. It does not, however, demonstrate that those particular conditions or reactions are
present only or primarily in people who would be thought of as
highly religious in the customary sense. Thus, the rate of mystical
experiences among those who attended churches devotedly was
found to be high, among infrequent attenders low, but among
nonattenders high. While that inverted bell curve does indicate
that occasional church attenders in our society are statistically unlikely to have mystical experiences, the rate of mystical experiences does not distinguish the people considered genuinely religious according to traditional indices from those who are not.

More interesting for my purposes, frequent attenders were found to be low in ethnic prejudice, infrequent attenders high, and non-attenders low. Again, the bell curve does not distinguish the people considered truly religious from the nonreligious.[35]

There is something peculiar about those results. What the investigations reveal is that, psychologically, those considered highly religious by traditional criteria and those considered thoroughly nonreligious by the same criteria in fact reacted in similar ways. Hence, on purely psychological grounds, so far as the evidence of these studies goes, both the frequent attenders and the nonattenders should be considered religious and contrasted with the infrequent attenders. But instead of developing their own psychological definition of religion, the investigators continued to rely on a criterion external to their discipline, the traditional conception of religion as a social phenomenon or activity.

To sum up, the fundamental criterion of most definitions of religion, and the hallmark of denotative definitions, has been the content of traditional beliefs, that is, their distinction between the "sacred" and the "profane" or between "supernature" and "nature." Confidence in the criterion derives from the indisputable observation that beliefs in gods and distinctions between sacred and profane conduct and objects have characterized what have traditionally been considered religions and religious individuals throughout history. Yet anthropologists, sociologists, and historians, when they speak as objective scholars, cannot assert empirical knowledge of a sacred realm or supernatural beings. Hence, they cannot assume that the distinctions formulated by those believers have any existence other than in the minds of those believers.

As was argued in chapter 3, what they believed may be part of our description of them; it cannot be our objective explanation of what they were doing. If scholars wish to distinguish religions and religious conduct from other kinds of human activity, they must use their own criteria. People have certainly believed in a distinction between the sacred and profane, but unless scholars can reformulate the distinction in their own terms, using their

---

35. Spilka, Hood, and Gorsuch, *The Psychology of Religion*, pp. 186-187, 270-274.

own objective knowledge, they cannot assume that beliefs about such a distinction are expressions of a fundamental human characteristic.

The danger in allowing the beliefs of traditional religions to delimit our conception of religious phenomena and circumscribe our explanations is that it becomes all too easy to disregard thinking and conduct that do not express those traditional beliefs but seem remarkably similar in nature. Frequently, scholars who concentrate on historical beliefs about supernatural forces and attitudes toward the sacred pay little attention to people who have strong beliefs that guide their conduct but do not believe in "gods" or distinguish between the "sacred" and "profane." All too often, wide-ranging worldviews and deep-seated individual convictions are dismissed as nonreligious, and as irrelevant to the study of religion, simply because they do not refer explicitly to supernatural beings and the sacred. Consequently, there has been surprisingly little interest in the major problem that the traditional terminology raises: why have some people been "religious" while others have not?

Typically, those who deny that "surrogate religions" are religions have not examined surrogate religions or ideologies and those who live by them closely. They have not demonstrated what "surrogate" religions are, how they differ from "real" religions, and why the difference is so fundamental as to place them in another category—or rather a pseudocategory, since it only typifies them as not "real" religions. They thus assume that belief in the supernatural and the sacred is a fundamental human aptitude—even though it is inexplicably lacking in many people.

To say with Otto that some people do not have religious experiences and emotions because they never come in contact with the "wholly other," or with Eliade that nonreligious people have emptied themselves "of all religion and all trans-human meaning," or with Berger that secularization is the removal of sectors of society and culture from "the domination of religious institutions and symbols"[36] is not good enough. Viewed empirically, it is superficial. It divides humanity into two types but only describes one, the "religious." While it asserts what people of the second

36. *The Sacred Canopy*, p. 107.

type are not, it does not explain what they are or why they differ. Yet if, as claimed, the distinction people have made between the supernatural and the natural or the sacred and the profane does express a fundamental human characteristic or fundamental kind of human thought, it has to be a characteristic or mode of thought that can be found in all normal human beings and can be examined in present rational empirical terms. We may therefore turn to a recent approach that has tried to do just that.

Chapter Five

Religion as Compensation

Rodney Stark and William Sims Bainbridge have recently proposed a very different theory of religion from those discussed in the last chapter. However much we may disagree with it, their work deserves close attention by anyone concerned to discuss religion objectively—though some may feel mine inordinate—precisely because they have attempted to be purely empirical. They have reformulated the distinction between the "sacred" and the "profane" in such agnostic terms that even those who do not believe in the distinction as customarily formulated must face the challenge carefully.

Stark and Bainbridge developed a manifestly explanatory definition of religion as the basis for a highly empirical, heavily statistical, and most enlightening sociological analysis of recent—and future—religious phenomena.[1] Three features make their approach particularly relevant for my present purposes. In the first place, unlike Peter Berger and Clifford Geertz,[2] they do try to justify their distinction between religions and surrogate religions by their own objective criteria. In the second place, more clearly than many definitions, their approach illustrates a fundamental characteristic of most definitions of religion, including those of Berger and Geertz: the insistence that religion is a social phe-

---

1. "Towards a Theory of Religion: Religious Commitment," *Journal for the Scientific Study of Religion* 19 (1980): 114-128; *The Future of Religion* (Berkeley, Los Angeles, London, 1985); *A Theory of Religion*, Toronto Studies in Religion, vol. 2 (New York, 1987).

2. The views of Berger and Geerz will be discussed in chap. 6.

nomenon. And, third, they base their arguments on an explicit conception of human nature.

Their fundamental conception of human nature owes much to economics and politics and little to philosophy, psychology, literature, or semiotics. They present a deductive model of religion based on seven axioms about human nature (which they call axioms, not because they are self-evident but because they explain so much). And perhaps because they have concentrated so heavily on American religious phenomena, the axioms present a market or exchange model of human conduct. They speak of religious economies[3] and depend heavily on the "mundane axiom" that "humans seek what they perceive to be rewards and try to avoid what they perceive to be costs."[4] Although that language only asserts that the pursuit of rewards at low cost is one dimension of human conduct, they apparently assume—as do many historians devoted to *Realpolitik*—that it is the only important dimension: "human action is *governed* by the pursuit of rewards and the avoidance of costs" (*FR*, p. 172, my italics). Not surprisingly then, their conception of religion is a modified reformulation of the deprivation theory of religion.[5]

Their conception of religion is hard to pin down because they hesitate between considering religion as a social organization, a set of beliefs, or the referent of those beliefs. In their article in 1980, their definition was: "*Religion* refers to systems of general

3. *The Future of Religion*, p. 504.
4. Ibid., p. 5; *A Theory of Religion*, p. 27. The latter has an appendix, pp. 325-350, in which they list their 7 axioms, 104 definitions, and 344 propositions about human conduct and religion. Since the argument of that book is couched in highly general and abstract terms, I shall usually cite the more discursive language in *The Future of Religion* rather than the equivalent assertion in *A Theory of Religion*; and I shall cite *The Future of Religion* as *FR* in the body of the text.
5. *A Theory of Religion*, p. 51. Cf. Bellah, *Beyond Belief*, p. 241: "Much of social science has relapsed into the positivist utilitarian idiom in which only 'hard and realistic' assumptions about human nature are allowed. In this idiom, human action is likened to a game in which every player is trying to maximize his self-interest or is concerned only with the *quid pro quo* in an exchange network, and where there is no place for the murky concepts to which Freud, Durkheim, and Weber were driven." But Bellah himself is not as far from a compensation view as that might suggest; see the passage on p. 245, quoted above, chap. 4, n. 4.

compensators based on supernatural assumptions."[6] The formal definition at the beginning of *The Future of Religion* is somewhat different: religions are "human organizations primarily engaged in providing general compensators based on supernatural assumptions" (*FR*, p. 8). A restatement in the middle of the book expands the definition and reformulates it slightly:

When rewards are scarce, or not available at all, humans create and exchange compensators—sets of beliefs and prescriptions for action that substitute for the immediate achievement of the desired reward. Religions are social enterprises whose primary purpose is to create, maintain, and exchange supernaturally based general compensators. (*FR*, p. 172)

Toward the end of the book, they return to the older formulation, defining "religion as a system of very general compensators" (*FR*, p. 432).[7]

Religion thus seems a general term for religions, and it is difficult to know whether they are thinking of religions as social organizations or sets of beliefs. Indeed, in their last book, they recognize that there are problems about defining religions as social organizations and indicate that religion can be defined either as a faith or a church, either as a cultural system or as a social system.[8] But since they use "monopoly faiths" as a synonym for religions that attempt to monopolize a religious economy (*FR*, p. 432), they apparently prefer to think of religions as social organizations, and their detailed analyses concentrate on religious organizations.

But there is a deeper uncertainty. In an "Aside on Faith," they say that "religion, in its *purest* forms, lies beyond the reach of all science and surely is not vulnerable to the definitions of two social scientists. . . . We leave its invisible aspects to others to comprehend and dispute" (*FR*, p. 14, my italics). Yet surely, human organizations do not lie beyond the reach of all science. Nor indeed do formulations of belief. The authors thus fluctuate between conceiving of religions as human organizations and as hu-

6. "Towards a Theory," p. 123.
7. The definition in *A Theory of Religion*, p. 39, is "Religion refers to systems of general compensators based on supernatural assumptions."
8. *A Theory of Religion*, p. 74.

man beliefs. And when they are thinking of religion as faith, they apparently include within it the invisible referents to which the beliefs refer. That raises the fundamental question of whether religion is a form of social organization such as a church, or what humans believe, or what their beliefs assert as real.

I shall discuss that problem later. Here I only wish to emphasize that although religious organizations purvey and depend for their existence on sets of ideas, that does not make them inaccessible to empirical analysis. Secrecy aside, religious organizations themselves do not have invisible and inaccessible aspects. Historians and sociologists have described and analyzed them and the ideas they proclaim almost *ad nauseam*. All that is in principle empirically inaccessible is, not the ideas on which they depend, but the unobservable referent of those ideas. Ideas, however, are not beliefs. An idea incapable of empirical verification becomes a belief only when an individual assents to it. That would suggest that while human organizations are highly accessible to empirical analysis, faith is a property of individuals that may be largely inaccessible, not because it deals with a different realm, but because the mental activities of individuals are difficult to examine empirically.

The main issue about their definition, however, is not whether religion refers to social organizations or to what individuals believe. The central and distinctive element of their definition is their conception of compensators. A compensator is "the belief that a reward will be obtained in the distant future or in some other context which cannot be immediately verified" (*FR*, p. 6). As they see it, people "pay" to gain compensators: they surrender certain values, certain immediately obtainable limited rewards, for the hope of a greater, but more distant and less certain, reward. To employ a term used by the authors, compensators are IOUs which those who accept them believe will be redeemed in the future. Compensators, however, vary greatly along a continuum from the specific to the general, from belief that the believer will be repaid by fairly limited concrete rewards in the relatively foreseeable future to belief in immense rewards, immeasurably distant in time and space, that no one can enjoy in this life.

At one end of the range are the deferred gratifications almost everyone experiences, the faith that if we give up certain specific pleasures or rewards now, we will relatively soon obtain greater political, economic, or social rewards that we desire. To give an example meaningful to academics, for struggling doctoral students who are willing to pay the costs of living poorly, working long hours, and conforming to the standards of some scholarly discipline, the compensator is the belief that they thereby establish a claim or receive an IOU from the system that will be repaid in the future by the rewards of professorial status.

The authors place magic in the middle of the range and distinguish it sharply from religion, for they do not consider supernatural assumptions a necessary characteristic of magic, although some magic utilizes supernatural assumptions. Magic provides relatively specific compensators. It promises tangible and fairly immediate rewards in this world by practices that do not rely on verifiable knowledge (*FR*, pp. 30-31). But because magic flourishes when scientific explanation is ineffective or unobtainable, its manipulations are not irrational (*FR*, p. 511). It is, however, highly vulnerable to later empirical disproof because its compensators promise tangible rewards in this world.

Religion stands at the far end of the continuum and involves the most general compensators, above all life after death. Its compensators promise immensely great and general rewards that human beings have sought immemorially, rewards that are not merely scarce but completely unavailable by natural means: knowledge of where we came from and where we are going, knowledge of the meaning of life, and survival of death (*FR*, pp. 7, 278).[9] Since no human being has ever achieved or observed them in this world, these rewards are, they argue, credible only on the basis of assumptions about supernatural agencies with conscious intentions whose powers exceed anything known in the

9. Cf. J. Milton Yinger, *The Scientific Study of Religion* (New York, 1970), p. 7: "Religion, then, can be defined as a system of beliefs and practices by means of which a group of people struggles with these ultimate problems of life. It expresses their refusal to capitulate to death, to give up in the face of frustration, to allow hostility to tear apart their human associations"; p. 12: "Religion is an organized effort to make virtue of our ultimate necessities"; p. 15: "Religion is man's attempt to 'relativize' these difficulties [foreknowledge of death, failure, frustration, injustice] by interpreting them as part of some larger good, some conception of the absolute that puts the individual's problems into new perspective, thus to remove or reduce their crushing impact."

natural world (*FR*, p. 7). Those compensators are, therefore, "for-ever secure from scientific assessment" (*FR*, pp. 30-31).

This economic and heavily rationalistic conception of religion certainly differs sharply from most approaches. It enables Stark and Bainbridge to reformulate the meaning of some major tech-nical terms in the sociology of religion such as "sects" and "sec-ularization," to give a fascinating analysis of religious activity from Catholicism to Scientology, and to argue an interesting thesis about the future of religion. But while their solidly empirical and heavily statistical analyses are enlightening, their general ap-proach raises profound questions.

Stark and Bainbridge conceive of humans as either rational or irrational. *Tertium nihil est.* They conceive of religion as "a ra-tional human activity,"[10] and they define mental illness as failure to conform to the prevailing theory of human action. They believe that if a single, logical, powerful theory of human action could be devised, it could serve as an objective standard of individual men-tal health. Indeed, they believe their own theory approaches such a standard![11] Yet their willingness to consider religion rational seems a little strange, for their only explanation of the creation of religious beliefs is that they are hallucinations of psychopath-ological individuals which appeal to others.

They do not discuss the origins of the great world religions, arguing that they are shrouded in time (*FR*, p. 171). The closest they come to discussing the major traditional forms of religion is in their analysis of modern sect movements. But since they define sect movements as schisms in existing religions, they cloak the origin of traditional religious beliefs, including those of Judaism and Christianity, in an infinite regress. Their explanation of sects is the old one that in religion nothing fails like success. Sects are depicted as an inevitable feature in the cycle of organized religion because of ever-present social pressures.

Sects are reactions against existing religions by adherents who observe internal contradictions between what the religion's com-pensators proclaim and how its most influential members act. If

10. *A Theory of Religion*, p. 84; see also pp. 114-115.
11. Ibid., p. 160: "To the extent that it [our theory] is complete, then mental illness objectively is the repeated failure to conform to its major propositions."

a religion adapts too well to the surrounding society, little social tension is involved in adhering to that religion and being a member of that society. Influential members of the religion can therefore enjoy the rewards provided by the surrounding society. But some adherents, who have achieved few of those rewards of accommodation, become dissenters. To compensate for their relative deprivation, they insist on faith that disdains earthly rewards and promises otherworldly gratification. The individuals who initiate sects are disgruntled people of middle rank or position, people who prefer to be leaders in a smaller group rather than subordinates in a larger one and therefore try to enlist people below them (*FR*, pp. 102-105).

The authors note that such conflicts have marked Christianity from its beginnings through the Middle Ages to the present; and they stress the schismatics' emphasis on poverty or deprivation. "When Martin Luther thundered against the worldliness of the church, he said nothing new" (*FR*, p. 114). But they do not discuss whether there was anything novel about Luther's specific ideas. Nor do they apply the thesis about otherworldly compensators to Judaism in the period of the first Temple, where it would be much harder to demonstrate. Indeed, they have little to say about Judaism. They categorize Reform Judaism as being not a sect with novel ideas but a "church movement," that is, a group that seeks to lower the tension between its religion and the surrounding society, and hence to reduce the social costs of adhering to the religion. Conservative Judaism is described simply as a sect that emerged out of dissatisfaction with Reform Judaism. There is no description of the supernatural assumptions or compensators of any form of Judaism (*FR*, pp. 122-124). Indeed, they pay remarkably little attention to the content of religious ideas of any kind. Even their careful statistical analyses of recent American sects say almost nothing about their beliefs.

Only in the chapter on the formation of cults do Stark and Bainbridge directly attack the problem of the creation of religious ideas. Their solution relies on three models of religious innovation: the psychopathological model, the entrepreneur model, and the subculture model (*FR*, pp. 173-177). The psychopathological model argues that religious innovation is the result of novel responses to personal and societal crises made by mentally ill individuals who often have their visions during psychotic episodes. In Stark and Bainbridge's terms, these individuals invent new packages of compensators. Their reactions may then lead to the formation of a cult if there are sufficient people in the society with similar problems. And if they are successful in founding a cult, the founders may achieve at least a partial cure of their illnesses. As might be expected, the authors rely on psychoanalytic theories and on some anthropological work that has used those theories for the validity of this model.

The second, entrepreneur, model might equally be called the hypocrite model, for it presents the founders of cults as individuals who consciously develop new religious ideas in order to sell them to others and thereby gain personal profit in terms of money and prestige. The entrepreneur may think up the new ideas himself or pick them up elsewhere, but whichever the case, he or she will tailor them to attract the prospective audience. As for the third, subculture, model, it focuses even less on the individual, conceiving of cults as the expression of new, usually small, social systems in which very small groups of individuals who interact intimately seek certain rewards and persuade one another to believe in some new compensators. But how hypocrites or subculture groups find new ideas is not explained.

Stark and Bainbridge explain the emergence and spread of new religious ideas, beliefs, or compensators by neurosis, psychosis, self-seeking, social pressures, or some combination of them. They thus recognize that religious ideas arise *within* individuals—and only certain individuals. They also remind themselves that "social movements are made of *individuals*. Cults do not make decisions—individuals do" (*FR*, p. 244; see also pp. 390-393). Yet they stay rigorously within the confines of their discipline. Save for their reference to psychopathology and self-seeking, they betray little interest in the thinking of individuals, treating them almost exclusively as participants in social relations.

Given their reliance on the psychopathic model of religious innovation, their conception of meaning systems, including religion, as logically related concepts seems paradoxical. More than that, it seems to disregard individual creativity and the whole realm of imagination totally. Individuals cannot have meaning systems, whether religious or not, unless they join organizations with such systems (*FR*, p. 392). Religion, as a rational activity, can be realized only by "specialized and organized social activities," a condition clearly met by conventional religions. And since they disregard nonrational thinking, they assert that "people often lack meaning systems."

One ought not base theories on the assumption that people usually will possess meaning systems, defined as systematic, coherent, and comprehensive frames of reference. To do so is to overintellectualize humanity, a common failing of social scientists. . . . Indeed, the widespread religious experimentation and seeking going on in our society surely suggest that many people do not possess an adequate religious meaning system. What else could they be looking for? Moreover, decades of research should have made it clear that humans have the ability easily to hold mutually contradictory and logically incoherent beliefs and opinions. Even when we construct attitude scales of items that *logically* imply one another . . . error types abound. (*FR*, p. 391, my italics; see also p. 367)

With these characteristics of Stark and Bainbridge's approach and the questions they raise in mind, we may return to the problem discussed in the last chapter, the use of beliefs about a distinction between the supernatural and natural or the sacred and profane as an objective criterion for religion. Is Stark and Bainbridge's definition of religion explanatory (functional) or denotative (ostensive)? Because of the key role or function they ascribe to "compensators," their definition seems manifestly explanatory, yet their insistence on "supernatural assumptions" seems to make it the classical denotative definition. Closer examination suggests that it is basically ostensive.

Although novel at first sight, their definition differs less from prior definitions than one might have thought. Where previous definitions used "supra-empirical powers" or the "sacred" as the distinguishing criterion of religions, Stark and Bainbridge use "supernatural assumptions." As they say in a preliminary definition, "religions involve some conception of a supernatural being, world, or force, and the notion that the supernatural is active, that events and conditions here on earth are influenced by the supernatural" (*FR*, p. 5). This definition is, therefore, a form of the traditional denotative definition. Although their most arresting concept is that of compensators, compensators become a criterion of religion only when combined with the criterion of supernatural assumptions.

The authors would doubtless disagree. They argue that their definition of religion is a logical consequence of their concept of the varying generality and empirical verifiability of compensators. Using that criterion, they deduce that the most general compensators are, and have to be, accompanied by supernatural assumptions. "Our analysis hinges on our conception of compensators and that the most general compensators are credible *only* if they are based on supernatural assumptions." They assert that the very general compensators of universal peace and plenty on earth provided by radical political organizations such as the Communist party are not only less general than those of religion (presumably any religion) but also, like those of magic, highly vulnerable to empirical disproof. The greatest rewards that compensators can offer are those "not directly available to anyone on this earth" that require supernatural assumptions and can never be disproved by science (*FR*, pp. 524-525).

Stark and Bainbridge seem to have the best of both definitional worlds. On the one hand, they give a criterion, the relative generality of compensators, that seems measurable and explanatory; on the other, they use the criterion of the supernatural, which—in generalizing terminology—makes the beliefs of those studied part of their scholarly definition. The crucial question is whether a clear dividing line between religious and nonreligious compensators can be inferred solely from the criteria of relative generality and empirical verifiability. If it cannot, then the reference to supernatural assumptions introduces a new criterion that makes their definition ostensive. And that, I would argue, is the case.

When the authors speak about compensators and their differing generality, the reader assumes that the compensators all perform the same kind of function and fall along the same continuum of increasing generality, the criterion for generality being the magnitude of the envisaged rewards and the degree of their empirical unverifiability. Least general are those compensators which, because they promise concrete, limited rewards in the proximate future, are most susceptible of empirical invalidation; most general are those which refer to rewards that, since they can never be observed in this life, are beyond empirical invalidation.

But is this a single continuum? Although Stark and Bainbridge treat compensators as differing only in generality along the same continuum, their compensators seem to be of two radically different kinds, expressions of two very different kinds of thinking, and they seem to fall along two different continua. What camouflages that dichotomy is the authors' conviction that all compensators are the product of the same kind of thinking, rational calculation, and differ only in generality. But does empirical unverifiability distinguish between religious and nonreligious compensators, and if not, do the authors therefore rely on a very different criterion, their subjective judgment about the value or desirability of different kinds of rewards?

To deal with the latter point first, the authors assert that life after death "is probably the single most urgent human desire" (*FR*, p. 6). But they do not examine that assumption or its various expressions in any detail, and while we might agree that most humans have wanted a good life that continues as long as possible, many people have seemed much more concerned about any obtainable rewards in this life than bliss in some imagined afterlife.[12] Throughout history, many who apparently believed in an afterlife, whether affluent or deprived, did not conduct themselves as if that were their most urgent desire, as the power of the Faust legend illustrates. While giving lip service to the possibility, they frequently, even habitually, conducted themselves in ways that ran counter to what their religion proclaimed necessary to obtain that afterlife. And certainly, the most urgent desire of many people today is not life after death but a better or bearable life here and now.

The authors' solution to that problem is apparently their proposition that "Humans prefer rewards to compensators and attempt to exchange compensators for rewards."[13] In other words, if people can get enough rewards in their daily life, they will be satisfied

12. According to one survey, belief in an afterlife can decline while belief in a god rises: see Theodore Zeldin, *France 1848-1945: Anxiety and Hypocrisy* (Oxford, 1981), p. 218. And nowadays, the problems of the quality of life and an easy death loom ever larger with the advance of medical science.

13. *A Theory of Religion*, p. 37.

by them and no longer hunger for compensators. Yet, as Pascal's wager reminds us, it is hard to see why people would abandon hope in an immense reward hereafter unless they had to. Few lives in any age are perfect beds of roses, and even people who have enjoyed many rewards here and now have also believed in an afterlife. Were life after death indeed the most urgent human desire, and people always did think of it as infinitely greater and more valuable than any less general reward, then all people would hope for it. Many people, however, both the relatively deprived and the relatively favored, have not believed. Consequently, it is difficult to assert objectively that individual life after death is the most general and urgently desired reward. It would seem that people have differed radically in their choice of compensators, not because of their rational calculus, given their situation, about rewards and compensators, but because of profound differences in their way of thinking about life.

The authors' formal criterion for the generality of rewards and hence of compensators is: "Rewards are general to the extent that they include other (less general) rewards." But we know that people who believe in an afterlife—as Jews in the period of the first Temple did not—do not always expect to enjoy in the hereafter all the lesser rewards they have enjoyed on earth, for example, sexual delight. To get around that problem, the authors introduce another criterion, the kind of reward and the value attributed to it, a strikingly subjective criterion: "Reward A is more valuable than reward B if a person will usually exchange B for A."[14] But if life after death were indeed the highest conceivable reward, we would expect people to give up less valuable immediate rewards if that were thought necessary to obtain a more distant reward of a different and incommensurably more valuable kind that satisfied their most urgent desire. Moreover, since evaluation of the value of different kinds of reward is a subjective matter, it would seem to lie outside the realm of rational thinking.

The basic problem in talking about the generality and value of rewards and compensators is: how they are to be judged, by whom, and when? On the one hand, the authors accept that the

14. Ibid., p. 28.

value of rewards is determined subjectively by human desires;[15] on the other, they assume that they can assess the value and generality of other people's compensators objectively. But it is hard to see how compensators can be judged objectively. What seemed very general to people in one period may seem very limited to others. From our perspective today, some compensators that Stark and Bainbridge would consider religious seem far less general than others potentially open to empirical invalidation.

Science now provides probabilistic empirical answers to the questions of where we came from, where we are going, and what life is of a generality far beyond that of many earlier and present religions. Consequently, compensators that refer to potentially empirically verifiable rewards can now be amazingly general— and distant. As science fiction indicates, the scope of beliefs about the shape of things to come has increased dramatically fairly recently. Thanks to space vehicles and the infrared telescope in space, our conception of time and space has been expanded by light years and our concept of infinity given new meaning. Genetics offers formerly inconceivable heavens and hells. But only we now can compare the generality of our scientific utopias with the compensations offered by ancient religions, for their adherents could not conceive of our utopias. The generality of compensators is thus historically relative. And if general compensators can be equated, as the authors do, with explanations of ultimate meaning, for example, answers to the question "Why are we here?"[16] their historical relativity is particularly obvious. Our present scientific explanations are far more inclusive and general than many previous "religious" explanations.

Even if we look only at traditional religions, the generality of their compensators is historically relative. From our vantage point, it is obvious that religions have varied greatly in the generality of the compensators they have offered—although Stark and Bainbridge pay little attention to that problem. They assume that "supernatural" rewards, those of magic being excluded, are by definition of the greatest magnitude. But beliefs about rewards in an imagined but completely imperceptible realm have varied

15. Ibid., p. 215.
16. Ibid., p. 39.

considerably. Anticipated rewards have ranged—for males—from fighting alongside the gods in Valhalla until they too are destroyed, from enjoying innumerable, ever-virginal, women, to— for both sexes—the almost totally unimaginable experience of infinite bliss that Dante tried to evoke. Moreover, had the authors examined conceptions of gods, they would have had to recognize that the powers attributed to gods have also varied greatly.

A different problem about generality is that Stark and Bainbridge pay little attention to the this-worldly effects of religious belief. They typically depict belief in general rewards in the distant future as compensation for failure to obtain scarce tangible rewards now.[17] Though they emphasize that the leaders of religious societies are rewarded with social power and prestige, they pay almost no attention to the way religious beliefs mold people's lives. In the first place, in addition to supernatural rewards, the adherents of most religions have also expected empirically unpredictable rewards on earth such as survival or the victory of their society. And some religions have emphasized this-worldly rewards almost to the exclusion of otherworldly rewards. In the second place, while the authors recognize that religions demand a self-imposed or self-ordering pattern of conduct, they say little about what individual adherents of religions must do to be seen by themselves and others as deserving of those rewards. They so stress the function of compensating for the evil of present deprivation that the function of providing guidance or understanding in the present is set aside.

The authors fail to emphasize that the payment for religious rewards is of two kinds, involuntary and voluntary. The relative deprivation of worldly power and its accompanying rewards that the authors stress is an involuntary payment. But believers also voluntarily impose additional costs on themselves that often demand strenuous self-control. An integral part of almost all beliefs in supernatural rewards is the belief that they are available only to those who voluntarily act in certain ways and refuse some immediate rewards they could obtain, such as certain forms of sexual gratification. Most of the beliefs of most religions are not descrip-

17. Ibid., pp. 11, 307-312.

tions of distant rewards but imperatives about self-ordering, descriptions of how to lead a good life here and now.

Maintaining the economic and legal metaphor, we may say that compensators are contracts that stipulate responsibilities for each party. They promise that reality will provide people general and often rather vague rewards in the indeterminate future on condition that people understand life here and now in a particular way and follow quite specific patterns of life. Compensators do not merely promise rewards hereafter to the involuntarily deprived; they usually dictate quite specifically how life should be lived in the present. Consequently, the appeal or power of compensators depends both on the attraction of the distant rewards and on the immediate psychological satisfaction of living according to a particular understanding and patterning of life. And it is by no means obvious which gratification is more compelling.[18]

It could be argued that what is most important psychologically about compensators is the pattern of living they dictate, not the distant rewards they promise. What most clearly characterizes religions is their imperatives about how life should be lived here and now, and those imperatives differ widely in kind and comprehensiveness. Whereas the rewards in another world proclaimed by the various Christian religions differ little, the specific forms of thought and action they stipulate as a condition for those rewards vary considerably. Hence, the promise of very general and distant rewards is not the only, and probably not the best, way of distinguishing between compensators.

The range of the convictions about present life that compensators specify may be more important. Compensators can be ranged according to the extent to which they provide a general understanding of present life and dictate conduct that provides the believers with appropriate and satisfying responses to present and future situations. And when that is done, it becomes much more difficult to draw a sharp line between traditional and surrogate religions—between, say, Communism and Islam.

18. In one of the last pieces he wrote, "Independent People," *New York Review of Books* 34, no. 15 (1987): 7, Arnaldo Momigliano noted that one aspect of Jewish society is "the well-known contradiction that Jews have notions of the next world and yet in practice attribute little importance to them."

If there are problems about the criteria to determine the generality of compensators, there are even more fundamental problems about the criterion of empirical verifiability, which is linked to another criterion, durability. Stark and Bainbridge argue insistently that what distinguishes nonreligious compensators from religious compensators is the former's vulnerability in time to empirical disconfirmation and hence their limited life-span. The authors therefore distinguish magic sharply from religion. So-called surrogate religions, such as Communism, are not religions because they cannot last.

But durability is also historically relative. Religions in the authors' sense, whether human organizations or sets of beliefs, have also lost credibility and had limited life-spans. Tribes with their general compensators based on supernatural assumptions have disappeared, whether because they died out or because their members converted to other religions. No longer do people base their compensators on supernatural assumptions about the Thrice-great Hermes. Indeed, even within Christianity, supernatural assumptions have changed remarkably. Were that not so, theologians would have been long out of business. Although the human desire for compensation may be everlasting, neither earthly nor supernatural compensators are.

Moreover, historical religions such as the Christian religions are providential religions; like Marxism, they assert that history will demonstrate the unrolling of a divine plan. And if history does not fulfill their expectations, if the world does not end within a short time, as it was expected at the outset, or if Christ's dominion over the earth does not become self-evident, as people in the Middle Ages believed it would, then the compensators must be modified by ingenious intepretation to overcome the empirical contradiction.

But there is a much more basic problem. Although an omniscient observer might be able to assess the durability and potential for empirical invalidation of compensators, that is not true for those who believe in them, for their beliefs exist and have not yet been invalidated. Believers at any given time do not know that their beliefs will later be demonstrated to be invalid. We may know that a rain dance did not cause rain, but those who participated did not. We may know that Hitler's promise of a millennial Reich was false, but those who believed in it did not. Empirical verifiability, like the generality and durability of compensators, is historically relative.

Neither the criterion of generality nor that of empirical verifiability yields the sharp distinction the authors seek to establish between human organizations or sets of beliefs that the authors considered to be religious and those they do not. By the criterion of generality, the two kinds of compensators overlap. Nor will the generality of compensators alone yield the sharp distinction between traditional religions and what have been termed surrogate religions that the authors wished to draw. To maintain that distinction, they had to introduce a further criterion in their definition, the criterion of "supernatural assumptions."

The fundamental problem about Stark and Bainbridge's conception of religion, leaving aside their considerable disregard for historical evidence, seems to be their assumption that religious thought is rational. Because of that assumption, they assumed that compensators were all of the same kind and fell along a single continuum. But when we examine their compensators more closely, they seem to be using two different criteria for them: on the one hand, the subjective assessment of those who have historically believed in certain compensators; on the other, their own present objective assessment that compensators have been invalidated empirically. And because they have used two different criteria, their compensators should be placed along two different continua.

On one continuum would be the rational compensators, compensators of varying generality that depend on rational empirical knowledge about earthly conditions and promise probable rewards in the future, rewards whose expectation makes present difficulties easier to bear. Such predictions may be more or less reliable, and the expected rewards more or less distant and more or less concretely conceived, but these expectations depend on a particular kind of thinking, the kind of rational empirical calculations that all who are not hopeless must make to survive.

On the other continuum would be the compensators that express feelings rather than calculations. They also promise gratification, whether in this life or some other one, but they express a very different kind of thinking. They are not the result of a rational empirical assessment of a person's situation, capacities, and environment. Rather, they are the product of the kind of thinking that has long found expression in children's stories and fairy tales in which people, often aided by magic, overcome hardship and live happily ever after in never-never lands that resemble known life but do not follow the same rules. Similar thinking is apparent in a remarkably similar genre, miracle stories, especially the miracles of the Virgin Mary.[19] And with this kind of thinking, it is but a small step further to imagine an unimaginable state of gratification in an unobservable existence.

This nonempirical thinking is very different from rational empirical predictions about particular, empirically definable, rewards that may result from acting in a carefully calculated way. It expresses the desire for a general state of being, happiness or salvation. What is desired is a global emotional state, whatever might produce it, and any particular rewards imagined are only metaphors to give that imagined contentment some concrete meaning or explanation. Far from being restricted to fairy stories, beliefs in Santa Claus, and the like, this is a kind of thinking in which all who are not suicidal are likely to engage. Most of us realize that the achievement of certain goals, initially envisaged as rewards, will not necessarily guarantee our happiness, yet we all, or almost all, believe that life is worth living, despite its hardships and despite our ignorance of how it originated and what is yet to come.

The faith that life is worth living and the hope that it will remain so, which carries us through hardships, does not spring exclusively, or perhaps even primarily, from a rational empirical assessment of the possibilities of specific conceivable rewards. As I shall argue later, it is our global reaction to everything that affects us.[20] That totality is something we cannot assess rationally and empirically. Of course, our thinking about the meaning of all we encounter is affected by our rational empirical knowledge, but that global reaction is not itself rational and empirical; and whether it involves beliefs about supernatural forces or not, it is

19. See, e.g., Italo Calvino, *Italian Folktales* (New York, 1980), particularly nos. 28, 41, 165, 186, 191, 197.
20. Below, chap. 9.

not at the mercy of empirical invalidation. It is the realm of attitude and imagination; it is our imaging of the value of our existence.

People react to what they encounter both rationally and nonrationally. Some people believe that their god is present in the
bread and wine consecrated by a priest of the Roman Catholic
religion, treat them as sacred, and distinguish them from the profane bread and wine they eat at regular meals; others, including
former Catholics, do not. Some people believe that the world they
perceive was created by a supernatural being who communicated
in human language with Moses; others, while perceiving the same
world, including those believers and their Bible, only think of
what they perceive as natural processes. Both sets of people are
reacting to similar empirical realities, but what they think about
them differs radically. Empirically, the difference lies not in any
distinction apparent in the realities independent of them which
they confront; it lies in how they think about them. And by that,
I do not mean the difference in *what* they think, but the difference in *how* they are thinking when they think about them religiously.

When pre-Christian Celts distinguished between one tree as
sacred and another as something they could cut for firewood, they
were thinking about a tree in both cases, but the nature of their
mental processes differed strikingly depending on the context in
which they thought about trees. The same is true of Catholics
who distinguish between the bread and wine of the Mass and the
bread and wine of their daily fare. The distinction people have
made between the sacred and profane did not depend on the
observable realities they encountered; it depended on their ability
to think about what can and cannot be perceived in two very
different ways; and that difference can be examined empirically.

Any analysis of nonrational beliefs about how life should be
lived, however, rapidly leads to questions about the origin and
meaning of ideas, and those are problems that Stark and Bainbridge carefully avoid. They are so concerned to demonstrate the
function of religious beliefs as rationally calculated compensators
for social deprivation that they have little interest in any other
dimensions of the ideas and actions they deem religious. They
have no interest in the vast vistas of "cosmization" that Peter Ber-

ger explores. They almost totally ignore the dense dimensions of religious belief that Clifford Geertz's definition embraces. Concerned only with the compensatory function of religious beliefs, they have little interest in their origin and meaning and no interest in symbolic thought or psychological processes.

In one sense they are well advised not to bring those matters into their analysis. As Neil Smelser put it,

Analytically, these frames of reference—the personality and the social—should be kept distinct. A description of a social system cannot be reduced to the psychological states of the persons in that system; a social system must be described in terms of roles, organizations, norms, etc. Similarly, a description of a personality system cannot be reduced to the social involvements of the person; it must be described in terms of distinctive psychological units.[21]

But by confining their approach to the social frame of reference and, even more narrowly, to an analysis of social institutions, Stark and Bainbridge neglect the other frame of reference and inevitably arrive at a one-sided and limited definition of religion. It is one thing to keep the frames distinct, quite another to pretend—save for some rudimentary axioms—that one of them does not exist, especially when the interaction between the two is so obvious to most observers that even the authors cannot avoid a reference to psychopathology and self-seeking.

They avoid problems of meaning or epistemology so far as possible in favor of institutional analyses. Yet, although they are suspicious of cultural explanations of meanings (*FR*, p. 366), they do acknowledge that "religion really is a meaning system" (*FR*, p. 390).

One thing is certain: Meaning systems do not hover above societies without visible means of support; meaning systems are not phenomenological smog banks. To exist, meaning systems must be the property of human beings and thus be sustained through human interactions. If that is so, then the place to look for meaning systems is not in an ozone layer of literary criticism or philosophical speculation, but in the concrete opinions and behavior of individuals, in the ongoing interactions

21. Neil J. Smelser and William T. Smelser, *Personality and Social Systems* (New York, 1963), p. 2.

among humans (that is, their social networks), in the division of labor, and within formal systems. (*FR*, pp. 391-392)

But their relative neglect of the role of individuals in creating social meaning systems and their disinterest in artistic imagination, epistemology, and problems of language make their approach very one-sided. However valuable their detailed analyses of sects and cults, their approach to religion only tells part of the story. While historians may find much that is useful in Stark and Bainbridge's work, they will hardly find its definition of religion adequate for their own purposes. Their thesis about deprivation may be usefully applied, for example, to the origin of the Franciscan sect, drawing attention to the reactions of a merchant's son who had aspired to knighthood. But the argument that the social skills of founders explains the success of sects will by no means yield the insight into the unique features of Francis's personality and thought that historians would feel necessary to explain his initial impact. Nor will it explain why myths about Francis that could hardly be considered rational were so important for the later success of the order.

The same would be even more obviously true for Luther. Luther's thoughts and actions provide a very well documented instance of innovation that produced a major religion, and Stark and Bainbridge could have used it to test their deprivation thesis about religious innovation. Presumably they would have explained any novelty in Luther's thoughts and actions as a result of his pathological condition. To justify their position, however, they would have had to delve into Luther's ideas and personality, but Erik H. Erickson's book,[22] whatever one may think of its precise thesis, does not even appear in their bibliography.

Since Stark and Bainbridge are sociologists, one can hardly blame them for remaining within their discipline and refusing to use conceptions referring to the personality frame of reference in their definition of religion. As noted above, it is remarkably hard to find any clear definition of religion in psychology other than implicit reliance on the self-definition of traditional religions. But that does not mean that what goes on within individuals should therefore be considered unimportant for a definition of religion.

22. *Young Man Luther* (New York, 1958).

However religion is defined, the definition must take both social processes and processes within the individual into account, for a maxim about human preference for rewards over costs hardly covers the rich ongoings within individuals. The problem is to find a way of distinguishing religious phenomena that shortchanges neither society nor the individual, neither rational nor nonrational thought. And there is a very different, almost antithetical, conception of religion that tries to avoid that one-sidedness—religion as the product of symbolic thinking.

Chapter Six

Religion as Symbols

As we have seen, the overwhelming majority of scholarly definitions of religion use the explicit beliefs of traditional believers as their criterion of religion. They disagree markedly, however, on whether religion is a social or psychological phenomenon. Or, more correctly, they hesitate. Perhaps because of their reliance on traditional religious concepts, most are unclear about how the distinction between the individual and society is relevant to discussions of religious phenomena. Although most of the scholars discussed thus far conceive of religion as a social phenomenon, they also recognize that much that they deem religious occurs within individuals.

Three recent definitions that have drawn considerable attention, at least among anglophone scholars, differ considerably from most of the approaches just discussed in that they pay considerable attention to both the social and the subjective element.[1] What distinguishes religion and religious people is not a particular kind of belief but the distinctive ideas, attitudes, and emotions aroused in individuals by their symbolic thinking. Peter Berger, Clifford Geertz, and Robert Bellah concentrate on semiotic networks or symbol systems, and they stress the interaction between individuals and their society rather than making a sharp distinc-

---

1. Much of the following discussion of these three approaches will be very familiar to scholars of religion, and were I only addressing them, I could state my reservations about these approaches more succinctly. I have discussed them at some length, however, because I could not assume that historians would be equally familiar with them.

tion between them. But whether they have avoided the problem of using other people's beliefs as their scholarly criterion of religion is another question.

The central novelty of Berger's sociological definition of religion is his relational concept of "cosmization," a term that denotes a complex projective theory about the nature of what we call "reality." That theory, developed by Berger and Thomas Luckmann in an earlier book,[2] is summarized at the beginning of *The Sacred Canopy* as a necessary preliminary for his definition of religion. The theory, which owes much to philosophical ideas, depicts our consciousness of reality as a purely human product, as the result of ongoing dialectical relations between the externalizing, objectifying, and internalizing activities of humans.

Humans, relatively instinctually unprogrammed animals, pour their actions out into the world in order to establish a precariously stable relationship with their world, one another, and their environment. Man, "biologically deprived of a man-world . . . constructs a human world."[3] The products of those actions then confront individuals as external objects, as existing in reality outside of man. Among those objectified products is that essential of human existence, society, which enables humans to reproduce and preserve themselves and their culture. It socializes those born within it so that their society also seems an external object to them, even though it is only the product of their joint activity. Through socialization, moreover, the individual also internalizes what is presented as reality by the society so that it is also subjective reality for the individual. Successful socialization thus produces "a symmetry between the objective world of society and the subjective world of the individual." But the social order and the reality it imposes is precarious because socialization is imperfect. Despite socialization and the social force exerted to protect a society's "knowledge" from dissent and denial, individuals may find the objective reality provided by their society subjectively implausible and cease to be coproducers of the social reality.[4]

2. Peter L. Berger and Thomas Luckmann, *The Social Construction of Reality* (Garden City, N.Y., 1967).
3. Peter L. Berger, *The Sacred Canopy* (Garden City, N.Y., 1969), p. 6.
4. Ibid., pp. 15-17.

Society is thus "a world-building enterprise" that imposes on individual experiences a nomos or meaningful order that rests on the foundation of language and builds up by means of language "the cognitive and normative edifice that passes for objective 'knowledge' in a society." It makes life and death meaningful for individuals and protects them from anomie and the terror of chaos so long as they do not separate themselves from it. "Whenever the socially established nomos attains the quality of being taken for granted, there occurs a merging of its meanings with what are considered to be the fundamental meanings in the universe. Nomos and cosmos appear to be co-extensive." And that socially objectivated "knowledge" or "reality" serves to explain and justify or legitimate the social order of society.[5] On that foundation, Berger then defines religion as

the human enterprise by which a sacred cosmos is established. Put differently, religion is cosmization in a sacred mode. By sacred is meant here a quality of mysterious and awesome power, other than man and yet related to him, which is believed to reside in certain objects of experience. This quality may be attributed to natural or artificial objects, to animals, or to men, or to the objectifications of human culture . . . the chieftain . . . space and time . . . localized spirits . . . great cosmic divinities.[6]

The specification of the "sacred" in Berger's definition would seem, as he insists, to make it a substantive or denotative definition that distinguishes religion from cosmization in any other mode. Yet the definition reduces religion to being but one form of cosmization, and cosmization is explained by its function of protecting biologically unprogrammed individuals from the terror of disorder or chaos and anomie.[7] The emphasis on the function of "cosmization" thus seems to move the definition into the explanatory category while, conversely, the specification of the "sacred" seems too vague to make it clearly denotative. Although Berger defines the "sacred" as the experience of awesome power, he does not produce criteria to determine when that apprehension

5. Ibid., pp. 19-29.
6. Ibid., p. 25.
7. A point well made, along with many others, by Van A. Harvey, "Some Problematic Aspects of Peter Berger's Theory of Religion," *Journal of the American Academy of Religion* 41 (1973): 82-83.

is or is not present. If we ask what distinguishes the profane from the sacred, we are only told that everything that does not stick out as sacred is profane, and that that dichotomization of reality is "intrinsic to the religious enterprise"—which does not get us much further. Berger also contrasts "the sacred" with "chaos," the terror of meaninglessness,[8] but since chaos is the opposite of any nomic order, religious or otherwise, that provides no distinction either.

Comparisons of specific examples of religious and nonreligious cosmization might have made the distinction clearer, but they are lacking. Although the weight placed on cosmization as a universal human activity would lead one to expect some discussion of non-religious cosmizations, there are none. Even Berger's definition of secularization only defines it as "the process by which sectors of society and culture are removed from the domination of religious institutions and symbols."[9] And surprisingly, he does not tackle a problem obviously relevant to his perspective, that of surrogate religions. Consequently, the reader may know what phenomena Berger is thinking about but remain very uncertain about the objectivity of Berger's distinction between religious and nonreligious cosmizations.

From the examples Berger gives of religious cosmization, it is obvious that his conception of the "sacred" is based on his knowledge of a broad range of what are usually considered religions, whether totemism, belief in gods, *dharma*, or a single god.[10] And he does present some very general characteristics that, he believes, distinguish religious cosmizations from nonreligious ones. "Religion is the audacious attempt to conceive of the entire universe as being humanly significant."[11] "Religion legitimates [socially defined reality] so effectively because it relates the precarious reality constructions of empirical societies with ultimate reality."[12] Religion conceals the "*constructed* character" of the institutional order of society by ascribing it to the universe.[13]

8. *The Sacred Canopy*, pp. 26-27.
9. Ibid., p. 107.
10. Ibid., pp. 34-35.
11. Ibid., p. 28.
12. Ibid., p. 32.
13. Ibid., p. 33.

The emphasis is on the totalizing or all-embracing quality of a "sacred" cosmos, its reach in time and space and the cognitive and emotional priority it gives to reality beyond human control. Yet this totalizing quality seems to be a question of degree rather than a criterion that makes possible any clear distinction between religious and nonreligious cosmizations. Adam Smith's "invisible hand," Herbert Spencer's "survival of the fittest," the mysterious march of material relations of dogmatic Marxism, or Nazism's faith in blood would seem to fit Berger's religious bill as well as totemism or *dharma*—or Calvinism.

Berger does not differ from Durkheim as much as one might have supposed from their radical difference in style of thought. Although Berger strongly emphasizes the dialectical relation between individuals and society, "reality" or religion is depicted primarily as a social product. Moreover, leaving convolutions about the case of Christianity aside, religion is seen as legitimating the social order—indeed it is difficult to differentiate from it—and as a method of social control that may involve the use of force. The unemphasized but central role that Berger attributes to language as the foundation on which religion rests also brings him closer to Durkheim and Saussure and to the hermeneutical approach of Clifford Geertz than might at first appear because of the great differences in their approaches.

For Durkheim, "the collective consciousness is the highest form of psychic life, since it is the consciousness of consciousnesses . . . that . . . sees things only in their permanent and essential aspects, which it crystalizes into communicable ideas."[14] Had Durkheim spoken of communicable signs or symbols instead of communicable ideas, or of a system of symbols instead of a system of ideas, the connection between his conception of meaning and that of his contemporary, Ferdinand de Saussure, and of modern semiotics would be more obvious. For even though Durkheim was probably unaware of Saussure's work, their epistemological attitudes were surprisingly similar.[15] The new intellectual climate that found expression in the work of Durkheim, Saussure, Otto, Freud, and Weber corroded positivism in many

14. *The Elementary Forms of Religious Life*, p. 492.
15. Jonathan Culler, *Ferdinand de Saussure* (New York, 1980), p. 79.

disciplines and raised the problem of "meaning" and "reality" in a way that was not fully apparent until the deconstruction wrought recently by symbolic philosophy, semiotics, and hermeneutics. Consequently, the distance between Durkheim's conception of religion and that of Berger is much less than one might expect after the passage of fifty momentous years. And the same is true of Geertz's conception.

Geertz's definition of religion, like Berger's, relies on the concept of the "sacred." According to Geertz, a religious system is made up of "a cluster of sacred symbols, woven into some sort of ordered whole,"[16] and those "sacred symbols function to synthesize a people's ethos—the tone, character, and quality of their life, its moral and aesthetic style and mood—and their world view—the picture they have of the way things in sheer actuality are, their most comprehensive ideas of order."[17] Formally defined, religion is

(1) a system of symbols which acts to (2) establish powerful, pervasive, and long-lasting moods and motivations in men (3) by formulating conceptions of a general order of existence and (4) clothing these conceptions with such an aura of factuality that (5) the moods and motivations seem uniquely realistic.[18]

Although Geertz does not specify the "sacred" in his formal definition, what he says before and after the definition makes it clear that "symbols" in the definition means "sacred" symbols. It is the distinction between the sacred and profane that identifies religion. The definition is, therefore, apparently denotative. The question of which symbols are and are not sacred is explained in a passage that needs to be quoted at length.

That the symbols or symbol systems which induce and define dispositions that we set off as religious and those which place those dispositions in a cosmic framework are the same symbols should occasion no surprise. For what else do we mean by saying that a particular mood of awe is religious and not secular, except that it springs from entertaining a conception of an all-pervading vitality like mana and not from a visit to the

16. *The Interpretation of Cultures* (New York, 1973), p. 129. This article, "Religion as a Cultural System," was first published in 1966.
17. Ibid., p. 89.
18. Ibid., p. 90.

Grand Canyon? Or that a particular case of asceticism is an example of religious motivation, except that it is directed toward the achievement of an unconditioned end like nirvana and not a conditioned one like weight-reduction? If sacred symbols did not at one and the same time induce dispositions in human beings and formulate, however obliquely, inarticulately, or unsystematically, general ideas of order, then the empirical differentia of religious activity or religious experience would not exist. A man can indeed be said to be "religious" about golf, but not merely if he pursues it with passion and plays it on Sundays; he must also see it as symbolic of some transcendent truths. . . . What any particular religion affirms about the fundamental nature of reality may be obscure, shallow, or all too often perverse; but it must . . . affirm something. If one were to essay a minimal definition of religion today, it would perhaps not be Tylor's famous "belief in spiritual beings" . . . but rather what Salvador de Madariaga has called "the relatively modest dogma that God is not mad."[19]

For Geertz, as for Otto, Durkheim, and Berger, the sacred is distinguishable from the profane by the awe provoked in individuals by their sense of being in contact with a fundamental order or unconditioned end that transcends them. Geertz assumes that awareness of this distinction is a given of the historical record or of human psychology which all recognize and which the scholar must accept. His appeal to common modern understanding of experience is manifest in the use of "we" and is reinforced by references to "transcendent truths," "Sunday," "spiritual beings," and, through de Madariaga, to "God." And Geertz tells us—although he states it in the objective voice—that unless we accept the distinction, we will have no criteria, no empirical differentia, for religious activity or experience.

But has Geertz provided empirical criteria that enable us to distinguish clearly between religious and nonreligious activity? His examples from daily life are rather unconvincing. If a visit to the Grand Canyon does not engender a conception of all-pervading vitality, a visit to the Amazon might; and a visit to the Canyon is certainly likely to make most people awed by their awareness of an order or reality that transcends them. A flat tire in Death Valley in proximity to an animal's skull might be even more convincing. And the example of the golf player indicates just how

19. Ibid., pp. 98-99.

indistinct the distinction is, for the transcendent truths to which the player might symbolically relate his golf—about play, mental and biological health, nature, and the relations between them all—might induce very powerful and long-lasting dispositions and yet be far from anything remotely resembling what have traditionally been considered religions.

But the element of the definition on which Geertz bases his most analytic argument for the distinction is not that of powerful and enduring dispositions, psychological awe before an all-pervading vitality, or conceptions of a general order. It is that of "factuality" or the "uniquely realistic."

It is this sense of the "really real" upon which the religious perspective rests and which the symbolic activities of religion as a cultural system are devoted to producing, intensifying, and, so far as possible, rendering inviolable by the discordant revelations of secular experience. It is, again, the imbuing of a certain complex of symbols—of the metaphysic they formulate and the style of life they recommend—with a persuasive authority which, from an analytic point of view, is the essence of religious action.[20]

This is the criterion Geertz uses to distinguish the religious perspective from commonsensical, scientific, or aesthetic approaches. He argues that whereas the commonsensical perspective accepts the realities of everyday life as fully factual givens to be mastered or accepted, the religious perspective moves beyond those realities to "wider ones," which it does not question or try to modify but accepts fully and uses to criticize daily reality. And whereas the scientific perspective engages in disinterested observation and systematic formal analysis with deliberate doubt that reduces the givenness of everday reality to probabilistic hypotheses, the religious perspective dissolves everyday reality in terms of what are accepted as wider nonhypothetical truths and does so with commitment rather than detachment. As for art, whereas the religious perspective is deeply concerned with fact and seeks utter actuality, art disregards the whole question of factuality.

Now, in one sense, I think I know what Geertz is pointing toward as the core of the religious perspective. It is the mood

20. Ibid., p. 112.

captured in the formula Berger uses in his discussion of masoch-
ism in religion: "I am nothing—He is everything." Or, more explicitly, "The lover, say, or the master is posited as total power,
absolute meaning, that is as a *realissimum* into which the tenuous
realities of one's own subjectivity may be absorbed."[21] In other
words, all the differentiated awarenesses of realities that constitute the everyday self are radically devalued in relation to belief
in an englobing will or order without which the individual cannot
face those everyday contingencies. Now it is easy to think of
highly emotional outpourings in which individuals known as
highly religious have expressed this sentiment or desire to be
submerged or united in ultimate reality or "God." And I would
agree that these are central phenomena that any definition of religion must cover and any explanation of religion must deal with.
But does this specification of the "really real" or *realissimum* distinguish the religious perspective qualitatively from the commonsensical, scientific, and aesthetic, as Geertz asserts?

What is presented here as the religious perspective is a relation
between belief and facts in which belief is given absolute priority
and becomes the absolute arbiter of facts. Yet, if we leave the
problem of the relation between language and reality aside for a
moment and examine Geertz's "really real" in commonsense
terms, one obvious problem, as Ralph Burhoe has pointed out,[22]
is that for many people today the most indisputable facts are those
on which most scientists agree, and the most comprehensive ideas
of reality are those about the universe provided by those theories
and facts. For such people the scientific outlook does formulate
"conceptions of a general order of existence" and clothes "these
conceptions with such an aura of factuality that the moods and
motivations inspired [by the conceptions] seem uniquely real."
Hence that outlook is a religion according to Geertz's definition.

That criticism suggests a more fundamental question. Is it true,
still in commonsense terms, that what believers in traditional religions conceived as comprehensive "sacred" orders have been
more real to them than the concrete realities of daily life? The

21. *The Sacred Canopy*, pp. 56-57.
22. Ralph W. Burhoe, "The Phenomenon of Religion Seen Scientifically," in
Changing Perspectives in the Scientific Study of Religion, ed. Allan W. Eister
(New York, 1974), p. 33.

answer would seem to be yes in marginal cases—for example, individuals during religious ecstasies or mystical trances. But relatively few believers in major religions experience such moods, and when they do, they divorce themselves so far as possible from other humans and from any conceptual consciousness of the common sacred symbols. Moreover, it can hardly be said that such moods "synthesize a people's ethos" or are the "most comprehensive ideas of order." Although mystics may be socially disruptive, when their conduct does express a people's idea of social and cosmic order, it relies on the participants' sense of present reality. Individuals in tribal religions who become possessed may seem to have departed completely from normal reality, but they act in ways clearly prescribed by the tribe's religious beliefs, their performance is a social act that requires witnesses, and those witnesses are as certain of their own reality as they are of the reality of the performance of the possessed. The expression of contact with supernatural reality depends on certainty of the reality of the group. One sense of reality does not override the other; they complement each other.

Whatever may be true for problematic marginal cases, for most indisputably religious people, belief in the reality of a transcendent order has not been rendered, as Geertz puts it, "inviolable to the discordant revelations of secular experience."[23] Were that the case, we would be hard put to it to explain the fact of religious change, conversion, and religious doubt.[24] As Jonathan Smith has put it, "the Babylonian Aiku festival and the Ceramese myth of Hainuwele are best described neither in terms of repetition of the past nor in terms of future fulfillment, but rather in terms of a difficult and incongruous present."[25] Without reference to people's recognition—whether explicit or tacit—of realities not adequately comprehended by their previous religion, it would be hard to explain cargo cults or Christianity. For most people, it is far from the case that belief determines reality or facts, or that realities determine belief. Rather, so far as they are distinguishable, they are dynamically or dialectically dependent on, but not

23. Above, n. 20.
24. A classic case, which will be discussed in chap. 12, is doubts about the consecrated bread of the Catholic Eucharist.
25. *Imagining Religion* (Chicago, 1982), p. 101.

totally determined by, each other. Realities or tangible experiences expressed as facts are as undeniable for most people as their religious beliefs.

Immediate experience of concrete realities is, however, connected differently with the comprehensive order in religious experience and scientific thought. In the latter, the tendency is to work from the bottom up, from the most undeniable facts toward larger and not necessarily integrated orders; in the former, the tendency is to think from the top down, from the believed order to the facts. In scientific thought, the recursive interplay of facts, theories, and premises is, if incomplete, explicit and conscious; in religious experience, the interplay of faith, beliefs, and realities is typically tacit (although some people may try to analyze it rationally). Indeed, one of the great advantages of ritual and myth is that they connect the indisputable here and now with a believed transcendent order by symbols that recognize them both without opening their relation to rational examination. That brings us to another central feature of Geertz's—and almost all scholars'—conception of religion, ritual.

> For it is in ritual—that is, consecrated behavior—that this conviction that religious conceptions are veridical and that religious directives are sound is somehow generated. . . . In a ritual, the world as lived and the world as imagined, fused under the agency of a single set of symbolic forms, turns out to be the same world. . . . Whatever role divine intervention may or may not play in the creation of faith—and it is not the business of the scientist to pronounce upon such matters one way or the other—it is, primarily at least, out of the context of concrete acts of religious observance that religious conviction emerges on the human plane.[26]

Here we are apparently at the heart or birth of religion, yet nothing in this passage implies or necessitates that the world as imagined is more real than the world as lived. What happens in ritual, as in religion generally, is a fusion in which both are important, so that there can't be one without the other. But if neither is felt as "uniquely real" or "really real," then the distinction between the sacred and profane becomes even hazier as a specification of religion, especially since it may be argued that ritual,

26. *The Interpretation of Cultures*, pp. 112-113.

although it may generate or strengthen conviction about religious beliefs, is not itself the original source of those beliefs.[27]

Geertz then describes the more public rituals as cultural performances and acknowledges that "all cultural performances are not religious performances, and that the line between those that are and artistic or even political ones, is often not easy to draw in practice."[28] Yet if it is through rituals that conviction of the validity of a religion is generated, then here if ever we should be able to observe the "sacred" or "consecrated behavior" and distinguish it from nonreligious behavior, but that is apparently difficult. It is not surprising that Geertz, like Berger, avoids the problem of distinguishing between religion and "surrogate" religions. Yet if we cannot observe whether something is consecrated or profane behavior, it becomes increasingly questionable whether Geertz's definition of religion is indeed ostensive or denotative.

A very different kind of problem involved in the reliance on a conviction about what is "really real" as a distinguishing mark of religion is that it is very difficult to determine what Geertz means by "real." His language, his reference through de Madariaga to "God," and his careful bracketing of divine intervention imply the existence of a cosmic order. Yet he does not discuss whether the symbols he himself uses and the sacred symbols he discusses, which make consciousness of a general order possible, have any real referents, whether they reflect, in whatever guise, any reality external to human thinking. He leaves open the possibility that that order has no extensionality outside a society's system of symbols, or outside of the social or intersubjective process that generates the symbols. Although the title of the article in which the definition appears, "Religion as a Cultural System," cannot settle the issue, it does imply that for Geertz the only awareness of order humans can have is that forced on them by their semiotic systems, by *their* society's interweaving of symbols into some sort of connected whole that synthesizes *their* worldview and ethos but is not determined by anything outside of them.

In a strange way, we come back to the Aryan myth, with its

27. See below, chap. 10.
28. *The Interpretation of Cultures*, p. 113.

debt to nineteenth-century philologists, and its confusion of languages with other realities, in that case biological reality. Language ceases to be a tool or means and becomes the only reality we encounter. Whereas before people were thought to worship divinities far beyond them, increasingly they are thought to worship symbols. For Otto, the man most influential in making the "sacred" *the* denotative specification of "religion," the ultimate order or reality was indeed divine, and awareness of it could not be expressed in words. For Durkheim also, what was worshiped was something real and external to the individual, though it was something created by human beings. The ultimate reality on which religion depended was the social order; and language, socially created "communicable ideas," was the expression of that order. But with Berger (as sociologist if not as Christian) reality, both the sacred and the profane, are a social product constructed on the foundation of, and by means of, language, which "nomizes by imposing differentiation and structure upon the ongoing flux of experience."[29] And for Geertz, religions are "complexes of symbols" that lie outside the boundaries of individual organisms "in that intersubjective world of common understandings into which all human individuals are born, in which they pursue their separate careers, and which they leave persisting behind them after they die."[30]

Given this commitment to a semiotic concept of culture,[31] it would seem, subject to Geertz's bracketing of divine intervention, that the "uniquely realistic" of religion is the pattern of relations determined by the structure of a people's language, not their *langue* but their *langage* or semiotic structure. If that is so, then religious faith is apparently the determination of (some) people to preserve the fundamental relations or structure of their semiotic network or sacred language at all costs (an attitude of which the French Academy would approve), even at the expense of specific assertions in speech or writing, in *langue*, that call that structure into question.[32] Not society but the structure of language is "God,"

29. *The Sacred Canopy*, p. 20.
30. *The Interpretation of Cultures*, p. 92.
31. Ibid., p. 50.
32. Although I disagree with Geertz's approach, I would agree with this

and anthropological hermeneutics of cultural symbols are theology, a comforting position for linguists—and also for those for whom the *Logos* is "God."

An even more extreme assertion of the centrality and irreducible reality of religious symbols is that of Robert Bellah. Despite my indebtedness to his work, I disagree with him for many of the same reasons I disagree with Geertz. I agree with his emphatic distinction between rational or cognitive and nonrational or noncognitive thinking, and I agree that religious symbolizing expresses people's sense of identity. As he puts it, religion is "a control system linking meaning and motivation by providing an individual or group with the most general model that it has of itself and its world."[33] But by treating both individuals and societies as actions systems,[34] he blurs the distinction between the individual and society.[35] Hence, when he describes religion as the most general mechanism for integrating meaning and motivation in action systems, religion is attributed both to individuals and to society, which permits him to place the emphasis where he wishes.

His preference, apparently, is to consider religion primarily as a social phenomenon and to view the religiosity of individuals as primarily a reflection of culture. In 1955, he thought that "human action is almost by definition symbolic action, which is another way of saying that it always involves culture."[36] In 1965, he declared that "many smaller units (individual personalities and groups) appropriate the symbols of their social and cultural environment in dealing with their own religious problems, though always with some degree of individual variation."[37] And in 1985, he and his collaborators felt that "a vital and enduring religious individualism can only survive in a renewed relation with established religious bodies."[38] Whereas I will distinguish between the

---

implication of his argument, albeit on the basis of a very different definition of religion. See below, chap. 7.

33. *Beyond Belief*, p. 16.
34. Ibid., p. 12.
35. I agree with Gerhard E. Lenski, *Power and Privilege* (New York, 1966), p. 22, that conservatives see systems where radicals see conflicts.
36. *Beyond Belief*, p. 261.
37. Ibid., p. 12.
38. Robert N. Bellah, Richard Madsen, William M. Sullivan, Ann Swidler,

individual and society, and will therefore emphasize the distinction between religions and the religiosity of individuals, he does
not distinguish them clearly and tends to subsume all religious
manifestations under culture.

What I disagree with most sharply, however, is his central thesis about "symbolic realism."

If we define religion as that symbol system that serves to evoke . . . the
"felt-whole," I am prepared to claim that . . . religion is a reality *sui
generis*. To put it bluntly, religion is true. This is not to say that every
religious symbol is equally valid any more than that every scientific theory is equally valid. But it does mean that since religious symbolization
and religious experience are inherent in the structure of human existence, all reductionism must be abandoned. Symbolic realism is the only
adequate basis for the scientific study of religion.[39]

This thesis rests on Bellah's sharp distinction between rational
or cognitive and nonrational or noncognitive thinking and on his
conviction that nonrational thinking communicates "nonordinary
reality that breaks into ordinary reality and exposes its
pretensions"[40] and that those deliverances cannot be explained or
invalidated by rational analysis. Since nonrational symbolic thinking is an innate property of human beings, its symbols are as real
as humans. And since its processes and the realities with which
it deals are not those of rational thinking, Bellah holds that it
cannot be explained in rational terms; it is irreducible.

The first problem with this kind of thesis, as Wayne Proudfoot
has so ably argued,[41] is that it confuses what Proudfoot calls "descriptive reduction" with "explanatory reduction." "*Descriptive reduction* is the failure to identify an emotion, practice, or experience under the description by which the subject identifies it."[42]

---

and Steven M. Tipton, *Habits of the Heart* (Berkeley, Los Angeles, London,
1985), pp. 247-248.

    29. "Christianity and Symbolic Realism," *Journal for the Scientific Study of
Religion* 9 (1970): 93; *Beyond Belief*, pp. 252-253. Ninian Smart, *The Science of
Religion and the Sociology of Knowledge* (Princeton, N.J., 1977), pp. 49-73,
takes a very similar position, although he uses "Focus," with a capital, for what
Bellah calls a symbol system.

    40. *Beyond Belief*, p. 245.

    41. *Religious Experience* (Berkeley, Los Angeles, London, 1985), pp. 190-
236.

    42. Ibid., p. 196.

In other words, if a description of a religious experience does not use or paraphrase the language with which the subject described and explained it, but describes it in different—for example, psychological—terms unknown to the experiencing subject, the description reduces the subjective experience to something else. And Proudfoot would agree that that procedure is illegitimate. To use his favorite example, if someone fears bears, mistakes a log in a forest for a bear, and is afraid of the "bear," what he fears is a bear, and his explanation of his fear is correct, even though his perception of a bear was erroneous. An observer's reductive explanation that he was frightened by a log would be a false description of the subject's mental state; logs do not frighten him. In other words, description of a religious experience must not be reductive.

But that does not exclude explanatory reductions. "*Explanatory reduction* consists in offering an explanation of an experience in terms that are not those of the subject and that might not meet with his approval."[43] While an observer may accept, indeed must accept, that the subject is afraid of bears, the observer may perfectly legitimately explain that on this occasion the subject was in fact frightened by a log, not a bear. The observer may also proceed to explain in various ways why the subject was so afraid of bears. And the observer can do all that without denying the reality of the subject's mental state and expression of it. As Proudfoot says, "This is perfectly justifiable and is, in fact, normal procedure."[44] And he proceeds to demonstrate the apologetic intent of arguments that confuse descriptive and explanatory reductions in order to deny the legitimacy of any reductionism.

Bellah fails to make that normal distinction, and his conception of explanatory reductionism is extreme. He even fails to distinguish between partial and total explanations of religious phenomena. He understands reductionism as scientific explanations that attribute observable functions to religion, and he uses as an example the Freudian interpretation of religion as a resolution of the oedipal problem. Since Freud reduced religion entirely to a psychological process and his theories have been challenged, the

43. Ibid., p. 197.
44. Ibid.

example may seem persuasive. But Bellah is apparently asserting not only that such total reductionism must be abandoned but also that any reductionism, even partial reductionism, is impossible. And that seems highly dubious.

The fourteenth-century belief that Jews caused the Black Death—a belief which brought death to thousands of Jews— would have been impossible had not Jews been a salient symbol in the religion and religiosity of Christians. But that particular belief about Jews, whatever its religious trappings, was obviously caused by people's overwhelming fear of death and by a kind of psychological reaction that can be observed in thoroughly secular situations. Because of their cultural conditioning and great fear, those people irrationally attributed to Jews the dissemination of the bubonic plague.

While we may grant the subjective importance of the belief for those who held it, we would not hesitate to state that the belief itself was scientifically false and obviously fulfilled certain psychological functions. And when we make such an assertion, we do indeed reduce a religious belief to a (false) empirical proposition that can be largely explained in rational empirical terms. The same would be true of any beliefs that used religious symbols to make false assertions about observable realities—for example, those involved in rituals to produce rain. Although Bellah claims that all reductionism must be abandoned, such partial reduction is clearly possible. Had he argued that religious symbolization could not be completely reduced to, or explained in, rational empirical terms, I would have agreed; to say that all reductionism of religious phenomena must be abandoned seems untenable. His conception of reductionism seems to be a straw man held upright by a dated conception of the imperialism of rational thought.

There also seems to be a confusion—that Aquinas would have deplored—of the concept of knowledge with that of faith. Bellah asserts that religion is true. He criticizes reductionism as the position "that the only *valid knowledge* is in the form of falsifiable scientific hypotheses,"[45] and says that religion exposes the pretensions of ordinary reality, by which he means that presented

45. *Beyond Belief*, p. 251, my italics.

by scientific thought.[46] But he also asserts that every religious symbol, like every scientific theory, is not equally valid, although he does not supply criteria for assessing the validity of religious symbols. Presumably his grounds would be nonrational. He thus applies the criterion of truth or validity to both religious symbols and scientific theories and considers both knowledge. Although he seeks to distinguish noncognitive thinking and religious symbol systems sharply from scientific thinking, he thereby muddies the distinction. Had he said that a religious symbol system was subjectively valid for those who maintained it, and that a scientific theory was rationally and empirically (or objectively) true, he would have avoided that ambiguity. But then he could not have made the striking assertion: "religion is true."

A religion cannot be valid in the same sense that a scientific theory is said to be true. If truth means scientifically verifiable knowledge, then a religious symbol—for example, the symbolic associations evoked by "Christ crucified"[47]—is not true. If understanding means what people believe to direct their lives, then that symbol is valid—but only for those who direct their life by that symbol. A religious symbol can be equated as to its truth with a scientific theory only if there is overlap. And since some nonrational beliefs do express propositions about observable reality, some beliefs may be analyzed scientifically and be shown to be scientifically false. Indeed, the symbol set that Bellah preaches (a very American religiosity of biblical traditions and the republicanism of the United States)[48] is full of assertions susceptible of empirical validation or invalidation. Conversely, a scientific theory can be equated with a religious symbol system only to the extent that the scientific theory depends on religious beliefs, as has also been the case.[49]

Nonrational and rational empirical thinking are very different, as Bellah insists. But they are not as inherently antagonistic as

46. Ibid., p. 245.
47. Ibid., p. xix.
48. *Habits of the Heart*, pp. 282-283, 295.
49. See Thomas S. Kuhn, *The Structure of Scientific Revolutions*, 2d ed. (Chigago, 1970). See also Amos Funkenstein, *Theology and the Scientific Imagination from the Middle Ages to the Seventeenth Century* (Princeton, N.J., 1986).

he seems at times to feel. Whatever the position of the early Wittgenstein, we can pursue rational empirical knowledge and still recognize our dependence on subjective personal or cultural understanding. Biologists can use their eyes to analyze the structure and function of eyes without believing they know everything about eyes or understand why our minds make all that they do of what our eyes transmit. While recognizing their reliance on nonrational modes of understanding that guide their lives, practitioners of rational empiricism can nonetheless explain, and in that sense reduce, aspects or characteristics of religion and religiosity, and they can do so without taking a stand as scientists on ultimate or total reality.

In this connection, it is striking that Bellah bases his defense of religion on the reality and inevitability of nonrational thinking but does not distinguish clearly between the nonrational thinking he considers religious thinking—valid or invalid—and the nonrational thinking he thinks perverse. His only indication of a distinction is his definition that religious thinking provides a very general model of the self and its world. Here he joins Berger and Geertz. But "perverse" nonrational thinking can also provide a very general model. In a surprising passage, Bellah declares that those who feel they are completely rational and pragmatic are most in the power of deep unconscious fantasies, that whole nations in the twentieth century have blindly "acted out dark myths of destruction," and that the Students for a Democratic Society were entrapped "in their own unconscious scenarios." But to say, simply because of some of the Nazis' pseudoscientific assertions, that they thought of themselves as completely rational and pragmatic is rather peculiar given the value they attributed to "thinking with the blood." The example does not provide a criterion for distinguishing between valid and less valid or perverse modes of nonrational thinking. It only demonstrates that nonrational thinking and myths can provide a very perverse general model of the self and the world. Nazism is hardly a good basis for his declaration: "This the price we have paid for . . . denying the central integrating role of myth and ritual, and letting our morality be dictated by our politics."[50] Where he draws the line between ide-

50. *Beyond Belief*, p. 254.

ology and religion is thus most unclear, as it is also in *Habits of the Heart.*

For Bellah, religious choice apparently consists of opting between symbol systems; and in the preface to *Beyond Belief*, he makes clear that the symbol system he finds most valid is that associated with the symbol "Christ." Indeed, when he first presented his thesis about symbolic realism in 1969, he argued that "religion is one" because man is one, and that students should be taught the meaning and value of religion along with its analysis, which doubtless explains the sharply critical reactions of two commentators who identified in some sense with Jews. With their knowledge of the use of Jews as a symbol in the symbol system of Christian religions, and with their fresh memory of the effect on Jews of governmentally supported Nazi teaching that emphasized nonrational beliefs and social integration, they could hardly fail to react negatively to the conclusion of Bellah's paper—which was almost a confession of faith:

> If this seems to confuse the role of the theologian and scientists, of teaching religion and teaching about religion, then so be it. The radical split between knowledge and commitment that exists in our culture and in our universities is not ultimately tenable. Differentiation has gone about as far as it can go. It is time for a new integration.[51]

And in response to the objections his stand provoked, Bellah declared:

> I do not wish to deny to any scholar the "neutral zone" within which he can carry out his studies. There is no obligation I would place higher than defense of that zone. But if a conception of religion which has in part grown out of the scientific study of religion has profound implications for the integration of my life, the life of my students, and the vitality of my culture then I intend to say so.[52]

Since I have no desire to make elements of my own religiosity a religion, other than my commitment to rational empiricism, I

---

51. "Christianity and Symbolic Realism," p. 96. For the strongly negative reactions to Bellah's thesis of Samuel Z. Klausner and Benjamin Nelson, see ibid., pp. 100-111.

52. Ibid., p. 115. This reaction seems to have been part of a reaction against the student movement of the 1960s. For Bellah's continuing struggle to develop a new integration see *Habits of the Heart.*

cannot follow Bellah here. As a historian, I am not a teacher of morality, although what I teach is relevant to moral judgments. I feel the best service I can provide my students is to encourage them to think empirically and rationally about history and, when acting in my role as historian, to leave it up to them to develop their own religiosity—which they will do anyway. Nor can I agree that *all* reductionism must be abandoned when we study religious symbolization. As will be obvious from what I shall say about mental processes, I agree fully that religious symbolizing can never be totally explained or reduced to rational empirical terms, but that is a far cry from saying that no reductive explanations are possible.

Indeed, to say that religious beliefs are nonrational or that parents indoctrinate their children with symbols is already a partial reduction that owes much to psychology and semiotics. To say that particular symbols—for example, "the Cross"—were developed partly because of historical circumstances, in this case the Roman use of crucifixion, is a partial explanation in rational empirical terms. And there are many obvious historical explanations of why "the Cross" took on new meanings at the time of the First Crusade of 1096. It is one thing to say that religious symbolizing is nonrational, that nonrational thinking is inherent in human existence, and that we do not know why we are here, but quite another to proclaim that religious symbolizing is therefore totally immune to historical and psychological analysis. Moreover, if it is granted that not every religious symbol system is valid, then it is quite permissible to assert that a nonrational symbol system is valid only for those who de facto use it.

Part Two

Proposals for a Historiographic Solution

Chapter Seven

A Definition of Religion

The ongoing debate about the conceptualization of religion in anthropology, sociology, and psychology confronts historians with a challenge. They may, of course, ignore the whole debate and rely on their personal and historiographic reflexes when discussing religious phenomena. But if they think the results of work in other disciplines valuable for historiography, they will take the debate seriously even if they do not take sides themselves.

Since historians deal with human action in the round, many will not find any of the definitions of religion in the other disciplines either satisfactory or necessary. While they may find ideas in the other disciplines valuable heuristically and use them eclectically to develop new interpretations, they may feel no need to define religion themselves. Some historians, however, those who deal with historical problems in which religion is central, may find the challenge harder to avoid. If they are at all aware that their detailed work rests on methodological—or cultural—preconceptions, their knowledge of the debate about religion in other fields should make them self-conscious about the way they conceptualize phenomena fundamental to their own scholarly enterprise. If they do become concerned, either they can choose among the available conceptions or definitions of religion, such as those discussed above, or they may consider and use them to clarify their own approach to, or conceptualization of, religion. In my case, although nothing seemed less desirable than yet another definition of religion, my dissatisfaction with those I had examined impelled me to examine my own preconceptions and try to pin them down by developing a definition of my own.

My definition of religion is similar to common usage and historical practice but attempts to avoid some of their ambiguities. In common usage, a religion is a social phenomenon: the beliefs and practices that have been persistently professed and commanded by leaders who claim supernatural authority, and that have been accepted, at least tacitly, by their followers; and the boundary of a religion is established by its special emphasis on beliefs and practices that distinguish its adherents from other religious people. From the point of view of an objective scholar, that usage has obvious drawbacks. If it denotes most historical religions clearly, it makes their beliefs the criterion of what religion is: religions are what the adherents of traditional religions have said they are.

Acceptance of such self-definitions as an objective criterion for religion is a renunciation of scholarly responsibility. It accepts as true assertions that are mutually contradictory and lack empirical validity. Thus adherents of one religion deny that other religions or some of their practices are truly religion. For example, although adherents of the Roman Catholic religion may assert that theirs is a universal religion, the self-definition is contradicted by the existence of other religions and by Catholicism's own obvious geographical and cultural concentrations. Moreover, reliance on the self-definitions of religions, with their emphasis on their unique beliefs, not only impedes recognition of the characteristics common to several or all religions, it also represses awareness of the extensive variation in belief and conduct among the adherents of a single religion.

To avoid those problems, to avoid incorporating the specific beliefs of particular religions in a definition of religion, we might use a generalizing comparative sociological definition that attempted to extrapolate what is common to what have customarily been considered as religions. To concoct one, we might say that religion is a set of beliefs about a superior, supra-empirical reality and the ways in which that belief is expressed.[1] But that approach

1. This definition is my conflation of those of Robertson, *The Sociological Interpretation of Religion*, p. 47; Michael Hill, *A Sociology of Religion* (New

has its own problems. In the first place, such a definition only camouflages the assumption that there are two different kinds of reality. In the second place, since it makes conduct a result of professed beliefs, it incorporates a bias in favor of socially proclaimed norms. It gives priority to publicly prescribed and expressed beliefs over the complexity of all the actual beliefs and observable conduct of individuals. In the third place, as that suggests, such a definition fails to distinguish what religions proclaim from what individuals in fact believe.

Most scholars who use some variant of this kind of definition assume or assert that religion is a group phenomenon in which individuals participate; individuals are thought of as religious because they belong to a religious group. Yet strangely enough, such sociological definitions apply equally to individuals who belong to no religion and are not even religious in the customary sense. If I believe there is supra-empirical reality in the sense that there is more reality, or more to reality, than I can presently observe empirically, and if I feel that it is superior in the sense that my existence is dependent on it (perhaps the infinite regress of preconditions that leads from my existence back to the astronomers' Big Bang and beyond), I have a religion by such definitions. Definitions of this kind thus fail to distinguish between a social phenomenon and a property of individuals, and the use of the single term, religion, makes it very hard to express the distinction clearly in historical writing.

The fundamental difference between my approach and that of most historians—and of most of the anthropologists, sociologists, and psychologists just discussed—is that I think that analysis of religious phenomena would be easier and more accurate if we distinguished much more sharply between a social phenomenon, religion, and a property of individuals, religiosity. My conceptualization therefore necessitates two definitions rather than one, a definition of religion and a definition of religiosity.

My definition of religion should cause few problems of comprehension because of its similarity to many recent definitions and to common usage. It differs most obviously from many definitions

---

York, 1973), p. 42; and Louis Schneider, *Sociological Approach to Religion* (New York, 1970), p. 6. See also Berger, *The Sacred Canopy*, pp. 25, 175-176.

in three ways. In the first place, while I take for granted that any definition must embrace what have traditionally been called religions, my definition also applies to so-called surrogate religions.[2] In the second place, whereas most definitions and discussions attribute religion both to society and to individuals, I want to distinguish sharply between the social phenomenon I call religion and the property of individuals I call religiosity. In the third place, in direct contradiction to most present sociological usage, instead of considering religiosity to be the internalization and expression by an individual of the norms and practices of his or her religion, I regard religion as a—partial—codification of religiosity. My definition of religion therefore depends on my definition of religiosity.

What I mean by religiosity and its implications for "surrogate religions" will be discussed in the following chapters. This brief chapter will only emphasize that my definition of religion differs from most in that it focuses on the social codification and prescription of belief, not on the content or source of those beliefs. It will also indicate my distinction between religion and religiosity.

> *By religion I mean those elements of religiosity that are explicitly prescribed by people exercising authority over other people.*

A religion thus depends on a particular set of social relations. To that extent, I am in agreement with most of the definitions discussed above and in very limited agreement with scholars such as Walter Burkert and René Girard who have recently attributed the roots of religion to a collective social action, to an original ritualized sacrifice that enabled members of a group to evade responsibility for violence and thereby functioned to restore social order.[3] Where I differ, and agree rather with Durkheim and Peter Berger,[4] is that I find the roots of religion rather in the mental processes that give individuals their sense of identity and con-

---

2. A consequence examined in chap. 11.

3. Walter Burkert, *Violent Origins* (Stanford, 1987); René Girard, *Violence and the Sacred* (Baltimore, 1977).

4. Emile Durkheim, *The Elementary Forms of Religious Life* Berger, *The Sacred Canopy*, especially pp. 16-20, 29-34.

ception of the realities surrounding them, an awareness they then try to share with others and may also try to enforce on others in order to protect their own identity. The result, if they succeed, is a religion.

As was true for Freud for different reasons, the example that most clearly illustrates my definition of religion is modern Catholicism because its final authority resides in a single person. Whatever the ultimate source of Catholic beliefs, an adherent of the Roman Catholic religion is one who obeys the commands of the Roman Catholic church in which ultimate authority, treated in practice for centuries as infallible, and legally so defined since 1870, belongs to the pope.[5] If any important question as to what or who is Catholic arises, the judgment must be ratified explicitly or tacitly by the pope. The precepts of the Roman Catholic church, expressed through its creed, Bible, theology, canon law, institutional organization, penitentials, homilies, and rituals, are almost innumerable. Few if any adherents are able to obey all of them. But so long as a person accepts papal authority and does not stubbornly and manifestly disobey major precepts that anyone can observe and that have been made known by the pope and those to whom he has delegated authority, then that person is considered a Catholic. The essential criterion is not total compliance with what the authority commands, still less with what it only advises or suggests, but willingness to submit to that authority when commanded. Conversely, in the last analysis, a heretic is one who stubbornly resists papal authority, is therefore excluded from the Catholic church, and is not or no longer considered a Catholic.

Reference to the authority of God aside, the ultimate criterion, in theory if not in practice, of what Catholicism is and who is a Catholic at a given moment is the decision of the pope, and a Catholic is one who accepts that authority. Even someone who

5. To maintain the clarity of the illustration, I have neglected the qualifications discussed in Brian Tierney, *Foundations of the Conciliar Theory* (Cambridge, Eng., 1955) and the arguments aroused by his later work, *Origins of Papal Infallibility, 1150-1350* (Leiden, 1972) and by Walter Ullmann, *The Growth of Papal Government in the Middle Ages*, 2d ed. (London, 1962). I shall argue later that the Roman Catholic religion, much as we know it today, only emerged clearly in the eleventh century.

opposed Catholicism and described its richness in pejorative
terms would have to accept that criterion implicitly, and would
probably use it explicitly as a condemnation. And this is how neutral historians have defined it in practice. Whatever else it may
be—and it is much, much more—essential to the Roman Catholic
religion is what has been prescribed by those exercising social
authority, and Catholics are those who accept the legitimacy of
that authority.[6]

The same kind of analysis could be applied to all other religions, although the analysis would be considerably more complicated because authority over adherents in many religions has been
much more diffuse or decentralized and less explicitly defined.
To pursue that analysis would take more time and space than I
can afford, but I think the conclusion would be the same: adherents of a religion are those who try to obey the prescriptions of
people exercising social authority, be it the pope or the adults of
a tribe. My conception of what religion or a religion is thus agrees
with the way the term is commonly used by historians, since what
they have typically referred to as a "religion" is the set of belief
and practices prescribed by religious authorities. In any case, the
definition clearly applies to or covers what have traditionally been
considered religions.

Yet however great the influence of religions—and it has been
and is still very great—what authorities prescribe and what adherents do is not the same. In practice, the people in authority
who have defined the Roman Catholic, Lutheran, Calvinist, or
other religions cannot and never have been able to control all the
thoughts and actions of their adherents that are relevant to their
precepts. They have been able to insist successfully only on the
performance of a fairly limited set of observable acts capable of
fairly precise definition, and on the absence of manifest disobe-
dience to other precepts and counsels that cannot usually be defined in precise terms of observable conduct. Beyond that, the
authorities have had to rely on exhortations and on providing
models or exemplifications of approved conduct (e.g., the lives of

6. To save space, I have excluded consideration of the role of earlier authorities—the apostles, early bishops, and church councils—in defining elements of Christianity that became precepts of Catholicism.

saints or the thoughts of approved thinkers) in order to instill in adherents a sense of how diverse personalities in diverse contexts have fleshed out the precepts and how adherents should act to be, not merely Catholics, but better Catholics.

Those who prescribe religions may seek to mold the lives of adherents as completely as possible, but there are limits to what can be enforced effectively even in the simplest societies. And in complex societies, there is a wide range of thought and action that may be influenced but cannot be controlled, and it is remarkably diverse. To continue the same example, it is possible to ensure that Catholics will profess the creed but impossible to control how each Catholic will think about or imagine his or her "God," impossible to control the associations consciously and unconsciously stimulated in each adherent when he or she hears or reads the word "Christ" or sees a picture or sculpture of Christ on the cross—or looks at another human being. Although all the people in a parish may be firm Catholics, the range of their reactions to stimuli of religious relevance will be very diverse.[7] Even among the saints, what contrasts, for example, between the reactions of Bernard of Clairvaux and Francis of Assisi. And how great the contrasts between Catholics in advanced and underdeveloped societies.

For obvious reasons, how a genuine adherent of a religion reacts, thinks, believes, and acts inescapably differs to some degree from the way all other adherents do. The moment we think of the millennial evolution of Judaism, Christianity, or Islam, of the diverse cultural, political, social, and economic conditions in which they have been present, and of their millions of adherents through history, each with a distinctive personality, my obvious point becomes painfully platitudinous. Even in a tribal context where socialization or religious indoctrination is omnipresent and physically compelling, each adherent is born at a different time, of different parents, under different conditions; each has unique physical and psychic characteristics; each has a distinctive social identity; and each has experiences and encounters challenges that

7. David Lodge, *How Far Can You Go?* (Harmondsworth, 1986) and Andrew M. Greeley, *Patience of a Saint* (New York, 1987) are delightful fictional depictions of variations in the religiosity of Catholics.

others do not. None think and act in precisely the same way even in the most carefully defined contexts such as ritual acts. Socialization may produce massive conformity; it cannot produce uniformity.[8] Although the impact of socialization varies heavily between different societies, I see no reason why the nature of the relation between socialization and personality should be any different.

Since the combinations of actual associations, thoughts, beliefs, and actions that are the meaning of a religion for those who adhere to it are not only as diverse as the individuals themselves but differ to some degree from what the authorities prescribe, they are not religion as I define it,[9] and I shall refer to such complexes of actions and reactions of individuals as religiosity, not religion. If I speak of the religiosity of Roman Catholics, I mean neither how Catholics are supposed to act nor the extent to which individuals devote themselves to living according to the rules, norms, and exhortations of the Roman Catholic church.[10] What I am pointing at is something infinitely more complex and variable: what each individual who, among many other beliefs, believes in some way that the pope's authority comes from Christ and that Jesus Christ is God does in fact think and believe about supra-

8. The same point is emphasized in a different way by Berger, *The Sacred Canopy*, pp. 15-18.

9. Here I agree, although for very different reasons, with Yinger, who insists that religion is a social phenomenon and refuses to call individual systems of belief religion: *The Scientific Study of Religion*, p. 12.

10. My dissatisfaction with the use of normative terms such as "piety" and "spirituality" in medieval historiography—e.g., *A History of Christian Spirituality*, ed. Louis Bouyer et al. (New York, 1963-1969)—and the logic of my own argument led me to discard the approach of scholars such as Gerhard Lenski, *The Religious Factor* (Garden City, N.Y., 1963), Rodney Stark and Charles Glock, *American Piety* (Berkeley and Los Angeles, 1968), and Spilka, Hood, and Gorsuch, *The Psychology of Religion*, pp. 6-8, 45-46, who measure individual religiosity by the degree to which the individual's thought and conduct conform to the expectations of particular traditional religions. For a discussion of those approaches, see Robertson, *Sociological Interpretation of Religion*, pp. 52-56. I then discovered that Thomas Luckmann had made the same point incisively in *The Invisible Religion* (New York, 1967), pp. 24-27, 69-74. See also Luckmann, "Social Structure and Religion in Modern Industrial Society," in *Science and Faith: International and Interdisciplinary Colloquium, Ljubljana, Yugoslavia, May 10-12, 1984* (Ljubljana and Rome, 1984), pp. 95-107.

empirical reality, and how—and to what extent—their confidence in such supra-empirical realities is expressed in their lives.

Since I have defined religion as elements of religiosity explicitly prescribed by people exercising social authority,[11] my immediate answer to the question of where the beliefs and practices prescribed by Catholicism came from should be apparent. The prescriptions—and counsels—of the Roman Catholic religion are a cumulative distillate of elements of religiosity which its authorities through the centuries proclaimed and their followers had to accept to be members of that church. Many of those elements were initially salient in the religiosity of the creators of Catholicism, including the elements continued from Judaic religiosity; many were elements introduced by the religiosity of those they sought to convert; and many further elements were introduced through the centuries as the authorities and adherents experienced new conditions. But central among the elements prescribed from the beginning was belief that the existing authorities had contact with, and commands and power from, a higher authority. With appropriate modification of the specifics, the same would be true of the Protestant and Judaic religions.

There is nothing revolutionary about what has just been asserted. Any history of Catholicism will describe that process of cumulative distillation; and the centrality of the exercise of authority in my definition of religion is consonant with the self-definition of the Roman Catholic religion at least on that point. And although the structure of authority in other religions may be very different, those who have exercised authority in them have acted no differently.

11. I do not consider those engaged in a common scientific discipline, e.g., physics, to be adherents of a religion, even though conformity to common presuppositions is usually necessary for recognition in the field. That paradigm is the expression of a consensus of individuals. They may exert great collective or social pressure on all entering the field to conform, but the presuppositions are not formulated and prescribed by individuals who exercise institutional authority over the whole field and who can demand belief in their prescriptions as a prerequisite for engaging in physics. Formally at least, the presuppositions are premises for hypotheses, not dogmas that may not be questioned. If they were dogmas, then that society would be a religion by my definition, and as a result, its adherents would not be able to belong to any other religion, which has certainly not been the case.

My definition of religion may, thus far, be acceptable to many. But it is incomplete, since I have not specified what I mean by religiosity. Disagreement is more likely to arise when I do, since I have made religiosity the source of the beliefs prescribed by a religion. Hence, before I discuss religiosity, I should make explicit how, in my more objective moments, I think we develop belief, acquire faith, or develop understanding as distinguished from how we develop objective knowledge. And here I must trespass on the epistemologists' domains.

Chapter Eight

Nonrational Thinking

Assertions about religion are peculiarly dependent on epistemological premises for they are assertions, not about knowledge, but about belief. How people think of religion depends on how they know or believe that humans act and react—and to what. More specifically, the underlying premise of any definition of religion—including sociological definitions—is some conception, however tacit, of the nature of human mental and psychological processes. But we cannot use the epistemological premises of believers in religions such as Augustine or Maimonides to understand religious beliefs. A definition that seeks to be empirical and objective cannot rely on a conception of mental processes that was accepted by believers in one religion but was and is anything but self-evident to thinkers in other religions—for example, divine revelation to Moses, divine illumination by Christ, or divine dictation to Mohammed.

The effort to explain human mental processes is as old as philosophy, and philosophers have long applied their convictions critically to religious beliefs. But only at the beginning of this century, when "religion" became an ontological concept for scholars, was there a concerted effort to use empirical descriptions of mental processes in order to understand religious phenomena. Not surprisingly, the epistemological stances of scholars differed and the debate of definitions described in earlier chapters began. And not too surprisingly, given all we have experienced and discovered, there has been an important change in epistemological assumptions. Although the approaches to religion of Berger and

Geertz owe much to earlier scholars, particularly Durkheim and Weber, one cannot help being struck, at least I cannot, by a noticeable difference in their conception of human awareness of reality, of the possibility of objectivity.

The epistemology of William James, the first great pioneer of the objective study of religion, does not place him entirely within the objective camp. At the outer limits of his thought about how humans can be aware of anything, his objectivity was explicitly tempered by his inheritance. He acknowledged that he had "over-beliefs" in "higher powers"[1] that influenced thought or "con-science," and those over-beliefs affected some of his avowedly objective discourse. Yet as a psychologist, he certainly sought to understand the workings of the mind empirically, and he applied that knowledge to religious experiences with most impressive re-sults. Durkheim also, but without any appeal to higher powers, believed he could be objective; the higher power that produced religious belief was society, something thoroughly observable, even though most people were unconscious of how their being part of society and guided by its common language influenced their consciousness. Max Weber is more difficult to place. Like Durkheim, he prized rationality and analyzed social structure and its influence on religious belief and action as objectively as he could. Yet he located the wellsprings of religion within the in-dividual and postulated a basic drive toward meaning, and he did not reveal his conception of the source of that meaning.

Rudolf Otto hardly belongs in any discussion of objective ap-proaches to religion. However valuable his terminology for reli-gious experience, and however much his emphasis on the emo-tional or psychological aspects of religion reflected the rising interest in psychological reactions, his conception of mental or psychological processes was so influenced by his Christian pre-conceptions that its only claim to objectivity might be the ref-erences to Kant. Freud, who carried the psychological emphasis so much further, needs even less discussion because his theories are so well known. He differed sharply from Durkheim and

1. William James, *The Varieties of Religious Experience: A Study in Human Nature* (New York, 1984), pp. 516-526. And see below, chap. 8.

Weber, if not from James, in that his fundamental research focused on the individual, and he certainly tried to explain belief in the "sacred" in terms of something he thought he could observe, psychological reactions to the will of the father.[2]

If we leap from the pioneering analysts of religion to recent ones, we can say little about the epistemology of many of the sociologists of religion since, typically, they do not make their conception of individual mental or psychological processes explicit. Instead, for obvious methodological reasons, they assume that religion is a social phenomenon and avoid psychological issues. Conversely, although recent psychologists of religion make their conception of psychological processes explicit, they typically take what they consider religious ideas as givens, assume they are a social phenomenon, and avoid discussion of their source. That is not true, however, of Berger and Geertz. Although both examine religion as a social or cultural phenomenon, both make their conception of how human beings think and feel fairly explicit, and a sea change in their conception of human consciousness and reality seems to separate them from the earlier students of religion.[3]

Whereas James, Durkheim, Weber, and even Freud sought to understand how humans related to an all-encompassing and undeniable reality or aggregate of realities that surrounded and impinged on them, in Berger and Geertz, as in Foucault and the literary deconstructionists, realities outside us have moved out of reach or become so shadowy that these scholars seem at times to verge on solipsism. In their more abstract discussions, if not their detailed analyses, they seem to disregard the impact of nonhuman forces on mental processes and discount the ability of humans to understand those realities. "Reality" no longer refers to everything known or unknown that exists but to what human beings think about it. It refers not so much to what human consciousness confronts, interacts with, and seeks to understand (including itself),

2. Sigmund Freud, *Moses and Monotheism*, trans. Katherine Jones (New York, 1955), pp. 152-156.
3. For an interesting discussion of that change in a very different form of expression, see Jane A. Hale, *The Broken Window: Beckett's Dramatic Perspective* (West Lafayette, Ind., 1987).

but to what people produce symbolically in their heads.[4] The title of Berger's earlier book with Luckmann, *The Social Construction of Reality*, makes reality a human product. Society is a world-building enterprise, and reality is what is produced by the externalizing, objectifying, and internalizing of human actions. When Berger seeks an anchor for his existence in a relation to any wider reality, he abandons objectivity and assumes the prayerful stance of the believer in *A Rumor of Angels*.[5]

With Geertz, heavily influenced by Suzanne Langer,[6] reality becomes the symbols that have emerged from the fluidity of the intersubjective world of common understanding. Religious belief and indeed all reality are apparently an almost purely mental product engendered by our actions and above all by our capacity to communicate with one another linguistically or symbolically. It is a word-building enterprise. No longer do human beings use symbols to denote and comprehend realities they perceive in and around themselves; rather, it is symbols that direct them, establishing their moods, formulating their conceptions of order, and creating their reality. Hence, for Geertz, the approach to culture should be hermeneutics. Reality has thus come to seem primarily a human creation, an imagining apparently little different from that of literary texts, about which, if we are to believe some of the more extreme applications of semiotics to literature, no empirically objective statement can be made. What a text means is what it activates in an individual's head at the moment. A major epistemological shift thus divides Berger and Geertz, as well as Bellah, from the pioneering scholars of religion.

Greatly as I have admired and been influenced by the work of those scholars, their approach did not resolve the problems that I, as a historian, faced in my effort to understand how the mutually incompatible claims of Judaism and Christianity were connected with the formation of antisemitism. For the reasons discussed in chapters 3 to 5, I felt that any conception that used particular beliefs—or symbolic expressions—about gods or the

4. A major influence here was Karl Mannheim, *Ideology and Utopia* (New York, 1936).

5. (Garden City, N.Y., 1970), subtitled: *Modern Society and the Rediscovery of the Supernatural*.

6. Suzanne K. Langer, *Philosophy in a New Key* (New York, 1942).

category of the sacred as the primary criterion for religion would only trap my explanation in the mental world of those I was trying to explain. But if I rejected those approaches, I had to reexamine my own. What assumptions underlay my approach to religious phenomena?

Little reflection was needed to recognize that my detailed work as a historian relied heavily on what I thought was known empirically about the human organism and its environment; and I found the recent work in cognitive science[7] more exciting and helpful in dealing with the epistemological problems of belief than structuralism and the deconstruction of texts. Even though, like most historians, my knowledge of the amazing complexity of human processes was and is severely limited, I had always relied on it tacitly, for I knew no better.[8] But when I thought out more explicitly what it implied for my conception of religion, I was surprised by the consequences, above all by the sharp distinction between religion and religiosity that seemed to follow.

Our ideas about what goes on in our heads is in flux, and so is our terminology for its dimensions.[9] Here I can only indicate briefly, and in scientifically imprecise and philosophically naive language that skirts obvious epistemological issues, the features of my limited knowledge of human mental processes that made me distinguish religiosity so sharply from religion. Much of what I say is platitudinous and has already been said better by those, like Bellah and Burhoe,[10] who base their views of religion on a theory or philosophy of action. Where I differ from them is primarily in my conception of the difference between rational, non-

7. See Howard Gardner, *The Mind's New Science: A History of the Cognitive Revolution*, paperback edition with a new epilogue (New York, 1987).

8. "Such a [substantive] theory of human nature is articulated by every historian in the accounts which he writes, and this theory of human nature may be seen as a 'speculative' philosophy of history" (J. L. Gorman, *The Expression of Historical Knowledge* [Edinburgh, 1982], p. 106).

9. For an excellent illustration of the complexity of the issues and the impenetrability of much of the terminology for any but experts, see Zenon W. Pylyshyn and William Demopolis, eds., *Meaning and Cognitive Structure* (Norwood, N.J., 1986).

10. Bellah, *Beyond Belief*, pp. 9-12; Ralph W. Burhoe, "The Phenomenon of Religion Seen Scientifically," in *Changing Perspectives in the Scientific Study of Religion*, pp. 15-39.

rational, and irrational thinking and its importance for understanding religious phenomena.

The individual human organism originates in intercourse, a social relation with the biological result of conception; mother and fetus remain connected until the trauma of birth, when the infant becomes a separate, if highly dependent, organism. Whether or not the infant initially distinguishes between itself and its mother or anything else or only does so after some months, a crucial change occurs within the infant in the preverbal stage before it is capable of symbolic communication: the infant becomes aware that not everything is an extension of itself. By the end of infancy, the articulation of self and the conception of others has not advanced far, and only gradually does the infant begin to imitate others,[11] to be able to engage in *mimesis*. But already at an earlier stage, the infant has become aware of a boundary between itself and everyone and everything else and of transactions across those boundaries.

Our consciousness of reality, including that of our own identity, depends, it seems, on our capacity to be aware of or perceive boundaries and transactions across them. When we "recognize" another human, we not only perceive a boundary that distinguishes that human being from everything in contact with it, but we perceive boundaries and relations within and constitutive of the individual right down, if necessary, to the fingerprints that differ even for "identical" twins. Were we to go deeper with scalpel and microscope, we would find cells with their membranes in proximity to, and interacting chemically and electrically across those membranes with, other cells, and finally we would reach the atomic activities underlying the genetic codes in the chromosomes of molecules of RNA and DNA. Within each individual, those boundaries, their relations, and the transactions across them that collectively constitute the structure of the individual are somewhat different. Moreover, the boundary that keeps them all together and identifies each individual is also defined by the external boundaries with which it is in contact, which differ for each individual.

11. See John H. Flavell, *Cognitive Development*, 2d ed. (Englewood Cliffs, N.J., 1985), pp. 128-129.

That the individual organism is thus unique is no news. It is less obvious that what constitutes the individual and gives it its unique identity is its structure, the relative stability of the boundaries that constitute it: the boundaries and their relations within the individual, the boundary of the individual organism, and the external boundaries with which it is in contact. Within the individual, the transactions between the cells, including the atomic activities involved, are fleeting, and the cells themselves decompose and are replaced throughout our life, almost the only exception, interestingly enough, being the neurons in our brain. What endure are the particular boundaries, relations, and transactions across them that form the boundary or distinctive patterns of the individual. When that complex of boundaries dissolves and its constituents disperse in new relations within other boundaries, the individual disappears.

Our consciousness occurs within those boundaries and is apparently our partial and ever-changing awareness of some of those boundaries and the transactions across them, our awareness of ourselves as active and reactive. Stimuli from within and without the individual produce reactions in our neurological circuits according to specifications we have barely begun to understand. The neurological transactions then produce other physiological reactions in the brain and elsewhere. Some but by no means all of these physical transactions are fleetingly converted into, paralleled by, or expressed as mental phenomena:[12] states of consciousness, awareness of boundaries and their modifications, imaging, emoting, symbolizing, verbalizing, integrating, cognizing, commanding, and the like, although we are conscious of only a very limited range of those states at any given moment. And only some of those conscious states—and here I disagree with some adherents of action theories—involve the use of symbols, if by symbols is meant, not the percepts or "representations" that are

12. I am here sidestepping the brain/mind or mentalist/physicalist controversy. That is an unresolved and fiercely debated issue among philosophers which a historian could not be expected to resolve. For a recent and fascinating approach from the physicalist side, see Kathleen V. Wilkes, *Real People: Personal Identity without Thought Experiments* (Oxford, 1988). I am also not concerned here with the issue that centrally concerns Wilkes, to wit, the characteristics of human personality, nor with the distinction between human beings and other forms of life.

debated by experts in cognition and artificial intelligence, but the tool by which human beings communicate with each other.[13] The resultant of these mental processes, whether involving symbols or not, is then converted back into, or paralleled by, physiological or neural transactions in the limbic region of the brain which stimulate further physical activity in the organism and on what lies beyond its boundaries—now even the moon. These recursive circuits thus act to maintain or modify the boundaries and transactions across them which are our existence and make us conscious of our existence as individuals and members of society within a nonhuman environment.[14]

Whatever the ultimate cause or basis in reality of our perceptions and conceptions of boundaries and the transactions across them, we cannot help thinking in terms of them any more than we can conceive of time and space without relying, however unconsciously, on our awareness of periodicities, whether of the sun, the vibrations of a quartz, quanta of energy, the length of our strides, or something else. And what is true of thought about physical reality is equally true of our thinking about our own awareness, that reflexive thought which makes us self-conscious and concerned about what we will do and be next.

We may be conscious of much, although never all at once, but the moment we think about our consciousness we are aware that

13. See, e.g., Oliver Sacks and Robert Wasserman, "The Case of the Colorblind Painter," *New York Review of Books* 34, no. 18 (1987): 25-34. In our consciousness of color, there is a three-stage process. The wavelengths of the light stimulating the three groups of cones in the retina are discriminated in the primary visual cortex, which can only make us conscious of varying shades of gray. The visual association cortex then computes estimates of light intensity in each area of the visual field in relation to the intensity of the whole image and makes us conscious of colors in the normal sense of blue, green, red, etc. Only after wavelengths have been discriminated in the primary visual cortex and then computed as colors by the visual association cortex do we think about color, symbolizing it and relating it to our memories, images, wishes, etc. to make it an integral part of our "lifeworld." "It is not clear that the experience, the phenomenon, of color can ever be explained (or explained away) by physiology or science: it retains a mystery, a wonder, that seems inaccessible, and that belongs in the sphere of the 'given,' not the sphere of questions and answers" (p. 32).

14. For a moving description of a, fortunately temporary, destruction of consciousness of part of an individual's existence that emphasizes the connection between physical and mental processes, see Oliver Sacks, *A Leg to Stand On* (New York, 1987).

it is ours and has limits. We realize that our consciousness is a mental process or series of momentary states distinct from, but located amidst, innumerable boundaries and transactions across them both within and without the organism. And to act and survive, each individual has to correlate and try to integrate the multitude of ongoing internal and external transactions of radically different kinds which affect it. But how? Not only is an individual not conscious of most of the transactions that affect it and incapable of controlling them consciously, but no individual has reliable rational empirical knowledge about most of the transactions of which it is conscious and wishes to control. The capacity of humans to think rationally and empirically—whether simply, practically, and pretheoretically or in sophisticated scientific ways— can discover and control only a fraction of the conditions on which the individual's existence depends. Even the knowledge of those who know how to split the atom is highly insufficient to assure their own continued existence; indeed, use of their knowledge may end all human existence. How, then, do individuals orient and direct themselves?

Since rational knowledge by itself, whether theoretical or pretheoretical, cannot assure survival, conscious effort to develop and preserve our identity, including our capacity to think rationally, has to depend ultimately on a very different mode of thinking or combination of mental processes, one that is not rational and is empirical only in the peculiar sense that it utilizes or associates sense perceptions or empirical knowledge in its own way. It is often referred to as symbolic thought. Yet since I am trying to analyze this process rationally, and since "symbol" is used so broadly and technically in semiology, logic, and cognitive science that it may be misleading to speak of symbolic thought, a better term for that associative mental process for my purposes may be nonrational thinking. And by that I do not mean irrational thinking. Irrational thinking I take to be defined by its opposition to rational thinking as the suppression or denial of what the capacity for rational thinking of the individual could demonstrate.

Despite Wittgenstein, it is certainly scientifically debatable whether there are two distinct modes of thinking.[15] Indeed, much

---

15. And, of course, philosophically debatable. For an argument against the

of the work on artificial intelligence has proceeded on the assumption that there is only one way in which brains/minds process inputs. But that view is opposed by others in the field,[16] so there is room for argument. It could also be objected that we think in more than two ways, that to lump everything that is not rational empirical thinking into one category as nonrational thinking is to fail to recognize significant distinctions within what I am terming nonrational thinking.[17] Yet even though the assumption that human beings think in two or only two fundamentally different ways cannot be confirmed scientifically or philosophically, there is certainly a gross difference between the two modes of thought at the level of human action that historians can observe and must deal with. And since that is where my problem lies, my distinction is intended to apply to that level.

Nonrational thinking may be fundamentally different from practical rational or scientific thinking, but it is not necessarily opposed to, or in contradiction with, rational empirical thinking and can, and usually does, use it in a subordinate capacity,[18] Aquinas's *Summa* being a wonderful example. There is no necessary conflict because many of the relations that nonrational thinking establishes between experiences and symbols are of a type that cannot presently be, or can never be, invalidated or validated by rational empirical thought.

Like rational empirical thought, nonrational thought comes in many forms, one obvious example being poetry, for instance Solomon's "Song of Songs" and the fascinating religious interpretations of it. What typifies nonrational thinking is that it typically gives the symbols it shares with rational thought a meaning very different from their meaning in practical or scientific discourse

---

distinction that is largely beyond my capacity and that of most historians because of its use of symbolic logic, see John F. Post, *The Faces of Existence* (Ithaca, N.Y., 1987).

16. As Francisco J. Varella made clear in "Perception and the Origin of Cognition," a paper presented at the Stanford University International Symposium on Understanding Origins, September 13-15, 1987.

17. It could be argued, for example, that analogical thought is a distinctive mode of thinking that provides a bridge between rational empirical and nonrational thoughts.

18. This nonrational use of rationality was characterized by Weber as *Wertrationalität*.

("your name is oil poured out"). Nonetheless, although many relations or beliefs established by the play of nonrational thinking may not be presently verifiable by rational investigation, some (intuitions?) may become susceptible of empirical validation or— a matter of great consequence—invalidation in the future. How nonrational thinking uses symbols has been well described by Victor Turner:

Such symbols exhibit the properties of *condensation, unification of disparate referents*, and *polarization of meaning*. A single symbol, in fact, represents many things at the same time; it is multivocal, not univocal. Its referents are not all of the same logical order but are drawn from many domains of social experience and ethical evaluation. Finally, its referents tend to cluster around opposite semantic poles. At one pole the referents are to social and moral facts, at the other, to physiological facts.[19]

That way of symbolizing corresponds with the human predicament, of which greater knowledge has only made us more aware, that of constituting at each moment a set of boundaries and relations directly and indirectly related to an infinite series of sets that range from what we know most concretely to what is beyond the reach of astronomy and so small that it eludes the molecular biologists. Our time and space have altered drastically. Of themselves and of a vast universe around them, humans have long been aware, but recently the universe has become immense by light-years, and we have also begun to realize the immense complexity that lies beneath what is immediately around and within us. Biochemists, biophysicists, neurologists, behavioral biologists, and psychologists have been demonstrating that the mental processes of which we are conscious are but the tip of an iceberg of almost inconceivably complex psychological and physiological processes.[20] Many of those processes within us we cannot control, and our control of the physical stimuli that affect us is limited. Nonetheless we consciously act. But how?

19. *The Ritual Process* (Ithaca, N.Y., 1977), p. 52; see also *Dramas, Fields, and Metaphors* (Ithaca, N.Y., 1975), p. 55.
20. See, e.g., Howard Gardner, *Frames of Mind* (New York, 1983); Melvin Konner, *The Tangled Web* (New York, 1983); R. C. Lewontin, Steven Rose, and Leon J. Kamin, *Not in Our Genes* (New York, 1984); Robert Ornstein, *Multimind* (Boston, 1986).

Like the existential predicament with which it deals, and like the outlook of traditional religions, nonrational thought has a holistic or global quality. It embraces a multitude of very different kinds of realities at once in a fluid interaction in a way that rational thinking never can. It does so not only because it demotes the logical coherence so necessary in scientific demonstration to a subservient role but above all because it is unconstrained by the taxonomic precision necessary for scientific thought. A single symbol has no single meaning; its meaning varies depending on the different ways in which it is related to other symbols at different times, even at almost the same time. It does not have to refer unambiguously or univocally to a single bounded entity or class of entities with common observable characteristics or to a single type of relation between such entities. In nonrational thinking, the significance of a symbol is fluid, and the boundary or transaction it indicates is elastic because a single symbol gets its meaning from its fluctuating relations to many other symbols, relations that are ambiguous and variable and cannot be established by rational empirical thought. What in logical empirical discourse would be a category error is a necessary characteristic of nonrational thinking and a necessity if we are to act.

To complicate matters further, although a symbol may have a highly stable and common meaning (set of relations to other symbols) for many people when used unambiguously in rational thought and discourse—and even a fairly stable set of evocations when used socially in nonrational discourse—what a symbol, even one commonly used in a society, evokes (its associations with other symbols) when a person is thinking nonrationally at one time may be very different from what it evokes at another. And what a given symbol evokes in one person always differs somewhat, and often differs greatly, from its nonrational significance for others in the same society because its nonrational function necessarily varies according to the pattern of each person's unique identity and experiences. That an evocative symbol in one society may have no meaning in another is too obvious for comment.

Nonrational thinking thus fluidly indicates and establishes for us a universe of relations between symbolized aspects of experience that could not be expressed if the symbols were employed unambiguously. It is our understanding of what we cannot express

as knowledge.[21] To paraphrase Giddens's language, it is the reflexive monitoring of our being.[22] By it we evaluate and try to
influence the infinity of activities through which we exist, including our capacity for rational thinking, for it is our nonrational
thinking that determines when and to what end we will use that
capacity. Our consciousness of hunger may direct our attention
to food but does not tell us where or how to get what we want
to eat. The same could be said of the skillful fashioning of a spear
in Neolithic times. The kind of thinking, perhaps about mighty
game, dead enemies, and the admiration of his fellows, that made
a man want a spear did not tell him how to make it, but it did
focus his capacity for practical reason on fashioning a tool to
achieve his ends.

Yet if the two kinds of mental processes are very different, we
alternate between them so rapidly and frequently that their interplay is very hard to distinguish. Indeed, so much of our
thought of both kinds is so habitual, so much a reflex, that most
of the time we are not aware of which way we are thinking. The
products of rational thinking, whether a tool, an action, a declaration, or a treatise, seem coherently rational only because they
are distillations from which the nonrational associations necessarily involved in their production have largely been eliminated. Yet
when we reflect, not on the final product, but on the fleeting
moments of consciousness that accompanied our effort to produce
that rational product, it is hard to discriminate when we were
thinking rationally and empirically about what we were doing or
experiencing and when nonrationally. While our Neolithic man
was making his spear, he doubtless alternated frequently between
practical rational thinking about what he was doing with his hands
and thinking nonrationally and emotionally about animals, other

21. This is a very elliptical way of taking a stand on the great philosophical
debate between figures such as Gadamer, Popper, Feyerabend, Rorty, Haber-
mas, Putnam, Searle, and others, a debate directly relevant to the study of
history. For overviews, see Terence Hawkes, *Structuralism and Semiotics*
(Berkeley and Los Angeles, 1977); John B. Thompson, *Critical Hermeneutics*
(Cambridge, Eng., 1981); Richard I. Bernstein, *Beyond Objectivity and Relativism* (Philadelphia, 1983); Howard Gardner, *The Mind's New Science*, 2d ed.
(New York, 1987).

22. Anthony Giddens, *Central Problems in Social Theory* (Berkeley and Los
Angeles, 1979), pp. 25, 39-42, 56-59.

humans, and gods. Indeed, during action, the interplay seems so intimate that Giddens has treated it as a single phenomenon that he calls practical consciousness: "tacit knowledge that is skillfully applied in the enactment of courses of conduct, but which the actor is not able to formulate discursively."[23]

Giddens thus treats both nonrational and rational empirical thinking as "knowledge," whereas I distinguish between nonrational understanding and tacit or explicit knowledge and will emphasize the importance of conflicts between them. We are all conscious that we think in at least two different ways. Even when we are thinking as rationally and empirically as possible, it takes but an instant's lapse in concentration for our thoughts to stray from the task we set our capacity for rational thought. Conversely, even when we are reacting nonrationally, intentionally bathing ourselves in poetic symbols, it may be difficult to extrude rational thoughts. Often that fluctuation is beneficial for rational thought, for the almost incessant alternation between nonrational and rational thinking reinforces our motivation to think rationally in order to solve a problem. Often it suggests ideas worth rational empirical investigation. Sometimes it is merely momentarily distracting. But the two modes of thinking can also conflict and lead to irrationality. Since nonrational thinking is influenced but not controlled by rational empirical thinking, it may conflict with what individuals think when they use their capacity for rational empirical thinking—or would think if they used it.

When the two modes of thinking harmonize, individuals feel comfortably integrated in themselves and in relation to the realities that impinge on them. But if individuals become aware of a conflict between what they believe and what they know or could know if they used their capacity to think rationally and empirically, doubts will disturb their peace of mind. When faced with such conflicts, "rational" people will reexamine their beliefs and their knowledge and modify them so that they can regain their ability to move freely between nonrational and rational thinking.

---

23. *Central Problems in Social Theory*, p. 57. I should emphasize here that I disagree with this use of the term "knowledge," since I reserve that term for discursive formulations and use "belief" to refer to understanding that cannot be expressed in rational empirical discourse; I think both kinds of thinking are involved in practical consciousness.

In some individuals, however, that awareness may induce irrationality, the preservation of belief by the suppression or compartmentalization of their capacity to think rationally and empirically about segments of reality and the projection on those realities of associations created by their nonrational thinking.[24] If that is so, and if, as I shall argue in the next chapter, our religiosity is a product of our nonrational thinking, then we may expect that, while religiosity may harmonize with rational empirical thinking, it may also induce irrationality, an issue to which we will return in later chapters.

24. If, instead, individuals repress consciousness of their nonrational processes, the effect is different. Rather than seeming irrational, they may seem hyperrational but so lacking in affect as to seem severely psychologically crippled. They are irrational in the peculiar sense that they will not or cannot allow their rational empirical thinking to recognize their own nonrational mental processes.

Chapter Nine

A Definition of Religiosity

However elliptical, cumbersome, and shot through with specific errors the foregoing discussion of the human predicament and nonrational thinking may be, if it also seems self-evident or platitudinous in its broad lines, that is all to the good. It may enable us to agree that religion is, along with aesthetic creations, the most enduring and general social expression of nonrational thought, and that religiosity is the most enduring form of individual nonrational thinking.

Structuralist and hermeneutic analysis can be applied so fruitfully to expressions of religious thought because, like literature, it is the expression of a fluidly interrelating whole in which the symbols used are meaningful only in terms of their total relations at a given moment, and the whole in terms of its parts. The devotees of semiotics are right: if one is seeking the whole meaning of a symbol for an individual at a particular time, as contrasted with its delimited meaning as a referent to a particular empirical reality, its meaning is inextricably dependent on the way that individual relates it at that moment to all or any of his or her other symbols according to a complex process of nonrational association. And there is, indeed, a whole that gives the parts meaning.

While individuals may believe that everything in the universe is in some way interrelated because a god or gods created the universe, what they are aware of is indisputably connected at that moment in a particular way in a totality much closer at hand: the brain or mind of the individual, a dynamic organization of a near-infinity of transactions of very different kinds. And in that non-rational mental universe, symbols are necessarily connected associatively without regard to logic and with multiple and fluctuating meanings. What a particular symbol means at a given moment varies depending on which other symbols are evoked by what the individual is presently experiencing.

In the consciousness of Catholics, for example, whether "father" will immediately be associated with "daughter," the "Son," the sacrament of "marriage," a "priest," an "abbot," the "pope," "God," or the "Devil"; what further associations will immediately be evoked by any of those other symbols; and how those associations will be expressed; all will vary, and may vary greatly, depending on the demands or stimulus of the immediate situation in which individuals find themselves—and on how they symbolize themselves. Religious thinking is an expression of that ever-creating universe of nonrational thinking. On this, I think, even scholars who support traditional religion but seek to examine it objectively may agree, for many base their arguments on the objective reality of symbols and the necessity for individual and social life of "noncognitive and nonscientific symbols," to use Bellah's language.

Nonrational thinking and religious thinking are so similar in function and content because both are reactions to the fundamental predicament of which humans are conscious. Like religious thought, nonrational thinking has a holistic quality. It expresses the individual's awareness of being a center tenuously poised among innumerable transactions across changeable internal and external boundaries; and as we move, it bounds that infinity by connecting it to a center. In our daily life, we are aware of physical entities with their boundaries, relations between them, and transactions across them; but when we think about it, there seems no end of them. At any moment, we experience some of them around us, but there are always more. The only limit we know to that frightening limitlessness is the one temporarily provided by our own self-centered consciousness, which constricts and structures our awareness of reality and thereby promises some control by defining the boundaries of reality paradoxically by the center of ourselves.

The same seems true of "gods." Many if not all conceptions of divinities similarly solve the fear of infinity, with all its implications of chaos, not by setting a boundary in the normal sense around reality but by having it emanate from and be controlled by supernatural centers whose powers establish the boundaries within which everything that human beings experience occurs. Human beings have long set limits to infinity by imagining supernatural powers which, like themselves, have *intentions* that establish a more permanent boundary for human identity than the shimmering mutability of individual consciousness in the face of infinity.

Nonrational thinking is, then, very close to what I mean by religiosity but not the same as it, for to define it simply as the process of nonrational thinking and action would be to include all unconscious mental activities and a host of highly transient conscious reactions. Nor do I equate religiosity with "personality," although they are also close, for personality is typically used to denote how individuals are seen as distinctive, not by themselves, but by others. By religiosity, I want to refer to something stabler and more accessible to the outside observer than the totality of nonrational processes, yet something central in the consciousness of the individual, not so much the process as its more enduring results in the consciousness of the individual. I want to distinguish between the total flow of processes and their result in much the same way that Giddens does by his distinction between system and structure, and with a similar emphasis on the duality of structure as something that both stabilizes and modifies.[1]

> *By religiosity, I mean the salient patterns or structure according to which the individual human organism consciously correlates all the diverse processes occurring within the organism with those that surround and impinge on it in order to develop, maintain, and ensure the coherence and continuity of the distinctive elements of its identity.*[2]

1. *Central Problems in Social Theory*, pp. 18, 69-76, 85.

2. This is very close to the position of Ward H. Goodenough, "Toward an Anthropologically Useful Definition of Religion," in *Changing Perspectives in the Scientific Study of Religion*, ed. Allan W. Eister (New York, 1974), pp. 166-169. I should also note here that a critical reader might object that this definition seems to exclude mystics, who are sometimes said to lose their identity in their union with their god or "Nothingness." I will only suggest that such experiences

By "salient," I am pointing toward the more general and stable boundaries and relations between them that structure our consciousness and dominate our patterning of the reality we inhabit mentally, the boundaries and relations to which lesser boundaries and relations are subordinated, the dominating structure of our consciousness. To put it another way, I am pointing to the most salient symbols—for example, "god," "love," and "death"—that are most richly, if most ambiguously, related to the greatest number of other symbols in our thinking. Salient also are our symbols for the boundaries between ourselves, other individuals, and the groups and societies in which and among which we live. A pedestrian example would be the frequency and different ways an individual growing up as a citizen of the United States connects the symbol "American" with other symbols in highly diverse connections.[3]

Whereas religion has been compared to a map with its fixity, religiosity in its fluidity might better be compared to the galaxy as seen from our perspective. Planets, stars, and comets move on paths determined by their velocity and gravity; stars are born and die, and meteors transfer mass from one orbit to another. Although structured, their relations to one another and the strength of their mutual attractions are constantly changing. Seen from our perspective, they move around us; they look different to us as we move and learn more about them; we cannot see them all at once; and those nearest us exert the greatest gravitational pull on us. Similarly, our religiosity is a fluid but imperfectly determined association of symbols of which we are only partly conscious at any moment, a constellation in which, although some symbols

---

involve a merging of the individual's identity with what is felt as eternal reality, and that that feeling can affect the individual's sense of identity once returned from the mystical experience, whether by strengthening his or her former sense of identity or, disruptively, by altering it.

3. My definition of religiosity is therefore very close to Van Austin Harvey's definition of a religion in *The Historian and the Believer* (New York, 1966), pp. 258-259: "A religion, abstractly speaking, may be regarded as a perspective, a standpoint in which certain dominant images are used by its adherents to orient themselves to the present and the future. It may be understood as a way of looking at experience as a whole, or better, as a way of interpreting certain elemental features of human existence." The difference is his apparent assumption that what he describes can be acquired only by adhering to a religion, and that he speaks of images where I speak of symbolic associations.

loom larger and are highly attractive at a given moment, all are constantly changing strength in relation to one another as we move from stimulus to stimulus.[4]

To express what I mean more simply, I might say that religiosity is the dominant pattern or structuring of nonrational thinking—and the conduct correlated with it—which the individual trusts to establish, extend, and preserve consciousness of his or her identity.[5] As would be obvious if I replaced "structure of nonrational thinking" with "beliefs in superior supra-empirical powers," this formulation owes much to the kind of sociological definition of religion I criticized earlier. The principal difference is that mine is a definition of religiosity, not of religion; it refers to a characteristic of individuals, not of groups.

My definition, moreover, does not demand that individuals believe that supra-empirical reality is different in kind from empirical reality, supernatural as contrasted with natural, sacred as contrasted with the profane. It is satisfied by any deeply rooted trust in relations that cannot be explicitly inferred or verified by the rational empirical thought of which an individual is capable—be it pretheoretical and practical or scientific and abstract. While englobing and utilizing what the individual knows rationally and empirically, and while often presenting its deliverances in the form of rational deductions from its premises of faith, religiosity subordinates rational empirical knowledge to its sense of realities beyond such knowledge. Hence I shall refer to such reality, here-

4. Daniel C. Dennett, "Why Everyone Is a Novelist," *Times Literary Supplement*, no. 4,459 (16-22 September 1988): 1016, 1028-1029, has used the analogy of "the centre of gravity," a term that has meaning but does not point to any real object, to provide an intriguing analysis of our sense of self. He argues that our sense of self is a fictional object of indeterminate, changing character that we are continually reforming. "We cannot undo those parts of our pasts that are determinate, but our selves are constantly being made more determinate as we go along in response to the way the world impinges on us" (1028). We are, so to speak, writing our own novel about ourselves addressed to ourselves. And Dennett concludes, citing Hume, that although no one has ever seen a self any more than anyone has ever seen a center of gravity, nonetheless the concept of self is, like center of gravity, a robust theoretical concept.

5. What I am suggesting is very close to what Giddens refers to as "ontological security": *The Constitution of Society* (Berkeley and Los Angeles, 1984), p. 50. See also R. D. Laing, *The Divided Self* (Harmondsworth, 1971), pp. 39-61, for "ontological insecurity."

after, not as supra-empirical, with its connotations of being above or superior, but as ultra-empirical. By ultra-empirical reality I only mean those entities and processes that lie beyond the boundaries of existing empirical knowledge so that their existence or characteristics cannot presently be confirmed by rational empirical thought.

It is obvious that I disagree with scholars such as Durkheim, Eliade, Smart, Berger, Geertz, and Bellah in that I distinguish two separate phenomena, religion and religiosity, where they see only one, religion. Less obvious is the fact that my definition of religion disagrees in a basic way with the well-known definition of religion that Geertz formulated in 1963 and the one formulated by Bellah in 1965. Geertz's definition equates religion with a set of symbols that act on people collectively. It makes symbols, not human beings or the external stimuli acting upon them, the active agent in religion and religious experiences. In contrast, my definition derives the symbols used by a religion from a characteristic of individuals, religiosity, and makes human beings who react to stimuli the active agents in establishing, maintaining, and modifying religions.

I fully agree with Geertz that religion is a social phenomenon, for I define religion as the prescription of elements of religiosity by people exercising social authority over others. And since religion is a social phenomenon, I agree that it is impossible without symbolic communication. I would also agree that the use of symbols in social indoctrination makes those symbols potent stimuli thereafter of patterns of nonrational thought or dispositions in many or all individuals. Yet, however great the molding power of social indoctrination, and I agree that it is very great, I do not believe that the meaning of symbols is purely the product of social interaction, nor that their meanings are fully determined by the semiotic system of a society. Whereas Geertz defines religion as a system of symbols that acts on humans collectively so as to produce moods and dispositions in them, I think that a religion and its symbolic proclamations are distinct from, and a consequence of, the religiosity of individuals. I also think that religiosity depends on processes in the individual that are prior to symbolic expression.

A symbol has no meaning by itself. Meaning is created,

grasped, activated, and communicated by individuals. Symbols acquire meaning only as individuals create, connect, and use them to encode and communicate their experiences. The range of potential meanings (especially nonrational meanings) of a particular socially available symbol may be largely the result of the way the symbol is related to other symbols in social interaction or by prescription through socialization—speech, rituals, dictionaries, law, and so forth. But the actual meanings of any symbol at any moment depend on how each individual relates that symbol to other symbols and to what that individual has experienced and is experiencing.[6] And since the way each individual experiences reality—including social interaction—is unique, the meanings of a symbol for each and every individual also depend on the unique way he or she links that symbol with his or her unique experiences. Whatever creeds, dictionaries, codes of law, or common usage may prescribe, the range of nonrational meanings that a symbol has for each individual is partly determined by the unique personal experiences with which that symbol was linked in the consciousness of the individual as he or she first internalized it and with which it became linked thereafter.

What is true of socialization with established symbols is also true of the creation of symbols. Symbols acquire meaning as devices to represent patterns of experience. While Jesus was alive, a cross meant nothing fundamental to his first followers. It became a salient symbol only as his followers gave rich meaning to his death in accordance with the meaning they sought to give to their own lives—as they were conscious of themselves. Thereafter, although theology would develop and Christians would indoctrinate their young in the meaning of "the Cross," its meaning for their children would be inextricably connected with their own differing formative experiences. Inescapably, the meaning of the symbol for successive generations of Christians differed in varying degrees from what it had meant for prior generations, and differed also

6. See Thomas Luckmann, "Hermeneutics as a Paradigm for Social Science?" in *Social Method and Social Life*, ed. Michael Brenner (London, 1981), pp. 219-230; *Life-World and Social Realities* (London, 1983), pp. 68-91; "Social Reconstruction of Transcendence," in *Secularization and Religion: The Persisting Tension: Acts, Nineteenth International Conference for the Sociology of Religion, Tübingen, 25-29 August 1987* (Lausanne, 1987), pp. 23-31.

for individuals of the same generation, because of their inevitable differences in gender, education, and economic and social status, and also because of their distinctive personal characteristics and experiences. Although the conceptual meaning of the major distinctively Christian symbols may seem more or less constant to us because of the relatively stable social prescription of their meaning, the nonrational meanings evoked by those symbols have always differed somewhat for each Christian individual because the religiosity of each was somewhat different—and the meanings of Christian symbols have differed even more obviously for non-Christians who have used them.

The fundamental disagreement here is about the role of language or symbolic expression of any kind. Since the issue is central in any discussion of religious phenomena, especially in Western culture ("In the beginning was the Word"), I need to make my own stance explicit. I do not think that the only reality of which we are aware is that provided in consciousness by language. Nor do I think, like extreme deconstructionists, that the only meaning that can be evoked by symbols is the present personal one, so that no objective statements may be made about the history and meanings of a text of Shakespeare. If I believed that, I would have to abandon my present endeavors as a historian.[7] My stance is influenced more by my experience of human actions and an interest in epistemology than by hermeneutics and semiology, which, however invaluable, concentrate so heavily on language, especially the language of imagination, that they neglect much else about consciousness and the use of language. At times, one feels that extreme semiologists think that Shakespeare, unlike us, never stubbed his toes on something he had not first perceived and named.

I agree rather with Searle so far as I am competent to understand him.[8] I think our intentional states or dispositions are nonsymbolic experiences that propose that something must be the

7. For an excellent discussion of the impact of linguistics and semiotics on historiography, see John E. Toews, "Intellectual History after the Linguistic Turn: The Autonomy of Meaning and the Irreducibility of Experience," *American Historical Review* 92 (1987): 879-907. Toews writes (p. 906) of "the hubris of wordmakers who claim to be makers of reality."

8. John R. Searle, *Intentionality* (Cambridge, Eng., 1983), pp. 5-29.

case to cause us to perceive something—for example, that our toe must have touched something that caused us pain. And I think that symbols or speech acts have meaning as—partial—representations of our experiences. However human consciousness and language originated, they were and continue to be molded from outside by the organism's transactions with wordless physical realities and forces. Awareness of some of those transactions, such as pain, is conscious, and some of the reactions of the organism to such transactions—for example, to withdraw the hand from the fire—are nonsymbolic acts or behaviors directed by intentional states or dispositions that are not symbols in Geertz's sense of an object, event, quality, or relation that serves as a vehicle of conception. These experiences simply *are*—although the individual may then re-present them by symbolic utterance or thought. What humans mean depends on, and is an effort to remember and represent in another medium, consciousness of being affected by, or directed toward, other realities—realities whose existence they must acknowledge if they are to survive. Humans therefore use their capacity for symbolizing and for rational thinking to try to discover what those realities are. Although the symbolic representations thus developed then feed back and affect perception, that could not occur without the prior existence of nonsymbolic dispositions toward stimuli.

My definitions of religion and religiosity thus rest on premises not about language or morality but about the processes of the individual organism. My approach most closely resembles the psychological approach of James, Otto, and Freud. Unfortunately, Otto's conception of what I would call religiosity was primarily a generalization of his own psychological experiences as a believing Christian, while Freud's explanation was an effort to illustrate the reach of his own, highly debatable, psychological theories; and neither examined the history of societies carefully. Yet both Otto and Freud tried, albeit in strikingly different ways, to explain "religion" without relying explicitly on the beliefs or symbolism of traditional religions as a premise. And both then found it necessary to rely heavily on their knowledge of individual psychology and to use novel terminology in their discourse about religion.

My approach is closest to the radical empiricism of William James. How close was a surprise to me because, although long familiar with some of James's ideas such as the distinction between the once- and twice-born, I had never examined his methodological approach until after I had developed my own position. When I did read his work carefully, I was both gratified to find how far he supported my approach and, at first, depressed to think how much time I had wasted by ignoring him. James's insistence on empirical objectivity had similarly led him to distinguish radically between "religious experience" or "the personal religion" and "external" religion. He distinguished sharply between "the feelings, acts, and experiences of men in their solitude, so far as they apprehend themselves to stand in relation to whatever they may consider the divine" and "institutional religion." Indeed, he distinguished so sharply between them that he recognized that some might question whether what he called personal religion should be called religion at all, and he was willing to accept almost any other name such as conscience or morality for the personal experience he was discussing.[9] Apparently, I had only followed his invitation, as he had not, and used "religiosity" for what he called personal religion or religious experience.

In the second place, my reasons for disagreeing with Geertz's and Bellah's emphasis on symbols closely resembled James's assertion: "so long as we deal with the cosmic and the general, we deal only with the symbols of reality, but *as soon as we deal with private and personal phenomena as such, we deal with realities in the completest sense of the term.*"[10] And my emphasis on nonrational thinking closely resembled James's emphasis on the central role of the subconscious: "*the fact that the conscious person is continuous with a wider self through which saving experiences come.*"[11] Indeed, my argument about the resolution of existential predicaments by nonrational correlations of experiences differed little from his conclusion that what was common to religious experiences was a sense of uneasiness that something was wrong existentially and a reaction or solution that gave the individual the sense of being saved from that wrongness.[12] And James's em-

9. William James, *The Varieties of Religious Experience* (New York, 1982), pp. 28-31.
10. Ibid., p. 498. James's italics.
11. Ibid., p. 515. James's italics.
12. Ibid., pp. 486-487.

phasis on the importance of what I call religiosity for psychological integration, and his insistence on differing degrees of religiosity, only made the similarity more obvious, as will be more apparent when I discuss the problem of degrees of religiosity.

There are, however, two major differences between James's approach and mine. In the first place, my distinction between religion and religiosity is even more radical than James's distinction between institutional and personal religion. James was uneasily content to think of both the property of individuals and the feature of societies as "religion" because he tended to deny any independence to the social phenomenon. He considered personal religion primordial and viewed institutional religion as but a deadened derivative from it. I differ fundamentally here and want to emphasize the difference. Although I agree that religion is dependent on religiosity and consider religiosity primordial, I think the difference between them is as basic as that between an individual and a society, and that each has its own distinctive characteristics and importance. I would not for a moment deny the importance of the influence of religions on religiosity.

Society cannot exist without individuals nor individuals without some social relations, however brief. But although societies and individuals are interdependent, the properties of the one are not the properties of the other. However much consciousness may owe to social interaction, it occurs only in individuals and can only be ascribed metaphorically or by generalization to a society. To say, for example, that a society was highly conscious of threats to its existence, means no more than that a very large number, but not all, of the members were conscious, in varying degrees, of some menace to their society, which they symbolized in similar if not identical ways.

Social interaction may produce and sustain languages. Societies may "remember" by preserving, repeating, and communicating representations of consciousness in material form through pictures, writing, and electronic recording, but societies do not think. Social cooperation may even produce machines that "think" in complex mathematical or syntactical ways. But societies and their machines only talk, remember, and think metaphorically since they are unconscious and without purpose of their own.

The greatest present challenge to such an assertion is the social product that is often thought of now as a model of mental processes, the computer. But without going into the debates about artificial intelligence,[13] I think that even though computers are far more complex and have far more unanticipated effects than water mills, they are no more conscious than water mills.[14] They depend for their existence and meaning on the consciousness and meanings of individuals who can think and act both rationally and nonrationally. Whereas computers only organize symbols according to the formal rules or language with which they have been programmed by human beings, human beings are directed by the nonrational thinking, often impossible to reduce to language, that gives them their sense of purpose. In and of themselves, computers—even the imaginary ideal machines or situations such as Turing's machine and Searle's Chinese room—have no consciousness or purpose because they are not directed by nonrational processes of their own.

What makes it so difficult to distinguish verbally between society and the individual is that language depends on social interaction, makes social interaction possible, and is its inevitable accompaniment. Language seems to bind individuals and society in a single universe of meaning. It is therefore easy to regard the symbols central in the functioning of both society and individual consciousness only as a social product, a product of what Geertz so nicely calls the realm of intersubjectivity. It is much harder to distinguish the social function of symbols from their meaning for individuals. Which attribution we make normally depends on the purpose at hand and the questions we are asking.

A law, as a product of social interaction and an element in social structure, can be viewed simply as a socially produced text, but we may also ask about its origins. At some point, the ideas comprised in that legal text originated in the minds of individuals as a result of their consciousness of experience, and individuals often had to invent new terms or give new meanings to old terms to express their purposes. Or, in the nonrational sphere, a coined word in a poetic phrase of Shakespeare was initially his effort to

13. See Gardner, *The Mind's New Science*, pp. 138-181.
14. On this, I agree broadly with John R. Searle, "Minds, Brains, and Programs," in *Mind Design*, ed. John Haugeland (Cambridge, Mass., 1981). See also Wilkes, *Real People*, pp. 32-48.

express his unique consciousness, although it now seems commonplace and a property of our culture. Though Shakespeare is inconceivable without Elizabethan society, he was radically different from it; and the same is true of all societies and those who compose them. Similarities not of structure but of function (self-protection, acquiring food, knowledge, etc.) may have long encouraged people to describe society by organic metaphors—to speak of heads of state, to conceptualize social institutions as corporations, and even to assert that society is an organism—but the difference between societies and individuals in structure and processes remains.

James would surely have agreed with assertions of this kind, and they may seem platitudinous to all but sociological or sociobiological determinists. But it does not therefore follow, as James assumes in the case of religion, that social products are merely impoverished reflections of richer realities in the consciousness of individuals. Rather, precisely because of their differences, both societies and individuals have their own rich complexity, and each depends on the other for its sustenance. Hence, I do not dismiss the social phenomenon of religion pejoratively as James's conception of "institutional religion" does. My conception assumes that, just as computers can perform calculations far beyond the capacity of any individual, so social organization combines, preserves, and transmits over time a range of elements of religiosity from many sources—David and Jesus, Francis of Assisi and Thomas Aquinas, Michelangelo and Mendelssohn—that is far richer and more enduring than the religiosity of even the most charismatic individual.

I also disagree with James in another way. What enabled him to dismiss "institutional religion" so easily was his belief in higher powers that *communicated* with individuals. Despite his remarkable objectivity, James's scholarly conception of religion was directly influenced by his "over-beliefs," by conceptions of religious experience drawn from his own experience of certain traditional religions and some not so traditional ones. Not only was he explicitly concerned to establish the *value* of religion, he proclaimed as a scholar that "there must be something solemn, serious, and tender about any attitude which we denominate as religious," that there must be passion and optimism about the whole of everything, that there must be an "enthusiastic temper of espousal."[15] Hence James felt able to deny that a merely philosophical or metaphysical conviction about life could be religious.

James's conception of religion thus had strong moral overtones derived from traditional religions, particularly Christian religions, as the examples he used to demonstrate the difference between a religious and nonreligious attitude make plain. He not only believed that individuals are conscious of being continuous with a wider (subconscious) self from which saving experiences and moral insight come; he maintained that the subconscious brought individuals into communication with "higher powers"; and he introduced that conviction not only in his concluding discussion of his "over-beliefs" but also in his scholarly definition of religion by his use of the term "divine." However pluralistic, even anarchic, his sense of directing higher powers, his will to believe made a premise from traditional religions central to his scholarly conception of religion. Here, as should be obvious, my conception of religiosity differs sharply in that it does not rely on any specific "over-beliefs." Instead of assuming that specific unseen powers endowed with consciousness, will, or motivation communicate directly with humans beings, I only accept that nonrational thinking about transactions with ultra-empirical reality has induced belief in such powers.

Both the constructive role attributed to religion by my definition and my refusal to accept belief in communications from specific supernatural powers as a scholarly criterion of religiosity make my distinction between religion and religiosity more radical than James's distinction between personal and institutional religion. My position is closer to that of Thomas Luckmann, even though I disagree with the priority he attributes to the social phenomenon. Like Berger, Luckmann holds that the subjective worldview that constitutes an individual's identity is only "the subjective expression of the objective significance of a historical worldview" that is provided by the society in which the individual was socialized.[16] And whereas he considers both the socially objectified worldview and the subjective worldview of the individual

15. *The Varieties of Religious Experience*, pp. 38, 48, 334.
16. *The Invisible Religion*, p. 70.

to be religion,[17] I differentiate much more sharply between them
and emphasize the relative autonomy of religiosity much more
than he does. I argue that personal identity is determined by
personal characteristics and experiences, that socially objectified
meanings are only part of those experiences, if a very major part,
and that the socially objectified meanings have in fact a somewhat
different meaning for every individual.

Yet to distinguish religion and religiosity so sharply creates a
new problem with interesting consequences. The adjective "religious" now has two quite distinct meanings depending on
whether it is derived from religion or religiosity, on whether the
adjective is applied to societies or individuals. Hence, if we ask
whether all people are religious, we can arrive at two different
answers. If "religious" is derived from religion, it is obviously false
to say that all people are religious, for all do not belong to a
religion. If it is derived from religiosity, it follows from my definition that all people are in some degree religious, since all individuals (save, e.g., infants and some severely brain-damaged
people) have some relatively stable patterns of nonrational symbolizing. But it does not therefore follow that all people are
equally religious.

If we look at people who are religious in the sense of religion,
people who unquestioningly adhere to a religion, we cannot help
recognizing great variations in the intensity of their adherence,
in the extent to which the prescriptions and counsels of their
religion mold their personality. That suggests that the extent of
an individual's religiosity is determined by the degree to which
his or her nonrational consciousness and conduct are harmonized,
interconnected, or integrated by some stable and salient structuring. If a large degree of such structuring is obvious, whether
in accordance with the precepts of a religion or as a result of the
individual's own efforts, or both, we can think of him or her as
religious. But if there is no such comprehensive patterning of
nonrational consciousness, if people exhibit no coherent set of
values or morality throughout the range of their conduct, we find
it difficult to think of them as very religious, even though in one

17. Ibid., pp. 50-76.

compartment of their life they may conform to the prescriptions of a religion.

One common characteristic of many prophets and saints seems to have been that, disregarding the content of their specific beliefs, and disregarding moments of revolutionary change or conversion from one set to another, they maintained their patterns of nonrational thought with remarkable consistency and expressed them in almost all of the wide variety of situations in which they found themselves. And they did so regardless of immediate danger, as for example in martyrdom. The value they placed on their consciousness of their distinctive identity was more important to them than physical comfort or even survival.

A classic medieval example here is the individuality of Francis of Assisi, who also, it may be noted, verged on what his religion deemed heresy and what had in fact been considered heresy in the case of the founder of the Waldensians. Perhaps the most remarkable example, however, is Joan of Arc, whose devotion to Catholic precepts, save that of the right of churchmen to control certain of her central convictions, was profound. But her insistence on her own identity was even stronger, with the result that she was both burnt as a heretic and rehabilitated as a saint. She was caught between the medieval Roman Catholic religion to which she adhered, with the politics of its social authorities, and her own religiosity in which the symbols of France and its king were centrally salient. And although initially condemned, her maintenance of her own religiosity later affected the religion she professed.[18] My distinction between religion and religiosity thus makes it easier to explain why some who seem very religious were not seen as proper adherents of a religion and, conversely, why all those who follow the precepts of a religion do not seem equally "religious." Some are highly religious in the sense of religion, some in the sense of religiosity, many, of course, in both senses, and some in neither.

People who do not adhere to or who oppose any existing re-

18. For an excellent discussion of Joan's self-image that illustrates what I mean by salient symbols of religiosity, see Marina Warner, *Joan of Arc* (New York, 1982), pp. 13-182. For a fascinating discussion of the nonrational association of salient symbols by other medieval people, see Caroline W. Bynum, *Jesus as Mother* (Berkeley, Los Angeles, London, 1982).

ligion may also be religious in different degrees. Many such people may manifest a relatively stable set of nonrational responses or expressions of personality in different contexts, yet those responses do not seem well integrated or connected; how they express or conduct themselves in one area of life seems unrelated to what they do in another. They compartmentalize their consciousness of life sharply, make little effort to integrate all that they believe, and seem unwilling or unable to utilize their capacity for rational thinking in many of the areas of activity in which they are necessarily involved. If asked to explain why they so value and devote so much energy and rational thought to certain activities but not others, say business and family, they give answers that do not stray far from the boundaries of those activities themselves, and they do not connect those activities with other obvious dimensions of their lives save by platitudes whose complex implications they do not examine. Their religiosity seems highly incoherent. Conversely, there are individuals who, while they do not belong to a religion, nonetheless conduct themselves in most areas of life in a way that manifests a common pattern or sense of connections, perhaps a deep sense of "morality." Einstein might serve as as a prominent example.

The extent of religiosity can be seen, then, as the degree to which a salient patterning of nonrational thought extends not only over time but also over the whole space or range of an individual's experiences. The extent of an individual's religiosity thus depends on the degree to which the individual mentally inhabits a stable and coherent (though not rigid) cosmos, regardless of whether or not he or she adheres to a religion.

Obviously, individuals can be religious in both senses, both devoted adherents of a religion and imbued with deep religiosity. The definition of religion as the prescription of elements of religiosity ensures as much. Yet there will always be differences between their religion and their religiosity, since their religiosity will always spring from and inform depths of consciousness and details of conduct beyond the effective control of any social authority. Moreover, individuals will differ in the importance they attribute to the various prescriptions they accept and to the authority that prescribes them. Nonetheless, so long as one fundamental and unquestioned component of the individual's religiosity is belief in the privileged relation or contact with ultra-empirical reality of some social authority and the necessity of obeying its major prescriptions of religiosity, the individual's religiosity will legitimate the religion's prescriptions of religiosity.[19] Though there may be tension between some aspects of an individual's religiosity and some particular beliefs prescribed by his or her religion, there will be no overt conflict.

People who adhere to no religion, however, may equally be deeply religious in the sense of religiosity. If individuals reject the right of the authorities of any religion to prescribe their religiosity, yet have some convictions that are also prescribed by religions in their culture—for example, belief that there is only one god or belief in the divinity of Jesus—they cannot be counted as adherents of a religion even though they may maintain their convictions about the meaning of their life intensely. Indeed, in the psychological sense, they may seem more religious than many adherents of religions, and some may found new religions. Similarly, people whose central convictions about the meaning of their life are not those of any particular religion may nonetheless seem very religious in their own way provided that their thought and conduct are directed by a stable, intense, and comprehensive pattern of nonrational thinking. They have their own cosmic confidence.

My effort to define religiosity has brought me to a very uncanonical position. It indicates that there are two types of expression of faith, one social and characteristic of religion, the other individual and characteristic of religiosity. The difference resembles the difference between the two senses of faith provided by dictionaries, the difference between faith as assent to propositions and faith as confidence or trust. Thus, whereas Catholic theologians have tended to stress assent to propositions about God,

19. The prescriptions of religious authorities may also, of course, be supported by people who do not believe the authorities have any privileged access to ultra-empirical reality. Some may support them out of cynical political motives. Others, because they recognize the limitations of their own personal experience and find little time to think out many matters for themselves, may accept many religious prescriptions as the fruit, garnered over centuries, of wisdom about how to live. But in both cases, the individuals are acting from prudential motives rather than from religious conviction, and their support of those prescriptions is only a secondary consequence of their own religiosity.

Protestants have stressed unlimited confidence in God—although neither religion emphasizes the one to the exclusion of the other. In any case, there is a profound difference between assent to prescriptions that can be expressed in words and a psychological disposition that can be encouraged but not enforced.

But if I make religiosity primordial, that does not mean I am taking a Protestant position. If there is a resemblance, I suspect it is a reflection of the fact that Protestantism came after Catholicism and placed greater stress on the individual. Though there had always been differences in religiosity, social recognition of their extent could not appear until a society and culture had emerged in which social authorities no longer enforced strict conformity to group norms. Yet if the Protestant spirit may have encouraged greater social awareness of religious diversity, Protestant religions rapidly discouraged further diversity. Once their founders had expressed their own religiosity, they or their followers soon disapproved of nonconformity. Luther rapidly retreated from the more radical implications of his concept of the priesthood of all believers; Calvin had Servetus burned. Not until the eighteenth or nineteenth century did public expression of nonconforming religiosity cease to be highly dangerous; and even in the twentieth century it is safe only in certain societies.

Be that as it may, my distinction between religion and religiosity differs from that of James, since it does not make the former merely the deadened reflection of the latter. Although I have made the prescriptions of religion dependent on religiosity, I have also recognized that religions act as rich independent variables that powerfully influence religiosity. Whatever theological implications my effort to remain empirical and rational may be thought to have, they were not intended, for I have tried so far as possible to avoid taking any theological stand, whether Judaic, Catholic, or Protestant, or any metaphysical stand, whether idealist or materialist. I have tried to stay within the bounds of rational empirical discourse. But to say that immediately raises the question of the extent to which religions and religiosities can be examined empirically.

Chapter Ten

The Empirical Accessibility of
Religion and Religiosity

Life depends on an infinity of microcosmic and macrocosmic relations of which only some fall within the range of rational empirical knowledge. Only a fool could fail to realize that we are always enmeshed in a vast diversity of transactions with what lies beyond our knowledge. There is therefore nothing surprising about our awareness of interacting with, or being related to, realities beyond our rational empirical ken. And since our knowledge of those transactions, on which our existence depends, is limited, our ability to describe and explain them objectively is limited. Yet if much about those transactions eludes our knowledge, they have left many traces. There is considerable evidence of how people have reacted to their awareness of relations with realities they could not know, and that evidence can be examined rationally and empirically, although it is much easier to examine religions than religiosities.

Religions and religiosities depend on people's conviction that through such interactions they have somehow gained some direct and directive understanding of realities about which they have no rational empirical knowledge. They may not be able to specify which transactions have yielded meanings or to explain very precisely what meanings they have grasped; but whatever meaning they have gained, wherever they acquired it, and however difficult it may be for us to describe it empirically, it guides their lives.

Such experiences of contact, however, are at least partially situated in the empirical realm, and to the extent they are, they and their preconditions and consequences can be examined empirically. Whenever people assert that they have had understandable contact with ultra-empirical reality, the modes of contact they affirm have a human ground that—in principle—anyone can examine. It is much easier, however, to examine empirically the human ground of religions and the modes of contact they assert than those of religiosities, because religions are social institutions, not psychological or mental processes.

It is very difficult for historians to describe and analyze religiosity empirically, which may be one reason why they have paid much more attention to religions than to what people have actually believed. In modern, pluralistic, democratic societies, evidence of the great diversity of individual thought and expression is plentiful, which makes it easy to conceive of religiosity as distinct from religion and to examine it in some depth. It is much harder to distinguish between them and to examine religiosity in earlier societies. Not only was there much greater pressure to conform in those societies, and hence less public expression of individual differences, but we have no direct evidence for the overwhelming bulk of individuals throughout history and hence no way of examining how they reacted individually. There is, however, much evidence for religions in past societies or cultures. And one characteristic of those religions is particularly valuable for empirical analyses: the particular way a religion professed that individuals could establish contact with the ultra-empirical.

Though we know little or nothing about most individuals throughout history, it is clear from the history of religions that religions arose because individuals believed that they had transactions with ultra-empirical reality that somehow conveyed understanding of its relation to empirical reality. They were convinced that they had experienced clearly recognizable moments of contact—or communing—with realities beyond the grasp of their knowledge, and that those contacts gave them a clear sense of direction. As their religious practices reveal, they felt that there were special channels through which some of the meanings or intentions of ultra-empirical reality had been revealed to them, and through which they could transmit their own meanings and intentions back. Because they believed in those channels, they believed they understood what the nature of ultra-empirical reality or realities implied for human action in the empirical realm.

Those who believed they had experienced such identifiable moments of contact may have been unable to describe their experiences adequately, convey fully to others the content of the understanding infused, or verify the guidance gained empirically, but their experiences were empirically situated. People could say when they had them, talk about them, and say what they implied for life here and now. Whatever Paul experienced on the road to Damascus, it did not make him taciturn or inactive. And whatever may be thought of Julian Jaynes's thesis about auditory hallucinations,[1] there can be no doubt that religious revelation has frequently taken the form of hearing voices speaking in humanly comprehensible terms about empirically observable matters. And when such revelations were institutionalized as social norms, religions emerged with their prescriptions for making contact.

What distinguishes religions is their proclamation that nonrational comprehension has been and can be achieved by specific modes of contact with ultra-empirical reality that can be described empirically. Their adherents may typically believe that contact was initially made through observable charismatic figures,[2] gods in human form or ancestors, wise men, or prophets who received communications from beyond which they then expressed in human language and shared with others. But they also believe that comprehensible contact continues. They believe that at certain moments or places, under certain conditions or through certain actions or privileged persons, all of which can be empirically described, they also, if properly disposed, will be in understandable contact with the empirically unintelligible.

Religions have to define modes of contact empirically because the religious experiences of individuals vary unpredictably, and those variations pose problems for those who have them and those

1. *The Origin of Consciousness in the Breakdown of the Bicameral Mind* (Boston, 1982).

2. Stark and Bainbridge, *The Future of Religion*, p. 356: "For cults to get started requires a founder able to attract others, to convince them to accept a new truth." See also Bryan Wilson, *Religious Sects* (New York, 1970), pp. 19-20.

with whom they want to share them. The more intense the sense
of contact, the more difficult it is to describe, repeat, or share
fully. However precious such moments may be felt to be, they
are rare and fleeting, and many adherents of religions never experience them with great intensity. Hence, both those who have
felt them intensely and those who have been told about them but
not experienced them are impelled to seek more reliable and repeatable or routine modes of contact—or ways of refreshing memory of intense experiences in the past. Out of this common urge
develop the socially provided modes of contact, the myths and
rituals that initiators and modifiers of religions develop, that religions prescribe, and that adherents practice with varying subjective reactions—the process Weber called the routinization of
charisma.

Necessarily, therefore, social modes of achieving contact with
the ultra-empirical differ decisively from individual modes. To be
a property of society, modes of contact must be actions jointly or
commonly performed by the members of the society. However
much the processes may consist of nonrational symbolic actions
such as rituals, how they are to be performed must be empirically
describable so that individuals can recognize them and cooperate
repeatedly in that joint or common action. Whatever nonrational
meaning may be attributed to a ritual, and however much the
subjective reactions of the participants may still differ, the mode
of contact must—in striking contrast with the processes within
individuals—be something that can be described or prescribed in
very concrete and detailed terms.

One obvious example would be the reading of passages in a
bible prescribed as canonical, another the Catholic Mass. Although the nonrational combination of roles, words, gestures, and
objects that constitute a Mass conveys powerful symbolic messages that have no empirically verifiable meaning, its proper performance has been described and prescribed in minute empirical
detail for centuries,[3] thereby making its repetition possible and
enabling believers to recognize empirically where, if properly disposed, they could make contact with their god. The same could

3. See Josef A. Jungmann, *The Mass of the Roman Rite: Its Origins and
Development*, 2 vols. (New York, 1951-1955).

be said with appropriate modifications of a fertility rite transmitted orally through generations.

A religion's modes of contact or channels of communication with ultra-empirical reality thus have self-evident empirical dimensions, and religions can be identified and distinguished from one another on that basis. Given my definition, the obvious mode of contact to start with is a religion's authorities and the society that obeys them. Those authorities are the fundamental mode of contact from which the religion's other modes of contact emanate; and the salvation promised by a religion depends on membership in the society defined by acceptance of that authority. Many other kinds of conduct may be commanded or advised, and all who are apparent members may not be promised salvation, but membership with the conduct necessary to maintain it is the first necessity. As it has been succinctly expressed, no salvation outside the church.

It might seem that membership is not essential, since the authorities and adherents of a Christian religion may entertain the possibility that adherents of other Christian religions—even of a non-Christian religion—may be saved. Yet so long as they refuse to leave their own religion or found a new and more embracing one, their continued adherence indicates their doubt that salvation can be as fully obtained outside their own religious society.[4] In any case, even if people who belong to religions—for example, tolerant polytheistic religions—regard other religions as valid for their own adherents, they agree that membership in religious societies is necessary.

The modes of contact and the promise of salvation offered by any religion thus have an identifiable social ground, and it is through that social ground that salvation is mediated to the adherents. To take the case of Catholicism again, salvation is believed to come from God through the Catholic church to those individual members who genuinely participate in the thought and conduct demanded of believers and participate in the sacraments operated by its priests. What is true of the Roman Catholic re-

4. If their refusal to leave their own religion is motivated simply by their desire to participate in a close human community, they may be highly religious in the sense of religiosity, but they are hardly religious in the sense of religion.

ligion is true of all religions; they prescribe that salvation comes to individuals from beyond through the mediation of the religious society to which they belong. Hence religions can be distinguished empirically according to their social characteristics.

There are many ways of characterizing religious societies. Sociologists have distinguished between churches, denominations, sects, cults, and movements, and those categories can be very useful for historians. Those categories, however, apply as well to Islam as Christianity. They do not distinguish between specific religions, a matter of great importance for the historian. If, however, a religion is defined as those elements of religiosity explicitly prescribed by people exercising authority over other people, then any collectivity whose authorities (however constituted) prescribe nonrational beliefs about modes of contact with ultra-empirical reality as a condition of membership is a religious society.[5] Historically, there have been many of them, and they can be distinguished according to the human authorities they acknowledged. We can identify the people who exercised authority over them, the way they organized their authority, and the relation of their authority to the organization of authority in society as a whole.

The location of religious authority in societies has varied greatly. In societies such as "primitive" tribes or early Islamic society, in which roles were little differentiated and there was no differentiated religious subsociety or suprasociety, the whole society was a religious society, and its authorities were the primary mode of contact with the ultra-empirical. The same can also be true of advanced societies in which roles are differentiated. When Henry VIII established the Church of England and made the king in Parliament its supreme authority, he was trying to remove the kingdom of England from the vast religious suprasociety of the Roman Catholic church and make the English kingdom an independent religious society in itself. In that society, prescription of elements of nonrational belief and conduct would be determined by the king (to whom James I would ascribe divine right); the prescriptions would be carried out by specialized agents the king appointed, the clerics; and their commands would be backed

5. It is therefore debatable whether a marginal case such as the Unitarian church constitutes a religion or an assembly of people with similar religiosity.

by the coercive physical power of royal government. In 1648, a very similar approach was expressed more broadly and epigrammatically in the Peace of Westphalia: *cuius regio eius religio*. But if religions can thus be identified specifically according to the people whose authority they support, they can also be distinguished more generally according to the type of society involved.[6]

One contrast between types of society and the relations of religious authority to society with which we are all familiar is that between a folk religion (which attributes religious authority to the elders of a primitive society and to almost all its institutions and almost all the conduct of its members) and a universal religion that legitimates no particular form of society (save its own religious organization). Herbert Stroup formulated an interesting variation of that contrast. He distinguished four kinds of religion according to their relation to society *as a whole*: religions of a people (e.g., Shintoism, ancient Judaism); religions closely supportive of a people (e.g., Hinduism); religions of withdrawal (e.g., early Buddhism); and religions of universal scope that transcend society (e.g., later Buddhism, Christianity).[7]

This categorization is suggestive and valuable, but it fails to take into account the social organization of complex modern societies or the existence and organization of the religious subsocieties within them or of the religious suprasocieties that transcend them. The categories jump from an all-embracing anthropological category, "a people," to "withdrawal" and "universal," categories that say nothing about the characteristics of the society from which individuals withdrew or of the new societies they formed. Stroup's categories do not recognize the difference between a "people" and a complex, differentiated society, the difference indicated by Ferdinand Tönnies's distinction between a *Gemeinschaft* and a *Gesellschaft* and Weber's distinction between traditional and rational-legal authority. Moreover, in my terms,

---

6. The next paragraphs are a revised form of ideas initially advanced in "From Ambrose of Milan to Emicho of Leiningen: The Transformation of Hostility toward Jews in Northern Europe," *Gli ebrei nell'alto medioevo*, Settimane di studio del Centro italiano di studi sull'alto medioevo, vol. 26 (Spoleto, 1980), pp. 316-324; revised and republished as "The Transformation of Anti-Judaism," in *Toward a Definition of Antisemitism*, chap. 4.

7. Herbert Stroup, *Church and State in Confrontation* (New York, 1967), pp. 136-152.

Stroup confuses religion and religiosity. If by "universal" is meant something that does not rely on or "sanctify" any particular form of social organization, then, although that may be possible for certain types of religiosity, it is impossible for a religion since acceptance of social authority is a necessary feature of religion.

To remedy those problems, we need two other categories to deal with religions supportive of social authority in complex, differentiated societies with their subsocieties. Religion in complex societies demands two categories because in such societies two different forms of superior social authority emerge as the result of increasing differentiation. The authorities of the traditional religion are deprived of the ability to employ physical sanctions independently; and their society of religion becomes distinct from the organization of what it considers "secular" society, which has its own values and is governed by its own authorities.

That differentiation causes no problem so long as the political authorities (hereafter, for convenience, the government) accept and enforce most of the nonrational prescriptions of the traditional religious authorities (hereafter the priesthood) and do not defy them. But since authority recognized as legitimate by the adherents of a religion is now differentiated and exercised by different people, conflict between those authorities and competition for people's loyalty may arise.[8] Whether on particular issues or more generally, individuals have to decide, however subconsciously and nonrationally, which authority they recognize as supreme in deciding particular issues for themselves and their society—a choice that increases tension in their religiosity and has major implications for their sense of identity. Thomas Becket, Joan of Arc, Thomas More, and Galileo are dramatic examples of people caught in such tension, as playwrights have long recognized. But such tension has claimed many other martyrs and been generally present in lesser degree in European civilization from the eleventh century to the present.[9]

8. An obvious medieval example is the conflict over the role of kings in episcopal elections after the pope had declared that bishops should be chosen only by clerics.

9. A less dramatic contemporary example is the tension aroused by the issue of prayer in governmentally controlled schools in the United States.

Thus, even in differentiated societies in which only one religion claims supreme authority, the religiosity of its adherents may in fact, on particular issues, be supportive of the supremacy either of the priesthood or the government. Indeed, religions themselves may differ in their prescriptions on this matter. Some may be supportive of the supreme social authority of the priesthood, some supportive of the supreme authority of the government. Whereas the Roman Catholic religion as prescribed in the thirteenth century very explicitly supported the supreme authority of the priesthood, although the religiosity of many Catholics did not, the Church of England after Henry VIII was obviously a religion supportive of the social authority of the government, as was the Lutheran church in Germany. But the clearest examples of systems of nonrational beliefs prescribed by people exercising social authority and supportive of governments are Nazism in Germany and Communism in Russia.

If we apply these sociopolitical categories to traditional religions, not only do Catholic and Islamic religions fall into different categories, but what is often viewed as one historic religion becomes a continuous modification of religiosity differently expressed in a succession of religions rather than a single religion. Take Christianity. Almost from the outset, the people whose religiosity attributed a supernatural dimension to Jesus divided into different societies that recognized different authorities. Even in western Europe during the Middle Ages, a period whose historians often write about "the Church" as if there had been only one church and one Catholic religion, there were changes in Christian religiosity and in the social ground of religion so revolutionary that it might be more accurate to speak of a succession of two or three Catholic Christian religions, an episcopal, a royal, and a third, more enduring, papal religion.

With the Reformation, of course, Christian religiosity in European culture and its extensions became highly diverse and was expressed—frequently in lethal ways—by many self-consciously distinct Christian religions, religions which can only be denoted by adding modifiers to "Christian" that point specifically to their different authorities, societies, and prescriptions. At the same time, because of the differentiation and competition of social authorities, the process much discussed by sociologists of religion as "secularization" accelerated as individuals and governments increasingly rejected the authority of traditional priesthoods.

I will discuss those modern developments later[10] and will concentrate here, however superficially, on the developments up to the Reformation. Since Christian religiosity grew out of Judaic, I will start by assuming with Stroup that early Judaic religion was the religion of a people, a set of nonrational prescriptions that defined and legitimated the institutions and conduct of a society whose members were biologically closely related and ethnically fairly homogeneous. By the Roman period, however, markedly different types of Judaic religion and religiosity had appeared within Israel.

If all accepted the Torah as a record of revelations, they obeyed different authorities who interpreted the Torah differently. There were, for example, Sadducees, Pharisees, Essenes, Zealots, and Hellenizers; many adherents were gentile converts or partial converts from a different religion or religiosity; and far more Jews lived in the Diaspora than in Palestine. The various forms of Judaism were now at best supportive of a people. Even if all Jews still looked to the Temple or Patriarch, they were no longer a people in the sense of a traditionally organized *Gemeinschaft* society whose authorities could autonomously use physical sanctions over all its members. The social—and to a considerable extent the ethnic—identity of the adherents was no longer adequately indicated by saying that they were Jews. Like Saul of Tarsus, they might also conceive of themselves both as Jews and as Roman citizens. Judaic religiosity was now only supportive of a people or the memory of a people ("next year in Jerusalem"). And with the destruction of the Temple and the decentralized reorganization of Judaism around synagogues and the authority of the rabbis—a decentralization that the invasions and fall of the Roman empire in the West would make more extreme—the social ground of Judaism became increasingly differentiated from the larger societies within which Jews lived. A new form of Judaic religion had emerged, one prescribed by the decentralized authority of rabbis rather than by the priesthood of the Temple.

10. See below, chap. 15.

As for the Jews who first followed Jesus, although their religiosity was overwhelmingly Judaic, they began to form a new society around a new authority who emphasized face-to-face conduct and disobeyed the social prescriptions of the established authorities of Judaism. This nascent religion (movement or sect) was thus less supportive of a people, and its exponents' religiosity had implications of universality. Then, with Saul/Paul and his converts, obedience to many prescriptions of Judaic law and attendance at synagogue were eliminated from the Pauline Christian religion, and many—and soon most—members had no significant biological or social ties with adherents of Judaism. The salvation promised by Pauline Christianity no longer required belonging to any particular people or membership in any form of society save one: the new subsocieties, based on households linked by apostles, that were formed by Christians in the interstices of the surrounding society to which they also belonged.[11] Seen from this perspective, early Pauline Christian religiosity can be described as a universalizing of Judaic religiosity.[12] But since its exponents rejected the authorities of Judaism and gradually established new ones, it gave birth to new religions with their distinctive religious societies.

With the spread of Pauline Christianity in the empire and its syncretic modification as many converts incorporated aspects or symbols of Greco-Roman culture in their Christian religiosity, a new form of Christian religion appeared.[13] However many traditional characteristics it retained, Roman society may be categorized as a complex, role-differentiated, and, in Weber's sense, rational-legal society, and Christians gradually followed that model and organized themselves in a more centralized and similarly role-differentiated society led by bishops, a church.

At first it stood apart from and was persecuted by the author-

---

11. See Wayne A. Meeks, *The First Urban Christians* (New Haven, 1983). As its subtitle, *The Social World of the Apostle Paul*, suggests, it deals with what I might call the social ground of Pauline Christianity.

12. As suggested by Schneider, *Sociological Approach to Religion*, p. 74 f. But I would disagree sharply with his formulation that it was a universalizing of Jewish religion. It was a universalizing of many elements of Judaic religiosity, but, since it rejected the authorities of Judaic religions, it was not a Judaic religion or the development of a Judaic into a universal religion.

13. See Peter Brown, *The World of Late Antiquity* (London, 1971), p. 82.

ities of the larger society. Then (with the conversion of Constantine, his official toleration of Christianity, and the subsequent adoption of Roman, Nicene, Pauline Christianity as the official religion of the empire by Theodosius I), that Christian religion and its society became institutionally and culturally tied to Roman society, and a special importance was attributed to the bishop of Rome. Christians in the empire were now members both of the empire, which now had a new religious significance, and the Church. The religiosity of many Christians therefore supported the social authorities of both the empire and the Roman church. Competition for supreme social authority was now possible, and one subject of controversy was proper treatment of Jews.[14]

Yet another type of Christian religiosity appeared in reaction to the success of that Christian religion in the empire, the religiosity of withdrawal of the desert fathers. They withdrew as individuals from society at large and formed little isolated societies, the new monastic communities in which the abbot had absolute authority; and to join such communities soon became known as entering "religion." Important in the late Roman world, that form of Christian religion became so influential after the fall of Rome that we often speak of the centuries in the West between the fall of the empire and the emergence of the papal monarchy in the eleventh century as the Benedictine Age.

But along with the spread of Christian monastic religions with their various rules, yet another type of Christian religion appeared after the fall of Rome which would dominate Europe until the eleventh century. With the conquest of the western empire by illiterate "barbarians," Roman legal-rational society in western Europe gradually dissolved, to be replaced by kingdoms of peoples whose mentality might be described as tribal or traditional. Their conversion to Christianity has often been described as "superficial," but that is a theological, not an empirical, judgment. They did convert, but in the process, because of the enduring presuppositions of their religiosity and the relatively undifferentiated character of their societies, they converted the former Christian religions and religiosity to Christian religions and religiosity sup-

14. See "The Transformation of Anti-Judaism," in *Toward a Definition of Antisemitism*, chap. 4.

portive of particular peoples. Thus, to choose but one example, the Franks saw themselves as chosen by God, whose rulers, such as Charlemagne, decided religious prescriptions, appointed bishops, and, when they did not simply disregard them, considered the bishops of Rome as in some sense their servants. However popes, surrounded by memories of their Roman past, and some other high ecclesiastics might view the matter, the religion of the Carolingian empire was a Frankish, Latin, Nicene, Pauline, Christian religion, and the supreme authority of that religion and religious society was Charlemagne.

That uneasy coexistence of Christian religions supportive of peoples—or semitribal kingdoms—with papal memories of a Christian religion supportive of the supreme social authority of the pope and priesthood lasted until the eleventh century, a century notable for growing tension in religiosity. It was also the century in which Europeans began to reorganize themselves into role-differentiated rational-legal societies. What is usually called the Gregorian reformation of the church or Investiture Contest was a struggle between the old royal Christian religions supportive of peoples and a new Christian religion prescribed by the pope that demanded that the religious authority of the priesthood and the society it controlled be sharply differentiated from secular government and be recognized as supreme.

Despite obvious compromises, the pope was victorious in the struggle against kings, and the papally controlled church became the religious suprasociety for all western Europeans—save rebels, Jews, and Moslems—whatever other societies they belonged to. The authorities of the new Christian religion then defined their church ever more sharply as a clearly differentiated, hierarchic society. They insisted on papal control of that society far beyond anything known in Roman times. They defined, created, and prescribed elements of Christian religiosity more thoroughly intellectually, legally, and ritually than had ever been done before. And they thus created the papal Latin Christian religion much as it would endure to the present.[15]

Those developments, however, also changed the character of

15. Richard W. Southern, *The Making of the Middle Ages* (New Haven, 1953), p. 133, reaches a very similar conclusion.

the monarchies of Europe. Since the religiosity of many of their subjects was still that supportive of peoples, and since the authorities of the Church still emphasized the religious legitimacy of properly subordinate kings, ascribed subordinate functions to them, and relied on them for physical support, royal government still had a Christian halo. The religiosity of Christians could therefore still support both kinds of social authority despite their different social grounds. But the priesthood's ever more detailed definition of its spheres of authority brought increasing conflicts between the priesthood and governments.

Friction increased as kings imitated the example of church organization and increasingly expressed their authority through rational-legal commands and territorial control. Kings gradually became rulers of complex societies rather than of peoples, and a Christian religiosity supportive of government, of the supreme social authority of kings, began to reappear.[16] Thereafter, conflict between the two kinds of religiosity developed rapidly within the confines of a single religion, a conflict no longer over symbolic actions, as in the Investiture Contest, but now over legal control of particular people and things, particularly those of political and economic importance such as political autonomy, jurisdictional boundaries, taxes—and Jews.

The bitter conflict between Pope Boniface VIII and Philip IV of France at the end of the thirteenth century (which coincided with the first massive expulsions of Jews) and many dimensions of the conciliar movement at the end of the fourteenth are but the most obvious instances of the violent struggle for supremacy between the two kinds of authority and the conflict of religiosities that it engendered. Not until the end of the Middle Ages, however, was there a successful challenge to the hegemony of the Christian, Roman Catholic, papal religion. Foreshadowed by developments such as the formation of the new Waldensian and Hussite Christian religions and the impact of Gallicanism on the

16. Thus Joseph R. Strayer, *The Reign of Philip the Fair* (Princeton, 1980), p. 387, speaks of the "royal religion" in France. See also ibid., pp. 237-313, esp. p. 295; and Strayer, *Medieval Statecraft and the Perspectives of History* (Princeton, 1971), chap. 19, "France: The Holy Land, the Chosen People, and the Most Christian King."

old religion, a new war of religions, the "Reformation," made some kingdoms and principalities independent religious societies—and others very close to it in practice. Luther's religiosity and the authority he gained gave birth to a new Christian religion that explicitly supported the supreme social authority of the government; Calvinists sought to make whole societies religious societies; and Roman Catholic religiosity came to support the authority of "secular" rulers as it never had before.

Thus, when we focus on the people who have asserted themselves to be religious authorities and on their relation to the surrounding society, we can distinguish religions empirically from one another by the people who designate themselves as primary modes of contact with ultra-empirical reality, who are accepted as such, and who prescribe elements of religiosity, and we can type religions according to the relation between their social authorities and other social authorities. Applying those criteria, I have argued that as social conditions and religiosity changed, new Christian religions appeared. But religions have other distinctive modes of contact that can also be examined empirically. If their authorities assert their own contact with ultra-empirical reality and prescribe belief in that contact, they also prescribe other modes of contact such as rituals in which all adherents can participate and come in direct contact with their god. The distinctive cultural characteristics of these modes of contact provide another way of distinguishing historically between religions.

What I have called the social ground of religion always involves more than social organization; there is also culture. Like any social organization, religions are rooted in and transmit distinctive cultural elements inherited from the past as well as those of the present. In most cases, many characteristics of their practices originated outside them in the practical conduct of everyday life. The older the religion, the more obvious the cultural debt because its fundamental prescriptions, including the location of its authority, were created in its formative period and contrast with the present culture. A further reason is that those who succeed to authority in a religion have to legitimate their authority by claiming to continue the privileged contact and modes of communication with the supernatural established by the founders.

That is particularly true of religions that originated in literate societies that could preserve the memory of their origins across centuries.

Myths of origin are replete with culturally specific allusions and
often attribute primordial contacts to specific localities. Rites use
distinctive verbal formulas, objects, gestures, and vestments that
originated in a particular culture. Language immediately imposes
a major cultural debt since it is so closely tied to culture, and
that debt becomes very obvious in literate societies when the
language in which the religion was first expressed becomes can-
onized as the sacred language. In Islam, the Koran, written in
Arabic and rich in local cultural allusions, was never to be translated into another language. The centrality of language in the
Greek and Russian Orthodox religions and for the Old Believers
in Russia needs no comment. And for centuries, the sacred and
legal language of Roman Catholicism was Latin, rich in Mediterranean cultural allusions to olive trees and the like. More than
that, the center of Catholicism was and is Rome, and the bishop's
vestments that now look so distinctive were originally simply the
garb of aristocratic Romans. The list could go on and on. Each
religion—and the modes of contact it prescribes—is marked by
distinctive cultural characteristics. However religions start, they
tend to become ethnocentric.

The resistance to changes in the myths and rituals of any firmly
established religion makes the debt to older cultures and the contrast with present culture particularly obvious. For that reason
and various others, many people think that religions once established do not change fundamentally. Yet for a historian, one of
the most obvious characteristics of religions is change. Religions
change, even old religions in literate societies, and new religions
appear.[17] Consequently, both old and new religions are marked
by recent cultural conditions, for example, the present use of local
vernaculars in the Roman Catholic Mass, the increasing acceptance of women in priestly roles in some Christian and Judaic
religions, or the role of psychological questionnaires in Scientol-

17. One of the more intriguing being cargo cults: see Jonathan Smith, *Imagining Religion*, pp. 98-101. For a general analysis of the emergence of sects or
cults, see Bryan Wilson, *Religious Sects*, and Stark and Bainbridge, *The Future
of Religion*.

ogy.[18] The obvious explanation is that major changes in sociocultural conditions have affected how people feel and think,[19] or, conversely, that even under stable conditions individuals may develop and propagate novel religiosities that influence sociocultural expectations.

The impact of changes in religiosity is, however, much harder to examine than that of social change, for religiosity is much less empirically accessible than social organization. The contacts with the ultra-empirical of individuals are much more invisible and evanescent than those prescribed by religions. Whereas religions may be so visibly stable that some believe their core has never changed, religiosity, including the religiosity of those in authority in religions, is remarkable for its diversity and mutability. For one thing, the culture of the moment has a far greater impact on individuals and their religiosity than on institutions and long-established religions. Even highly conservative individuals inevitably live here and now and are immediately and heavily influenced by their immediate social and cultural ground—families, friends, neighbors, teachers, knowledge, technologies, games, art, goods, politics, and so on. And because of their distinctive genetic, psychological, and mental characteristics, individuals, including those who exercise religious authority, do not react identically to even the most intimately shared and common of social grounds, their families—as the amazement of parents at the differences between their children testifies.

Religiosity is difficult, often impossible, to analyze empirically because its modes of contact are in an important sense subjective and private. Individuals may experience a sense of understanding while participating in socially instituted channels of contact with ultra-empirical reality—for example, reading the Bible or communion through the Eucharist—or the moments may be highly personal as in mysticism. But in either case, the consciousness of meaningful contact is a property of individuals. Even though social action may have made possible or stimulated consciousness of being in contact and communication with ultra-empirical real-

18. For Scientology, see Stark and Bainbridge, *The Future of Religion*, pp. 263-283.
19. E.g., Wilson, *Religious Sects*, p. 228: "The proposition that sects arise in conditions of social change is a truism."

ity, that consciousness itself necessarily occurs within individuals, is somewhat different for each, and is difficult or impossible to communicate fully to others.

Individuals who believe they have experienced awareness of meaningful interaction between their empirical humanity and ultra-empirical reality explain it in different ways. Some may attribute it to a social action, a ritual; some may attribute it totally to a particular and striking ultra-empirical intervention, a miracle; some to some revelation unilaterally offered by the ultra-empirical reality; and others may ascribe it rather to their own efforts or those of others to discover how to communicate with what is beyond them. In Augustine's *Confessions*, we have a classic description of both a long effort to achieve communication and comprehension and an individual's sudden sense of a supernatural revelation.

Here in a nutshell we have the difference between religion and religiosity. While the modes of contact of a religion are social institutions, prescribed actions and formulas of belief that can be empirically described and that adherents can therefore perform cooperatively and repeatedly, the modes of contact of religiosity are processes in the consciousness of individuals which they cannot repeat at will or convey effectively to others so that others can repeat them more or less identically. Although individuals who feel they have had meaningful contact with ultra-empirical reality may be able to describe empirically their conduct and beliefs about the cosmos before and after the experience, the actual experiencing of the contact cannot be shared.

In some conversion experiences, such as Augustine's decisive moment or Saul of Tarsus's revelation on the road to Damascus, the contact may seem a divine intervention so unexpected and overwhelming that it is unrepeatable and almost impossible to describe. In mystic experiences, the occurrences are similarly unpredictable, and the resulting sense of communion typically indescribable. The same is true of less dramatic experiences of communion. Since any individual's consciousness of contact, however excited by social stimuli, is necessarily subjective, dependent on personal characteristics, individual experiences, and immediate stimuli, it is necessarily variable. The mental and psychological processes (and the external stimuli) involved cannot be reliably repeated and may be so subconscious or difficult to describe as to be incommunicable. No individual can fully communicate his or her experience to others or prescribe it successfully for them. Whatever the uniformity of social conditioning, there will always be a significant remainder of conditions necessary for the experience that cannot be shared or intelligibly conveyed.

Yet if consciousness of contact may be almost inaccessible to empirical analysis, the context of its occurrence, the environment, and the human condition and actions that preceded and followed such experiences are empirically describable, at least in large measure or in principle. The experiences occur in particular social and cultural environments, are accompanied by describable individual actions, and have consequences for people's conduct thereafter. In principle, therefore, these enabling conditions can be described and examined empirically. In practice, however, it is only in rare cases that historians can describe and analyze in any detail the empirical dimensions of instances of individual consciousness of contact with ultra-empirical reality.

For most of the human past, the paucity of evidence makes it impossible even to delineate the overwhelming bulk of the population as individuals, let alone analyze how their individuality might have molded their consciousness of contact with the ultra-empirical. Even when there is a fair amount of evidence, it usually concerns a few individuals who left enduring traces because of their social importance; and that evidence often concerns their public, frequently official, stands rather than their private thoughts and moods. Historians may labor to collect all the evidence about such individuals and construct some idea of their personality, but the result for anything but the more recent periods is meager.[20]

There are, of course, exceptions. Strangely enough, we may know a lot about the consciousness of ultra-empirical reality of individuals for whom we have almost no concrete biographical information because their literary or artistic works have endured—for example, Sophocles or Shakespeare. More frequently,

20. Robin Lane Fox, *Pagans and Christians* (New York, 1987), provides a dazzling panorama of religious life from the second to the fourth centuries, but, because of the nature of the evidence, we learn much more about religion or public attitudes than about religiosity or individual consciousness.

however, we have considerable knowledge because individuals tried to express their understanding of reality, not through the filter of fiction but directly, philosphers and theologians being an obvious example. Yet even here, Aquinas's exclamation as he neared death, "all I have written seems to me like so much straw compared with what I have seen and with what has been revealed to me,"[21] is a salutary reminder of the difference between didactic prose and living experience. Far more revealing of the consciousness of contact with the empirically unknowable of people in the past are the autobiographies and diaries of mental and psychic development left by rare individuals such as Marcus Aurelius or Augustine of Hippo. Yet these too were written with a purpose and intended for others, and they may omit or pass lightly over experiences that we would consider important but their authors deemed insignificant, irrelevant to the purpose at hand, or improper in the prevailing culture, to say nothing of the impact of those powers of repression of which we are so aware since Freud.

It nonetheless remains true that because of the depth of his self-examination in the *Confessions*, supplemented by his extensive theological writings, we can penetrate further into Augustine's consciousness than that of anyone else in antiquity,[22] and perhaps no one has done so better than Peter Brown.[23] In the terms I am using, Brown has given us a remarkable—and highly empirical—study of an individual's religiosity and demonstrated how unique it was. Thanks to that fairly extensive information about Augustine's social ground, capacities, and highly personal

21. F. C. Copleston, *Aquinas* (Harmondsworth, 1955), p. 10.

22. C. N. Cochrane, *Christianity and Classical Culture* (New York, 1944), pp. 399-455, attributes the "discovery of personality" as a philosophical concept generally to Christianity and specifically to Augustine, but he did not mean that personality or consciousness of individual identity did not exist before Augustine or Jesus, and I am arguing that they have existed as long as society. Augustine's novelty seems to lie in his having conceived of that consciousness in such a way as to make its examination and public expression of profound importance. I am therefore in disagreement with Colin Morris, *The Discovery of the Individual* (New York, 1972), who is able to argue that the discovery of the individual occurred in Western culture between 1050 and 1200 only because he does not distinguish clearly between the social importance attributed to individuality or self-expression and the individual's actual consciousness of being distinct from others.

23. *Augustine of Hippo* (Berkeley and Los Angeles, 1967).

experiences, and thanks also to Brown's sensitive interpretation, how Augustine came to feel in contact with ultra-empirical reality becomes fairly explicable. But far from fully. While we may in varying degrees be able to empathize with Augustine, we none-theless remain aware of how distinctive the complex and contin-uous, though often dramatic, modifications of his highly distinc-tive religiosity were, and how impossible it is for us to be conscious of those experiences as he was.

The plenitude of Augustine's subjective experience of meaning can never be ours, his nonrational understanding can never be ours. We can, however, make objective statements *about* the pre-conditions of those experiences and *about* his expression of them. Indeed, our recognition of the difference between him and our-selves may stimulate us to attempt to explain his experiences in ways that he never did. We know that he had much in common with us as a human being, but also that, because he was himself and of his period, his reactions to and conceptions of natural phe-nomena, geography, people, and so on differed greatly from ours, and that his salient symbols therefore differed from ours. We can then analyze those similarities and differences to provide our own explanation of his experience of contact with ultra-empirical real-ity. At the extreme we might explain aspects of his subjectivity in ways he would never have imagined. While he acknowledged how important his mother was for his development, we might attribute a psychological significance to their relations that he could never imagine—a tactic we apply with little reservation to the religious fantasies of people in the present whom we consider mentally disturbed. In this and other more reputable ways, we can seek to explain some characteristics of his religiosity.

It should be emphasized and reemphasized, however, that these partial explanations do not explain his religiosity away, for in the last analysis, although Augustine was similar to other peo-ple in many ways, his totality and his consequent consciousness of contact with his god were—like that of someone as idiosyncratic as the English poet Christopher Smart—unique. Yet if his life as a whole and the consciousness of contact with ultra-empirical real-ity that accompanied it were unique, the characteristics he shared with others enabled him—so far as his language permitted—to describe many elements of his religiosity with enduring consequences. And, as a vast bibliography testifies, elements of his religiosity have profoundly influenced Christian religiosities and religions to this day.

Because Augustine's introspection and expression of it were highly exceptional in his own day and long after, we can discuss his religiosity objectively in some detail, as we cannot do for multitudes who lacked his opportunities and powers of self-examination and self-expression. For centuries after Augustine, there is remarkably little direct evidence of individual states of consciousness. Only from the eleventh century forward, as Colin Morris has emphasized,[24] does such evidence increase notably, but still only for exceptional men and women—for example, the evidence provided by Hildegard of Bingen and other mystics who focused on their interior states.[25] With the so-called Renaissance, more evidence becomes available. But only with Calvinism and the self-examination it stimulated does rich evidence for less prominent people become noticeably more plentiful.[26] With Romanticism in the late eighteenth century, however, and with the new concern with psychology in the nineteenth, the evidence increases greatly, providing much of the data for William James's novel empirical analysis of religious experiences. And thanks to Freud's technique of free association and other techniques of psychological research, we now have a much greater awareness of the complexity of consciousness and nonrational thinking.

One major result of that far more abundant data is indicated by James's title for his pioneering study: *The Varieties of Religious Experience*. The closer one could examine individual consciousness, the more apparent the diversity of religious experiences or religiosities became. Although social indoctrination and language

24. *The Discovery of the Individual.*

25. See, e.g., John F. Benton, "Consciousness of Self and Perceptions of Individuality," in *Renaissance and Renewal in the Twelfth Century*, ed. Robert L. Benson and Giles Constable (Cambridge, Mass., 1982), pp. 263-295; the fascinating analyses of Caroline Walker Bynum, *Jesus as Mother* (Berkeley, Los Angeles, London, 1982) and *Holy Feast and Holy Fast* (Berkeley, Los Angeles, London, 1987); and the argument for the connection between the new sense of self and the awareness of new boundaries made by Ivan G. Marcus, "Hierarchies, Religious Boundaries and Jewish Spirituality in Medieval Germany," *Jewish History* 1 (1986): 7-26.

26. See, e.g., Paul Seaver, *Wallington's World* (Stanford, 1985).

ensured that people in the same culture used many common symbols to express their religiosity, how and why they associated them as they did clearly varied enormously. And, as is obvious in James, the discovery of that diversity in turn drew attention to the difference between religions and the religious experiences of individuals. But even with that vastly increased evidence for religiosity and the great advances in our knowledge of how the brain and mind function, our ability to examine empirically the stimuli and reactions that form any individual's structure of religiosity remains very limited.

To sum up, the political, economic, social, and cultural conditions, the events, and the biographies that constitute the human ground of both religions and religiosities can, in varying degrees, be described and analyzed empirically. But religions are far more susceptible of objective description and explanation than religiosities, which is doubtless why historians have concentrated on them. Although the referents of the thoughts prescribed by a religion may not be susceptible of empirical validation or invalidation, its authorities and their prescriptions of beliefs about ultra-empirical reality and modes of contact with it are out in common view and can be examined in precise empirical detail. (I am leaving out of consideration the historian's problem of finding sufficient evidence or the anthropologist's problem of finding reliable informants about secret myths and rites.)

Religiosity, however, is not susceptible of direct observation. An individual's consciousness of contact with ultra-empirical reality or realities and the complex internal processes that produce it are psychological or mental events that are not immediately accessible to others. They can be known to others only after they have been socialized, that is, transformed by symbolic expression and represented according to the conventions of some society's language or artistic mode of expression and the expressive abilities of the individual. And even in the case of people as gifted as Augustine or Bach, that expression not only transforms but also filters the experience, giving understandable expression to only some of its multiple components or dimensions.

It follows from the fact that religions are easier to identify and describe empirically than religiosities that it is easier to discuss conflicts between religions than conflicts between religion and religiosity or conflicts between faith and knowledge within an individual's religiosity. Sociopolitical events are out in the open for many to see and leave many traces. We can describe wars of religion in detail. But the religiosity of individuals is not usually a matter of public discussion and leaves few if any traces for the historian to examine.

Even when there is apparently considerable evidence for the religiosity of individuals, it may be misleading. As every medievalist knows, the many medieval biographies of people deemed unusually holy, the "Lives" of saints, were a genre of religious literature that had its own license and sought official approval. It was quite acceptable to borrow items from earlier "Lives" and to omit any details that did not fit the approved models. And even when we do have considerable reliable evidence of religiosity in the past, it is usually only for unusual individuals who were impelled to make a record of their religious reflections or for highly exceptional individuals such as Francis of Assisi and Luther who modified their religion or created a new religion. Yet even though our evidence may be limited and may have been molded to conform to a particular religion, when we do have sufficient evidence, we can usually detect a tension between the religiosity of individuals and their religion.

We can, therefore, describe and analyze empirically religions and the conflicts between them in the past. And as the evidence increases as we approach our own day, we can describe people's religiosity and the conflicts between their religiosity and their religion in more and more detail. But when we examine twentieth-century religions and religiosities and the tensions within and between them, a new problem suddenly arises. What should we count as a religion? What is the difference, if any, between religions and what have been termed surrogate religions?

Chapter Eleven

Physiocentric Religion

Any analysis of antisemitism, especially of the modern period, confronts an apparently empirical historical question. Can the antisemitism expressed in the twentieth century by people who explicitly rejected Christian beliefs be explained in purely secular terms, or was it also a religious by-product? For students of religion in general, the historical issue is whether we are living in an irreligious age. Those questions confront us with a fundamental issue about the categorization of religious phenomena, the one camouflaged by the term "surrogate religion." What has happened to religion in the twentieth century?

Ever since Bernard Lazare, a number of scholars have emphasized the difference between medieval and modern antisemitism, between religious and racial antisemitism. They did so because they thought in conventional terms of the Middle Ages as a religious period and of the nineteenth and twentieth centuries as a predominantly secular period, as have many other scholars, both those who favor the trend and those who deplore it. Thus, sociologists of religion of both persuasions have recently devoted considerable attention to what they label as secularization,[1] and they have usually dismissed phenomena that look remarkably like religious movements, such as Communism and Nazism, as merely secular substitutes for religion, surrogate religions.[2] By my defi-

---

1. See, e.g., Berger, *The Sacred Canopy*, pp. 105-171; Hill, *A Sociology of Religion*, pp. 228-250; Robertson, *The Sociological Interpretation of Religion*, pp. 235-241.
2. Robertson, *The Sociological Interpretation of Religion*, p. 38.

nition of religion and religiosity, however, religious attitudes have been as plentiful in the nineteenth and twentieth centuries as in the thirteenth, and Communism and Nazism can be categorized as religions.

Perhaps the most impressive recent argument that we are living in an increasingly secular age is that of Ernest Gellner in *Nations and Nationalism.*[3] His description of the changes in conditions and mentality in the modern period and his assertion that traditional religions are in decline before the advance of the rational pragmatic spirit are most persuasive, as is his explanation of nationalism. And though he does not deal with religious phenomena in any depth, his analysis of nationalism nonetheless relies on a conception of religion that divides history into a religious and secular period in a fashion reminiscent of Auguste Comte.

Gellner states that nationalism "is *not* the awakening of an old, latent, dormant force, though that is how it does present itself."[4] He asserts that nationalism does not have deep roots in the human psyche, for it is only a rare, recent, and so far brief phenomenon.[5] More generally, he argues that "one may not invoke a *general* substrate to explain a *specific* phenomenon" because the substrate may generate many surface possibilities. "What is crucial for its [nationalism's] genuine explanation is to identify its specific roots. . . . In this way, specific factors are *superimposed* on to a shared universal human substrate."[6]

The argument seems slightly tendentious, especially if the substrate is not clearly specified. True, one may not be able to explain why the Smiths' house was destroyed without identifying that there were matches in the house and a young boy who liked playing with them. But it remains true that oxygen was necessary for it to occur and that what occurred was combustion, not the leveling of the house by an earthquake. Newton would hardly have discovered the law of gravity had he only been concerned to explain why specific kinds of objects fell under specific conditions. And Gellner himself describes nationalism as a widespread and pervasive force, "a flame that springs up so strongly

3. (Ithaca, N.Y., 1981).
4. Ibid., p. 48, Gellner's italics.
5. Ibid., p. 34
6. Ibid., pp. 34-35, my italics.

and spontaneously in so many disconnected places" that it easily becomes "a devouring forest blaze."[7]

Gellner's penetrating analysis of the appearance, characteristics, and future of nationalism is very sociological and political, and also apparently deterministic, despite a brief disclaimer.[8] The agents that determine history, at least the history of nationalism, are political, economic, and sociological trends or abstractions: communities, cultures, societies (preagrarian, agrarian, and industrial), states, markets, industrialism, productivity, education, communication, literacy, education, clerisies, growth (economic and cognitive), mobility, and the like. They explain "why all this must be so."[9] No attention is paid to the variety of social realities that James J. Sheehan has emphasized.[10] The thinking of individuals is considered largely irrelevant in the genesis of nationalism, and nonrational thinking, so far as it is not simply dismissed as false consciousness,[11] only appears as an impediment to peaceful consensus and social entropy.

Gellner conceives of nationalism as the political principle that the political unit or state and the national or ethnic unit (primarily resulting from common language) should be congruent. The sentiment of nationalism is the satisfaction aroused by the satisfaction of that principle or the anger aroused by its violation.[12] He stresses the causal role of universal literacy, communication, priestless unitarianism, egalitarianism, cognitive innovation, and economic and cognitive growth in the emergence of nationalism. Despite the horrors of our times, he considers rational cognition "the secret of the modern spirit." And he defines rationality as follows: "By the common or single conceptual currency I mean that all facts are located within a single continuous logical space, so that statements reporting them can be conjoined and generally

7. Ibid., pp. 125-126.
8. "This attitude [Gellner's] does not spring from any generalized contempt for the role of ideas in history. Some ideas and belief systems do make a very great difference" (ibid., p. 123).
9. Ibid., p. 140.
10. "What Is German History? Reflections on the Role of the *Nation* in German History and Historiography," *Journal of Modern History* 53 (1981): 1-23.
11. *Nations and Nationalism*, pp. 124-125.
12. Ibid., p. 1.

related to each other, and so that in principle one single language describes the world and is internally unitary."[13]

I can only agree with much that Gellner says. I have stressed the importance of rational empirical thinking, and it would be difficult to discuss nationalism in detail without taking into account his analysis of the sociopolitical developments that stimulated nationalistic religiosity. What I miss is any suggestion that nonrational thought plays any fundamental role in directing the use of rational capacities, any mention of Kuhn's analysis of the importance of nonrational factors in scientific advance. And though Gellner emphasizes the importance of language and literacy, there is little consideration of the problems of language and communication and their relation to reality that semioticists have made so obvious, despite the fact that their work is very useful for deciphering how people have conceived their individual and social identity and for understanding religions.[14]

Gellner is little interested in religion. Though it plays a major role in his model of historical progress, his conception of it is highly reductive, not to say harshly negative. In a fashion reminiscent of Comte, Gellner considers religion a dubious legacy from the past. He accepts Durkheim's view "that in religious worship [preindustrial] society adores its own camouflaged image," but he maintains that in the nationalist age, "societies worship themselves brazenly and openly spurning the camouflage." He speaks of the aridity and sterility of medieval Scholastic thought and asserts that "enlightened" modern theologians have little interest in the doctrines of their faith and treat them with a comic auto-functionalism.[15] He apparently thinks of theologies as idiosyncratic cognitive systems that are being gradually dissolved by shared neutral knowledge.[16] He stigmatizes as blinkers repellent to men of liberal tendencies "the self-absolutizing, critic-anathematizing official faiths of late agrarian societies, which indeed are generally so constructed as to be logically invulnerable from outside and

13. Ibid., p. 21.
14. Though he discussed some of those issues brilliantly later: *Culture, Identity, and Politics* (Cambridge, Eng., 1987), pp. 152-184.
15. *Nations and Nationalism*, pp. 26, 56; see also pp. 58, 142.
16. Ibid., pp. 78, 117.

perpetually self-confirming inside."[17] He argues that high cultures need churches to sustain them in agrarian societies but need states in the nationalistic age, and he seems relieved that there has been a transition from "a culture-religion to a culture-state."[18] He speaks of our present society as "a society whose entire political system, *and indeed whose cosmology and moral order*, is based in the last analysis on economic growth, on the hope . . . of a perpetual augmentation of satisfactions,"[19] a position almost identical with that of Stark and Bainbridge.

One problem raised by such language is that of discerning how Gellner distinguishes between culture and religiosity or religion, or between a modern "rational" cosmology and an outdated religious cosmology. Apparently, religions are expressions of the culture of the social elite in preindustrial societies, a culture that is restricted to that elite and functions to adorn and legitimate its coercive social order. By contrast, in modern advanced national states, because of the play of abstract sociological forces, "culture is now the necessary shared medium, the life-blood or perhaps rather the minimal shared atmosphere, within which alone the members of the society can breathe and survive and produce."[20] Yet it is not clear why the cultures of earlier social elites count as religions, while mass culture in the industrial age does not.

Gellner considers culture as fundamental and ever-present and dismisses religions as secondary, time-bound phenomena. But without a clear definition of culture, the distinction is hard to follow. A definition of culture as broad as "a system of ideas and signs and associations and ways of behaving and communicating"[21] assures that religion is an expression of culture, for culture includes everything and anything human beings habitually think and do. But what distinguishes religions from the fashion in clothes? What makes preindustrial culture, but not industrial culture, religious? From my approach, what Gellner describes as

17. Ibid., p. 120.
18. Ibid., pp. 72-73.
19. Ibid., p. 32, italics mine. The distinction between an age of religion and one of mass culture closely resembles Arendt's chronological distinction between religious and racial antisemitism.
20. Ibid., pp. 37-38, 141-142.
21. Ibid., p. 7.

culture in the nationalistic period sounds remarkably like the expression of a range of religiosities that have in common the high value they attribute to rational empirical thinking and pragmatic efficiency but that diverge remarkably in their nonrational symbolizing of self, society, and cosmos.

While I find much of Gellner's analysis highly illuminating, I was struck by its neglect of a phenomenon perhaps more evident in California than in Cambridge, England. In California, which is often thought of as postindustrial society, where mobility has been extreme and economic growth outstanding, and where Silicon Valley is a symbol for logical precision and cognitive expansion, extending even to dreams of artificial intelligence, the advance of the "rational spirit" has been paralleled by the search for a different kind of lifeblood than that described by Gellner. A surprisingly high percentage of the economically favored who are most affected by those social developments attend churches. Although traditional religions are less influential than in many other parts of the world, some 80 percent believe in "God," whatever that symbol means for them. As Californians jog through life to defer death, gurus of various sorts and techniques such as transcendental meditation flourish, and a surprising number of people have sought to give meaning to their lives by joining single-action causes such as antinuclear or animal-rights movements.

What I find lacking is any serious examination of what Gellner calls belief systems, under which rubric he equates what I call religiosity and religions. As nearly as I can make out, he sees them as rationalizations to legitimate the acquisition of scarce goods, and in one sense I agree with him. The social boundaries that individuals symbolize to structure their sense of identity are frontiers on which they depend for material protection and satisfactions. But that is not the only function of social symbols; they also locate. And there are other equally basic needs which those boundaries do not satisfy. There is the need for individual self-esteem—which helps explain why no amount of material possessions is ever enough and prestige is so valued. There is the desire for power, which is not only a means of acquiring possessions but also an expression of self-determination and the desire for its recognition. And underlying both of those is the need for self, for that certainty of individual identity amidst an infinity of transactions with the known and unknown that has led some people to spurn all but the minimum of material goods and others even to choose death.

Gellner emphasizes and reemphasizes that the rational spirit and a technology that can liberally satisfy material needs have drastically altered mentality in industrial societies. He argues that those developments are moving people toward a universal—nonreligious—culture in which, although languages may differ in phonemes and vocabulary, life and thought will be largely standardized.[22] Nonetheless, he doubts that all barriers to communication will disappear. He acknowledges that "some measure of patriotism is indeed a perennial part of human life"[23] and expects that "an international plurality of sometimes fairly diverse high cultures will no doubt (happily) remain with us" because of the infrastructural investment already made in them and their coincidence with national boundaries.[24] But he does not make clear why he is happy that divisions between certain "independence-worthy"[25] cultures are likely to endure, nor does he examine the source of their durability.

He acknowledges that formidable barriers and fissures do inhibit the trend to social homogeneity or entropy: genetic differences associated with social disadvantages; the limpetlike persistence of clusters of "intimate and pervasive values"; conspicuous social inequalities; and, to a much lesser degree, differences of language.[26] Yet, though he recognizes "that some deeply engrained religious-cultural habits possess a vigour and tenacity which can *virtually equal* those which are rooted in our genetic composition,"[27] he does not explain why they are so strong. Though well aware that competition for scarce goods and wars are commonplaces of history and are prominent features of the industrial age, he pays remarkably little attention to the attitudes that create social and cultural boundaries and cause conflicts.

With its emphasis on the rational spirit and lack of interest in

22. Ibid., pp. 114-122.
23. Ibid., p. 138.
24. Ibid., p. 121.
25. Ibid., p. 119.
26. Ibid., pp. 67-75.
27. Ibid., p. 71, italics mine.

nonrational and irrational thinking, Gellner's model of modern social psychology is of little use in explaining the appearance of new religions in industrial societies. It is of even less use in explaining the localized, if all too broad, phenomenon of the "Final Solution" in a highly industrialized society. If social mobility enabled by the spread of the rational pragmatic spirit is, as he argues, the most powerful trend in recent history, then the "Final Solution" should not have happened. Not only were Jews in Germany leading exemplars of that spirit and mobility, but Germany was a highly industrialized society when Hitler emerged, and the Nazis were not adherents of an old religion.

What seems lacking is an analysis of consciousness. Or rather, the analysis emphasizes rational cognition and disregards nonrational and irrational thinking, simply dismissing them as false consciousness. But there is no such thing as false consciousness; individuals either are conscious or they are not. Even if we describe someone as semiconscious, we do not mean they are falsely conscious. The ideas a person expresses may be judged false by some present or later standard of rational empiricism, but they are nonetheless expressions of real consciousness. Moreover and more important, they only express part of it, for consciousness always involves more than rational empirical thought. Not only is nonrational thinking part of our consciousness; it guides our use of our rational empirical capacities. For one person to express his own religiosity by condemning another's as false consciousness is a case of the stove calling the kettle black.

The fissures and barriers that impede a universal culture of rationality are not merely the result of past social inequalities and traditional religions, important though those have been. They are rooted in basic human characteristics that have been present throughout history and are as active as they ever were. For Gellner, religions are crippling legacies from the past; religious thought and action are outmoded in modern industrial societies and will be of even less importance in the future. Yet if we distinguish between religion and religiosity, the religious future is less clear. As Gellner knows, and as those who worry about "secularization" fear, religions have disappeared, and even the most deeply institutionalized literate religions are in decline. Yet if people can live without religion and religions are not necessary characteristics of societies, the same cannot be said of religiosity. Hence, the potential for new religions is still present, which brings us to the problem of "surrogate religions."

Communism and Nazism resemble traditional religions in so many ways that they are often called surrogate religions. Unfortunately, scholars of religion have not paid close attention to them, even as a basis for comparison and even though a main topic of their recent discussions has been the trend denoted as secularization. Most have avoided the problem by definitional prescription. Since they define religions as beliefs about "gods" or the "sacred"; and since the so-called surrogate religions explicitly deny the existence of gods or a supernatural realm in the customary sense, they decide that "surrogate religions" are not religions and therefore do not require their close attention.

Yet if one defines religion solely in present rational empirical explanatory terms, that sharp distinction disappears. Some scholars have therefore categorized "surrogate religions" as religions.[28] Even Stark and Bainbridge, who deny that they are genuine religions, found it necessary to pay serious attention to them precisely because of their effort to analyze religion in purely rational and empirical terms.[29] For my part, I shall disagree both with those who deny that any "surrogate religion" is a religion and with those who count them all, including nationalism, as religions. I will argue that dogmatic Marxism and Nazism are religions but that nationalism is not.

As Léon Poliakov has remarked, "The notion of religion is so hard to define that it is sometimes difficult in retrospect to draw a clear dividing line between religion and nationalism as between religion and scientism."[30] But the line is easier to draw if we define religions as societies whose authorities explicitly prescribe nonrational beliefs, if we distinguish religiosity sharply from religion, and if we refuse to confuse the religiosity from which a

28. Or at least as functionally equivalent to a religion. See, e.g., Ward E. Goodenough, "Toward an Anthropological Definition of Religion," in *Changing Perspectives in the Scientific Study of Religion* (New York, 1974), pp. 168–169, 189, and, with serious reservations, Yinger, *The Scientific Study of Religion*, pp. 196–200, 584.

29. See above, chap. 5.

30. *The Aryan Myth* (New York, 1974), p. 304.

religion emerges with the religion that is later prescribed. From this perspective, scientism and nationalism are not religions; they are prominent changes in the religiosity of most Europeans— whether Catholic, Protestant, or atheist—in recent centuries.

By the sixteenth century, Christendom was crumbling both institutionally and mentally. Thereafter, western Europeans were increasingly divided in religiosity and between different Christian religions, and Christian religions were increasingly challenged by expressions of new types of religiosity. The names of Machiavelli, Luther, Galileo, Hobbes, Descartes, Locke, Newton, Hume, Rousseau, Condorcet, Kant, Adam Smith, Darwin, Hegel, Comte, Marx, Freud, Weber, and Einstein are only some obvious signposts of the radical changes in mentality we summarize by labels such as "Renaissance," "Reformation," "Capitalism," "Scientific Revolution," "Enlightenment," and "Industrialism." To them could be added the signposts of technological advance, starting with that classic trio, gunpowder, the printing press, and the compass, and ending with the atomic bomb, the pill, the computer, and genetic engineering.

Perhaps the most important change in religiosity in recent centuries has been the value increasingly placed on rational empirical thinking and its practical application. Striking demonstrations of its reach and power, particularly in the physical sciences, made its value so obvious that a growing number of educated people and doubtless many others who were less educated came to value their rational empirical capacities in ways that decisively altered the hold of traditional beliefs. They felt that nonrational beliefs should not inhibit their capacity to think rationally and empirically about anything that interested them. They expanded the range of their rational empirical thinking ever more widely and allowed it to exercise a veto over nonrational beliefs in ever broader domains. And despite their differing and changing beliefs, the knowledge that resulted was significantly cumulative and very disturbing. Not only did it challenge many traditional beliefs, it fundamentally changed the conditions under which people lived.

In the countries most affected, the pragmatic application of new rational and empirical techniques dramatically increased material resources, improved knowledge, extended communications, and enlarged social organizations. As a result, people in the modern period became increasingly disembedded—to use another of Giddens's terms. Where before people had trusted the security provided from birth by their nest of kinship groups and familiar localities, now they had to depend increasingly on relations, ultimately global relations, with people they had never known and localities they had never seen. The segmentary boundaries that had theretofore organized their social lives were dissolving; and as they did, their old ways of symbolizing their social identity began to lose their force. To preserve their sense of identity, people had to symbolize their social identity in new ways. And because their confidence in their social identity was threatened, they reacted by expressing an ancient characteristic of religions and religiosity—sociocentrism and ethnocentricism—in a new and strident way.

We are so accustomed to thinking of monotheistic religions with their self-proclaimed universality as the highest and most evolved form of religion that we often forget one of the most obvious characteristics of religions, the one Durkheim emphasized. Societies tend to have their own religions, or at least their own variant of a religion, and religions are societies. Most religions throughout history have supported the identity of particular peoples and their social hierarchies, and most peoples have had their own religion. That was taken for granted in antiquity, and the first enduring monotheism was the religion of a people who believed themselves chosen. Moreover, the distinctive characteristics of particular societies are reflected in their distinctive religious symbols. Though religions may be expansive, they have a social and cultural base.

One of the earliest components of religiosity is the way young people symbolize the boundaries of their immediate physical and social transactions. As their experience widens, their religiosity acquires broader temporal and spatial dimensions and uses more symbols, but those primary symbolic associations—between self, warmth, stomach, mother, father, sister, uncle, love, hate, family, home, good, bad, and so on—remain remarkably powerful and, however subconsciously, attract others into their orbit. Since religiosity is the structuring and coordinating of all that the individual experiences, there is, as Freud and many others have insisted, a constant impulse to coordinate the later symbolizing of

broader experience with that primary symbolization—both positive and negative—of the most immediate human relations. In
other words, religiosity is initially not only self-centered but
highly sociocentric and ethnocentric. And the religiosity of many,
perhaps most, individuals remains so throughout their lives. Unlike prophets, theologians, monks, and metaphysicians, whose
talk or silence focuses on infinity to give meaning to the here and
now, the horizons of most people's religiosity stay close at hand.
The most salient symbols of greatest affective power are those for
self, family, and immediate society, while the socially provided
symbols for what lies beyond that immediate horizon become salient only during rituals or in times of crisis.

Because sociocentrism and ethnocentrism are such prominent
features of most people's religiosity, they have always exerted a
steady pressure on or rather within religions. Sometimes, when
sociopolitical developments weaken old social boundaries and
bring new ones into existence or when individuals form new
cosmic ideas, as in the time of Paul, the religiosity of some individuals may condemn ethnocentrism, and religions can appear
which proclaim their universality. But the prevalence of religiosity
that accords high value to symbols of distinctive social and cultural
identity continually pressures religious authorities to formulate
their religion so that its symbols reinforce valued social and ethnic
boundaries. Even apparently universal religions easily become
barely camouflaged imperialisms.

Nowhere is this more obvious than in Christianity with its early
division into religions with political, linguistic, social, and gender
boundaries and, in western Europe, its emphasis on Rome. Even
when the papal victory in the eleventh century temporarily over-
came the early medieval Christian religions supportive of particular peoples and proclaimed a European Catholic religion, that
development was accompanied by an even clearer split between
Greek-speaking and Latin-speaking Christians and open war
against Islam. And despite the apparent triumph of an international religion within western Europe, by the late thirteenth century the pressure of sociocentric and ethnocentric religiosity was
once more legitimating the religious authority of kings and splitting European Christendom. Thanks to the support of their subjects, Edward I of England and Philip IV of France were able to

challenge papal authority successfully; and during the schism and conciliar movement, Europe divided on religious issues according to political divisions.

There is no better example of Christian religiosity supportive of the supreme social authority of kings than that of Joan of Arc. She believed she had a divine mission to free France from the English by military victory and have the dauphin crowned at Reims. Her god legitimated her king, and she died at the stake because she would not abandon the faith that gave her life meaning. Thereafter, she became a symbol of France. Although Voltaire mocked her legend, by the late nineteenth century she was the symbol and heroine of France both for Catholics and for agnostics or atheists, for Péguy and Claudel as for Michelet and Anatole France. No wonder Marina Warner titled the last chapter of her study, "Saint or Patriot?"[31] Patriotism is indeed a perennial part of human life, as Gellner stated, because it is an expression of religiosity. But it is only one way of symbolizing social identity under particular conditions; under other conditions, fundamental social identity may be symbolized by the tribe, the city, or the nation.

By the sixteenth century, a new theory of the divine right of kings had been formulated, and several kings and princes were deciding which Christian religion their subjects should observe. As in the early Middle Ages, Christian religions were supportive of particular kingdoms. Thus, well before industrialism and the appearance of nationalistic religiosity in the nineteenth century, the religiosity of many Christians was infused with patriotism and very supportive of the authority of kings over their subjects and territories. Then, as kings fell or became primarily symbols of a highly integrated society and its common culture, legitimated by the history of that people rather than by the authority of "God," Christian patriotism became Christian nationalism. Indeed, by the late nineteenth century, Christian and national symbols had been so closely associated in the religiosity of many adherents of Christian religions that it is difficult to know whether to describe them as nationalistic Christians, Christian nationalists, or simply

31. Warner, *Joan of Arc*, pp. 255-275.

nationalists who went to church and worshiped their society there, as Durkheim in effect said they did.

If religiosity is the salient structure according to which individuals consciously correlate their experiences to maintain their distinctive identity, then nationalism is the expression of one, but only one, function or dimension of religiosity—its symbolizing of social identity under particular historical conditions. The associations of nationalism symbolized people's social identity but not the cosmic processes on which they depended for their identity as individuals. Consequently, nationalism was fully compatible with adherence to religions that provided cosmic reassurances of identity and promised personal salvation. Manifestly, it was compatible with Christian religions. When the symbols of people's identity as Spanish, French, English, German, and so on became as important in their religiosity as Christian symbols or more so, most people did not abandon their churches and Christian beliefs. Even when "Motherland," "the Flag," and other symbols used to express the distinctive character of their culture and society became more salient than Christian symbols, Christian symbolic associations and beliefs could still be very salient, as they were in England.

The triumphant words of Gilbert and Sullivan's song, "For he is an Englishman," did not mean their hero was not a Christian. A proper Englishman was Christian. Indeed, one reason England proved so well adapted to this period was that there was little conflict between the old and new symbols, for there had long been a distinctively English church. Since the dominant Christian religion of England was English, controlled by its government and widely accepted by its subjects, most English people were unaware of any conflict between their Christianity and their nationalism. Perhaps that is why most felt little need to search for new symbolic definitions of their social identity and were so immune to the appeal of the new physiocentric religions of Communism or Nazism. It was so easy to think of English virtues and strength as power given by their god.

> God of our fathers, known of old—
> Lord of our far-flung battle-line—
> Beneath whose awful Hand we hold
> Dominion over palm and pine—

> Lord God of hosts, be with us yet,
> Lest we forget, lest we forget.[32]

Ironically, the fourth line of Kipling's "Recessional" (1897) associates the English with the triumphal hopes of Solomon and the Jews of Psalm 72 (Vulgate 71)—and with the Catholic conception of the triumph of Christ and their church which was so important to Peter the Venerable and led him into one of the feeblest rationalizations in his treatise against the Jews. Kipling also distinguished between "we," the English, and the "Gentiles" or lesser breeds without the Law, metaphors that associated traditional Jewish and Christian symbols with the salient symbols of English nationalism.

The same use of traditional but less explicitly Christian religious symbols is evident in Rupert Brooke's "The Soldier" (1915). So also is the "divine grace" of England.

> If I should die, think only this of me:
> That there's some corner of a foreign field
> That is forever England. There shall be
> In that rich earth a richer dust conceal'd;
> A dust whom England bore, shaped, made aware,
> Gave, once, her flowers to love, her ways to roam,
> A body of England's, breathing English air.
> And think, this heart, all evil shed away,
> A pulse in the eternal mind, no less
> Gives somewhere back the thoughts by England given;
> Her sights and sounds; dreams happy as her day;
> And laughter, learnt of friends; and gentleness,
> In hearts at peace, under an English heaven.[33]

In England, a royal Christian religion blended so easily with nationalist religiosity that Westminster Abbey was a shrine for both kinds of religiosity. But in other countries, Christian and nationalist symbolizations of social identity could come in conflict because Christian religions did not coincide closely with political boundaries or were associated with class divisions.

During the French revolution, many nationalists in the country

---

32. *The Oxford Book of English Verse, 1250-1918*, ed. Sir Arthur Quiller-Couch (Oxford, 1939), p. 1076.

33. Ibid., p. 1134.

of Voltaire came to reject the dominant Catholic religion explicitly. Prayers to "Notre Père qui est aux cieux" were replaced by "Allons enfants de la patrie," and many of those children came to view Catholicism with deep suspicion, in no small part because it was not purely French. Moreover, the Catholic authorities had opposed the revolution, and Catholicism was closely linked with the social barriers the revolutionaries fought to overthrow. The new nationalist religiosity therefore tended to be heavily "laïque," explicitly rejecting the symbols of the old religion and creating new ones of its own.

Saint Joan of France and the bellicose Marianne had no bodies to be enshrined, but art made them symbolically ever-present. And in the Pantheon, the bodies of other saints of "la Patrie reconnaissante," including Voltaire, Lazare Carnot, and Emile Zola, the defender of Dreyfus, were brought to cohabit cryptically with the Christian symbols that no depictions of France's past could avoid. The religiosity of most people, both those who were and those who were not Catholic, became overwhelmingly nationalistic and professedly rationalistic ("c'est logique"), sometimes with strange results. Many firm adherents of Catholicism have been not only strongly nationalistic but also firm supporters of the "laïque" educational system.

German nationalism had a much more painful birth. England and France had been politically united societies with one overwhelmingly dominant Christian religion for centuries. Germans entered the nineteenth century politically and religiously divided. They were linked by a common language and the culture it carried, but for centuries they had only had a facade of political unity, and Napoleon destroyed even that. Even when Germany was united in 1871, its boundaries neither included all contiguous German-speakers nor eliminated the strong regional loyalties within the formerly autonomous territories. "Symptomatic of these signs of the continued incompleteness of Germany was the difficulty of finding any agreement on the question of national symbols."[34] At first, Bismarck, the creator of the new Germany, was the principal symbol; only after the national trauma of World War I was "Deutschland, Deutschland über alles" made the na-

34. Gordon A. Craig, *Germany 1866-1945* (Oxford, 1980), p. 58.

tional anthem. The very stridency of many German expressions of nationalism reflected the fact that Germany has had a serious problem of national identity since 1867.

National identity was even more of a problem in the Austro-Hungarian Empire. The Hapsburg monarchy ruled over a variety of ethnically diverse peoples whose growing nationalism spurred movements for independence. The monarchy tried to offset those centrifugal tendencies by favoring its German subjects and emphasizing its Catholicism, but it was undermined from within by the struggles for independence of its non-German subjects and the opposition of liberals, and it was challenged externally by competition with, and the attraction of, the triumphant Germany of 1867. *Grossdeutsch* nationalists such as Georg Schönerer sought union with Bismarck's Germany, while Austrian nationalists such as Karl Lueger worked to develop a Catholic Austrian nation.[35] Challenged on all sides, the monarchy could not stand the strains of the First World War and was dissolved in 1918. Yet if the greatly reduced Austrian republic that emerged in 1919 was far more homogeneous ethnically, and if the dominant religiosity of most Austrians was both Catholic and nationalistic, there was still bitter hostility between Catholics and nonbelieving socialists, and between those whose Pan-Germanism favored union with Germany and those whose Catholicism favored an independent and Catholic Austria—some even to the extent of seeking the return of the Hapsburgs.

Nationalism came even later to the Russian empire. During the nineteenth century, it was very backward in social and political organization in comparison with developments in western Europe. Religion and government were tightly linked; the social hierarchy was very inflexible; and the population was ethnically very diverse. For most of the nineteenth century, the religiosity of the illiterate masses in Russia, so far as it was not purely local, was a patriotic Christianity that focused on the Tsar and was encouraged by the highly Christian "Official Nationalism" he supported,[36] not the nationalistic religiosity so prevalent in western

35. Carl E. Schorske, *Fin-de-siècle Vienna* (New York, 1981), pp. 116-146.
36. See, e.g., Nicholas V. Riasanovsky, *Nicholas I and Official Nationality in Russia, 1825-1855* (Berkeley and Los Angeles, 1959) and *A Parting of the*

Europe. Opposition before World War I, like so many other developments in Russia, was inspired by socially revolutionary ideas
from western Europe rather than by nationalist sentiments—although the relatively small number of Slavophiles came close. Nor
were the leaders of the revolution of 1917 strongly influenced by
nationalist sentiments.

Although the revolution was certainly a political revolution with
international consequences, it was above all a social revolution
that overthrew the old authorities and their symbols. Christian
and royalist symbols were rejected even more completely than in
France not only because the new authorities were Marxists but
also because the Tsar was closely associated with Russian Orthodox Christianity and the old social hierarchy. But the old symbols
were not immediately replaced by nationalist ones. The symbols
of the new regime were initially explicitly internationalist. Only
after the new totalitarian dictators had imposed their beliefs on
their Soviet citizens, and after the regime had faced great foreign
opposition and been subjected to internal ethnocentric pressures,
did something closely resembling nationalism in western Europe
emerge in the Soviet Union, and even then, as is so apparent
now, it was in competition with regional ethnic loyalties.

Nationalist symbols became increasingly prominent in people's
religiosity in Europe in the nineteenth and early twentieth centuries, affecting adherents of different religions and those with
none. Expressions of nationalism were often replete with traditional religious symbolism. In harmony with Christian religiosity,
nationalism emphasized the progressive and "providential" un-
folding of history. It was the strident expression in response to
new political, technological, and social conditions of a primeval
function of religiosity, the symbolization of the social and ethnic
frontiers of individual identity. And because its symbols fulfilled
only one of the functions of religiosity, it could be expressed by
those who adhered to different religions and those who adhered
to none.

The fact that it was so widespread and vocal by the early twentieth century may partly explain why Durkheim asserted that re-

---

Ways (Oxford, 1976), and Léon Poliakov, *La causalité diabolique* (Paris, 1980-
1985), 2: 88-92, 102-107.

ligion was in effect people's worship of their society. From my point of view, Durkheim was right in recognizing what surrounded him as a religious phenomenon but wrong in categorizing it as religion. When he wrote that religion was above all "a system of ideas with which *individuals* represent to themselves the society of which they are members, and the obscure but intimate relations they have with it,"[37] he was—if we change "ideas" to "nonrational symbols"—describing what I would call religiosity. Yet he was only describing one aspect of religiosity, since it also involves symbolization of self and ultra-empirical reality. Moreover, he simplified matters even further by confusing that partial dimension of religiosity with all religion.

He was able to equate religiosity and religion, the property of individuals and the characteristic of societies, because he attributed consciousness to society and made individual beliefs dependent on it. He maintained that society had a collective consciousness that inspired beliefs in individuals. But that puts the cart before the horse. Consciousness only occurs in individuals. Though members of a society may hold many similar nonrational beliefs, they are not identical, and we may only speak of an aggregate of similar attitudes. Only when the authorities of a society formulate nonrational beliefs as ideas and compel adherents to conform to them do those ideas become a defining characteristic of the society. And by that criterion, nationalism alone was never a religion.

Nineteenth-century governments did not institute religions of nationalism. Politicians did express nationalist attitudes, and governments appealed to them and established rituals that reinforced them in order to justify taxes and military sacrifice. Yet, although governments exerted pressure against opinions they disliked, they neither formulated nor prescribed beliefs about the creation of the nation or about ultra-empirical forces on which it allegedly depended. Even when revolutionaries sought to establish their own government of a nation, their declarations were primarily concerned with political, not religious, norms; their constitutions dealt in detail with the organization of human government, not with cosmic forces and proper worship of them.

---

37. *The Elementary Forms of Religious Life*, p. 257, my italics.

The American Declaration of Independence said that all men were created equal and endowed with "inalienable rights" by the "Creator," but promptly prescribed religious liberty as one of those rights. The French Declaration of the Rights of Man and the Citizen assumed a "Supreme Being," pronounced that men and citizens had "sacred" rights, and alluded to Rousseau's mythical conception of the general will, but one of the sacred rights it declared was the right to speak, write, and publish freely. The Declaration of the Rights of the German People in 1848 did not even allude to a supernatural power; to the contrary, it declared that no one had to reveal his religious convictions and that everyone could practice his religion in public or private. Though these declarations relied heavily on the abstract ideas of political theorists such as Locke and Rousseau, their references to ultra-empirical realities were strikingly elliptical, and they left large liberty to the citizens to believe as they wished. Also significant, since convictions about history were so important in nationalist attitudes, they made little allusion to historical events; they simply assumed political frontiers.

If we are looking for what might be called credos of nationalistic religiosity, diffuse though they were, we have to turn to the rhetoric in which individuals such as Maurice Barrès, Heinrich von Treitschke, Giuseppe Mazzini, and others expressed their religiosity. They and many other lesser figures expressed their nationalism vigorously and formed cultlike movements to express and spread their convictions. The movements resembled political parties but differed from them. They included people of different parties, and many were called leagues, apparently to differentiate them from the pragmatic realpolitik competition between particular interests within the nation.

Yet if the oratory and publications of these nationalists included allusions aplenty to the workings of "God," "Reason," and "race" in history, they did not define beliefs about those forces and they created no new religions. Unlike the Christian view of history, their nationalistic history was not based on any cosmic premises of its own; it relied on existing beliefs, which was why it could blend into traditional religions. And though many governments, supported by intense social pressure, came very close to prescribing dogmatic beliefs about national history and the superiority of the nation around the end of the nineteenth century, especially during World War I,[38] none clearly crossed the line.

History was important to nationalists because it revealed the nation's origins and advance. But if historical thinking can subserve religiosity, it also influences it, for it is the meeting place of rational empirical and nonrational thinking. Perhaps nowhere are religion and the results of rational empirical thinking more inextricably intertwined than in the writing of history, at least in the West with its historically oriented religions, for in no other intellectual endeavor, except perhaps adjudication, are the two modes of thinking so intimately involved. Even as an academic discipline, historiography discusses values, straddles the humanities and the social sciences, and is divided between proponents of history as literature and history as science or, at present, between exponents of historiography as narrative and of historiography as analysis.

History and religion overlap and compete. Not only do Christian—and Judaic—religions provide myths of origin that biologists and geologists can dispute, they make assertions about the direction, dynamics, and details of history that historians can dispute. Conversely, historical scholarship describes where individuals and groups originated and how they came to be as they are today. On a limited scale, histories respond to some of the same questions that religions claim to answer. And since historians have their own religiosity, they may create their own myths of origin or reinforce myths created by others.

As I insisted at the outset, what makes the connection between religion and historiography so inextricable is that historians cannot avoid discussing religion. Biologists may dispute religious beliefs, as Thomas H. Huxley did so vehemently, but they can pursue their work without ever referring to religious phenomena. Historians cannot. Try as they may to be objective and to set aside their religious conditioning and ethnic or national prejudices, they have to deal with religious ideas and actions. Most historians are forced to make explicit assertions about religious phenomena be-

38. By that I mean positive prescriptions of belief, not the efforts of governments to censor expressions of attitudes of which they disapproved, such as those in Germany between 1871 and 1918; see Craig, *Germany 1866-1945*, pp. 199-206.

cause those they study made their religious convictions explicit, and other historians make implicit judgments when they assume that the historical actions they describe were unaffected by religious beliefs. Even when historians bracket religion by using traditional religious language to categorize and describe religious conduct, offering little explanation of their own of that conduct and leaving it up to their readers to understand it as they wish, they are making a decision about religion, however tacit.

Historiography reflects religiosity, and changes in religiosity find expression in histories, as is obvious from nineteenth-century historiography. Foreshadowed in the eighteenth century, the nineteenth century saw a great increase in historical writing that was little concerned with Christian themes and often anti-ecclesiastical or even anti-Christian. In the second half of the century, the belief in "scientific" historiography almost completely expelled Christian conceptions of providence from the historians' domain and replaced them with national myths. History became an academic discipline; historians acquired new social importance; governments supported historical research and archival revelation; and historical education came to be organized along political lines to explain the evolution of nations.

Many, perhaps most, historians, especially those who attracted the widest audiences, devoted themselves to their own national past—as many still do. And those who were most conscious of their national identity—especially the more literary historians who gave free rein to their religiosity—wrote what we now recognize as highly nationalistic histories. In the fashion now condemned as Whig history, they recounted myths of origin and became the retrodictive prophets for the dramatic epiphanies and noble victories over evil of the nation. Their message passed to the politicians and schoolmasters who drew on their writings to deliver "homilies" for national salvation enriched with many historical references. Yet, although governments supported historians and historical indoctrination, historians did not create national religions; though they greatly influenced people's religiosity, they were not recognized as social authorities. What might seem to be religions of nationalism only appeared in the twentieth century when people exercising social authority claimed privileged access to a new understanding of cosmic reality and prescribed that history be rewritten according to their beliefs.

The new nonrational beliefs on which they relied reflected the value attributed to rational empirical thought. Ever since the sixteenth century, a small but growing and increasingly influential number of Europeans had placed a very high value on their capacity to think rationally and empirically. Their conclusions disturbed many members of the social elite, particularly those exercising traditional religious authority. And if it was disturbing enough when rational empiricism introduced ideas about the natural world which raised doubts about traditional religious beliefs, it became much more disturbing when those techniques were applied to human relations in general—to politics, economics, social organization, and human beings themselves. By the nineteenth century, especially with emergence of the social sciences, the results of the new religiosity in which the symbols of rational empirical thinking were so salient had become clearly revolutionary, encouraging atheism and opening prospects of an uncertain future very different from the more or less stable cosmos people had imagined before.

In reaction to that uncertainty, some nineteenth-century thinkers of a theoretical turn of mind developed new theories about human development and salvation—Hegelianism, Marxism, social Darwinism, and Aryanism—which, like Christianity, suggested new certainties. Initially their theories were only presented, however apodictically, as the outcome of rational empirical thought or metaphysical speculation. Nonetheless, like all paradigmatic changes, their theories were motivated by nonrational beliefs and made assertions about realities well beyond rational empirical verification. So long as they were only regarded as hypotheses open to criticism, they were impressive rationalizations of religiosity of greater or lesser heuristic value for further inquiry, not religions. They developed into religions only when people who thirsted for new certainties began to accept their theories as gospel and to rationalize their experiences and act according to their new beliefs.

The spread of religiosity that prized objectivity so highly, undermined traditional beliefs, and disturbingly disregarded social frontiers had provoked a reaction with destructive implications for rational empirical thinking itself. If many welcomed—in varying degrees—the new ways of thinking and the possibilities they opened, many others felt deeply threatened, for the advance and application of rational empirical knowledge was undermining their sense of identity. And though they too were influenced by the social value now attributed to rational empirical thinking, they used the new techniques of knowledge very differently.

Many people were impelled, again in varying degrees, not to be objective but to appear so. They were concerned not to strive for objectivity but to use and manipulate the new rational empirical techniques so that the results would support beliefs that affirmed their distinctive social or ethnic identity. Since they could not ignore the changes around them, they reinterpreted them to suit themselves. Appealing very selectively to new knowledge, they modified their symbols of social identity, of their reference groups, to affirm their distinctive identity more broadly than before but still as narrowly as possible. Most symbolized themselves as members of a nation, but many did not find that foundation sufficiently all-encompassing or cosmic. Instead, thanks to the new theories about class and race, they were able to symbolize themselves also or even primarily as something that transcended time and space, as members of a class or race, thereby attributing a cosmic significance to their identity that transcended national boundaries.

Already before World War I, "true believers" in the Marxist and Aryan theories were forming movements that resembled cults or sects and preparing the way for the imposition of new religions in Russia and Germany after the war. Govermental Marxism and Nazism fulfilled the functions of a religion and had similar characteristics—prophets, canonical texts, martyrs, shrines, rituals, and the heavily indoctrinated priesthoods of their controlling parties. Lenin and Stalin dogmatically prescribed—to put it mildly— belief in dialectical materialism and promised a future classless paradise. They imposed on Soviet citizens a set of nonrational beliefs about the causes of good and evil, about their identity and salvation, and about the privileged role of the Soviet Union in the cosmic process. Hitler similarly promulgated a set of nonrational beliefs about his subjects' identity and future, including

belief in the purity of pure Aryan blood and a millennial Reich—
a myth already deeply suffused with German nationalism. The
governments of both societies thus formulated and prescribed beliefs about entities, forces, and states whose existence, like that
of the Christian Father, Son, Holy Spirit, and paradise, had never
been empirically established. And we should emphasize that despite the value both sets of beliefs attributed to a particular country, they were based on a faith or premises that purported to
provide the meaning of the whole human condition and the direction of all human life.

Since Lenin, Stalin, and Hitler very forcefully ordered their
followers to organize their lives according to a prescribed set of
explicitly formulated nonrational ideas or beliefs, Soviet Marxism
and Hitler's Nazism are religions by my definition. Their beliefs,
which could not be publicly questioned, defined the distinctive
identity of their adherents and laid down how they should think
and act. They reified or dogmatized what had once been debatable hypotheses about cosmic forces as indisputable ontologies
like those of traditional religions. Common to both was the effort
to control thought, to subordinate their adherents' capacity for
rational empirical thinking to expressions of nonrational thinking
explicitly prescribed by the government. Common also was their
adherents' faith in their authorities' privileged understanding of
reality.

The parallels with traditional religions are obvious. Nonetheless, most scholars do not classify dogmatic Marxism and Nazism
as genuine religions because they did not proclaim the existence
of "gods" in the customary sense and because their adherents ad-
amantly refused to recognize the existence of a supernatural
realm.[39] They seemed concerned only with the triumph of the
proletariat or the victory of the Aryans in this world rather than
the salvation of souls in some otherworldly paradise. Yet the difference is not black and white. Earthly concerns do not clearly
distinguish so-called surrogate religions from traditional religions.
Many traditional religions have been greatly concerned with this
world, and some have paid little attention to any other. Moreover,

---

39. For discussions of the issue, see Robertson, *The Sociological Interpretation of Religion*, pp. 38-42, and Wilson, *A Sociology of Religion*, pp. 243-244.

the Marxists and Nazis did promise a future paradise for the collectivity in which the memory of the individuals who strove for it would be preserved.

Surrogate religions may deny there is life in the usual sense after death, yet there is still the penumbra of an afterlife. It is reflected in assertions that individuals did not live and die in vain. Whether said in praise of those who died in a war, revolution, or labor conflict, the thought reflects the conviction that, although cosmic processes may be mindlessly impersonal, human beings, individually and collectively, are part of those processes and will endure in their effects. Without their contribution the cosmos would be somewhat different. Life continues, if not individuals, and the future is potentially paradise.

There is, however, a fundamental difference. Almost all traditional religions have attributed consciousness and intentions to unobservable forces with which they believed they could communicate; believers in the so-called surrogate religions do not. They explicitly deny the existence of any radically different realm of being controlled by unobservable conscious forces. They deny any difference between what they can observe in nature and the ultimate forces and unobservable entities in which they believe. And they believe that the unrolling of history will only provide further revelations of the underlying or transcendent processes whose effects they can observe directly here and now.

The fundamental difference between traditional and so-called surrogate religions is that the ultimate or transcendent processes proclaimed by the latter may be meaningful for human beings but are themselves mindless as a stone. They have direction but not intention; they produce effects of which they are not conscious. Like the gods, they are immensely powerful: human existence depends on them, and human salvation consists in acting in harmony with them. But they are not "gods" for they lack willpower. Alone in the cosmos, human beings are conscious and have willpower, and even their willpower may be an illusion.

With the development of science and the appearance of the so-called surrogate religions, the old problem of free will and determination was rephrased. Where the issue for centuries after Augustine had been whether "God" determined all that would happen and whether salvation was predetermined or at least partially dependent on the exercise of human will, the issue that now arose was whether the physical processes of the cosmos determined all that happened and whether belief in human free will was a delusion or unimportant epiphenomenon. As Isaiah Berlin put it, "For Hegel, for Marx, for Spengler (and for almost all thinkers for whom history is 'more' than past events, namely a theodicy) this reality takes on the form of an objective 'march of history.' "[40] We should note, however, that Berlin uses customary religious language here, and that it is misleading; when mindless cosmic processes, not "gods," explain human suffering and salvation, such beliefs can be called a theodicy only metaphorically.[41] Though the cosmic processes these historicists assert may be orderly and creative, they have neither consciousness nor purpose; they simply are.

To categorize religions or religiosity of this kind as surrogate is only to say that the contents of their beliefs differ from those of traditional religions. And to call them ideologies does not distinguish them from traditional religions, for traditional religions can also be considered ideologies.[42] I therefore want to suggest a different approach. Since what we term surrogate religions and the religiosity that underlies them are so strikingly similar in form and function to traditional religions and religiosity, it might clarify the issue if we conceived of both as religions or forms of religiosity, but as different species, and if we denoted each positively according to its distinctive empirical characteristics.

Since the fundamental difference would seem to be that traditional religions place their trust in nonhuman powers endowed with consciousness while so-called surrogate religions do not, we might differentiate the two kinds of religion, and the religiosity underlying them, as psychocentric and physiocentric. Traditional or theocentric religions can be called psychocentric because they proclaim that unobserved entities with the mental attributes of consciousness, intention, or willpower control human destiny.

40. *Historical Inevitability* (London, 1954), p. 10.
41. Similar objections apply to the term "pantheism."
42. "Ideology" may be a good term for the theories of thinkers such as Marx and the policies they advocated, but it is misleading when applied to the dogmatic prescription of their hypotheses that makes them immune to criticism and converts them to nonrational beliefs.

Surrogate religions and religiosity can be called physiocentric because the cosmic forces or entities they proclaim are unobservable physical forces or processes that themselves lack intention or consciousness. As George Mosse said of the German Volkish ideology, "The essential element here is the linking of the human soul with its natural surroundings, with the 'essence' of nature."[43]

Since what I am now calling psychocentric religions are what most definitions have considered to be religion, and the only kind of religion, it may seem that I have merely reintroduced the old distinction between the natural and supernatural or the sacred and the profane, replacing time-honored language with barbaric neologisms and extending the meaning of "religion" to the point of meaningless. But there is an important difference. As I argued at length earlier,[44] most scholarly definitions of religion include references to processes and entities that cannot be observed and explained empirically; they base their conception of religion on the content of traditional religious beliefs. But not only my definitions of religion and religiosity but also my distinction between psychocentric and physiocentric religions use as criteria only entities or processes that are very close to us and that we can observe empirically, at least in principle.

Of course, we know empirically that people have believed in gods; and when we describe their beliefs, we must try to describe them in terms that would have been acceptable to the believers.[45] But, to repeat, *their* explanation of their own state of mind can no more be *our* scholarly conception and explanation of them than an ancient description and explanation of an illness that we would categorize as cancer could be our modern medical diagnosis of that state. Whatever our paradigms of existence, if we are striving to be objective, we can categorize and explain religious phenomena only in our own rational empirical terms. We know that the believers believed, and we can say that *they* believed in gods, but *we*, from our perspective as historians, cannot say that was what they were doing, for our rational empirical thought does not

43. *The Crisis of German Ideology* (New York, 1964), p. 4.
44. In chaps. 3-5.
45. See above, chap. 6 at n. 42.

permit us to say that there are gods (in their meaning of the word) that can cause, or be the object of, belief.

We can recognize that they symbolized their projections as gods, the forces of production, or biological selection without using their symbols to formulate our own explanations of their beliefs and conduct. Attribution, projection, and transference are well-known mental processes. Bodies, mental activities, and our awareness of them are also observable phenomena. If I say that people in the past attributed certain psychic characteristics to nonhuman forces they could not observe, I am discussing their conduct in terms that do not conflict with their description of their state but that use our empirical knowledge of human conduct to categorize and partially explain it. And if I apply the same procedure to so-called surrogate religions, I can similarly describe their adherents as attributing certain physical characteristics to nonhuman forces they could not observe.

Hence, without departing from our empirical knowledge, we can say that adherents of both kinds of religion attributed to the unknown beyond them, or projected or transferred on it, characteristics or qualities with which they were familiar in their everyday life. We can also say that both types of attribution confirm their believers' sense of the value of their existence by making their identity the project or product of great unseen cosmic forces. And since both kinds of projection seem to express the same kind of mental process and fulfill the same function, we may conceive of them as two different species of religion and religiosity.

I might have called them idealist and materialist religions, but that would have suggested a sharp "either/or" distinction rather than a matter of emphasis. The attributions of psychocentric religiosity and religions stem from and emphasize our awareness of minds at the expense of our awareness of bodies; their most salient symbols refer to psychic characteristics.[46] Physiocentric religions do the reverse. But in most cases, though each emphasizes one

---

46. A particularly clear example is the conception of the twelfth-century Islamic philosopher Averroes, that the universe is imbued throughout with intelligence by the intelligence of the prime mover.

or the other, each also incorporates elements of the other. In neither is there usually a radical separation of consciousness and matter. In most psychocentric religions, the cosmic forces or gods not only create and control physical processes, they are often embodied themselves; in physiocentric religions the cosmic forces, however mindless, create human consciousness and determine human will. From this point of view, Hegel is, as he is in other contexts, a watershed between two ways of understanding.

Moreover, if physiocentric religions are a recent phenomenon, the novelty of the religiosity underlying them should not be exaggerated. Symbols that refer to objects, place, social location, and bodily characteristics have long been, if not dominant, nonetheless very salient in psychocentric religions and religiosities, as Eliade and Douglas have insisted in different ways.[47] Christian religions and religiosity have certainly attached great symbolic value to particular places, objects, and bodily functions, above all the body of Jesus of Nazareth. Nor should we exaggerate the difference in relative endurance of psychocentric and physiocentric religions. Stark and Bainbridge have emphasized that what I have called physiocentric religions have a shorter life-span than psychocentric religions, because they are more directly related to rational empirical knowledge and therefore more subject to empirical disconfirmation. But psychocentric religions have also changed, diversified, and disappeared as their adherents encountered new conditions and acquired further knowledge. Yet, that said, it remains true that only recently did symbols referring to physical phenomena become so dominant in some people's religiosity that they developed or were attracted to physiocentric religions.

I do not think that Europe passed from a religious to a secular age. If we conceive of religion and religiosity as I have defined them, what we see instead is that, in response to radically new conditions and a radical change in mentality, old dimensions of religiosity were expressed in new ways and a radically new kind of religiosity developed that engendered a new kind of religion. When nationalism is viewed in this light, it loses much of its

---

47. Eliade, *The Elementary Forms of the Religious Life*; Mary Douglas, *Natural Symbols*, 2d ed. (New York, 1973).

novelty; it is the expression under new conditions of a basic characteristic of religiosity that has been manifest in psychocentric religions through the centuries. Conversely, however, the novelty of the physiocentric religiosity of the true believers in Marxism and Aryanism and of the physiocentric religions prescribed by dictators in the Soviet Union and in Germany only stands out all the more clearly.

Religions may disappear, but religiosity continues. It may seem ephemeral because it is a property of individuals that varies in structure from individual to individual, dies with the individual, and differs greatly from locality to locality and generation to generation. But unlike any religion, it is a permanent feature of history, for, whatever its ultimate source, it is an enduring property of human beings. Hence, new religions, whether psychocentric or physiocentric, can still appear in highly industrialized societies, and they have appeared, especially in times of crisis. They may prove to have shorter life-spans than the great traditional religions of the past, but their source, religiosity, will still be there. So also will tensions between nonrational and rational empirical thinking, perhaps all the more so because the challenge of rational empirical thinking is now so all-encompassing. To speak of challenges to religious belief, however, brings up another complicated issue, that of religious doubt.

Chapter Twelve

Religious Doubt

Everything said thus far leads to one major conclusion that may be obvious but is central for any analysis of religious history. There is a continual tension in all societies between religion and religiosity, between the prescriptions of religious societies and what individuals actually feel and think, as well as tensions within the religiosity of individuals. In those tensions lies the potential for religious creativity but also for religious doubt and conflict. In Western societies, the tensions have often been so severe that many individuals became aware of them, and some had serious doubts about their religion that made them lukewarm believers or impelled them to press for changes in their religion, convert to another one, found a new one, or refuse to belong to any religion. And I shall restrict myself here to tensions within Western culture, although I think my argument, appropriately modifed, would apply to other cultures whose rate of change was slower.

Throughout the history of Christianity, there have obviously been times when adherents who believed wholeheartedly in the divinity of Christ were nonetheless conscious of a great tension between some of their convictions and what they were required to believe and do if they were to remain adherents of the particular Christian religion they professed. One example can stand for many. About 1379, the English poet William Langland ironically described great men who talked about Christ as if they were clerics, found fault with God the Father, and churlishly criticized the theologians. The conservative Langland wanted these doubts repressed, but, significantly, he could express them very lucidly himself.

Why . . . did our Saviour allow the Serpent into the Garden of Eden, to beguile the first woman and then the man . . . and lure them to hell? And why should all their seed suffer the same death, for their sin alone? . . . Your own teaching contradicts itself in this matter; for if we are to believe what you priests tell us of Christ in the Gospel, He taught that "The son shall not bear the iniquity of the father." In that case, why should we who are now living be corrupted and destroyed for the deeds of Adam? There is no sense in it, for as the Scripture says, "Every man shall bear his own burden."[1]

Religious creativity, the development of new religious attitudes and new religions, has received much attention from historians. The phenomenon of religious doubt, which often accompanies creativity, has not. Although philosophers from Descartes to Popper have examined doubt as an epistemological problem or technique for rational empirical thought, and although recent scholars such as Kuhn and Foucault have analyzed the importance of nonrational thought for rational doubt, there has been less analysis of doubts about nonrational beliefs, particularly those of religion. Scholars have begun to examine "unbelief" conceived as a rejection of the prescriptions of a traditional religion in their entirety,[2] but they have paid little attention to the intermediate phenomenon of doubt, and even less to one of its most typical forms, partial doubt, that is, doubts about particular beliefs.

Doubts—consciousness of conflicts between beliefs and between beliefs and knowledge—deserve close attention in any discussion of religious phenomena. They have been a prominent feature of religious history since antiquity. One could start with the account in chapter 4 of Exodus of the rod that turned into a snake

1. William Langland, *Piers the Ploughman* (Harmondsworth, 1975), p. 115. Questioning of the concept of original sin had, of course, appeared much earlier. For a recent discussion of the early phase, see Elaine Pagels, *Adam, Eve, and the Serpent* (New York, 1988).

2. E.g., Rocco Caporale and Antonio Grumelli, eds., *The Culture of Unbelief* (Berkeley, Los Angeles, London, 1971); Paul W. Pruyser, "Problems of Definition and Conception in the Psychological Study of Religious Unbelief," in *Changing Perspectives in the Scientific Study of Religion*, ed. Allan W. Eister (New York, 1974), pp. 185-200.

so that Moses could prove to the people of Israel that he had received a supernatural revelation. In Europe from the eleventh to the sixteenth century, Catholics frequently voiced anticlerical sentiments that demonstrate a variety of doubts. And if we come to the present, there is the obvious conflict between what the authorities of Catholicism prescribe and what many of its adherents in the United States believe about abortion, homosexuality, artificial contraception, married priests, women as priests, and the like.

Religious doubts are obvious throughout history, and historians have described specific instances in detail. How to explain them is less clear. One approach is simply to avoid the problem by relegating it to the realm of mystery that historians should not attempt to penetrate. Frequently, the doubts of adherents of a religion are described in theological terms and the matter left there, on the ground that historians should not engage in theological arguments. An alternative approach, typical of Marxist analyses, is to explain away the inability or refusal of individuals to accept some beliefs or practices of a religion, especially if it is pronounced, as the expression of what are categorized as nonreligious motivations, for example, as revolutionary or reactionary social protest cloaked in the language of religion. More widespread is the approach that treats religious belief implicitly as superstition. Doubts are explained as the result of the spread of knowledge that reveals the falsity of the claims of religions. But both of those approaches only avoid the problem of belief, Marxist or other. Although it seems obvious that religious change throughout history is the result of the interaction between group norms and individual convictions, between social developments and individual actions, neither the Marxist nor the rationalist approach pays adequate attention to the actual nonrational beliefs of individuals, including their own.

If, however, we recognize that religion and religiosity are distinct and can clash in ways that lead to religious doubt and change, we can discuss religious doubts without becoming implicitly involved in a theological argument or a denial of the indispensability of nonrational convictions. We can, for example, avoid falling into the contradiction in terms involved in saying— or implying—that their religion impelled some adherents of the

Catholic religion to disagree with the pope and, in some cases, to leave the priesthood or the Roman Catholic religion. And we can do so without going to the opposite extreme of explaining away their thoughts and actions as the expression of nonreligious or evil impulsions. We can simply say that the religiosity of some Roman Catholics impelled them to doubt certain prescriptions of their religion, and that the ensuing conflict was an exacerbation of the ever-present, but usually hidden, tension between the Roman Catholic religion of any period and the religiosity of its adherents. We can recognize that such tension has been a potential source of religious change without making value judgments about those changes. The same considerations apply to discussion of recent tensions in other religions, for example, debates about women and the ministry in Protestant and Judaic religions. It also becomes easier to discuss religious change.

Although the continuity of certain formulated beliefs such as those attributed to Moses, Jesus, and Mohammed is striking, it is obvious that people's religions and religiosities have changed dramatically in the course of history. Yet historians often have difficulty in talking about religious change because they use the same term, "religion," to refer both to the social phenomenon and to the property of individuals. It is typically assumed that the individual's "religion" is an expression or consequence of the social phenomenon of religion.[3] Historians may, indeed, indicate that there is something individual about a particular person's religious attitudes, but typically that individuality is seen as only adjectival, as but a variation of, or reaction against, a social property, as but a supplementation, emphasis, derivation, or dilution of the beliefs prescribed by the authorities of established religions or religious communities. The social phenomenon remains the prime mover, and the individual seems to be reacting only to its impulsion.[4] Thus Robert Bellah and his coauthors argue that in the United States "it would seem that a vital and enduring religious individ-

3. In harmony with Durkheim.
4. This seems true of one of the best books on medieval heresy, Robert I. Moore, *The Origins of European Dissent* (New York, 1977), in which religious disagreement is seen as the result of reactions against the shortcomings of the Catholic church.

ualism can only survive in a renewed relationship with established religious bodies."[5]

Without a term that denotes succinctly what individuals actually believe and do religiously, it is difficult to discuss their thought and action without falling into the error of analyzing their religiosity according to the criteria—for example, spirituality or piety—established by the religions prevailing in the individual's culture or in the historian's culture.[6] But that seems ridiculous when applied to many figures who would usually be described as very religious. If spirituality is conceived to be devotion to the beliefs and practices of a religion, then we would have to say that an individual like Luther lacked spirituality at the time that he had come to doubt several beliefs of the religion he had professed, was disobeying its authorities, but had not yet founded a new religion of his own.

The refusal to distinguish clearly between the religious characteristics of a society and those of the individual and to recognize the inevitable tension between them is deeply embedded in common language by the lack of any generally accepted substantive term for the religious property of individuals. That absence can probably be explained by the pervasive influence on the languages of Western civilization of the authorities of traditional religions who wished to maintain that only people who accepted their authority and belonged to a religious society could be properly religious. In any case, that cultural inheritance poses severe problems of terminology for those who wish to discuss religious phenomena without relying on the premises of those faiths. Even William James, who wanted to distinguish the individual phenomenon sharply from the social, was caught in the thrall of the single term available in the language and reduced to contrasting individual experiences with institutional expressions.[7] A glaring

5. *Habits of the Heart*, pp. 247-248.

6. See above, chap. 7, n. 10.

7. Sixty years after James's book, Eric Dodds could find no better way to distinguish which third-century religious phenomena he was going to discuss than to say that his lectures would be concerned not "with the external forms of worship" but with "religious experience in the Jamesian sense," with the personal experience of individuals: E. R. Dodds, *Pagan and Christian in an Age of Anxiety* (New York, 1965), p. 2. Wayne Proudfoot's title, *Religious Experi-*

example of the problems that arise is the use of the terms "popular religion" and "high religion" to describe the beliefs and practices of people who adhered to one and the same religion. But the difficulty disappears if we recognize that those people adhered to the same religion but differed in religiosity and speak of the religiosity of the educated and the uneducated.

It is, of course, important for our historical understanding to know whether acceptance of the authority and basic precepts of a religion was part of various people's religiosity—as it was for most people throughout history. And it is important to know how the authorities of a religion at any given time categorized individuals—as Catholics, devout, pious, impious, sinners, heretics, Protestants, Puritans, pagans, unbelievers, atheists, capitalists, and so forth. But it is equally important to treat the religiosity of individuals in its own right, to know what the religiosity of those individuals actually was, both as they were conscious of it and as we scholars now understand it. Without a term that acknowledges that the religious beliefs of individuals can vary independently of social prescriptions of belief and conduct, it is very difficult to explain the crucial phenomena of religious change and religious doubt, for those phenomena cannot be explained concretely without focusing on individuals as independent variables.

That religiosity can be an independent variable is usually recognized in the case of major religious innovators. Thus Weber's discussion of charisma focused on the religiosity of exceptional individuals and presented them as independent variables, and many historians of religion have done the same, whether because they believed those individuals had received revelations or because their independent influence was so obvious. But we should never forget that multitudes of less exceptional individuals had their own religiosities, which were also independent variables in varying degrees. And the independence of their religiosity also affected religion and religious change, whether because it was simply a fact with which the authorities of religions had to come to terms as best they could, whether because it impelled people to follow charismatic leaders, or whether because it led many

---

ence, reflects a similar difficulty in finding a way to distinguish clearly between the social and the individual phenomenon.

people in recent times to abandon without fanfare their adherence to any religion.

Changes in religion and religiosity and the doubts that typically accompany them may be sudden and disruptive or gradual and imperceptible, and they may be explained in many ways. In many early, small, preliterate societies, tension between what the tribe's nonrational beliefs prescribed and the religiosity of its individual members was doubtless minimal, except perhaps for occasional unusual individuals. Because conditions changed slowly and beliefs were transmitted orally, beliefs could be modified imperceptibly from generation to generation, and religions in those societies could adjust relatively easily to suit new conditions and attitudes. At the opposite extreme stand the dramatic changes in literate societies in which, because religious prescriptions had been enduringly codified, they were hard to modify despite the pressure of massive changes in environmental and technological conditions and in knowledge and mentalities, revolutions such as that symbolized by Luther's famous statement: "I cannot do otherwise, here I stand, may God help me, amen."

In between those extremes there is a range of tension between and within religion and religiosity, a more or less troubling awareness of conflicts between the authorities of religions and some of their adherents and of conflicts within the religiosity of those adherents. The more complex the society, the greater the likelihood of tension, conflict, and doubts. Even in literate societies, however, tension was frequently not very disruptive because it was relieved by gradual modifications or interpretations of the prescriptions that defused the conflict. At other times, however, particularly in the case of the dramatic tensions that have characterized Western civilization at least from the time of Socrates, the tension has been considerable and socially and psychologically disruptive. I need not list the conversions, sects, so-called heresies, executions, and religious wars that litter Western history.

However particular changes in religions and religiosities are explained, it would seem generally true that the degree of religious tension, the speed of religious change, and the prevalence of doubts are closely related to the type of society and the rate of environmental and social change in general. But environmental and social change affects religions and religiosities differently, particularly in role-differentiated societies; the more rapid the change, the greater the tension between them.

It follows from my concept of religion that every religion prescribes some form of social organization. That implicit or explicit self-definition of the religious society is a distillate of many experiences widely dispersed in time and space and of many people's thoughts about them, but it is a prescription, not an empirical definition of the society. It is what the authorities of a religion prescribe that society ought to be rather than an analysis of what it is empirically.[8] Individual adherents, however, necessarily have different, more empirically realistic and personally oriented, conceptions of society. Although heavily influenced by social prescription, the individual is closer to the ground; to survive, he or she has to give more weight to what is as contrasted with some prescription of what society ought to be. An inevitable part of the sense of identity of individuals is their self-centered consciousness of being concretely involved in specific relations with other individual members of a particular society at specific times and in specific places.

In small, relatively unchanging societies in which individuals are forcefully indoctrinated in a common culture, know each other, engage in the same activities (save for gender differences), and have very similar experiences, the discrepancy between social norms and the individual's consciousness of social relations will be minimal. But if a society expands and the rate of social and cultural change increases, integration will be strained. Individuals will experience change in localized ways that contrast with the conception of society as a whole authorized by religious authorities. Tension between the form of society prescribed by a religion and how the society is actually symbolized in the nonrational thought or religiosity of individuals will increase.[9] If the discrepancy between them becomes blatant and overtly discussed, doubts will arise, and there will be pressure for religious change.

Doubts, whether specific doubts about particular elements of a religion or doubt about a religion as a whole, may arise for many

8. E.g., the contrast between John of Salisbury's *Policraticus* or Aquinas's *De regimine principum* and Machiavelli's *The Prince*.

9. The importance of the social ground of religions and religiosities is massively demonstrated in Stark and Bainbridge, *The Future of Religion*.

reasons. Changing social conditions and technologies can make many individuals aware of new needs, new possibilities, and new attitudes that do not harmonize with some of the practices and values prescribed by their religion. Some individuals may become critical of religious prescriptions because of individual disputes with religious authorities over specific material possessions, attitudes, or types of conduct. Some unusual individuals can have personal experiences that seem more compelling insights into the meaning of life than those provided by religious authorities. Some, especially in sophisticated literate societies, can find that their rational empirical knowledge makes them doubt some or most beliefs of their religion.

There are doubtless many kinds of religious doubts, but for reasons that will become apparent in the next chapter, I want to distinguish broadly between nonrational and rational empirical doubts. By nonrational doubt, I mean an uncertainty about beliefs, values, or a cosmology that is inspired, not by any conflicting rational empirical knowledge, but by the appeal of other beliefs. Individuals may feel that their own pattern of nonrational symbolizing or that of a different culture or society they have encountered provides a better understanding of all they have experienced than the nonrational beliefs current in their society. They may therefore begin to doubt their former beliefs. By contrast, rational doubt arises when people become aware of a conflict between their rational empirical knowledge and some of their nonrational beliefs and begin to doubt those beliefs. But since one kind of conflict may stimulate the other, adherents of a religion may experience both kinds of doubt at the same time.

Nonrational doubt is the uncertainty that encourages conversions from one religion to another. As individuals grow up in any society, they acquire a variety of beliefs through social indoctrination. As they live, however, they may—and usually do—develop some beliefs of their own. Many of those beliefs may not conflict with what they had been taught, but some may. If they do, and if the individuals feel that their personal beliefs give them a better understanding of what they experience, who they are, and what they should do than those they have learned, they may reject some of the beliefs they had been taught. If they are not very reflective, they may reject those particular beliefs without reflecting on their connection with other inherited beliefs. In that case, their rejections are little more than reservations about some aspects of what they have been taught and may have once believed. But if their own beliefs lead them to question some central beliefs of their religion, they may come to doubt the authority of those who prescribe the beliefs and turn to new authorities, whether themselves or different people. Alternatively, some individuals may feel no more than a diffuse dissatisfaction with their religion without developing any conscious alternative but then encounter a different profession of belief that seems more appealing, perhaps one provided by missionaries of a different religion, and accept it.

Nonrational doubts about beliefs seem to arise from the impact on societies and individuals of changes in environmental conditions, including technological advance, and the desire for power or awareness of lack of power those changes inspire. Conversions that affect whole groups are classic expressions of such tension. Members of one culture may feel that their encounter with another culture has enlarged their horizons, confronted them with new problems, exposed them to powerful mental or physical techniques of which they had hitherto been unaware, revealed the limitations of their previous experience and understanding of the world about them, and thereby changed their conception of their identity and potential role. They may then come to feel that the religion of the society they have encountered is more powerful than their own religion because it embraces a much wider range of experience and apparently enables its adherents to do things they themselves have been unable to do. They may then convert, either because they want to become members of a more politically powerful society or, as in the case of the Germanic invaders of the Roman Empire, because they wish to dominate a more sophisticated society they have conquered.[10]

10. The refusal of most Jews to convert or assimilate despite centuries of existence as a relatively powerless minority within powerful societies may be partly explained by the conviction of being a chosen people and the promise of future power provided by messianic belief. But it also suggests that Judaism, perhaps because its monotheism demands obedience to certain practices but assent to very few prescriptions of nonrational belief about the nature of reality, has provided a remarkably flexible and comprehensive symbolization of existence in known and unforeseeable situations.

Conversions can also be caused by developments within a society. As a result of their personality and experiences, individuals may develop nonrational beliefs of their own that conflict with, and cause them to doubt, some nonrational prescriptions of their religion. In many cases, as with mass conversions, individuals unsettled by such doubts seem to be reacting to their awareness that they lack the power and prestige of the social superiors who control their religion. Individuals discomforted by the feeling that the value of their identity is not adequately recognized—or is explicitly denied—by the prevailing values, beliefs, and practices of their religious society may reject that religion and, if possible, join another religion or create a new religion that supports their beliefs about their identity.

Thus some priests and peasants in fourteenth-century Europe felt their value as humans was not recognized by the prescriptions of their society and proclaimed that all the descendants of Adam and Eve were equal in status and that the religious and political hierarchy should be abolished. Luther certainly felt that the Roman Catholic religion had not adequately recognized the value of German identity. Blacks have similarly felt themselves fully human in societies that denied it and, when possible, pushed for social change, often led by their ministers, and joined religions that insist on their equality or superiority. Women have felt themselves equal or superior to men in societies that denied it and tried to have the value of their identity recognized by religions. In these and other cases, the conflict between self-image and some beliefs prescribed by society has provoked doubts, the propagation of new beliefs, and sometimes new religions. Since these doubts are reactions to relative deprivations, they may seem to fall under the deprivation theory of religion, but since they are often efforts to overcome deprivations by changing conditions here and now, the fit is dubious.

Rarely, however, is disagreement purely nonrational. Typically, individuals whose nonrational beliefs conflict with those current in their society will try to rationalize their beliefs, at least to themselves. They will use their capacity for rational empirical thinking to demonstrate to themselves, and possibly to others, that the beliefs with which they disagree are empirically false or that those who prescribe them do not really believe them. And when they do, they often find themselves in the company of individuals who followed precisely the reverse path and were not socially disadvantaged or powerless.[11] These are the individuals who, in large part because of personal capacities and social opportunities, have been able to develop their rational empirical capacities and applied them to problems in a way that made them doubt some of the beliefs prescribed by their religion. Thus both nonrational thinking and rational empirical thinking—Jesus or Socrates—may unsettle religious beliefs, create pressure for religious change, arfd be dealt with similarly by social authorities. But nonrational and rational doubts pose different problems for historians and must be dealt with differently.

Nonrational beliefs and doubts resist rational empirical explanation. Theologians, metaphysicians, philosophers of art and law, and the like may engage in rational and hermeneutic analysis of different textual forms of thought that express nonrational thinking and the conflicts between them, but to do so, they have to abstract those patterns of thought from their concrete human and material environment. By contrast, empirical analysis of what individuals actually believe, the sources of their beliefs, and changes in them requires intensive examination of particular historical instances in all their complexity. Until rather recently, however, most historians tended to take nonrational beliefs as givens and then examine their expression in social norms and the impact of the norms on individuals. But that is changing. Recently, cultural anthropologists, social psychologists, and historians of mentality have been making the importance of nonrational ideas for the organization and action of particular societies increasingly obvious. And they have been increasingly successful in explaining how particular beliefs arose and changed.[12]

If we want to examine the development of actual belief as contrasted with social norms, we have to examine individual lives, for belief is an activity of individuals; ideas or prescriptions are not beliefs until individuals assent to them. Unless we conceive of people as social robots, we must examine individuals to dis-

11. Despite some Marxist hypotheses that depict intellectuals as a dominated fraction of the dominating class.

12. E.g., Lynn Hunt, *Politics, Culture, and Class in the French Revolution* (Berkeley, Los Angeles, London, 1984).

cover how in fact they correlated what went on inside them with what impinged on them from outside. And that is very difficult. The evidence of cultural norms, social ideas, and common forms of social conduct may enable us to draw general inferences about common formulations of belief and their causes, but they do not permit us to assert that any particular individual actually believed those ideas or to describe how he or she believed them.

In historiography, the obvious place to look for actual beliefs, whenever there is sufficient evidence, is biographies—with fictional biographies such as those of Proust and Joyce in mind to remind us of the flow of associations that biographers can only rarely catch.[13] Biographies of individuals and their times have often been denigrated as an inferior form of historiography, but if well done they are the fullest description of what individuals actually believed and did and how their beliefs changed. Yet even when there is plentiful evidence for individuals, we still have to rely heavily on their own expressions of nonrational thinking, and those expressions are only a very partial representation of all that went on in their minds. To make matters worse, historical evidence of their expressions is incomplete.

We can describe their nonrational thought only partially. And if we go further and try to explain why they believed or doubted as they did, our explanation is limited not only by our limited information but also by our inability to explain the ultimate mysteries of our own existence. As many psychiatrists might agree, the specific nonrational beliefs and doubts of individuals can be explained only very partially and vaguely except in cases of severe abnormality. Historians, who lack the immediacy of access to individuals of psychiatrists, are in a much worse position to explain them.

Rational doubt, our second broad category, is much easier to

13. A particularly valuable example for my present purposes is *The Auto-biography of Malcolm X* (New York, 1966), since it traces the evolution of the religiosity of an exceptional person, who grew up under conditions that most intellectuals have not experienced, and describes a religion that has not affected most of them directly. Because most who read it will be struck by the difference from their own experience, they will less likely be able to understand Malcolm X's religiosity in terms of their own assumptions about religion; and for that reason, they may pay more attention to the complexity and uniqueness of Malcolm's nonrational associations.

examine and explain empirically, for it is not entirely in the non-rational domain. It is the result of consciousness of a conflict between nonrational beliefs and rational empirical knowledge; and if one pole of the conflict resists description and explanation, the other pole is much more accessible. We can examine rather directly what people knew, and we can, to a large extent, explain rationally and empirically how that knowledge had been developed, for knowledge can be shared and its sharing leaves many traces. We can assess the knowledge available to individuals, and if we can ascertain their nonrational beliefs, we can see whether there was a latent conflict. Indeed, in many cases we are spared the labor of detection because the individuals affected by rational doubt expressed their doubts and their reasons for them openly.

The tension between nonrational and rational empirical thinking and the reactions it may arouse are very obvious in advanced societies that attribute great importance to rational empirical thinking, provide theoretical training in techniques of rational empirical thought far beyond those needed for the immediate needs of everyday life, and encourage its application in many domains. If Socrates is a symbol of that attitude, a classic medieval example is the conflict that arose in medieval Europe, beginning in the eleventh century, between the affirmations of faith and what could be demonstrated by the application of the increasingly dominant Aristotelian logic to assertions about observable and unobservable phenomena. It became so acute by the thirteenth century that some thinkers were reduced to holding that some propositions were true by faith but false philosophically and, conversely, that some propositions were true philosophically but false by faith.[14]

The best-known modern example is what used to be described as the warfare between religion and science, a battle recently renewed in U.S. courts between Christian fundamentalist believers in creation according to a literal reading of the book of Genesis and those whose account of creation derives rather from the evolutionary theories of Darwin, Mendel, and Lyell. Yet if such flagrant tensions and doubts are easy to document from recent history, we may suspect that similar, albeit less dramatic, tensions

14. The classic discussion of that medieval tension is Etienne Gilson, *Reason and Revelation in the Middle Ages* (New York, 1938).

occurred in primitive societies untouched by Aristotle or Darwin when unsettling major changes in environmental and social conditions or encounters with other cultures brought knowledge of hitherto unknown possibilities.

Conflict between nonrational and rational empirical thinking can occur because human beings create and use symbols in two different ways but use many of the same symbols to express both kinds of thoughts. On the one hand, they develop symbols to denote realities they have experienced, connect them rationally and empirically, and use them to express their knowledge. On the other, they create and use symbols to organize their nonrational understanding of their existence and to act. Conflict can arise when people use the same symbols to express both modes of thinking and confuse one meaning with the other.

Some symbols are not used in both kinds of thought, for some do not denote entities that people have observed and have only nonempirical meanings, for example, "God" or "heaven." They are second-level symbols, symbols of symbols. They do not have observable referents other than to what goes on in people's minds. Although scholars may employ such symbols when describing nonrational associations in the minds of the people they are studying, the symbols themselves have no objective empirical meaning. For those for whom they are subjectively meaningful, however, they are very significant and emotionally arousing because they symbolize—and are reminders of—whole networks of nonrational associations central to their sense of identity.

Most symbols used in nonrational thinking, however, are not of that kind; they are first-level symbols. Like "mother," "church," "water," or "blood," they can have both rational empirical and nonrational meanings. Pieces of wood at right angles may "cross" or be "The Cross." These symbols can therefore have different meanings depending on which way people are thinking. And since the consciousness of reality that each mode of thinking produces is different, they can conflict. When people are thinking rationally and empirically, they use the symbols common to both modes of thinking to focus attention on what they know or can know about the characteristics of some bounded entities or processes which they can observe and with which they can interact. But when people are thinking in the nonrational mode, the empirical realities the symbols denote are no longer the primary focus of consciousness. The meaning evoked by interaction with some realities depends not simply on what could be known about the realities themselves and their empirical relations to other realities, but on the relations established by an individual's nonrational association of the symbols for those realities with many other symbols whose referents cannot be connected rationally and empirically with the reality—for example, nonrational thinking about circumcision. The resulting understanding is very different in character from the knowledge people have of reality when they are thinking rationally and empirically.

But the way the different meanings are expressed can overlap, and when they do, they may conflict and cause doubts. The two kinds of meaning overlap when people express nonrational associations or beliefs in language identical in form with that of verifiable rational empirical propositions, for example, "Jews have horns," "all history is the history of class struggle," "Jesus rose from the dead." Since the symbols and syntax used in such expressions of belief are the same as those used in rational empirical discourse, people can readily mistake those expressions of religiosity for rational empirical propositions. But when they do, faith is confused with knowledge, and the nonrational associations asserted as "true" become susceptible of empirical verification or disproof.

Overlap does not necessarily lead to a conflict between the two modes of thinking. So long as the beliefs stemming from people's nonrational symbolizing do not contradict what they do know about reality, or could know if they used their existing capacity to think rationally and empirically, there is no denial of the independent existence of the reality with all its known, knowable, and as yet unknowable characteristics. People can still alternate freely between nonrational and rational thinking about reality without any awareness of conflict or doubt.[15]

15. Hence, what we call magic, the nonrational effort to manipulate empirical realities to achieve desired results here and now, is no more irrational or superstitious than any other action to better our empirical condition that expresses our nonrational understanding of reality and does not conflict with our present knowledge. It has been incorporated into most religions because it is an expression of religiosity.

Conflict is also unlikely to arise when the overlapping meanings concern physical realities that exist only because people created them to serve as symbols. Writing and flags owe their existence to human beings. Although writing and flags are composed of chemical and biological materials that exist independently of human intentions, people combine them to create physical symbols that evoke strong emotions, and individuals may be assaulted for showing contempt for them. But their nonrational significance does not necessitate any denial of their empirical characteristics. "This is our flag" may be said with deep nonrational meaning, but that meaning does not conflict with the person's knowledge of the mundane physical characteristics of the flag.

Conflicts are most likely to arise when people use physical realities that exist independently of how people may symbolize them, as if they were symbols like words or icons and then treat those independent realities as if they were simply nonrational symbols. For people not only denote their interaction with independent physical realities by symbols; they also make independent realities serve as symbols. They use realities they have directly experienced and denoted (e.g., the fluid symbolized as "blood") as symbols in their nonrational thought and actions (e.g., making someone a "blood brother") because *some* of the characteristics of those realities make them useful as similes or metaphors for, or reminders of, something else (e.g., family, cultural, or biological relations)—*Blut und Boden*.

In Western culture, there is no better known example of the use of independent realities as symbols than the symbolization of Jesus of Nazareth as Christ, and no better example of the expression of a belief as an empirical proposition than the assertion that he was resurrected from the tomb and did not really die. Since no one claimed to have witnessed the act of resurrection, it could neither be verified nor denied objectively—although considerably later accounts affirmed that Jesus had been seen on earth by his disciples after his death. But because the assertion was, statistically, so improbable and supported by so little evidence, it introduced a conflict between nonrational and rational empirical thinking that provoked doubts at the time and ever after. Paul of Tarsus described those doubts in almost Aristotelian terms.

Now if Christ is preached as raised from the dead, how can some of you say that there is no resurrection of the dead? But if there is no resurrection of the dead, then Christ has not been raised; if Christ has not been raised, then our preaching is in vain and your faith is in vain. We are even found to be misrepresenting God, because we testified of God that he raised Christ, whom he did not raise if it is true that the dead are not raised.[16]

Christian faith was embodied in Jesus; and after his death, beliefs about his body were fundamental for Christian faith.[17] Its resurrection was the guarantee of his beliefs and his followers' salvation. The body of Christ, in life, death, and resurrection, became the salient symbol to which other symbols were associated to give it different meanings in theology, in ecclesiology (as a metaphor for the Catholic church and the society of Christians), in art, and in ritual. Indeed, the re-creation or reenactment of his body in the Eucharist would be the central ritual of Christianity. And the clearest example of the problems that can arise when expressions of religiosity are mistaken for empirical propositions is provided by the history of the Eucharist.

For centuries, people in the Mediterranean region cultivated grain and grapes, made bread and wine, and were highly knowledgeable about them. So basic were they as shared comestibles that, like salt, they were used as symbols of commensality, of permanent or temporary participation in a community with its values and traditions. But there was no conflict between what people knew about bread and wine and what they believed about themselves or their guests. Even when people went further and used bread and wine in highly ritualized ways, more as nonrational symbols than as substances that satisfied hunger, there was no conflict. In the feasts of Purim and Passover, comestibles have been used for centuries as similes to remind Jews of historical experiences, but that symbolic use has not necessitated irrational denial of any of the empirical characteristic of the bread and wine.

Conflict arose only when use of those physical realities as nonrational symbols necessitated denial of some of their known or

16. 1 Corinthians 15:12-15.
17. As is true to a lesser extent of Mohammed in Islamic thought.

knowable characteristics. When, or if,[18] Jesus of Nazareth took bread and wine and said that it was his body and blood, his manifestly nonrational utterance was identical in form with a rational empirical proposition. Nonrational thinking about bread and wine therefore overlapped rational empirical thinking about them in propositional form. Still, so long as his followers understood the utterance contextually as a command that they use bread and wine ritually as nonrational symbols to evoke his presence in thought or remembrance, there was no conflict. But when some of his followers understood his utterance both as a command and as a proposition about a change in the physical reality of the bread and wine themselves, they confused metaphor with empirical proposition and introduced a latent conflict between their nonrational and rational thinking about bread and wine.

The conflict remained latent for centuries because people continued to think of the bread and wine as but part of the total ritual context rather than focusing their attention on the physical characteristics of the bread and wine by themselves. Conflict only emerged in the Middle Ages, when people's attention came to concentrate on the consecrated bread and wine as objects in and of themselves.[19] Many people, perhaps most, gradually became aware of a conflict between what they knew about bread and wine—and about human flesh and blood—and the prescribed belief that when a priest consecrated bread and wine during the Mass, they changed into the real body and blood of Jesus of Nazareth. Doubtless many people still gave the matter little thought, but in the first half of the eleventh century, a number of people not only doubted the belief but rejected it entirely and were branded by the Catholic church as heretics. By the middle of the eleventh century, the problem had become a major theological issue, and for the next century and a half concerned theologians sought ways to express their faith in a way that did not clash directly with their knowledge.

By the end of the twelfth century, theologians had developed

18. Hyam Maccoby, *The Mythmaker* (San Francisco, 1987), pp. 111-115, argues that Jesus did not say it.

19. The most extreme form of this isolation of the object came in the later Middle Ages with the practice of keeping a consecrated host continually visible in a monstrance.

the doctrines of concomitance and transubstantiation in order to reconcile their faith and their reason, and in 1215 the pope made the doctrine of transubstantiation dogma. While the doctrine affirmed that there was a real change and relied on the premise of divine intervention in the Eucharist to explain it, the argument used all the prevailing, basically Aristotelian, techniques of knowledge to explain how there could be such a change without its being empirically detectable—save in the case of certain miracles.[20] In effect, the solution reformulated the belief about the Eucharist so that the affirmation of faith was no longer identical with a simple empirical proposition and, hence, not as manifestly subject to empirical disconfirmation and open to doubt. But since the doctrine still asserted that it was "true" that there was a physical change in the bread and wine themselves, it still confused faith and knowledge. And although it had become very dangerous to express doubts in the heyday of the Inquisition, the dogma left many people unconvinced. They had to handle the resulting tension as best they could, and some reacted irrationally.

20. See James J. McGivern, *Concomitance and Communion: A Study in Eucharistic Doctrine and Practice* (Fribourg, 1963); Jean de Montclos, *Lanfranc et Béranger: Le controverse eucharistique du XIe siècle* (Louvain, 1971). Aquinas's solution is a fascinating example of the complexity of the rationalization involved and of the extent to which nonrational thought and assertions of empirical knowledge still overlapped: *Summa theologica*, IIIa, lxxiv-lxxxiii.

Chapter Thirteen

Religious Irrationality

Irrationality is usually thought of as a characteristic of individuals, and to understand how it affects religious belief, we should start with the individual. But what of societies? Can societies—in particular, societies that prescribe religious beliefs—be characterized as irrational, and if so, how and how much? To answer that question we must look at historical societies. After some preliminary consideration of the nature of irrationality, I shall therefore turn to the historical example I know best, the one most directly relevant to the formation of antisemitism, medieval society.

Religious belief has often been described as irrational, but the expression is highly ambiguous and conceals basic issues. It can mean either that religious beliefs are not based on reason or that they conflict with reason and that religious believers are therefore irrational. That ambiguity can be avoided if religious beliefs are described as nonrational, as the product of a fundamental and inescapable mode of thinking that is not rational empirical thinking but does not necessarily conflict with it and may use it in a subordinate capacity. Religious beliefs can then be seen as neither rational nor irrational. But if religious beliefs as expressed conflict with and inhibit rational empirical thinking, they are both nonrational and irrational.

Nonrational thinking associates symbols in very diverse ways, and rational thinking is its servant, as is so obvious in philosophical theology. Like servants, however, rational thinking has, so to speak, a mind of its own. It performs functions that its master will not or cannot perform, and it does so according to its own procedures. Consequently, there can be conflicts in which each seeks to have its own way. Often, the result is a cooperative solution in which each preserves its dignity. But sometimes the master is so threatened that the servant is dismissed. As some individuals seek to maintain their confidence in their identity in the face of conflicting realities that threaten it, they may defend the beliefs that give them confidence by inhibiting their capacity for rational thinking in varying degrees. They may become irrational.

Irrationality takes many forms, and psychologists and psychoanalysts have divided sharply and at times bitterly in their efforts to describe and explain them. Since I have no competence in that arena, I will only be concerned here to indicate what I mean by irrationality. I am not concerned with the kind of mental malfunction that has physical causes and makes people incapable of rational empirical thinking on any subject—for example, drugs, brain trauma, or Alzheimer's disease. Their thinking is not irrational in the sense that interests me. Although their thinking may conflict with the observer's rationality, there is no conflict between the way they are thinking and their own capacity to think rationally and empirically, because they do not have that capacity. They might be better described as completely nonrational, meaning that, temporarily or permanently, they have no rational capacities, a well-known problem in law.

What I mean by irrationality is closer to what are typified as neuroses, which only interfere with rational thinking and action in certain areas. Although such irrationality may be affected by biochemical processes, it seems to have primarily mental causes and to be remediable in some measure through mental treatment. We are all aware of the conflicts that arise from that most human of habits, wishful thinking. We all engage in nonrational thinking about people and institutions with which we identify, from which we expect much, and about which we may be very well informed—for example, our child, political party, football team, or country. Yet if we use our capacity for rational observation, we are often forced to recognize that what we believed about them is not the case, and we have to adjust our beliefs to accord with realities we cannot deny. But some people can and do deny truths about those they love that are very apparent to others.

We all know people who assert strong opinions about certain subjects but do not use the powers of rational thinking of which we know them capable on other similar subjects. We often speak of someone's bias or prejudice in favor of or against some individual, group, or institution, their seemingly willful refusal to pay attention to awkward facts. When their biases are not too dangerous or crippling, neither we nor they are much bothered by them. We may even admire their loyalty and strong sense of identity, if it does not threaten us. If the matter is not very important and the suppression circumscribed, we may simply say that that person is overly emotional about certain matters. And not infrequently, we recognize that individuals can be rational about a subject at one time and highly irrational at another. We know there are times when it is unwise to discuss certain matters with a person and wait for better occasions.

But if individuals obviously, continuously, and increasingly suppress their ability to think and act rationally and empirically about some important matters, and if their actions seriously threaten themselves and others, we are likely to think of them as irrational and in need of psychiatric help. To explain their conduct, we turn to psychological theories—with greater or lesser confidence. But most of us, including most historians, have only a superficial understanding of those theories, and the ability of historians to diagnose or explain individual irrationality in the past is highly limited. We can, however, recognize that irrationality generates epistemic problems, and the following simple-minded assertions are intended primarily to indicate the kind of problems that arise.

It would seem—if we leave brain damage aside—that as individuals develop, the organism reacts so strongly to certain experiences or associated stimuli that it becomes durably patterned to respond similarly thereafter to similar stimuli or the symbols for them. For better or worse, those associations (or coordinations of various physiological and psychological reactions to stimuli)[1] become a highly stable characteristic of the psychosomatic structure of individuals; and the symbols they use to express them become central to their nonrational symbolizing and their sense of identity thereafter. If the relations thus established and sym-

---

1. See the works cited above, chap. 8, n. 20.

bolized then prove more or less congruent with what individuals experience later, including their rational empirical thinking, the result is a comfortably integrated individual. But if they do not, individuals will find themselves in a "double bind," caught between two unreconciled messages or meanings. And since their nonrational symbolizing is so important for their sense of distinctive identity, rational empirical thinking becomes a challenge to their sense of identity.

When faced with such a challenge, many individuals maintain their capacity to think rationally and recognize that it contradicts some important beliefs stemming from their nonrational symbolizing. They may then try to harmonize their faith and their knowledge by reexamining, expanding, or otherwise modifying their knowledge. If that does not succeed, however, they are still able—although often reluctantly and painfully—to modify their faith and with it their sense of identity. But some cannot.

Some individuals have apparently been so strongly and inadaptively imprinted that they hang on to their beliefs and suppress the capacity for rational empirical thinking they show on other subjects. Although application of that capacity to their subsequent experiences would clearly raise questions about some of their beliefs, which they express as, and consider to be, empirical propositions, they nonetheless maintain them and suppress any doubts. Their illogical and often highly emotional efforts to support their beliefs indicate that they are still subconsciously aware of doubt, aware that use of their rational empirical capacities would reveal how unfounded some beliefs central to their sense of identity were. But the fear that their identity is insecure and ill-adapted to survival only makes them refuse, or be unable, to think rationally and empirically about the challenged beliefs.

People who have been so strongly imprinted that they cannot adapt to new experiences and new knowledge suppress or compartmentalize their capacity to think rationally and empirically about some aspects of reality; they cease to be able to move freely between nonrational and rational thinking on certain subjects. More than that, not only do they refuse, or are unable, to acknowledge the knowable characteristics of certain realities, they also project on them, or attribute to them, characteristics that the realities do not possess, attributes that are the creation of their own nonrational thinking and express their sense of their own identity.

The process of projection, if not our concept of it, existed long before Freud, and its power has long been recognized in practice. For centuries, people have used it to ensure that they or others would be perceived as possessing desired qualities. Uniforms have long been used to block certain perceptions of social and individual realities and emphasize others. Whether regalia, priestly garb, judicial or academic robes, the clothing of soldiers, or the fashion of an elite, symbolic uniforms have served not only to identify authority and function but also to legitimate power and prevent others from thinking of the weaknesses and remarkable diversity of the human beings beneath the impressive appearances. And that reminds us that, although projection is a psychological process within individuals, it, like nonrational beliefs, can be induced by social action.

The most paradoxical example of conscious intent to substitute projection for accurate perception of reality is Freud's technique for overcoming it. To improve reality testing, he stimulated patients to concentrate on their nonrational associations and express them in a ritualized context to an analyst behind their backs. One major result was transference, the projection onto the highly attenuated—but undenied—reality of the analyst of associations that had little or nothing to do with him or her. Indeed, the psychoanalytic encounter can be considered the proving ground for the concept of transference, and its goal as the effort to wear away neuroses by making patients increasingly aware of their inappropriate transference of emotions, of the blatant conflict between their projections and the empirical reality of the analyst.

It should be emphasized, however, that the patient does not deny the existence of the person conducting the analysis. Although people may systematically inhibit their capacity to think rationally and empirically about some independent realities, or be manipulated so that they will, nonetheless they do not deny the existence of the realities on which they project their beliefs. Rather, they deform their perception of those independent realities so as to make them conform to their nonrational symbolization of them. Although they may suppress their capacity to perceive many observable characteristics of certain realities or the lack of certain observable characteristics, they still acknowledge some observable characteristics of those realities, for they still confront those realities and feel the need to do something about them. None, save the completely nonrational, suppress their rational empirical capacities completely, for to do so would entail rapid extinction. Indeed, it is that continuing, if restricted, confidence in rational empirical thinking that may make it possible to overcome irrationality—but it is also what can make irrationality so lethal. However the SS perceived Jews, they knew that Jews had bodies of different ages and genders and could be killed.

If irrationality is a psychological reaction of individuals that has epistemic consequences for them, it is also a social phenomenon because the irrational beliefs of individuals can be formulated as ideas, communicated to others, and expressed in social norms and institutions, as is all too obvious in the case of Hitler. He not only had irrational beliefs about Jews but also used his social control to express his beliefs and to suppress the availability of rational empirical knowledge that conflicted with them. If irrationality as a psychological phenomenon is only a property of individuals that affects their religiosity, as an epistemic phenomenon it can affect societies and religions.

Religious irrationality originates as a characteristic of religiosity—and it seems to be a reaction to rational doubt. Whether individuals become irrational seems to depend on what they do when they become aware of a conflict between what they themselves believe, or have been told to believe by their religion, and what they know, or suspect they could know if they thought rationally and empirically. Needless to say, individuals experiencing such conflicts react in very different ways depending on their personality and social situation. If they are adherents of a religion, as has been the case for most of history, they are likely to experience great psychological stress. Not only do they have to deal with the conflict between their own nonrational and rational thinking, they must also face the conflict between their faith in the authorities of their religion and their disbelief in some of its prescriptions—with all its potential for bitter social conflict between themselves and those authorities.

Even adherents of a religion who are not strongly committed to their religion and sense a conflict between their knowledge and some prescriptions of their religion face hard choices. They may not feel that the religion's authorities are their fundamental contact with ultra-empirical reality; indeed, they may consciously doubt that they are. But while that may make it easier for them to trust their empirical knowledge and reject certain beliefs prescribed by the religious authorities, it increases the social pressures on them. On the one hand, if they keep their doubts and convictions to themselves, they have to conform outwardly while rebelling inwardly, an uncomfortable position in any heavily religious society. On the other hand, if they assert their convictions openly, they are likely to be condemned by the authorities as "heretics" (people who choose for themselves rather than conforming to the society's norms) and be repressed by incarceration, death, or expulsion from the religious society—which may mean exclusion from their family. And even if they can face that social pressure and are able to leave their former religion safely, they then face the choice of converting to another religion, founding a new one, or renouncing adherence to any religion whatsoever. Maintaining the capacity to think rationally and empirically can be very difficult, particularly in societies dominated by religions. Many have found it hard or impossible to do so.

There are many individuals, however, for whom the authorities of their religion are so fundamental in their symbolic structuring of their identity that they cannot imagine defying their religion's prescriptions and being excluded from their religious society. Hence, if some of these individuals have knowledge that makes them doubt certain prescribed beliefs, and if the authorities do not modify the prescriptions so that they harmonize with their knowledge, these individuals can only wrestle with their doubts privately. If they remain conscious of their doubts and agonize over them in solitude, they can maintain their rationality; but if they try to avoid awareness of them by inhibiting their capacity for rational thinking, they will lapse into irrationality.

Of all these reactions to doubt, the most important for a study of antisemitism is the one least likely to attract notice in history books: the repression of doubts by individuals who remained adherents of a religion. For one thing, it is hard to detect, particularly in earlier societies; the evidence about individuals is often simply too meager. Moreover, in many historical societies—and some contemporary ones—individuals have had to keep quiet about their doubts for fear of punishment. And even in societies where that threat is not present, individuals who want to preserve their faith in their society and to repress any doubts about social authorities are unlikely to express their doubts publicly. Consequently, their doubts leave few traces. As a result, we often tend to view people in the past—and in some contemporary societies— as far more uniform in belief than they were or are.

That there were doubts in the Middle Ages is obvious from the evidence of those who did not suppress them. At Orleans in 1022, for the first time since 385, some Christians burnt other Christians because, among other things, they did not believe in the literal humanity of Christ. Members of several other dissenting movements not only doubted Christ's humanity but also doubted that Christ was really present in the Eucharist or that prayers for the dead were of any value.[2] Yet if there is plentiful evidence that many individuals had doubts, direct evidence of individuals who had doubts but suppressed them is hard to find. I shall therefore start with a clear example.

As we saw earlier, the belief that Jesus Christ was physically present in the consecrated bread and wine of the Eucharist had become the object of widespread doubt by the middle of the eleventh century, and the authorities of the Catholic religion responded by modifying the formulation of the belief, but they also prescribed in 1215 that Catholics had to believe it. Since the religious authorities had developed formidable means to repress open dissent by 1215, and since these were strengthened by the organization of the Inquisition starting in 1231, it became very dangerous to express doubts openly. Heretics such as the Cathars continued to do so amongst themselves, but most kept quiet. Only very occasionally is there evidence of the harrowing underworld of individual efforts to suppress doubts.

A delightful story reveals the anxiety that such efforts could cause. Joinville recounts what William of Auvergne, bishop of Paris (1228-1249), told him. A great theologian, whom William did not name but who was presumably a well-known teacher in

2. See Jeffrey B. Russell, *Dissent and Reform in the Early Middle Ages* (Berkeley and Los Angeles, 1965); Moore, *The Origins of European Dissent.*

the University of Paris, came to the bishop and confessed with tears that he could not believe in the Eucharist "as holy Church teaches" (the dogma of transubstantiation), but said he knew that the disbelief was a temptation of the Devil. Bishop William asked if the temptation gave him pleasure. The theologian said no, it troubled him as much as anything could. The bishop then asked whether, for any reward, he would say anything against the Eucharist or other sacraments of the church, and the theologian responded that no torture would make him say such a thing. The bishop then asked whether, after a war, the king would owe more to a castellan who had successfully guarded a castle on the border of the kingdom or to a castellan who had guarded an unthreatened castle near Paris. The theologian of course said that more was owed to the frontier castellan. Bishop William, with his untroubled faith, then compared himself to the castellan near Paris and the theologian to the frontier castellan and declared that God owed four times the grace to the theologian who was at war in tribulation yet had guarded the faith and would not abandon it for any earthly reward.[3]

Doubtless many people were never troubled by the dogma because they gave the question of the real presence little thought. They compartmentalized their thinking so that rational empirical thinking did not interfere with the nonrational assurance they gained from the Mass. But many others could not avoid awareness of a conflict. If Joinville's story is heartwarming because the bishop tried to comfort the theologian instead of condemning him, it provides a clear example of how individuals could become conscious of a tension within their religiosity and of a conflict between their religiosity and their religion. And it vividly illustrates the acute psychological stress that such awareness could engender.

If the theologian could handle that stress at considerable cost, it impelled others to irrationality. Many who could not escape awareness of the conflict felt their identity so threatened that they repressed their capacity to think rationally and empirically and projected their own nonrational meaning on realities so strongly that they perceived what they wanted to perceive. Desiring

3. Geffroi de Villehardouin and Jean de Joinville, *Memoirs of the Crusades* (London, 1951), pp. 146-147.

"proof" that Christ was indeed physically present in the Eucharist, some Christians "saw" what they wanted to see. They "saw" the consecrated wafer turn into flesh or blood; they "saw" an infant on the altar; they "saw" a child or a thirty-year-old man on a cross.[4]

Thomas Aquinas took these projections very seriously. Although he asserted that Christ's body could not be seen in the sacrament by any bodily eye but only by the spiritual eye, he argued that, as a result of divine action, the eyes of some believers were affected so that they saw flesh and blood, and he also maintained that, in some cases, there were real, visible, physical changes.[5] By the later Middle Ages, after the institution of the feast of Corpus Christi in 1264, many also came to believe that Jews—who manifestly disbelieved in transubstantiation—tortured consecrated wafers in order to harm Christ, and that the wafers bled.

With the example of William of Auvergne's theologian and of the reactions of many other nameless Christians to the Eucharist in mind, we can turn to an example where the individual's doubts can only be inferred. Peter the Venerable, the last great abbot of Cluny (1122-1156), provides a striking example of efforts to suppress doubts. His treatises are almost entirely devoted to arguing against doubts and disbelief. He wrote a major treatise against the Petrobrusian heretics who, in direct opposition to the beliefs on which Cluny was founded, rejected the Eucharist, veneration of the Cross, infant baptism, and the authority of priests, and accepted only those parts of the New Testament that they believed were reports of eyewitnesses. Peter also wrote a little treatise to correct some of his own monks at Cluny who had noticed that Jesus never said openly in the Gospels that he was God. He was also responsible for the first translation of the Koran and wrote a treatise against Islam. He wrote another treatise on miracles, for they functioned to save people from disbelief. And he wrote a long and most interesting treatise against the Jews in

---

4. See Peter Browe, *Die Eucharistichen Wunder des Mittelalters* (Breslau, 1938). These "miracles" are an extreme example of what social psychologists call attribution. See Spilka, Hood, and Gorsuch, *The Psychology of Religion*, pp. 18-29.

5. *Summa theologica*, III.76.7-8.

which he mentioned or imagined almost every objection that Jews might make to Christian beliefs and recognized that most of the standard Christian counterarguments would never convince Jews.

Peter said that he wrote his treatises to convince the disbelievers of the error of their ways, but he knew his treatises would not convert them, and he also said that he was writing to confirm weak Christians in their faith, and that seems to have been his main purpose. He was so concerned with the problem of preserving faith that, in his polemic against the Jews, he made a fascinating effort to analyze why people have faith. The argument demonstrates how badly Peter wanted rational empirical proof of his nonrational beliefs. Unfortunately for him, he was convinced that many of his nonrational beliefs were empirical propositions, tried to prove them by empirical arguments, and could only produce weak arguments. He seems to have recognized as much subconsciously, for he knew that his "proofs" would not convince Jews. Yet he refused to admit to himself that his arguments were not rationally and empirically convincing. Instead, he condemned Jews for their failure to think rationally, depicting them as animals lacking in reason because they would not agree with him. And in striking contrast with his contemporary, Bernard of Clairvaux, whose untroubled faith did not rely on rational empirical thinking, Peter's frustration made him hate Jews bitterly.[6]

William of Auvergne's theologian and Peter the Venerable are only two examples of individuals who wrestled with doubts they wanted to repress. We know of their doubts because they left obvious traces. But most others did not. Although a few more examples could be provided, it would be hard to find many.[7] Nevertheless, I strongly suspect that the indications we have are only the tip of an iceberg. We know that many were susceptible to doubts because they expressed them; they became the now nameless followers of known leaders who preached their doubts openly, propounded alternatives, and were condemned by the authorities and undoubting adherents of the church. There are

6. See "Peter the Venerable: Defense against Doubts," in *Toward a Definition of Antisemitism*, chap. 8.

7. For example, we know of one eleventh-century monk, Otloh of Saint Emmeran, who came at times to doubt the reliability of the Bible and even the existence of his God: Morris, *The Discovery of the Individual*, pp. 79-82.

also many passing indications in humorous expressions that many people who were not great theologians and never joined religious movements dealt with their doubts by taking the authorities and prescriptions of their religion lightly. They doubted internally but conformed publicly and only expressed their doubts in a safe manner among their peers.

Others, however, neither resolved their doubts theologically nor took the beliefs they had been taught lightly. Instead, they defended their beliefs by imagining that the threats to their faith were external. They attributed cosmic evil to other human beings—heretics, sorcerers, witches, and Jews. Not only did they regard these human beings as symbols of opposing beliefs; they also believed that they engaged in secret inhuman activities that attacked their Christ and undermined their society.

In 1233, Pope Gregory IX issued a bull that asserted that heretics in Germany assembled in secret meetings in a cave during which they kissed the anus of a mysterious black cat and, after the lights were extinguished, engaged in promiscuous, often incestuous and homosexual, orgies. Gregory did not invent the fantasy. As Norman Cohn has demonstrated, it can be traced back to antiquity. It was preserved and transmitted to the Middle Ages and repeated by several medieval writers, and the later accusations against witches derive from it.[8]

Its appearance in western Europe coincides with the appearance of doubts. In the eleventh century, some Christians asserted—without any evidence—that the quietly thoughtful Christians who had been branded as "heretics" at Orleans engaged in ritualized sexual orgies and cannibalism. Writers of the twelfth century made the accusation against other "heretical" groups, and the rumors were still very much alive in the thirteenth century. Between 1231 and 1234, a fanatic inquisitor, Conrad of Marburg, conducted a persecution of "heretics" in Germany. Among other things, he accused his victims of rejecting Catholic beliefs about the Eucharist and conducting diabolical rituals. His accusations were obviously derived from the old fantasies about orgies. But

---

8. Norman Cohn, *Europe's Inner Demons* (New York, 1975), pp. 1-59. See also Edward Peters, *The Magician, the Witch and the Law* (Philadelphia, 1978), pp. 33-44.

whereas in the eleventh and twelfth century writers had only made the accusation after people had already been condemned and killed as heretics on other grounds, Conrad used these accusations as grounds for executing many people and was able to persuade Gregory IX of their truth. In fact, his accusations were so wild and claimed so many lives that many in Germany did not believe them. When he was killed in 1234, most Germans, including the emperor, breathed a sigh of relief.

Nonetheless, as everybody knows, the Inquisition used the same fantasies in the later Middle Ages to persecute the women they identified as witches, and Protestants acted similarly later. And as we shall discuss later, similarly chimerical beliefs were used to justify the killing of Jews from the twelfth century to the present. No one had ever observed human beings doing what the accusations alleged, and the only "evidence" for them was confessions extracted by torture. Nonetheless, these irrational fantasies developed by certain individuals were accepted and transmitted by writers distant from the alleged events and by popular rumor. They were then used by individuals and institutions to intensify hatred against people thought to hold opposing beliefs and justify their extirpation.[9]

That fact raises the question of social irrationality and of the irrationality not of individuals but of religions. We know that very large numbers of Christians through the centuries have had chimerical beliefs about heretics, witches, and Jews, and that what they thought seemed false to many then and seems egregiously false to any well-informed person now. And we know that those fantasies, which had started as expressions of individual irrationality, were accepted by many Christians, including ecclesiastical authorities, and became an institutionalized characteristic of medieval and early modern society. It would seem that the Catholic religion not only was nonrational but also began, in the eleventh century, to be to some extent irrational.

All the Catholics and Protestants who believed these fantasies were not, of course, irrational. Most knew no better. They were not suppressing their capacity to think rationally and empirically.

9. See "Historiographic Crucifixion," in *Toward a Definition of Antisemitism,* chap. 12.

Rather, they were relying on the epistemic organization of their society to provide them with knowledge about matters beyond their personal ken. But what their society provided them was false. They themselves were not irrational; they were the victims of social irrationality.

Social irrationality springs from the common tendency to mistake expressions of nonrational beliefs for rational empirical propositions. That does not lead to irrationality so long as the beliefs stated as objective truth (e.g., god exists), do not conflict with what can be demonstrated by prevailing rational empirical thinking. The beliefs can be accepted as hypotheses and some may later be demonstrated empirically. Social irrationality arises only when many people assert as true expressions of belief that could be demonstrated at the time to be empirically false (e.g., Jews have horns). Created by individuals driven to irrationality by their need to reinforce their nonrational beliefs, such propositions may then be accepted by others who do not assert them from their own knowledge but are willing to accept what others assert as true when it reinforces their own beliefs. We might, therefore, define social irrationality as cooperative and partially institutionalized efforts to reinforce beliefs central to people's sense of social identity by projections that necessitate the suppression of available knowledge and that incite action in accordance with those projections.

Because most of those who have been affected by it were not themselves irrational, social irrationality has long been hard for contemporaries and later observers to recognize. When a nonrational belief is asserted as an empirical proposition but is in contradiction with what can be known, and is in fact known to some, relatively few people may have the knowledge to contradict it. Most people lack the opportunity to observe the realities that the symbols of irrational assertions denote. Even today, rational empirical knowledge about Jews or Communists is distributed most unevenly; most know little about the real characteristics and conduct of the human beings denoted as Jews or Communists. For many people, Jews and Communists exist only symbolically as "Jews" or "Communists" in their minds, and the meaning of those symbols for them depends primarily on their nonrational associations.

In the second place, many people are unaccustomed and unable to think rationally about abstract matters. They have difficulty drawing general inferences from what they know concretely—for example, from their direct knowledge that all the human beings they know are individuals who vary markedly to the inference that Communists cannot be identical. And third, irrational beliefs are propagated in a way that dissuades people from thinking about them rationally. The people who repeatedly and emphatically proclaim irrational beliefs typically present them as "facts" in the context of emotional expressions of nonrational belief intended to incite action to implement and defend their beliefs; they stimulate their audience to think nonrationally and deaden their capacity for rational thinking. Homilies are one example, and Hitler's harangues are an extreme example.[10]

But because the irrational beliefs of individuals can be expressed as if they were empirically true, and can be accepted as such by rational people, irrational ideas can influence social policy and institutions, including religious societies. Religions or religious societies can therefore be considered irrational to the extent that their authorities act so as to support irrational thinking and discourage rational empirical thinking that would challenge irrational ideas. Hence, if we wish to decide whether a religion is in some degree irrational, the question is whether the authorities of the religion legitimate irrational ideas, and if so, how and how much.

In the case of the medieval Catholic religion, the answer cannot be clear-cut. The broad answer is that the highest authorities did not explicitly prescribe irrational beliefs but supported some tacitly. Thus, bishops and priests supported the idea that, as a matter of empirical fact, Jews ritually crucified Christian children, and they authorized shrines that insitutionalized the idea. And although popes never officially prescribed that adherents had to believe that idea, they never pronounced the accusation false, and they countenanced the shrines, most notoriously in the case of Simon of Trent. The same is true of the accusation that Jews profaned the consecrated bread of the Eucharist to harm Christ.

10. Similar points have been made in a systematic way by Raymond Boudon, *L'idéologie* (Paris, 1986).

Popes and priests also explicitly supported, by legislation, the belief that Jewish doctors intentionally poisoned their Christian patients—even though kings and aristocrats who had much closer knowledge thought the belief false.

Significantly, however, the religious authorities treated some other irrational beliefs very differently. After the German emperor had conducted a careful examination, known throughout Europe, of the accusation that Jews engaged in ritual cannibalism, and after he had prohibited the accusation, the pope finally condemned it. During the Black Death, relying on the massive evidence of Jewish mortality available to any reasonable observer, the pope also condemned the accusation that Jews were causing the Black Death. It would therefore seem that religious authorities were willing to support irrational ideas that strengthened faith in their authority when evidence of the falsity of those ideas was not widely available. But they refrained from doing so when the evidence that the beliefs were false was so readily available that many influential people would recognize their falsity.

The explanation of the difference in reaction would seem to lie in the fact that, although the Catholic religion was the established religion of medieval societies, the priesthood was competing with governments for social authority, and the survival of the religion depended on the maintenance of its authorities. Knowledge that demonstrated the falsity of certain beliefs was widely available to all in the upper levels of society. Hence, if the higher religious authorities supported those demonstrably false beliefs, the non-priestly authorities would assume that the religious authorities knew the ideas were false and were being hypocritical, which would weaken their legitimacy and their authority relative to the governments. It was therefore in the interest of the priesthood not to support such manifestly false ideas and to give only tacit approval to less manifestly false beliefs without prescribing them officially.

That line of analysis suggests that in well-established religions whose adherents belong to all strata of society and whose authorities belong to the upper strata, most (but not all) in authority in the religion will use their capacity for rational empirical thinking and refrain from prescribing patently irrational beliefs that could then be demonstrated to be false. But they may tacitly countenance some other less demonstrably false beliefs. And that is probably true also of the religions of less intellectually sophisticated societies.

But that cautious policy may not be followed by religions without social standing. The authorities of a new religion or sect that is fighting for recognition against massive disbelief, and is seeking any recruits from any social level it can get, may not feel constrained by considerations of rationality. When Luther was fighting bitterly to spread his new religion among Christians, and when Jews refused to confirm his beliefs by converting to his new religion, he reversed his original position on Jews and supported the traditional medieval accusations in violent language. Similarly, the authorities of religions that appeal primarily to the less educated in an intellectually sophisticated and religiously pluralistic society such as ours may disregard rationality in their effort to maintain their existence. Fundamentalist Christian religions do not rely on the well-educated for their membership, and they show little regard for empirical rationality.

If religions may be irrational in the sense of prescribing or countenancing particular irrational beliefs, they may also be irrational in a more fundamental sense. Religions can encourage rational empirical thinking, but they can also discourage or suppress it, and such suppression has been very evident in Western civilization. Socrates is perhaps the most famous single victim, although Galileo would be another example. The stereotypical example of the institutionalization of such suppression is the Inquisition or Holy Office, and Stalin's Russia and Hitler's Germany provide all too recent examples of it, with George Orwell's *1984* being its most famous fictional depiction. Such suppression continues in dictatorships now, and efforts to suppress knowledge can also be found in democracies, as the debates over textbooks in the United States indicate.

One obvious present expression of religious irrationality is what is known as fundamentalism. Fundamentalists of whatever religion are those who ardently maintain certain prescribed beliefs about life and about how they should act that manifestly conflict with available and well-established contemporary knowledge. Of course, that knowledge may not, indeed cannot, be definitive, but fundamentalists refuse even to try to coordinate belief and knowledge. Although they treat their beliefs as if they were empirical propositions, they refuse to think rationally and empirically about empirical propositions that they know contradict their assertions; and they attempt, by force if possible, to suppress diffusion of that conflicting knowledge. They avoid conscious doubt by treating faith as knowledge and avoiding knowledge. To call them fundamentalists is highly appropriate, for they treat nonrational thinking as if it were not only fundamental but also the only significant mode of thinking.

Social irrationality seems a prominent characteristic of European civilization, and not just because we are better informed about it. It seems to be a side effect of that evolution of rationality which Weber thought was peculiar to Western culture. From the ancient Greeks to the present many people in European civilization and its extensions have valued rational thinking highly, if not always empiricism, labored to develop that capacity, and encouraged the creation of social institutions such as universities to foster it. So highly has rationality been valued that although some of the nonrational beliefs of the Catholic religion were stated as empirical propositions that could easily be doubted, the Catholic religion has strongly supported the rationalization of its beliefs in a way that assured the further development of rational thinking— even though Catholic authorities have also sought at times to suppress its conclusions, particularly when rational thinking was combined with empiricism.

A good argument can be made, and Weber laid the basis for it, that manifest irrationality can only appear in certain societies. If irrationality is considered to be the result of doubts resulting from a conflict between nonrational and rational thinking, it can arise only when people differentiate sufficiently clearly, in practice or conceptually, between their nonrational and rational empirical thinking so that they are aware of the difference. Only then can they become aware that there are two different ways of thinking and recognize conflicts between them. Although "primitive" people do use their rational empirical capacities pretheoretically to solve their practical problems, they do not seem to be aware of it as a distinctive way of thinking; the interaction between their two types of thinking is so immediate that they are hardly aware of it. As it is often put, they do not distinguish between the "sacred" and the "profane."

But when people develop abstract rules of procedure for rational empirical thinking about anything (logic, statistics, methods of observation), they do become aware that there are two different ways of thinking. Although they do not create the capacity to think rationally and empirically, they come to recognize its distinctive powers. And once they make that differentiation, or engage in second-order thinking about how they think, they are potentially faced with challenges between their affirmations of belief and their assertions of knowledge.

Whatever the causes, the Greeks of antiquity did just that, even though they did not differentiate their thinking as explicitly as we do; and their development of rationality opened the way for individual and social irrationality.[11] Indeed, according to one theory, their pursuit of rationality led directly to racism. Christian Delacampagne has argued that the development of rationality led the Greeks to categorize the natural phenomena they observed, including human beings, and arrange them on a hierarchical ontological scale that placed Greeks above non-Greeks and men above women, and made slavery a "natural" condition. He has also argued that belief in reason kills religion, replacing gods and myths of origin with the forces of nature and scientific explanations of origins.[12]

I thoroughly agree with Delacampagne's emphasis on the crucial importance of the development of reason in the sense of rational empirical thinking about how we think, that is, philosophy and psychology. But I disagree strongly with his thesis that it led directly to the death of religions and to racism. Thus, his argument about the Greeks fails to recognize that although classification may be a rational activity, when the Greeks applied that

11. For interesting hypotheses about the development of rationality by the Greeks, see the articles by Julius Moravcsik, Arthur W. H. Adkins, Joseph Margolis, Dallas Willard, and Wallace I. Matson in *Language and Thought in Early Greek Philosophy*, ed. Kevin Robb (La Salle, Ill., 1983). See also G. E. R. Lloyd, *The Revolutions of Wisdom* (Berkeley, Los Angeles, London, 1987).

12. *L'invention du racisme* (Paris, 1983); revised edition, *Racismo y occidente* (Barcelona, 1983).

capacity to non-Greeks, slaves, and women, they subordinated that capacity to nonrational sexual and ethnocentric premises that were salient in their sense of unique identity. More generally, I cannot agree that religion and reason are necessarily incompatible. As should be clear by now, I think that religiosity is a fundamental characteristic or capacity of human beings, and I have argued that religious beliefs are menaced by reason only when they are affirmed in the same form as rational empirical propositions, are considered to be empirical propositions, and are contradicted by rational empirical knowledge available at the time. But when they are, irrational beliefs can arise.

Irrational beliefs appear when individuals confuse nonrational beliefs central to their sense of identity with knowledge, attempt to defend those beliefs against rational doubts by suppressing their own capacity to think rationally and empirically about the characteristics of certain objects, events, and people, and attribute empirical characteristics to them that have never been observed. And since there is no better example of the horrors potentially stemming from such attributions than the treatment of Jews in European civilization, and no doubt that religion played a major role in that treatment, the final section of this book will illustrate the implications of my approach to religion by applying it to explain antisemitism.

Part Three

The Religious Roots of Antisemitism

Chapter Fourteen

From Anti-Judaism to Antisemitism

Antisemitism, I shall argue, both in its origins and in its recent most horrible manifestation, is the hostility aroused by irrational thinking about "Jews." But Jews have also been the object of all the more usual kinds of hostility that have been directed at other major groups, especially enduring ethnic groups that competed for scarce resources. If we look first at the kind of hostility that preceded and prepared the way for antisemitism, the contrast will become obvious.

Since I am primarily concerned with the European antisemitism that led directly to the "Final Solution," I shall not discuss pagan attitudes to Jews in antiquity. Certainly, many pagans in the Roman Empire were strongly, even violently, anti-Judaic; indeed, a few individuals may have been antisemitic in my sense. But for various reasons, some of which were sketched in chapter 2, I do not think their attitudes significantly influenced the formation of antisemitism in western Europe, whereas a connection between Christianity and antisemitism is undeniable. We must, therefore, examine the hostility of Christians that preceded the appearance of Christian antisemitism, the hostility usually referred to as anti-Judaism.

As I observed at the outset, the term "anti-Judaism" was used at the end of the ninteenth century by Bernard Lazare to distinguish the centuries-long religious opposition of Christians to Judaism and Jews from nineteenth-century antisemitism. But both

Jewish and Christian scholars soon came to describe instances of hostility against Jews at any time from antiquity to the present as antisemitism. And so long as they accepted that usage, Christian scholars could no longer rely on a chronological argument to disculpate Christianity from responsibility for the Holocaust. If they wished to absolve early Christianity, they had to find a way to distinguish between anti-Judaism and antisemitism in antiquity as well as in the modern period.

Several Christian scholars, therefore, sought to distinguish between the hostility in antiquity of which they did not approve and the Christian rejection of Judaism on theological grounds of which they did approve. Yet if they were able to do so by arguments based on Christian premises, they were unable to demonstrate an empirical distinction between the two kinds of hostility. Their historical investigations only demonstrated ever more clearly an undeniable connection between Christian hostility in the first century and the horrors of twentieth-century antisemitism.

Empirical distinctions can be drawn, however, if religious phenomena are conceptualized in the way I have presented. It can be argued that anti-Judaism is a nonrational reaction to overcome nonrational doubts, while antisemitism is an irrational reaction to repressed rational doubts. And when this distinction is applied, the historical picture that emerges is very different from either the chronological distinction between a period of religious and a period of racist hostility favored by Hannah Arendt, or the theological distinction between two forms of hostility in the ancient world favored by many Christian scholars.

Jesus of Nazareth was neither anti-Jewish nor anti-Judaic—to say nothing of antisemitic. The historical Jesus was a Jew whose religiosity was deeply Judaic and whose only religion was Judaic. He was born in Bethlehem into a society in which the dominant religion was a Judaic religion closely supportive of a people, and in which the religiosity of almost all members was deeply influenced by nonrational Judaic beliefs so that they symbolized themselves as Jews. The Jews, however, were divided among several competing Judaic religions or sects.[1] If all Jews accepted Hebrew

1. See Jacob Neusner, William Scott Green, and Jonathan Z. Smith, eds., *Judaisms and Their Messiahs at the Turn of the Christian Era* (New York, 1987).

Scripture as divine revelation, as individuals they differed somewhat in religiosity, and as members of society they looked to different human authorities to determine the meaning of Scripture and prescribe their conduct.

Jesus certainly symbolized himself as a Jew in his own language, whatever other symbols were salient in his sense of identity, although he had little need to do so explicitly when almost all he spoke to were Jews. But as he developed, he associated that symbol and those usually associated with it with symbols that were salient in his own religiosity in a way that made his religiosity differ markedly from that of many other Jews—although it apparently had much in common with the religiosity of those who accepted John the Baptist as a privileged contact with the god of Judaism. In any case, Jesus' religiosity found expression in beliefs—for example, in the proximate end of the world and how individuals should prepare for it—that set him apart from most other Jews and seem to have caused him to have nonrational doubts about some prescriptions of the dominant Judaic religion and to seek to modify them.

The initial conflict between the followers of Jesus and Paul and the majority of Jews who did not join the Nazarene movement was a conflict over nonrational beliefs, and above all over one belief. The limited evidence from a later period permits only speculation about the precise characteristics of Jesus' personality, religiosity, and expressed beliefs. Yet we can be sure that he asserted, like Moses or the prophets but in his own way, that he had a direct contact with the god of Judaism denied to other contemporaries; and he persuaded others to believe him. We might speculate about what it was that made his beliefs appealing to their religiosity.[2] But whatever sociological and psychological explanations be given, his followers associated Jesus nonrationally with the Judaic symbols they associated with their god, symbols

2. There must always be an affinity between the message of a charismatic and the needs of his or her audience. The deprivation theory would suggest that the affinity in this case was a shared reaction of the socially disfavored against the upper classes. A variant of it, based on a possible reading of the uncertain evidence of the Gospels, would be that what appealed, perhaps particularly to Paul, was Jesus' emphasis on the value or salvation of the individual rather than that of the religious society.

such as Moses, Messiah, Christ, and Israel, and with other symbols connected with their daily life that were central in their sense of identity, such as neighbor. And as Jesus became a salient symbol in their religiosity, their sense of identity and of the meaning of Judaism changed.

A new religious movement developed around Jesus composed of Jews who accepted him as a direct contact with their god, the god of Moses. Yet, though they used most of the same Judaic symbols as other Jews to express their own faith, some of their nonrational beliefs conflicted with those of many Jews. Jesus and his followers apparently questioned some of the prescriptions of the dominant Judaic religion—or at least the conduct of those in authority—in a way that encouraged doubts about the legitimacy of the religious authorities and led to Jesus' condemnation. Assuredly such questioning was the case for those who continued to believe in Jesus and risk persecution after his condemnation by those authorities had led to his condemnation and execution by the Romans. They had to reject that prescription at least.

Yet to describe Jesus and his early followers as anti-Jewish or categorize their attitude as anti-Judaism makes sense only if we neglect the religiosity of Jews and think of Judaism as a single religion. To describe them as anti-Judaic contradicts the way we use "Christianity." We denote as Christians any people at any time who have symbolized themselves as Christian because they believed that Jesus was in some fundamental sense supernatural, and we use the term Christianity to refer to the thoughts, actions, and religions connected with that belief by people who have symbolized themselves as Christians. Similarly, we should not identify Judaism with any particular Judaic religion. Rather, we should denote as Jews those who have symbolized themselves as Jews because they believed that the fundamental revelation about ultra-empirical reality came through Moses, and we should use the term Judaism to refer to all the thoughts, actions, and religions connected with that belief by people who symbolize themselves as Jews.[3]

3. One value of distinguishing between religion and religiosity is that it permits a distinction between those who are Jews in the sense of being adherents of a Judaic religion and those who are Jews in the sense that their religiosity uses many Judaic symbols even though they do not adhere to any Judaic religion.

We cannot then describe Jesus and his immediate followers as anti-Jewish or their attitude to Judaic religions as anti-Judaism. Although their religiosity may have conflicted to some extent with that of many other Jews, they symbolized themselves not as Christians but as Jews, and they relied heavily on long-established Judaic symbols and beliefs to establish their own sense of identity. The criticisms of the scribes and Pharisees attributed to Jesus in the Gospels accuse them of being hypocrites; they are not criticisms of the religion over which they presided. Some of Jesus' first followers may have disliked some other Jews, but since they symbolized themselves as Jews, they could not hate others simply for being Jews. Moreover, although they rejected some beliefs prescribed by existing Judaic religions, and although they formed their own religious subsociety or subsocieties that recognized Jesus as a superior religious authority (including the subsociety that met in the portico of the Temple and followed the Law), they were only creating a new Judaic sect or potential Judaic religion that they hoped would become the religion of all Jews.

In its origins, Christianity, like Pharisaism, was neither anti-Jewish nor anti-Judaic. Whatever the conflicts with other Jews or Judaic religions, the followers of Jesus could become anti-Jewish or anti-Judaic only if they accepted Christ rather than Moses as their most fundamental contact with their god and the primary symbol of their identity and refused to accept the authority of any Judaic religion, even though they might still symbolize themselves as Jews.[4]

Many who followed Jesus never took that decisive step. They were the Judeo-Christians who stayed in the middle, endured for about a century, were increasingly rejected by other Jews and Christians, and had largely disappeared by 135. The decisive change came with Paul and his decision to devote his efforts to converting non-Jews to his understanding of Jesus' message. Just as Jews had sought to convert gentiles to their Judaic religion, so Paul and others such as Philip, Barnabas, and Mark sought to persuade them to believe in Jesus. And as Paul's proselytizing succeeded, his attitudes changed.

I cannot enter here into the present lively debate about Paul's

---

4. Hence, I would consider the "Jews for Jesus" movement as anti-Judaic.

thought and his attitude toward non-Christian Jews and the dominant Judaic religions. Despite arguments to the contrary, it still seems plausible that he maintained that Jews who did not believe that Jesus was a direct contact with their god would not be saved. But even if Paul was against Judaic religions to that considerable, if considerably ambivalent, extent, I do not think he hated non-Christian Jews, for he still identified himself as a Jew.

Paul's religiosity seems initially to have been universal in outlook, individuals and their religiosity being more salient in his consciousness than any particular society or religion. "There is neither Jew nor Greek, there is neither slave nor free, there is neither male nor female; for you are all one in Christ Jesus."[5] Jews and non-Jews would be saved, he insisted, if they as individuals accepted Jesus as their fundamental contact with "God"— indeed, as their god. Hence, he did not demand that his non-Jewish converts identify themselves as Jews. Just the reverse. He told them that they should not obey many prescriptions that were common to every Judaic religious society. If his religiosity, like that of Jesus, was distinctively Jewish, he did not think salvation depended on adherence to a religion, possibly because he believed the end of the world at hand. Unlike those who first followed Jesus, the religiosity of Paul and his followers had at first no institutional base. Initially the Pauline movement was neither a sect within Judaism nor a religion outside of it; it was a sharing of religiosity with any who would accept it.

Although Paul used synagogues as a springboard and his messages were permeated with Judaic symbolization, his preaching neither supported nor rejected the members of any Judaic religious society, nor indeed any other existing society. A Jew or a non-Jew could be a Christian. And just as Paul did not expect Jews who followed him to give up all their prior symbolic associations and conduct, neither did he require his non-Jewish adherents to reject all the symbolic associations and practices that had hitherto given them their sense of identity. They could recognize the appeal of his beliefs without having to symbolize themselves as Jews or abandon all their Greek and Roman associations.

His appeal was remarkably successful, and precisely because it

5. Galatians 3:28.

was—and because Paul was not operating within an established religious society—he soon confronted the problem that faces anyone whose social expression of religiosity attracts many individuals, the problem of social organization, of the routinization of charisma. Unlike Francis of Assisi, Paul accepted the burden wholeheartedly. He tried to organize his followers into religious societies that accepted his prescriptions. In his epistles, our earliest direct evidence for the consequences of Jesus' teaching, we can see him striving to exert authority over his followers to ensure that they would believe and conduct themselves as he did. The result was the little societies of households headed by Christians in various cities: the beginning of new Christian religions supportive of the authority of Paul. And with the birth of Christian religions, there could now be tension between Christian religions and Judaic religions—and between the religiosity of Christians and their Christian religion.

The emergence of the new Christian religious societies generated new intergroup attitudes and intergroup politics. The new Christian societies reacted to each other, to Jewish society, and to the greater surrounding society of the empire; and the Roman and Jewish authorities reacted to the new Christian societies. The Roman persecutions and the gradual conversion of Greco-Romans to Christianity are too well known to need discussion and are irrelevant here, but the reaction of Jews is important.

The Jewish authorities reacted strongly against Christians initially, but paid less and less attention to Christians thereafter. Since the overwhelming majority of Jews had not been attracted by the new Christian religiosity, the Jewish authorities did not feel particularly threatened by the relatively small schismatic movement. They had even less cause to worry when Paul made it possible to be a Christian without being a Jew, for most Jews did not wish to abandon their self-identification as Jews and were not attracted to the Pauline Christian movement. Moreover, since most of the adherents' of the Pauline movement were not Jews, the rapid expansion of the movement was not a serious threat to the authorities of the Judaic religions. As for the Christians who still adhered to their Judiac religion, the Judeo-Christians, they were a problem, as is any sectarian movement within a religion. But they were only a minor problem, which was solved by occasional persecution and their exclusion from the synagogues about the year 80. Of far more concern for the Judaic authorities than these conflicts with Christian movements was the conflict with the Roman authorities that led to the destruction of the Temple and the dispersion from Jerusalem.

Although the Jewish authorities did circulate scurrilous stories about Jesus and his followers, which were known in their medieval form as the *Toledot Jesu*, they were very brief and were the kind of slander that religious authorities frequently tell about those they consider heretics. What is striking is that the authorities of the new Talmudic Judaic religion ignored Christianity almost completely, save for those stories. Those who explain the development of Talmudic Judaism as a retreat from Greco-Roman thought in reaction to the success of Christianity are almost certainly wrong. The efforts of Jews to maintain their identity in the face of the riots against Jews in Greek cities, the wars with Rome that resulted in the destruction of the Temple, and the dispersion of many Jews from Jerusalem and Palestine provide a more obvious explanation.

For Christians, however, Jews and Judaism remained crucially important. Although Jews posed no serious or enduring physical threat to the survival of Pauline Christianity, the very existence of Jewish religiosity and Judaic religions posed a fundamental problem for Christians and the new Christian religions, for it was an internal problem, a birth trauma. Christians could never escape their awareness of competing with Judaism. Even before there was a distinctive Christian religion, the early followers of Jesus and Paul had challenged the legitimacy of the authorities of the dominant Judaic religion and tried to attract others to their beliefs about Jesus. And when new Christian religions with non-Jewish adherents were formed on the basis of those beliefs and sought to legitimate their independence, they had to make their rejection of the Judaic authorities an explicit and integral part of Christian belief.

From motives common to most sects, the adherents of the new Christian religions were necessarily anti-Judaic in the sense that they had to demonstrate the superiority of their Christian religions to any Judaic religions. But their arguments were ambivalent precisely because their claim to legitimacy rested on their

Judaic inheritance. People in antiquity expected religions to be old, with the result that Christians sought to claim antiquity by insisting that their religion was a continuation of Judaic religion.[6] They were partly right and partly wrong. On the one hand, Christian religiosity had started as a form of Judaic religiosity, and the emerging Christian religions maintained many elements of religiosity prescribed by Judaic religions; on the other, the emerging Christian societies were not a continuation of any Judaic religion, for they had rejected the authorities of all Judaic religions and were developing their own.

Their struggles to establish their own identity were fraught with tensions, including the tension with Judaism. Although Paul stressed faith, hope, and love, the Christian religions emerged out of conflicts and doubts. As his epistles make clear, Paul and his followers were troubled not only by the disbelief of non-Christian Jews and Greco-Romans but also by their own nonrational doubts and diversity of belief. That diversity should not surprise us. Belief in Jesus and baptism was no more open to rational proof or disproof than belief in the authority of the High Priest or the Pharisees or circumcision. And since faith in Jesus was still primarily an individual phenomenon and there was no social authority that could impose its prescriptions on all Christians, diversity of religiosity produced manifest diversity in the beliefs about Jesus.

People became Christian because they had had nonrational and rational doubts about the beliefs with which they had grown up and were powerfully attracted by the new beliefs they encountered. But their new religiosity was unsettled. Not only had most of Paul's converts not grown up in a society permeated with Jewish symbols, they had not grown up in a society in which Christian symbols, nonrational associations, prescriptions of carefully formulated beliefs and rituals, and their institutional organization were taken for granted. In fact, the most distinctive Christian beliefs—for example, about the Trinity—had not yet been stably formulated. And because both their religiosity and the formulation of Christian beliefs were in a state of flux, the religiosity of individuals had an impact on the development of the beliefs and

6. See Simon, *Verus Israël*, pp. 87-124.

organization of Christian religions that would be impossible later. Inevitably, there were sharp disagreements as individuals sought to organize religious societies and to formulate and prescribe their beliefs.

The first centuries of Christianity were a period of massive syncretic borrowing and organizational development, accompanied by political struggles, great theological debates, the gradual definition of the canon of the New Testament, and schisms. And one inescapable issue among many others was the relation between Christianity and Judaism. The symbols and many of the symbolic associations of Jewish religiosity would have been salient in Christian religiosity even if, like Marcion (died about 160),[7] Christians had been willing to accept that theirs was a brand-new religion, deny the authority of Hebrew Scripture, and reject much of what would become part of the canonical New Testament. But all the main Christian religions did accept translated versions of Hebrew Scripture as divine revelation. The conflict between Christian and Judaic religions was thus enshrined within Christianity in the division of the Christian Bible between the Old and New Testaments, the belief in the old and new Covenants, and the New Testament's testimony to Jewish disbelief.

Jews and Judaic religions posed a problem for Christian religiosity and Christian religions that Christians could not avoid, for it was the result of tensions within the religiosity of Christians and between Christians. They could not help asking and trying to explain why the vast majority of Jews had been unwilling to accept the Christians' beliefs about Jesus. Jesus was a Jew who lived and died in the Jewish society of Palestine; he and his disciples relied on Jewish Scripture; and many Jews in Palestine had seen him. Why, then, had most not believed him? Jews were thus the very incarnation of disbelief in Jesus. And because they were, not only could they inspire doubts but Christians who were seriously bothered by their own doubts could hardly avoid thinking of Jews.

If Paul and other Christians had been thinking rationally and

7. Jaroslav Pelikan, *The Christian Tradition*, vol. 1, *The Emergence of the Christian Tradition* (Chicago, 1971), pp. 71-81.

empirically about the problem, they—like any modern historian—could have found obvious explanations for Jewish disbelief by examining the divisions of Judaism at the time and the alternative explanations then available for Jesus' actions and death. But to accept those answers would have emphasized that Jesus' divinity was anything but self-evident and that the reaction of non-Christian Jews to Jesus was easily comprehensible. In fact, several passages in the Gospels indicated that he had not made his identity obvious, but to insist on that obscurity would only have strengthened doubts about his divinity. Instead, Christians increasingly insisted on the failure of Jews to recognize what Christians asserted to have been manifest to men of good will.

Among the variety of Christian reactions to enduring Jewish disbelief, three main nonrational reactions stand out: belief in the deficiency of Jewish understanding; the deicide accusation; and the belief that historical events demonstrated that God was punishing the Jews for their deicide. The reactions are clearly related; together, they constitute the core of Christian anti-Judaism. Yet if we, looking back, can see the relation between them, they only emerged gradually, one after another. And although they fused, they remained conceptually distinct. I shall therefore deal with each separately.

The first reaction to Jewish disbelief was the effort to explain why Jews did not believe as Christians did. Paul was very aware of the need for such an explanation. Whatever he now believed, he knew that he had not initially believed in Jesus, and he knew that most Jews who knew what he knew neither believed in Jesus nor interpreted Scripture as he now did. Paul could not avoid the problem of explaining the conflict in nonrational beliefs. He resolved it in a self-righteous way whose consequences he could not have foreseen.

Precisely because his religiosity was Judaic and monotheist, Paul could not acknowledge that he was proclaiming a new god and active in establishing a new religion. There could only be one god, the god who had revealed himself to Jews and whose revelations were preserved in the Hebrew Scriptures. Why then did most other Jews who revered the same Scriptures refuse to see life as he did? In his frustration, Paul asserted that the god of the

Jews had blinded most Jews to the meaning of their own Scriptures and even to their god's presence among them so that they were now inferior in righteousness.

In effect, in the terms I have been using, his paradoxical assertion was equivalent to the proposition that the capacity of most Jews to think nonrationally had been weakened, an idea so implausible that Paul considered the phenomenon mysterious and could only explain it by divine action. A modern parallel would be the Nazi assertion that Jews were unable to appreciate fundamental values because of the mysterious action of biological forces. Instead of assuming, like polytheists, that people and individuals have had different gods because they were different people, monotheists have been monopolists; they have insisted imperialistically that there was only one valid faith or genuine sense of human identity, and that all sane people should believe in their concept of a supreme being.

Paul's belief in Jewish blindness was a nonrational and nonempirical intepretation of the conflict of nonrational beliefs. But it had implications for the interpretation of empirical events since it purported to explain something empirically observable, the difference in beliefs. It therefore suggested that other events could be explained in the same way. Not surprisingly, the Christians who followed Paul came to expect that events of history would confirm their belief in Jesus. If they had to defer and reinterpret the expectation of the end of the world which had been so important for the beginning of Christianity, they could, in the meantime, interpret other occurrences in present times as empirical confirmations of their faith. When the Romans were victorious in the Jewish wars, destroyed the Temple, and dispersed Jews from Palestine, Christians thought those hard-won successes of the Roman army demonstrated that their god was punishing contemporary Jews for their condemnation of Jesus and continuing disbelief in him.

But if events during Jesus' life and after confirmed their beliefs, then those before Jesus must do so also. By the time of Eusebius (died ca. 340), Christians had revised history before Christ to correspond to their interpretation of the conflict between Jews and Christians after Christ; they polarized the actors of the Old Testament into bad Jews and good Hebrews and thought of themselves as the descendants of the Hebrews and the true Israel.[8] By the beginning of the fifth century, Augustine of Hippo would see all history as a confirmation of his faith, and his writings would influence Christians for centuries to come to see it the same way. Jews were not only blind to the divinity of Jesus; they were unable to understand their own history.

As James Parkes emphasized, Christians gradually reinterpreted Hebrew Scriptures and the past of Jews in accordance with their own nonrational beliefs in a way that anyone who does not share Christian beliefs—and even someone like James Parkes who did—must consider a distortion. Even though some literary scholars assert that a text has no fixed meaning or that we cannot know what it meant to those who composed it, we can be sure that whatever the Hebrew Scriptures meant to those who composed them, they did not mean what Christians, who lived much later and whose religiosity had developed under very different conditions, said they had meant. Nor had Jews done what Christians said they had done.

The Christian understanding of Jewish history is a perfect example of the failure to distinguish between nonrational and rational empirical thinking. But it was not irrational. We, looking back with our techniques of rational empiricism and historical analysis, can recognize what they were doing. And we would be irrational if we ourselves failed to distinguish between the two modes of thinking about the past. But since neither Jews nor Christians had developed those techniques, they were not suppressing their capacity for rational empirical thought. They were not being irrational as they molded their beliefs about the past to confirm their distinctive identity. They were writing religious history, myths of origin, not the empirical history of religions, something most Christian historians of Christianity would continue to do until the nineteenth century—and many still do in the twentieth.

If the first main nonrational reaction to the challenge of Jewish disbelief was to make historical events a demonstration of Jewish blindness, the second and most famous was the accusation that the Jews were responsible for the death of Jesus Christ. As ob-

8. See Simon, *Verus Israël*, pp. 86-124.

served earlier, the affirmation of the physical resurrection of Jesus of Nazareth, symbolized as Christ, was identical in form with an empirical proposition. As such, it aroused doubts at the time and has ever since. But from an early date, many Christians hated Jews who were not born when Jesus died because, they said, the Jews had literally killed their god.

Paul, who was thoroughly aware of the doubts about Jesus' resurrection, accused Jews of blindness but not of killing his god. That accusation did not appear clearly until the Gospel attributed to John, which is usually dated about the end of the first century, when it had become obvious that most Jews were not going to believe in Jesus. Nonetheless, the accusation owed much to Paul, for it relied on his assertion of the supernatural blindness of the Jews. As Jesus' life and death became more remote in time and space, and as more and more gentiles converted to Christianity, it became easier to think of "Christ" as "God" than of Jesus as human. But if Jesus had died on the cross because of Jewish disbelief, either Jesus was only a dead human or the Jews had killed the Christ. Since Christians proclaimed that their god had appeared empirically, many were therefore impelled to protect themselves from doubt by insisting that "Jews" were so deficient in understanding that they had not only misinterpreted their own Scriptures but had, in some concrete sense, killed "God."

The deicide accusation camouflaged Christian awareness that the continued existence of Jewish disbelief challenged Christian belief. The accusation enabled Christians to repress doubts about Jesus' resurrection by imagining that no one who was not blind could have encountered Jesus without perceiving he was God. Indeed, not to recognize their God seemed so implausible that some Christians found it easier to attribute it to ill will than to ignorance. Some apocryphal gospels alleged that the Jewish authorities really had believed; they had known that Jesus was God but killed him nonetheless. As Thomas Aquinas would put it much later, the ignorance of the Jewish elders was affected ignorance, "for they saw manifest signs of his Godhead; yet they perverted them out of hatred and envy of Christ."[9] Jews were not simply blind, they were malevolent.

9. *Summa theologica*, III.47.5. For an overview of this development, see

Many, probably most, Christians in the Roman Empire did not in fact hate Jews, but some did, especially some in authority who were later considered as peculiarly authoritative and given the title of Church Fathers. But at the time, they felt their authority challenged. The most famous example is John Chrysostom,[10] but Ambrose was not far behind. Had the Roman Empire in the west continued, hostility against Jews might have increased greatly and become irrational, but it did not.

With the fall of the western Roman Empire, the deicide accusation lost significance. When the Germanic conquerors converted to Christianity, they understood it according to their own religiosity, and they converted the religion of Ambrose, Jerome, Chrysostom, Augustine, and the other authorities into a Christian religion supportive of particular peoples. They took for granted that each people, including Jews, would have its own religion; they conceived of Christ as the mighty god, bringer of victories, depicted in the Old Testament. They paid little attention to the account of the humanity of Jesus in the New Testament and were little concerned with his suffering and death. Although they believed their god had appeared on earth, they apparently could not imagine that anyone could really have killed him. Consequently, they thought of Jews as they were depicted in the Old Testament and saw them as a model rather than as Christ-killers.[11]

By the end of the eleventh century, however, conditions had changed radically. Jews in northern Europe were a small and largely defenseless group who lived surrounded by Christians whose religiosity and religion were changing significantly. During the eleventh century, many Christians had recently come to think of Jesus as he had been in empirical reality, to think of him, not simply symbolically as a distant all-powerful divinity, but also historically as a poor suffering human on the cross. One symptom of the change was that, whereas European Christians had been using "Jerusalem" primarily as a symbol for heaven, now the symbol evoked emotional responses to the earthly city, the symbol of

---

Jeremy Cohen, "The Jews as the Killers of Christ in the Latin Tradition, from Augustine to the Friars," *Traditio* 39 (1983): 1-27.

10. See Wilken, *John Chrysostom and the Jews*.

11. See "The Transformation of Anti-Judaism," in *Toward a Definition of Antisemitism*, chap. 4.

Jesus' empirical death and resurrection.[12] The renewed interest in the observable city manifested itself throughout the century by the increase in pilgrimages to it. Another symptom of the change in mentality was the Investiture Contest, the great struggle in the middle of the century to establish a European Christian religion that looked only to the authority of the pope. And when, in 1095, the pope of the new religion called on his adherents to liberate Jerusalem where Jesus had died from Moslem unbelievers, he and others were surprised at the wide response.

One response was the official crusading armies; the other was what is known as the People's or Peasant Crusade. The popular crusaders came from an area in northern Europe that had suffered from severe social dislocation. Those who joined the movement came primarily from the lower segments of society. They left the society where they counted for little and took off to fight the unbelievers. They set off on their own before the official crusade in groups with little organization. But before they left, and in defiance of the religious authorities, some of these groups slaughtered any Jews they could lay their hands on who refused to convert.[13] They did so, they said, because Jews had killed their Christ and were Christ's worst enemies.

In fact, the Jews of 1096 had had nothing to do with the death of Jesus (except that they approved of it); and had Jesus really been immortal, even Jews at the time could not have really killed him. But what non-Christian Jews could and did do in Jesus' lifetime—and have done ever since through the account of them in the New Testament and their presence in the midst of Christians—was to challenge Christian ideas about Jesus. Their existence and disbelief reinforced any doubts that were lurking consciously or subconsciously in the minds of Christians. And here it is well to remember that some small Christian movements or

12. Joshua Prawer, "Jerusalem in the Christian and Jewish Perspectives of the Early Middle Ages," in *Gli ebrei nell'alto medioevo*, Settimane di studio del Centro italiano di studi sull'alto medioevo, vol. 26 (Spoleto, 1980), 2:739-812.

13. Jonathan Riley-Smith, "The First Crusade and the Persecution of the Jews," *Studies in Church History* 21 (1984): 51-55, argues that the bands that committed the major massacres were ably led by experienced nobles, but I remain unconvinced about the number of knights in these bands and how disciplined they were.

"heretics" had already been expressing doubts about Jesus' divinity or his humanity in the first half of the eleventh century.

Jews were therefore a real threat to any Christians who were sensitive to threats to their identity. Some Christians sensitive to doubts, like Anselm[14] and Peter the Venerable, sought by rational arguments or rationalizations to overcome their doubts and preserve their assurance of the value of their identity; some, like William of Auvergne's theologian, would learn to live with them; some would suppress doubts by killing heretics. But several bands of the popular crusaders of 1096 tried to extirpate Jews. These groups seem to have been made up of people whose sense of identity had been seriously undermined by rapidly changing social conditions that they could not control or understand and to which they could not adapt successfully. Their present life gave little assurance of the earthly value of their identity, and in their dissatisfaction they sought a new one. As their refusal to obey ecclesiastical or governmental authority and their generally disorderly conduct indicate, they had little faith in those authorities. Yet if their unsettled religiosity conflicted with their religion and made them doubt its authorities and their prescriptions, they had been brought up in that religion—however unsophisticated their understanding of it—and the symbol of Christ was salient in their sense of identity. Whatever else they were, their religiosity was Christian.

When the distant pope summoned Christians to fight to liberate Christ's tomb from Moslem unbelievers, the message mobilized them to escape from their uncertainties. It associated "Christ" with "fighting," "revenge," and "feud," symbols prominent in their culture, and probably peculiarly salient in their own frustrated lives. Holy war thus gave a new integration to their

14. In or about 1097, Anselm, the greatest medieval theologian before Thomas Aquinas, doubted the standard explanation of why his god had suffered death and wrote *Cur Deus homo*, the famous treatise that gave his own explanation of why God had had to become man and die in order to save human beings; he was directly influenced by his awareness of Jewish disbelief: see Richard W. Southern, *Saint Anselm and His Biographer* (Cambridge, Eng., 1966), pp. 88-91. The increased sensitivity to challenges to Christian beliefs is indicated by the great increase in polemics against Jews in the eleventh and twelfth centuries: see the articles by David Berger and Jeremy Cohen and my comment in "AHR Forum," *American Historical Review* 91 (1986): 576-624.

lives that emboldened them to defy the local authorities of their religion. But when they thought of fighting, revenge, and Christ's death, the symbol "Jews" immediately came to mind, for they had been taught that "Jews" were responsible for his death. What better expression of their newly reinforced religiosity than to avenge the death of their Christ by attacking those responsible for his death?

It is highly significant, however, that these violent groups first summoned Jews to convert and killed them only if they refused. To the killers, the threat of Jewish disbelief to their sense of identity was even more important than their desire for vengeance. There could hardly be a better confirmation of their faith or better reassurance of the security of their identity as Christians than— as in show trials—the willingness of Jews to recognize the error of their ways and become Christians. But most of the besieged Jews refused, preferring to die rather than abandon their own identity. They rejected baptism, fought to defend themselves, and expressed contempt for "the hanged one." When they could no longer defend themselves, many expressed their disbelief in the most extreme form by preferring suicide.[15] And since the unofficial crusaders were unable to make living Jews serve to reinforce their belief in Christ and the value of their own identity, they tried to eradicate the threat of disbelief by killing Jews. Their religiosity was so threatened that, though the Jews' challenge to their identity was only mental, they could respond only by defying the authorities of their own religion and killing the overt disbelievers.

The suicides and massacres of 1096 were horrible, yet it is difficult to characterize the killers as irrational (though some may have been). If they hated Jews because of doubts about the value of their own identity and killed Jews to stifle those doubts, they were nonetheless correct in thinking that Jews did not believe in Christ and mocked those who believed in "the hanged one." Moreover, the killers did not project on Jews any characteristics

---

15. See Robert Chazan, *European Jewry and the First Crusade* (Berkeley, Los Angeles, London, 1987).

Jews did not have, such as horns.[16] They killed Jews because they were Jews, because Jews were people in the midst of Christendom who stubbornly rejected the nonrational beliefs of Christianity and persisted in adhering to their Judaic religion to the point of martyrdom. The killers were no more irrational than the Catholics and Protestants who killed each other in the Thirty Years War. Yet if they were not irrational, their reaction to their awareness of conflicting nonrational beliefs had brought them to the verge of irrationality. And from then on, the crusades would embed the stereotype of Christ-killer in all ranks of society.

The third main reaction to Jewish disbelief was the efforts of Christians, as they gained political power in the Roman Empire, to use Jews for their own ends. By the fourth century, Christian religions supportive of the supreme social authority of the priesthood had existed for some two centuries within the complex differentiated society of the Roman Empire. By 313, the Catholic religion had acquired sufficient support so that its authorities could compete with the authority of the government and persuade the emperor to recognize and protect it. And once they had gained that measure of political power, they were able to influence the Roman government to deny Jews access to influential occupations, prohibit them from building new synagogues, and restrict their intercourse with Christians.

It was a fateful precedent. Even though Christians may not have been conscious of it, the results of their legal efforts to restrict and degrade Jews reinforced their belief that empirical historical events would confirm their faith in Jesus Christ. They had long believed that their god was punishing Jews for their disbelief and deicide by depriving them of political power and dispersing them. Now they could use their power to make sure that the condition of Jews would continually demonstrate divine punishment. Jewish social degradation could be used to confirm their Christian beliefs.

The germ of the idea that Jews existed to serve Christians can be found in Paul's explanation that the disbelief of Jews was part

16. See Ruth Mellinkoff, *The Horned Moses* (Berkeley, Los Angeles, London, 1970), pp. 121-137.

of the divine plan to bring salvation to the gentiles. That explanation rapidly became a commonplace and was given its most
influential reformulation by Augustine of Hippo at the end of the
fourth century.[17] Augustine extended Paul's concept of Jewish
blindness dramatically so as to make the existence of Jews useful
to Christians. Jews were dispersed everywhere so that they could
serve Christians. Because they disbelieved yet preserved the
Scriptures they could not understand, they were testimony that
the Christians had not invented Christ. The presence of Jews
dispelled doubts about Christianity. And Augustine made the fundamental implication of this manner of thinking strikingly explicit:
"The Jew is the slave of the Christian."[18]

Empirically, of course, Jews were not the slaves of anyone
when Augustine wrote, but Jews were being enslaved in another
sense. Within the minds of Christians in order to silence their
doubts, the symbol "Jews" was being made the slave of Christian
nonrational beliefs, with potentially dire consequences for the
realities the symbol denoted. Ironically, while Christians were
accusing Jews of stubborn blindness to the salvation offered them,
they themselves were becoming increasingly blind to the empirical reality of Jews. As they would do with the bread and wine
of the Eucharist, many Christians, when they perceived real Jews,
began to think about Jews as if they existed physically only as a
symbol that expressed Christian faith. There are few clearer examples of that thinking than Pope Innocent III's assertion in 1208.

Thus the Jews, against whom the blood of Jesus Christ calls out, although they ought not to be killed, lest the people forget the Divine
Law, yet as wanderers ought they to remain upon the earth, until their
countenance be filled with shame and they seek the name of Jesus
Christ, the Lord. That is why blasphemers of the Christian name ought
not to be aided by Christian princes to oppress the servants of the Lord,
but ought rather to be forced into the servitude of which they made
themselves deserving when they raised their sacrilegious hands against

17. *The City of God*, ed. and trans. Marcus Dodds (New York, 1948), 2.277-
279; 18.46.
18. Ibid. The idea that Jews should serve Christians had already been advanced by Tertullian (died ca. 220): Simon, *Verus Israël*, p. 102.

Him Who had come to confer true liberty upon them, thus calling down His blood upon themselves and upon their children.[19]

By the thirteenth century, as a result of the efforts of ecclesiastics, kings, and barons to exploit Jews, each for their own ends, Jews had been given a degraded legal status that set them apart from all others in European society and denied them even the protection usually accorded serfs.[20] Their shame and punishment thus seemed obvious. Yet if Jews were increasingly denied this-worldly opportunities, their right to live and practice their own religion was still protected, above all by the pope.

By 1250, the Catholic religion and almost all Catholic Christians, although deeply impregnated with elements of Judaic religiosity, were violently anti-Judaic. The authorities of the Catholic religion taught that the old Judaic religion had been superseded and assumed that those who practiced it would go to hell. Most Catholics knew little about Jews but disliked them in varying degrees. Yet, although some Christians during the various crusades had tried to extirpate Judaism and Jews by force, they had done so in defiance of the authorities of their religion. For although the authorities prohibited most intercourse between Christians and Jews, they nonetheless defended the presence of Jews and their religion in their midst, as they could use the degraded state of Jews as empirical evidence in support of Christian beliefs.

The only time the authorities tried to deny Jews their religion was when they feared it could no longer serve to confirm Christian belief. Christians had long taken for granted that the religion of Jews was what Christians, relying on their own interpretation of the Old Testament, thought it was. But they were wrong. Talmudic Judaism had developed after Christ, and the Babylonian Talmud, completed by 600, was accepted by European Jews in the eleventh century.[21] Christians, however, were largely unaware of the change. The few Christian scholars who were aware

19. Solomon Grayzel, *The Church and the Jews in the Thirteenth Century*, 2d ed. (New York, 1966), p. 127.

20. See "*Tanquam servi*: The Change in Jewish Status in French Law about 1200," in *Toward a Definition of Antisemitism*, chap. 7.

21. See Jacob Katz, *Exclusiveness and Tolerance* (Oxford, 1961).

of the existence of the Talmud had little understanding of it and paid little attention to it. In the middle of the thirteenth century, however, the ecclesiastical authorities became very aware of Talmudic Judaism after Nicholas Donin, a Jew who had converted to the Catholic religion, denounced the Talmud to the pope, who then ordered that it be carefully examined.

Only then did the Catholic authorities realize that the religion of contemporary Jews was not the superseded and fossilized Judaic religion they had imagined and blamed Jews for practicing. They discovered the existence of the Talmudic Judaic religion and were shocked. As the pope put it, Jews were now using a huge book, the Talmud, not the Bible, as their fundamental divine revelation. Of course, Christians had been interpreting their own Bible for centuries; Christian theologians had written many and massive commentaries; and for centuries, the authorities of the Catholic church had been prescribing how Catholics were to understand the Bible. Yet, somehow oblivious to all that, the pope blamed Jews for putting their own intepretation on their Bible, and he commanded that all copies of the Talmud and the commentaries on it be burned.

The commission that investigated the Talmud provided several rationalizations for the condemnation, but central was the objection that Jews were teaching their children to understand their Bible according to the Talmudic interpretation, not according to the Christian interpretation, and that that interpretation would make it harder to persuade Jews to acknowledge the superiority of Christian beliefs. Although the authorities already considered the Jews damned for their Judaism, when they discovered that contemporary Jews were practicing a religion that did not harmonize with Christian beliefs about Judaism, they considered Jews doubly damned and sought to eradicate Talmudic Judaism. Jews had to conform to the image Christians had made of them and practice what Christians told them was their religion.

The results of the condemnation were tragic for Jews, but the papal campaign was only partially successful precisely because, as even the pope was forced to recognize, the Talmudic religion really was the religion of contemporary Jews. And thanks largely to Paul, Christian theologians had long believed that Jews must be preserved because they still had a central role to play in providential history: their remnant would be saved at the end of time. Consequently, while still trying to censor passages of the Talmud, the authorities allowed Jews to continue to practice their Talmudic religion. Christians may have wanted to ensure that the existence of Jews and their beliefs did not contradict Christian beliefs, but the Catholic authorities were sufficiently realistic to recognize that Jews were an independent reality and that toleration of Jews meant qualified toleration of Talmudic Judaism. They could, however, and did try to deal with it as they had dealt with Hebrew Scriptures: they could try to interpret the Talmud so as to confirm their Christian beliefs.[22] A new stereotype was born, that of the mysterious Talmudic Jew.

Thus, to defend their nonrational beliefs about Jesus of Nazareth, Christians came to believe that Jews were mysteriously blinded, had killed god, and were therefore being divinely punished. By 1096, because of changes in Christian mentality, "Jew" had become much more salient as a symbol of the killing of Christ in the religiosity of many Christians, and hostility toward Jews had increased greatly, particularly in northern Europe. By 1250, many Christians, including popes, had expressed those anti-Judaic beliefs in extreme ways. Nonetheless, the degradation of Jewish legal status, the crusading massacres, and the condemnation of the Talmud were nonrational, not irrational, reactions to the conflict between Christians and Jews. Though xenophobic and violent, they were a response to real characteristics of Judaism and Jews. But something more had now appeared. No longer was anti-Judaism the only kind of hostility directed against Jews; a century earlier, a new irrational hostility had surfaced in northern Europe.

If antisemitism is defined as chimerical beliefs or fantasies about "Jews," as irrational beliefs that attribute to all those symbolized as "Jews" menacing characteristics or conduct that no Jews have been observed to possess or engage in,[23] then antisemitism first appeared in medieval Europe in the twelfth century. By then, the symbol "Jew" was evoking violent hostility, even

22. See Jeremy Cohen, *The Friars and the Jews* (Ithaca, N.Y., 1982), pp. 60-195; Robert Chazan, *Daggers of Faith: Thirteenth-Century Missionizing and Jewish Response* (Berkeley, Los Angeles, London, 1989).

23. See "Toward a Definition of Antisemitism," in *Toward a Definition of Antisemitism*, chap. 14.

though, or partly because, most Christians knew little about them. Most Christians in western Europe, particularly in north-western Europe, had had little opportunity to observe Jews at all closely, and most had little interest in knowing more about the people they had been taught to regard as inferior. They knew Jews were human beings like themselves, they knew that Jews had different religious beliefs and practices, but they had little knowledge of what Jews actually believed and what their religious practices were—save that they had been told they were old, use-less, and bad. At worst, Jews were killers of Christ, but nothing more. The capacity of most Christians to determine whether ap-parently empirical assertions about contemporary Jews were true was therefore severely diminished. That ignorance, when com-bined with the rapidly rising hostility against Jews as killers of Christ, made Jews an inviting target for irrational projections.

Shortly after 1096, some individuals began to attribute to Jews characteristics that neither they nor any others had observed. Whatever other motives were at work, the characteristics they projected on Jews were clearly inspired by their own doubts about the body of their Christ and their need to overcome them. Just as some Christians reacted to bread and wine as if they could see the body and blood of Jesus of Nazareth and were thereby re-assured of his real presence, so some began to react to contem-porary Jews as if they were still trying to kill Christ, thereby demonstrating the truth of beliefs about Jesus and the Jews.

We can pin the origin of the first such fantasy down to a single individual. In 1144, the body of a child was found near Norwich, England. Nothing about the boy was religiously significant save that someone had killed him at Eastertide. But about 1150, Thomas of Monmouth, a monk who had come to the cathedral priory some four years after the event, created the fantasy—with considerable help from the boy's family and a Jewish convert to the Catholic religion—that Jews had crucified the boy and that they conspired annually throughout Europe to crucify a Christian child in order to express their hatred of Christ, whom they could no longer attack directly.[24]

---

24. See "Thomas of Monmouth: Detector of Ritual Murder," in *Toward a*

The falsity of the fantasy should be apparent, although many have believed it right down to the twentieth century.[25] Indeed, it was immediately recognized as a fantasy by many of Thomas's fellow monks who were there at the time of the crime and stated that there was no evidence that Jews had even murdered the child, let alone crucified him. But by depicting Jews as still concerned to kill Christ and describing the miracles surrounding the alleged victim, the fantasy confirmed beliefs about the death and resurrection of Jesus. And since it gave added credence to threatened religious beliefs, it found a receptive audience. Thomas disseminated his fantasy by word of mouth and by the account he wrote of it. Others picked up the story and spread it further. The belief was then translated into action. Jews in various localities were accused and killed for the alleged crime; shrines to the alleged victims were constructed in churches and cathedrals across Europe with the explicit approval of bishops and priests and with the tacit approval of popes who failed or refused to condemn the accusations or the shrines.

A century later, a different fantasy about ritual murder appeared in Germany, the fantasy of ritual cannibalism. It can be seen as a halfway stage between the original fantasy of ritual murder by crucifixion and the fantasy about Jews and the Eucharist that appeared later. The central European ritual, performed innumerable times daily across Europe, was the Eucharist, the symbolic eating of Christ. Ever since the eleventh century, however, many who could not help thinking that the consecrated bread and wine were only bread and wine had had serious doubts about the real presence of Christ in the Eucharist. But if it could be shown that even disbelievers in Christ believed in the efficacy of a similar but evil ritual, doubts about the efficacy of the Christian ritual might be overcome. Any "evidence" to that effect was therefore most welcome to some.

Between 1231 and 1234, Conrad of Marburg was exciting Germans—and the pope—with accusations that "heretics" in Germany rejected the Eucharist and engaged in their own horrible

---

Definition of Antisemitism, chap. 9. It should be noted that belief in a Jewish conspiracy was present from the very beginning of irrational beliefs about them.

25. "Historiographic Crucifixion," in *Toward a Definition of Antisemitism*, chap. 12.

secret orgies. Almost immediately after, on Christmas day of 1235, while those ideas were still fresh in everybody's mind, five boys were found dead after their parents' mill at Fulda had burned down. The few Jews at Fulda were immediately accused of killing the boys to obtain the blood they needed for their rituals, and all were slaughtered. The accusation was brought to the attention of the German emperor; and early in 1236, after an unusually careful investigation, he pronounced the charge false and forbade anyone to accuse Jews of ritual cannibalism. Eleven years later, even the pope pronounced against it. But the rumor continued to spread and brought more shrines and death to many Jews then and thereafter.[26]

Yet another fantasy appeared at the end of the thirteenth century. Like the fantasy of ritual murder by crucifixion, it corroborated the belief that contemporary Jews were still trying to harm Christ by attacking his body. And even more directly than the ritual cannibalism fantasy, this accusation was connected with the doubts many Christians had about the Eucharist. The new fantasy accused Jews of attacking Christ through the consecrated host or wafer of the Mass. What is remarkable about the fantasy is that although some Christians had reported seeing signs of Christ in the Eucharist for centuries, the fantasy about Jews did not appear until the late thirteenth century, just when it had become very dangerous for Christians to admit to any doubts about the dogma of transubstantiation, and shortly after the institution of the feast of Corpus Christi to honor Christ's eucharistic presence.[27] The fantasy obviously functioned directly to confirm the dogma when many people badly wanted confirmation. It assumed that even

26. See "Ritual Cannibalism," in *Toward a Definition of Antisemitism*, chap. 11.

27. Poliakov, *Du Christ aux Juifs de cour*, p. 75, and R. I. Moore, *The Formation of a Persecuting Society* (Oxford, 1987), p. 38, state that there were accusations of host profanation at Cologne in 1150 and at Belitz in 1263. Their evidence, however, comes from chroniclers who wrote much later and anachronistically introduced into their account the later accusation that Jews attacked the host to injure Christ. The first clear evidence for such accusations comes from about 1290, whereafter they proliferated rapidly: Friedrich Lotter, "Hostienfrevelvorwurf und Blutwunderfälschung bei den Judenverfolgungen von 1298 ('Rintfleisch') und 1336-1338 ('Armleder')," in *Fälschungen im Mittelalter*, Monumenta Germaniae Historica, Shriften, vol. 33, part 5 (Hannover, 1988): 533-583.

Jews really believed in transubstantiation although they would not admit it—except under torture.

The greatest slaughter of Jews at any one time in the Middle Ages was caused, however, by a totally different fantasy. It was occasioned by the death not of a few children but of millions of Christians. When the Black Death was devastating the population of Europe between 1347 and 1350, there were three main explanations of the horror. One was an effort, however erroneous, to explain it scientifically. But for those who could neither accept the uncertainty of their knowledge nor be as lighthearted about their salvation as the protagonists of Boccaccio's *Decameron*, there were two religious explanations. One was the kind of explanation often used to explain great disasters. Since it was unthinkable that God would do evil or permit such evil without a good purpose, God must be punishing people for their sins or testing their faith.[28] The other explanation was that cosmic forces of evil were at work: the Jews, in league with the devil, were destroying Christians.[29]

The explanation that God was punishing sins or testing faith was not very reassuring. If people's sins were so grievous that God was even killing many devoted priests and monks, as well as innocent children by the thousands, that implied profoundly disturbing questions about anyone's salvation. And if God was testing faith, it raised disturbing questions about God's goodness. Yet once the plague was thought of as a result of human actions, there was a way out of that hellish dilemma. It became possible, and was much more reassuring for personal salvation, to blame someone else. Although the pope had emphasized something widely known, that Jews were dying like Christians, Jews were nonetheless accused of conspiring to poison the wells in order to destroy Christendom, and thousands were killed.

It would be hard to find a clearer example of irrational scapegoating; and the fact that the people known as flagellants were particularly active in inciting attacks on Jews reveals something

28. The explanation also used by Jews to account for the massacres of 1096; see Chazan, *European Jewry and the First Crusade*, pp. 161-168.

29. Séraphine Guerchberg, "The Controversy over the Alleged Sowers of the Black Death in the Contemporary Treatises on the Plague," in *Change in Medieval Society*, ed. Sylvia L. Thrupp (New York, 1964), pp. 208-224.

about the mental processes at work.[30] These self-selected volunteers of both sexes and various social ranks went around in groups from town to town, thereby helping to spread the plague. In each town they stopped to whip themselves in a violent public ritual in order to purge themselves of their sins, set an example of atonement, and stop the plague. Their conduct thus conformed to the explanation that God was punishing people for their sins. The flagellants seem to have been people particularly beset by internal conflicts that fear of the plague had made even more acute.

The plague apparently heightened their consciousness that they had not been thinking and acting in accordance with the prescriptions of their religion. But it apparently also made many angry at the failure of their religion to satisfy their needs and inspired them to defy religious authority. Although the flagellants started with masochistic self-abasement, many soon began to attack local priests, the closest symbols of religious authority, and to claim supernatural authority for themselves. They also disregarded papal commands and attacked Jews, even though their travels should have made them more aware than most that Jews were dying of the plague like Christians. They seem to have had confidence neither in themselves nor in their religion and to have acted desperately to restore their self-confidence by extirpating Jews, the incarnate symbol of disbelief.

Thus, by the late Middle Ages, in order to dispel doubts about their religion and themselves, many Christians were suppressing their capacity for rational empirical thought and irrationally attributing to the realities they denoted as "Jews" unobservable characteristics. These four fantasies—that Jews ritually crucified Christian children, used human blood and flesh in their rituals, tortured the wafers of the Eucharist, and sought to destroy Christendom by sowing the Black Death—are the clearest examples of irrational efforts by Christians to use Jews to repress doubts about their beliefs and strengthen their faith in their Christian identity. But there were other irrational projections, including the attri-

30. Philip Ziegler, *The Black Death* (New York, 1971), pp. 84-109; Robert S. Gottfried, *The Black Death* (New York, 1983), pp. 69-74.

bution of physical characteristics that existed only in the imagination of Christians.[31]

"The Jews" had become the great symbol of hidden menaces of all kinds within Christendom. In a rapidly changing Europe suffering from economic depression, social discontent, ecclesiastical divisions, bubonic plague, and endemic and devastating wars, many Europeans were prey to lurking doubts that sapped their self-confidence. They struggled to repress them but remained anxious, and many gave expression to their unease by attributing to Jews evil characteristics that made the goodness of Christians obvious by contrast and attributed their problems to an external source. Many believed that individual Christians and Christendom as a whole were threatened by a secret conspiracy of Jews who stole their children (like gypsies), crucified them, and ate them; who poisoned Christians old and young; who were still trying to torture their Christ; and who were working to overthrow their values and society. The conspiracy was imaginary, but the fear and hatred the image engendered were all too real. Indeed, the hatred was peculiarly intense because what these Christians feared was buried deep within themselves. They feared and hated their own doubts about beliefs basic to their sense of their identity, doubts they could neither acknowledge consciously nor eradicate subconsciously.

They hated Jews, it should be emphasized, because they were Christians. They created and believed chimerical fantasies about Jews because Christian symbols, including "Jew," were very salient in their religiosity and they wanted to preserve their faith in Christ. Their fantasies were the expression of one kind of Christian religiosity, initially only the religiosity of a few Christians but soon shared by many. So far as the evidence permits, the fantasies can be traced back to particular localities and to the irrational religiosity of individuals. Yet if some irrational individuals created these chimerical beliefs and others rapidly found them appealing, despite the disbelief of many at the time, many more Christians soon came to believe them, not because they were irrational but because they trusted what their society communicated, for, although the authorities of the Catholic religion condemned some

31. See Poliakov, *Du Christ aux Juifs de cour*, pp. 140-161.

of the fantasies, they gave explicit or tacit approval to others, and governments did the same. The fantasies were given widespread social expression and incorporated in European historiography, literature, and art. They became deeply embedded in the mentality of millions of normally rational Christians. Thus, by the later Middle Ages, it had become very difficult for many not to believe the fantasies, particularly the less educated. Consequently, many Christians were willing to participate in the killing of thousands of Jews for actions that no Jew had ever been observed to commit.

These irrational massacres were very different from the first great massacre in Europe. Those who died in the massacre of 1096 were killed because of what they really were, Jews who adhered to Judaism, rejected and despised Christian beliefs, and approved of the death of Jesus. Similar massacres occurred in northern Europe at the time of later crusades. And even though the new hostility against Jews as usurers contributed to the later massacres, the hostility was still, for the most part, only xenophobic, for Jews were in fact disproportionately engaged in moneylending in northern Europe by the late twelfth century. Moreover, despite that additional cause of hostility, the numbers of Jews killed at the time of successive crusades declined sharply because governments, which were profiting from their exploitation of Jewish moneylending, had grown stronger and were able to prevent or limit the massacres.

Governmental protection and use of Jews in the twelfth and thirteenth centuries, however, only increased hostility against them, and to that hostility was now added the new irrational hostility expressed by the chimerical fantasies. In the course of the thirteenth century, rulers found it increasingly unwise politically, and unrewarding economically, to protect Jews and began to dissociate themselves from the Jews. More than that, they put into effect the policy advocated by the antisemitic movements of the late nineteenth century: they began to expel Jews. By the end of the fifteenth century, Jews had been expelled from most of western Europe; where they were not, they were isolated in ghettos to protect Christians from them.

Those expulsions were accompanied by the new wave of massacres that began at the end of the thirteenth century. Though all the old anti-Judaic and economic motives doubtless played their part, these massacres were triggered, not by a summons to crusade and the attendant accusation of deicide, but by the new irrational accusations of conspiratorial ritual crucifixion, ritual cannibalism, host desecration, and well-poisoning. Someone would accuse the Jews of one of these crimes, and the accusation would inspire mobs to roam from town to town killing Jews for a crime no one had ever seen them commit. These massacres claimed far more victims than the earlier ones connected with the crusades, and the Jews who were killed did not die as martyrs in defense of their Judaic faith; they were the defenseless victims of their killers' delusions. In these attacks we can see, for the first time in European history, a clear parallel to Hitler's delusions and the victims of the camps. Socially significant antisemitism first emerged in medieval Christendom,[32] and it became ever more deeply rooted as the Middle Ages drew to an end.

32. As Poliakov clearly recognized in 1955. He asserted that what should properly be called antisemitism, antisemitism in its classic form, only became widespread in the fourteenth century and was then a specifically Christian phenomenon: *Du Christ aux Juifs de cour*, pp. 116, 126, 140.

Chapter Fifteen

The Revolution in Religiosity

By the fifteenth century, Catholic Christian antisemitism was deeply embedded in European culture, and it remained so right down to the twentieth century. But the religions of Europe and the religiosity of most Europeans changed greatly after the fifteenth century, and as a result a new kind of antisemitism appeared in the nineteenth century. Though often borrowing from Christian antisemitism and collaborating with it, it explicitly rejected the Christian beliefs that Christian antisemitism defended.

Were one forced to identify the major changes in the modes of thinking, experiences, living conditions, and social organization of Europeans after the fifteenth century, some obvious candidates would be the great advances in rational empirical knowledge, the vast increase in material resources and production, the rapidly expanding contacts with the non-European world, the development of the social organizations we call nation-states, the growth of patriotic and national sentiments, and the weakening of Christian religions. Of these related trends, the last is most directly relevant to changes in attitudes toward Jews, for what had set Jews apart was not their unwillingness or incapacity to engage in intellectual and economic activities, to travel, or to be loyal to the country in which they resided, nor was it their biology; it was their religion and its significance for Christians.

There was what can only be considered a religious revolution between the sixteenth and the twentieth century. For millennia, almost all human beings had believed in gods and adhered to psychocentric religions, but then, very rapidly when measured on the scale of human history, there was an unprecedented spread of disbelief. By the late twentieth century, after a period of transition of some three centuries, though most people in Europe and the European colonies still adhered to psychocentric religions, albeit often only halfheartedly, more and more people were able to live without them.

The hold of Christian religions declined gradually but steadily after the fifteenth century. No longer was there a single overwhelmingly dominant Christian religion, and the percentage of the population that adhered with deep conviction to any particular Christian religion was in continuous decline. After the sixteenth-century wars to defend old religions or establish new ones came revolutions to overthrow established religions. At least for some of the participants, the English civil war of 1642 was already a struggle to make religion voluntary, and the American and French revolutions at the end of the eighteenth century and those of 1848 explicitly rejected the ultimacy of the authority of any religion.

Without citing all the historical studies of the growth of toleration, one can safely say that the trend from the sixteenth to the nineteenth century was toward the establishment of the right of individuals to believe what they wanted, provided their actions conformed to laws they could agree on through some nonreligious procedure. In 1640, Milton expressed his hope for the future.

Under these fantastic terrors of sect and schism, we wrong the earnest and zealous thirst after knowledge and understanding which God hath stirr'd up in this City. What some lament of, we should rather rejoyce at, should rather praise this pious forwardnes among men, to reassume the ill deputed care of their Religion into their own hands again. A little generous prudence, a little forbearance of one another, and som grain of charity might win all these diligences to joyn and unite in one generall and brotherly search after Truth; could we but forgo this Prelaticall tradition of crowding free consciences and Christian liberties into canons and precepts of men.[1]

If we set aside Milton's assumption of Christianity and intolerance of "Popery," we might say that Milton's prayer had been largely fulfilled in western Europe by the end of the nineteenth

1. John Milton, *Areopagitica*, in *The Complete Prose Works of John Milton*, ed. Don M. Wolfe et al. (New Haven, 1953-1962), 2:554.

century. Since his distinction between precepts of men and free consciences is almost identical with my distinction between religion and religiosity, what he foresaw can be restated in my terms as the trend from the seventeenth century to the twentieth for the authority of religions to be increasingly called in question and the autonomy and legitimacy of religiosity emphasized. In western Europe by the end of the nineteenth century, religion was increasingly seen—as has been said so frequently of the twentieth—as something voluntary and personal, as something that belonged primarily to the "private" sphere.

The first symptom of the trend was dissatisfaction with papal control of Christian religion. Though evident as early as the thirteenth century and growing in the fourteenth and fifteenth, it was only a peripheral challenge through most of the Middle Ages. By the sixteenth century, however, dissatisfaction had become common as rulers sought to harmonize their religion with their authority and as revolutionary intellectuals formulated their own sense of personal and social identity. Foreshadowed by Gallicanism and the establishment of a separate Inquisition for Spain, drastic dissatisfaction first erupted in Germany. Whatever the precise nature of Luther's bellicose religiosity, theological concerns, and attitude to the state, he addressed his Bible and many of his tracts in German to Germans. And whatever his intentions for the Christian man and his expectations of how he would exercise his new freedom, his revolt against Rome and Catholicism and his appeal to Germans initiated an age in which religions tended more and more to coincide with political and cultural boundaries—nowhere more obviously than in England, and nowhere with less success than within the frontier of the German empire.

Aided by the writers, composers, and artists whom they patronized, rulers worked to "patriotize" or, as we would say, to nationalize religion, whether by controlling Catholicism within their boundaries or by supporting and controlling the new Protestant religions. Patriotic symbols became increasingly salient in the religiosity of their Christian subjects, who increasingly took for granted that their religion sanctified their present political loyalties as well as promising them future bliss—or damnation. Even kingdoms that had no religion of their own, as most did not, had their own distinctive or vernacular form of a broader religion, or at least their own peculiar combination of several religions and their own peculiar way of dealing with that fact, with the result that adherence to one of the religions had very different consequences depending on where the adherent was.

The fragmentation of Christendom into different warring Christian religions encouraged doubts about Christianity itself. It was now patent that people of all ranks could and did disagree about Christian beliefs; and if many could disagree as to which were valid Christian beliefs or which was the genuine Christian religion, then some could doubt that any Christian religion or even any Christian belief was valid. In fact, such doubts were already being expressed more or less covertly in the seventeenth century by the intellectuals known as *libertins* or freethinkers, and a term and concept unknown to the Middle Ages reappeared, "atheism."

In the classical world, "atheism" had been a charge leveled against people who had gods but did not worship the gods of the society in which they lived, for example, Jews in the Roman Empire. By contrast, in the Middle Ages, when there was only one recognized god, people spoke of infidels or heretics, not atheists. In the sixteenth century, however, symptomatic of the stresses introduced by religious pluralism, "atheist" reappeared in the European vernacular languages and became widely current in the seventeenth. Initially, it had the same basic meaning as in antiquity; Christians of one kind referred pejoratively to Christians whose theology differed as atheists. Then, in the eighteenth century, with the appearance of the Deists, who believed in a god on philosophical grounds but rejected Christian revelation, the term was applied particularly to them, though they themselves denied being atheists.

The second half of the eighteenth century brought a much more radical change in meaning. In large measure as a result of the scientific revolution, some intellectuals, most notably Baron d'Holbach, now rejected any belief in "God." And, significant of the changing atmosphere, not only were these men called atheists by others; they proudly described themselves as atheists. Thus, by the later eighteenth century, some educated people were both fully aware of their doubts and also, unlike Descartes, able to live without a religion, some even finding satisfaction in savaging old beliefs and the gullibility of their adherents. Their need for self-assurance was apparently sufficiently satisfied by their material security and their pride in contributing to the dramatic advance of knowledge, to Condorcet's Progress.

By the middle of the nineteenth century, atheism in the new meaning of the term was expressed ever more openly and made a central intellectual issue by thinkers such as Comte, Feuerbach, and Marx, and in 1882 Nietsche proclaimed the death of God. Indeed, by the late nineteenth century, the religiosity of many positivists had become so self-confident that it seemed almost a religion, though in fact it was, as with Bertrand Russell, a rejection of religion. By the beginning of the twentieth century, atheism and agnosticism were still not widely accepted, but it was possible to be openly atheistic or agnostic without serious penalties, and atheism had become a characteristic of many less intellectual people, both Marxists and non-Marxists. As the century wore on, nonrational and rational doubts had become so widespread that "God" was no longer a very salient symbol in the religiosity of many—though it might still figure there as a negative symbol for a variety of rejected beliefs or "superstitions."

Atheists fell into two schools. For Comte, Feuerbach, and Marx, the bottle was still half-full, or even fuller. The loss of a god and eternal individual life would be more than offset by the improvement of life that could be envisaged once those alienating illusions were abandoned. Other atheists were fundamentally pessimistic, most notably Schopenhauer and Nietzsche, whose final outlooks are perhaps better described as anomic than atheistic. Not only the existence of a god but the value of human existence and being itself were questioned, questions to which the existentialists of the first half of the twentieth century would try to provide an answer.

These intellectual atheists criticized traditional beliefs and one another's ideas, influenced other members of the educated social elite, and fought the battles that made it safe to express atheism openly. But their thinking was not simply a debate about ideas; it was also a reaction to changing political, social, and economic conditions that affected less educated people in similar ways. By the twentieth century, many people who had never read what the intellectuals had written came to doubt the existence of "God"

and question the meaning of their lives. According to one estimate, by 1985 there were some two hundred million atheists, or
a billion throughout the world if those totally disinterested in the
issue are included,[2] and most had not become atheists or agnostics
because they had devoted concentrated thought to the problem;
their doubts and disbelief were rather an almost unconscious reaction to all they had experienced.

The gradual loss of certainty is obvious. The multiplication of
Christian religions, the conversions from one to another, and the
appearance of Deists provide clear evidence of swelling nonrational doubts. Even more obvious is the growth of rational doubts
from Pascal through Hobbes and Descartes to the warfare between religion and science in the nineteenth century and the reactions to those doubts of fundamentalists in the twentieth. The
unparalleled development of rational empirical knowledge in Europe and North America and its application to natural phenomena
and many aspects of human conduct challenged or overthrew
many traditional beliefs, and those rational doubts reinforced any
nonrational doubts people already had about Christianity.

The trend is clear. Yet, revolutionary as it was, its extent should
not be exaggerated. Most Europeans in the late nineteenth century still adhered to Christian religions. Most still believed in a
god, and those who no longer believed in the god of Christianity
were not thereby freed from the influence of Christian symbols
and beliefs. However much the Christian "God" might be dying
in the minds of intellectuals and many who were not intellectuals,
"His" existence was still taken for granted by most people during
the nineteenth century and well into the twentieth, and Christianity was still culturally omnipresent.

Though weakened, Christian religions were still well-established, well-endowed, and influential societies; and some were
coextensive with political societies and backed by their governments. Adherence to Roman Catholicism was particularly strong

2. Cited in Michael J. Buckley, *At the Origins of Modern Atheism* (New
Haven, 1987), p. 27. Buckley's book is a fascinating study of the development
of atheism and the reaction of Catholic thinkers to it in the seventeenth and
eighteenth centuries. For a brilliant analysis of these intellectual trends from
the seventeenth century to the present, see Hans Küng, *Does God Exist?* (New
York, 1981).

in Mediterranean Europe. In Italy, Catholicism was almost as much a patriotic religion as Anglicanism was in England. Much the same was true of Spain as a result of the government's control and enforcement of Catholicism. In northern European and North American societies, the authority of Christian religions was much weaker. The influence of Catholicism was seriously challenged by governments as well as by Protestants and intellectuals; scientific and technological advance was more rapid; social conditions were changing much more rapidly under the impact of industrialization; and individuals were much more likely to experience religious pluralism as a fact in their dealings with their neighbors.

In Germany, the dominance of Christian religions was challenged during the revolution of 1848 and then by Bismarck's *Kulturkampf*[3] from 1871 to 1887. Even in Austria, where there was no internal opposition from Protestantism, the influence of Catholicism was seriously threatened in the later nineteenth century by the political ascendancy of the liberals, particularly in Vienna.[4] In France, where disbelief in Christianity had first been expressed most directly, the rejection of Christian beliefs was associated with the new form of government, and a significant minority were open disbelievers. The only major country in the north which had a firmly established and relatively unchallenged national religion was England, provided that we distinguish England from Great Britain.

The vast majority of the English could adhere more or less untroubledly to the Church of England, for adherence involved little strain in their religiosity. The Church of England imposed relatively few constraints on the thoughts or loyalties of its adherents save that they should love England. It had a remarkably flexible or ambiguous theology that could live with scientific advance; its requirements for membership were minimal; it was supported by the government; and it supported English nationalism. Moreover, given the democratization of the government, adherents of other Christian religions in England had little reason to fear that their religion would be persecuted. Adherence to a

3. The term was coined in 1873 and indicates the depth of the upheaval in Germany.

4. See Carl E. Schorske, *Fin-de-siècle Vienna* (New York, 1981), pp. 140-144.

Christian religion thus involved few conflicts with the trends of the period and little tension in most people's religiosity. As a result, in contrast with much of northern Europe, Christian religiosity was relatively unchallenged and Christian indoctrination almost universal. Indeed, the most striking religious trend in England around the middle of the nineteenth century was not disbelief in Christianity; it was the evangelical movement, which affected Nonconformists as well as Anglicans and is thus evidence that a change in religiosity can transcend the boundaries of religion.[5]

Opposition to Catholicism or disbelief in any Christian religion had spread very unevenly across Europe, characterizing some regions and individuals much more than others. Yet even in northern Europe, where religions were most obviously losing their grip, the influence of Christianity remained strong, for European music, art, and literature were impregnated with Christian symbols and ideas, and education made them a prominent part of the mental furniture even of those who explicitly rejected traditional religions. Particularly tenacious were the symbols used by Christians that were not explicitly Christian: the symbol "religion" itself and that symbol of symbols, "God." If the Christian god had not created the world, then god the clockmaker had; and although the French revolutionaries hated Catholic priests, they nonetheless tried to divinize Reason before settling for a Supreme Being. Most striking, however, is the oath taken by recruits of the Nazi SS: they swore obedience to Hitler unto death, "so help me God," *So wahr mir Gott helfe.*

The inertial pressure of established religions and the expectation that people should have a religion thus remained strong, Comte's "Religion of Humanity" being one of its more bizarre expressions. Most people still took for granted that they should belong to a religion, whether an old or new one—which may help explain why new Christian and non-Christian religions proliferated from the late eighteenth century onward, especially in the United States, where no single Christian religion had ever en-

5. For an excellent depiction of the problems involved in openly abandoning belief in Christ in England, see Noel Annan, *Leslie Stephen: The Godless Victorian*, 2d ed. (New York, 1984).

joyed hegemony over the whole of that loosely integrated and
rapidly changing society.

Even among the exponents of science, many, perhaps most,
were unable or unwilling to live without the additional certitude
provided by religions. They remained, at least nominally, Christians (or Jews) and continued to rely in diverse ways on traditional
Christian (and Judaic) beliefs and rituals for the conduct of their
personal and social lives. By doing so, they perpetuated the assumption that rational empirical thinking should be subordinated
to religion and based on it, and they reinforced that assumption
in the population at large, most of whom were even less able—
or less permitted—to live without cosmic beliefs that made their
identity seem secure.

Most people could not and did not devote their time to scru-
tinizing the mysteries of the universe. Preoccupied with their immediate mundane responsibilities, they relied on the authorities
of their society for their understanding of their cosmos, and their
social indoctrination ensured that Christian symbols would be salient in their religiosity. Save for Jews, Marxists, and dogmatic
atheists, and even for many of the latter two, most people were
raised in Christian religions and had some knowledge of the
Christian Bible and beliefs. Even more or less nominal adherents
used the rituals of their religions as social rites of passage whether
they believed in them or not. Hence, though secondhand knowledge of scientific advances might lead many to question particular
Christian beliefs, most remained adherents of the traditional
Christian religions, many sincerely devoted, many unthinkingly
so.

For those, whether aristocrats or peasants, who still lived much
as they had under the *ancien régime* and whose mentality had
not yet been transformed by advancing knowledge and industrialism, adherence to Christian religions was almost axiomatic.
Their inherited religion seemed the natural accompaniment of
their traditional social standing. Whatever religious doubts they
might have, they could still rely on their social standing to reassure them of the solidity of their identity. As for those who were
following new ways of life and profiting from the new conditions,
they could—to reformulate Weber's and Tawney's theses about

capitalism and Protestantism—restructure their religiosity by associating their god with their new roles in society and the material rewards they brought. If they had any doubts about the ultimate basis of their existence, they could offset them by a belief in openended progress expressed by symbols such as the "invisible hand" and reassure themselves of their identity as capitalists. They could also rely on their nation's success and future promise and identify themselves by the symbols of nationalism.

Many, however, neither fitted the old symbolizations of social identity nor profited from the new. The advance of industrialism had introduced new forms of exploitation and created new social conflicts. What satisfied many was a disaster for others. In certain regions and social categories, the rapid changes in social organization and social norms had uprooted people from their old securities without providing them with new social identities of which they could be proud. Dissatisfied with themselves and denigrated by others, many were prey to nonrational and rational doubts about themselves, about their society, and about the universe. Their tension-riddled religiosity clashed with the certitudes proclaimed by the elites of their society. By the beginning of the twentieth century, a trend concealed by the endurance and multiplication of Christian religions had become manifest: the growing number of people who were dissatisfied with old religions yet hungered for something to replace them.

As a result of the religious revolution and in striking contrast with the Middle Ages, a growing number of people in the late nineteenth century did not believe in any psychocentric religion or indeed in any religion at all. Of these, some were self-confident positivistic atheists or agnostics whose religiosity was coherent and relatively untroubled by doubts. Like Comte, their faith in their capacity for rational empirical thought, in human progress, in their nation, and even in cosmic processes compensated for—or blinded them to—any uncertainty they might feel about what lay beyond their grasp. Some, indeed, like Hegel and Marx, sought answers to the questions about life which psychocentric religions had claimed to provide and sought to develop far-ranging cosmologies that provided new answers. But many others could neither believe in any existing religion nor answer their questions about the meaning of life for themselves. Their unaided religiosity was too incoherent, too amorphous, to assure them of the significance of their identity.

In the Middle Ages, tension in religiosity had been primarily the result of doubts about the beliefs prescribed and enforced by a long-established religion, and that kind of tension continued to exert its pressure down to the twentieth century on both Catholics and Protestants. But by the nineteenth century, a new kind of tension had appeared that was almost the exact opposite. It might be termed agnostic anxiety. It was the anxiety of people who could not believe in any existing religion but who also doubted themselves. They were unable to symbolize their experience of the world around them in a way that reassured them of their worth. And because of their anomie, they hungered for a way of symbolizing their universe that they could associate with the way they symbolized themselves. Consequently, they were ready to recognize the authority of beliefs preached by others whose symbolizing of the universe made the symbols by which they symbolized themselves—for example, "workers of the world"—positively salient and thus reassured them of their importance in the universe.

Some returned to modified forms of the old psychocentric religions that had been remolded to take their condition into account, for example, Christian socialism, and some turned to new psychocentric religions. But others found relief in the physiocentric religions discussed in the last chapter, many demonstrating their gratitude by their willingness to die for them. *The Authoritarian Personality* is perhaps the best analysis of a prominent characteristic of physiocentric religiosity: its tendency to dualism, to thinking in terms of black and white, right and wrong, capitalist or Communist, Aryan or non-Aryan.[6] But psychocentric religions have also had their dualistic strain between the spirit and the flesh, the soul and the body, the saved and the damned. The dualistic strain in Christianity, which Paul had expressed so clearly, caused tensions in Christian religiosity and religions that

6. T. W. Adorno, Else Frenkel-Brunswick, Daniel J. Levinson, and R. Nevitt Sanford, *The Authoritarian Personality* (New York, 1950).

theologians sought long and hard to resolve.[7] The dualism in physiocentric religions, however, was almost exactly the reverse of the Christian dualism and generated a different kind of tension.

Whereas psychocentric religions are based on beliefs about unobservable and largely unpredictable psychic forces that are difficult or even impossible to invalidate empirically, physiocentric religions are based on beliefs about unobservable material processes whose existence is supposed to be immediately demonstrated by what is observably going on immediately here and now. Physiocentric beliefs are therefore particularly susceptible to empirical disproof, as Stark and Bainbridge have emphasized. The beliefs prescribed by physiocentric religions demand that what one can see, hear, feel, and touch must never conflict with what one believes. Hence, physiocentric religiosities and religions are much more open to challenge and productive of irrationality— or hypocrisy—unless their fundamental beliefs are in conformity with rational empirical knowledge and are formulated in terms so abstract that what they predict is as far beyond direct observation as was the dogma of transubstantiation asserted in the thirteenth century. The tragedy of the twentieth century was that Hitler was able to institute a physiocentric religion so susceptible to empirical challenge that it could be maintained only by massive irrationality.

7. See Hans Liebeschütz, *Synagoge und Ecclesia* (Heidelberg, 1983).

Chapter Sixteen

Physiocentric Antisemitism

The dramatic changes in European societies, religions, and religiosities between the sixteenth and the twentieth centuries inevitably affected attitudes toward Jews—whose societies, religiosity, and religions also changed. Just as the fall of the western Roman Empire and the infusion of new elements of religiosity had brought a hiatus in the development of Christian attitudes toward Jews, so the fall of medieval Christendom and the modifications of religiosity that accompanied it were another watershed. As was the case between 500 and 1500, hostility against Jews first declined from about 1500 to 1800 but then increased sharply, culminating in the paroxysm of antisemitism of the mid-twentieth century.

Initially, violence against Jews and the salience of the symbol "Jew" declined in western Europe. After the expulsions from the thirteenth to the fifteenth century, western Europe was nearly *judenrein.* Many Jews fled to Islamic territories, and many others settled in eastern Europe, where accusations of ritual murder and the massacres they provoked would pursue them down to the early twentieth century. In western Europe, however, not only were there few Jews but the internal challenges to Christian faith of the Reformation and Enlightenment distracted attention from them. Christian beliefs were now seriously threatened by the manifest disbelief not of Jews but of born Christians. The religious wars between Christians and the efforts of some Europeans to destroy the faith of others loomed far larger than any alleged conspiracy of the few Jews remaining in Europe. Although xenophobic stereotypes and chimerical fantasies about Jews remained deeply embedded in European culture, Europeans now faced indisputably real, widespread, and even more intimate menaces to their faith. As a result, first the Jesuits and then the Freemasons came to be seen as the principal conspiratorial enemies within Europe.[1]

The struggles between Christians had other consequences that also, if indirectly, favorably affected attitudes toward Jews. For one thing, both Protestant and Enlightenment thinking brought belief in miracles into disrepute, and the Catholic Reformation followed suit to a lesser extent. For another, theology became more philosophical and placed less emphasis on Christian revelation.[2] Hence, fewer nonrational beliefs were stated in the form of rational empirical propositions and accepted as such. Thus the Protestant denial of transubstantiation made it difficult if not impossible for Protestants to accuse Jews of attacking Christ by profaning the host. Even in Catholic areas, accusations of contemporary profanations became less plausible. In the third place, the fact of religious pluralism, the Calvinist emphasis on the Old Testament, the greater familiarity with a wider world in an age of discovery, and the rising pragmatic dislike of religious wars gradually brought a generally more tolerant religious atmosphere.

Beginning in the middle of the seventeenth century, the governments of several of the countries from which Jews had been expelled became willing—both for religious reasons and out of self-interest—to accept the presence of Jews as Marranos or under restrictive conditions.[3] Then, starting in the late eighteenth century, after the authority of Christian religions had been openly challenged by Enlightenment thinkers, Jews were gradually emancipated legally in most countries. Encouraged by those more favorable attitudes and policies, Jews migrated back from eastern to western Europe in increasing numbers during the nineteenth

1. See Jacob Katz, *Jews and Freemasons in Europe, 1723-1939* (Cambridge, Mass., 1970); Léon Poliakov, *La causalité diabolique* (Paris, 1980-1985), 1:56-78, 95-100, 111-112, 147-182.

2. Buckley, *At the Origins of Modern Atheism*, pp. 344-363.

3. For a general overview, see *A History of the Jewish People*, ed. H. H. Ben-Sasson (Cambridge, Mass., 1976), pp. 733-749.

century, especially after 1880. They settled particularly in cities,[4] where, though generally regarded as inferiors, a minority became prominent in finance and several professions and gained some political influence. As could only be expected given the embedded anti-Jewish stereotypes, their success in the competition for scarce goods attracted the attention and aroused the resentment of many non-Jews, for many people still thought of Jews as the outsiders par excellence within European society.

In fact, Jews were loyal to the countries in which they lived; those who had long lived there were highly assimilated; and the newer immigrants, especially the more successful, assimilated rapidly. But assimilation was far from complete. Most Jews maintained and wished to maintain their Judaic religiosity and religion and thought belief in Christ folly or worse. But most Europeans— and their descendants abroad—had been brought up on the New Testament account of Jesus' life and death, and Christian symbols were still salient even in the religiosity of those who did not believe. Whether or not they thought much about Jesus, they associated their history with Christianity, and they attributed Jesus' death to "the Jews," whom they thought different and inferior. Old stereotypes remained common coin.

Xenophobic hostility was aggravated by the reaction to the eighteenth-century emphasis on reason known as Romanticism. It reinvigorated trust in nonrational thought, reinforced traditional forms of religious expression, spawned new ones, and revived interest in what seemed the most religious period of European history, the Middle Ages. Interest in medieval history was further strengthened by the rising nationalism, for nationalists looked back to the Middle Ages as the period in which their nations first took form. Both Romanticism and nationalism thus worked to make Jews seem a people apart, for when people read histories of the Middle Ages, they encountered antisemitic beliefs and were reminded that Jews had been excluded from the medieval kingdoms. Literature did the same, as Sir Walter Scott's *Ivanhoe* reminds us. Economic self-interest, Christian preconceptions, nationalistic xenophobia and historiography all com-

---

4. Peter G. J. Pulzer, *The Rise of Political Anti-Semitism in Germany and Austria*, rev. ed. (Cambridge, Mass., 1988), pp. 9-15.

bined to reinvigorate old xenophobic stereotypes of the Jews as rootless, disbelieving, parasitic, usurious cowards.

Many who felt threatened by industrialism, urbanism, capitalism, socialism, rationalism, and all the other activities that were destroying their sense of security associated them in contradictory ways with Jews and accused the Jews of instigating them. Since some Jews were indeed prominently involved along with many non-Jews in those activities, there was a kernel of truth in the charges, just as there had been in the medieval stereotype of the Jew as moneylender. But in fact, as in the Middle Ages so in the nineteenth-century, the trends were overwhelmingly the result of what non-Jews had been doing; despite Marx's and Sombart's theories about Jews and capitalism, the changes would have occurred had there been no Jews.

The stereotype of parasitic usurer served social xenophobes on both the right and the left throughout Europe, especially after the economic crash of 1873. Many conservatives who felt menaced by the economic developments, which they understood much less than Marx and Sombart, blamed them on the Jews. They made "the Jews" the symbol of social disintegration, condemned the liberals who cooperated with them, and thereby absolved themselves of any responsibility for the present state of affairs. Conversely, people whose dislike of contemporary conditions led them to advocate radical social change also blamed Jews for present evils. Socialists of various persuasions began to proliferate in the latter half of the century, and many, regardless of whether they were Catholic, Protestant, or atheist, and regardless of their nationalism or dislike of it, were very hostile to Jews. They had been indoctrinated to believe that Jews secretly siphoned off the wealth of workers, and they viewed bankers and the bourgeoisie as the devil. Not surprisingly, they saw in "Jews" a symbol of all they hated. Toussenel, Proudhon, Blanqui, and Marx were prominent propagandists of such attitudes, as was also Drumont, who was socialistic in his own unprincipled way.[5]

However misguided, these xenophobic reactions from the right

5. George L. Mosse, *Toward the Final Solution: A History of European Racism* (New York, 1978), pp. 152-155; Jean-Denis Bredin, *The Affair: The Case of Alfred Dreyfus* (New York, 1986), pp. 293-296.

and left should not surprise us. The nineteenth century was a period of strong nationalistic xenophobia in general, and many people were being adversely affected by economic developments. During the Middle Ages, Christians from peasants up to popes had stereotyped Jews as parasitic usurers who threatened the social fabric, and the stereotype had been retained ever since by both Catholics and Protestants. Yet if xenophobic hostility against Jews increased throughout Europe in the later nineteenth century, how intense it became varied depending on the degree of social tension and on how recently Jews had become prominent in different countries.

If we leave aside Russia, where Christian antisemitism continued almost unabated, hostility was strongest in Austria, Germany, and France, where social tension was high and Jews newly prominent.[6] These countries had been racked by revolutions and radical changes in their form of government and unsettled by economic change, and the number and influence of Jews had recently increased far more noticeably than in other countries, especially after the great migrations from Russia after 1880. According to one estimate, at the end of the nineteenth century there were 5,000,000 Jews in Russia, a little less than 2,000,000 in Austria-Hungary, 600,000 in Germany, some 180,000 in England, 80,000 in France, and 100,000 in Holland.[7] If we remove England and Holland from consideration, since Jews had long been able to reside there and people had become used to them, the figures for Austria, Germany, and France could serve as a rough index of the new prominence of Jews and the intensity of xenophobia in those countries.

The new prominence of Jews was most obvious in the Austro-Hungarian Empire. Jews had migrated to Hungary and Austria from Bohemia, Moravia, and Galicia in great numbers in the nineteenth century. By 1910, Jews constituted about a quarter of the population of Budapest. In Vienna, from which they had been

6. Hostility was present everywhere, but what there was in England, for example, was relatively unimportant in comparison with Austria, Germany, and France; see Colin Holmes, *Anti-Semitism in British Society, 1876-1939* (London, 1979).

7. *Histoire des Juifs en France*, ed. Bernhard Blumenkranz (Toulouse, 1972), pp. 347-348.

almost completely barred prior to 1848, they had come by 1890 to constitute about 12 percent of the population and had acquired, as has been said with some exaggeration, "complete domination of Viennese cultural life in the generation before 1914."[8] Since the Dual Monarchy was already riven by competing nationalisms that threatened the power of the Austrians, many conservative Austrians were peculiarly sensitive to the influx and influence of Jews.

In Germany in 1890, of a total population of about fifty million, a little over a half million (1 percent) were Jews. But there had been a very considerable internal migration to the major cities. Between 1816 and 1895, when Germans were struggling to develop their sense of nationalism, Jews as a percentage of the population of Berlin, the capital of the new empire, rose from 1.7 percent to 5.1 percent. And as in Austria, although to a lesser extent, a minority of Jews—and converted Jews—became socially and culturally influential.[9]

The same pattern was repeated on a much lesser scale in France. While the general population rose from about 30,000,000 to about 39,000,000 between 1809 and 1900, the Jewish population rose from about 47,000 to nearly 100,000 in 1870 but then dropped sharply with the loss of Alsace-Lorraine. By 1900, there were no more than 80,000 Jews, or about 0.2 percent of the total population. As elsewhere, however, most had settled in the major cities. Yet even in Paris where the vast majority (some 50,000) lived, they constituted only about 1.7 percent of the Parisian population of about 3,000,000.[10] But, as elsewhere, some Jews had become socially and financially prominent even though most were poor.

It is not surprising that many in these countries viewed Jews xenophobically, but their motives varied depending on the reference groups by which they symbolized their social identity,

8. Pulzer, *The Rise of Political Anti-Semitism*, p. 13; for the general statistics for both Austria and Germany, see pp. 3-14.

9. Ibid., p. 10; Paul W. Massing, *Rehearsal for Destruction* (New York, 1949), pp. 3-5.

10. Phyllis Cohen Albert, *The Modernization of French Jewry: Consistory and Community in the Nineteenth Century* (Hanover, N.H., 1977); Jean-Marie Mayeur and Madeleine Rebérioux, *The Third Republic from Its Origins to the Great War, 1871-1914* (Cambridge, Eng., 1984), p. 108.

whether a religion, an aristocracy, a nation, the aggregate of workers, or some combination of reference groups. The hostility of rural landowners, for instance, differed from that of urban workers. Their justifications for their hostility also varied depending on their upbringing, but they varied less. For obvious reasons the most widely used justifications were the old Christian preconceptions about Jews, for they transcended social and political frontiers. But how they were used depended on whether people were Catholics, Protestants, Deists, or atheists.

Not surprisingly, medieval stereotypes were most used by Catholics. In some regions, Catholic attitudes toward Jews had changed little since the Middle Ages, and where that was not the case, older attitudes could still be found in particular groups. Since the medieval xenophobic stereotypes and chimerical fantasies were perpetuated in Catholic shrines, hagiography, and art, Catholics who reacted xenophobically were particularly prone to reinvigorate the centuries-old stereotypes of Jews when Catholicism was challenged, as it was severely in the nineteenth century.

The competition between the Catholic and Protestant religions had been stabilized within most countries, but Catholicism faced new challenges in the nineteenth century even in areas where it was still the religion of the vast majority, the challenges summed up as "modernism." Pope Pius IX reacted vigorously against them in his *Syllabus of Errors* of 1864 and by his proclamation of papal infallibility in 1870. Although Leo XIII (1878-1903) tried to adapt medieval theology to changed social and political conditions, he faced considerable opposition from conservative Catholics, and Pius X (1903-1914) promptly returned to a condemnation of any attempt to "modernize" the Catholic faith.

In the Austro-Hungarian Empire, the Catholic church was not threatened by Protestantism—save externally by the possibility that Pan-German sentiment might lead to the incorporation of Austria in the new German empire—but the church's authority was challenged within Austria by the liberals, who became politically dominant after 1848 and who tolerated Jews and associated with them. Conservative Catholics therefore associated the liberal trends they hated with the increasing numbers and prominence of Jews. And since they were also highly sensitive to ethnic differences because of the competing nationalisms in the Austro-

Hungarian Empire which threatened Austrian dominance, many were very aware of the increasing presence of Jews and hostile to them.

The first highly influential accusation against Jews came in 1871. August Rohling was a Catholic canon who came from the Rhineland and was made professor at the University of Prague. In 1871, he published *Der Talmudjude*, a very derivative work that repeated almost all the medieval accusations, including that of ritual murder. Though it later received wide notice, going through many editions, being the subject of a famous legal case in Vienna in 1883, and influencing Wagner among many others, at first only the Catholic press in Austria, Germany, France, and Italy paid attention to it.[11] By 1880, during the pontificate of the "liberal" pope, Leo XIII, such charges were being made in Rome. The Jesuit journal, *Civiltà Cattòlica*, founded in 1850, had become a semiofficial voice of the papacy, and by 1880 it was publishing bitter attacks on Jews, including repetition of the old accusation of ritual murder.

Since most Austrians were Catholic and since Jews had become so prominent in Vienna, politicians who appealed to Catholic hostility against Jews soon gained a wide hearing. Georg von Schönerer, though nominally a liberal, began attacking Jews on economic and nationalistic grounds by 1878 but failed to gain much of a following. But when Karl Lueger opportunistically allied with Catholic circles in the 1880s and cynically exploited the political potential of hostility to Jews, he gained wide support and was finally elected mayor of Vienna in 1897.[12]

If conservative Catholics in Austria felt threatened by rationalism and liberal government, conservative Catholics in Germany were even more threatened. Although Catholicism was fully recognized and there were only a little over half a million Jews in Germany, about 60 percent of the population was Protestant, primarily Lutheran, and only about 35 percent Catholic.[13] To

11. Dirk van Arkel, *Antisemitism in Austria* (Diss., University of Leiden, 1966), pp. 14-34; Katz, *From Prejudice to Destruction*, pp. 219-220, 256, 267, 277, 285-286; Mosse, *Toward the Final Solution*, pp. 138-141.

12. Pulzer, *The Rise of Political Anti-Semitism*, pp. 143-154, 158-162, 171-182.

13. Gordon A. Craig, *Germany 1866-1945* (Oxford, 1980), p. 181.

make matters worse, not only were Protestant scholars such as David Strauss, Julius Wellhausen, and Adolf Harnack questioning Christian beliefs fundamental to Catholicism, but Germany was the home of the most highly developed thinking about metaphysical matters in the nineteenth century, and much of that thinking rejected Christian beliefs completely.

Since Catholics were themselves a minority, the more liberal favored religious toleration and the emancipation of Jews, but conservatives opposed Jewish emancipation. As early as 1848, two Catholic theologians, Sebastian Brunner and Bishop Konrad Martin of Paderborn, were warning people about the danger of Talmudic Jews. After the full legal emancipation of Jews between 1869 and 1871, and with the beginning of the *Kulturkampf* in 1871, Catholic attacks on Jewish influences intensified. Works that misrepresented and attacked the Talmud, such as that of Rohling, were disseminated more widely, and some Catholics blamed the persecution of the *Kulturkampf* on Jews and even expressed a degree of racism.[14] But precisely because they were a minority, Catholics had relatively little influence on the government's policy toward Jews save when they allied with other groups.

In France, the political situation was very different, and conservative Catholics felt threatened for different reasons. Catholicism had been the dominant religion for centuries, and in 1870, out of a total population of about 36,000,000, there were only some 600,000 Protestants and some 80,000 Jews. But if Protestantism and Judaism were no serious threats, rationalism and republicanism were. The Catholic church was losing its hold, especially in the cities and among males. Disinterest in, or distrust of, the Catholic church had become much more open after the establishment of the Third Republic and what has been called the end of the notables, the sharp decline in the prestige of the entrenched conservatives in the countryside.[15] Moreover, the defeat

14. Uriel Tal, *Christians and Jews in Germany* (Ithaca, N.Y., 1975), pp. 85–93; Massing, *Rehearsal for Destruction*, p. 15.

15. As it had been for some time, Catholicism was in retreat, especially in major cities. What is very difficult to establish is the number of people whose ancestors had been Catholic but who were themselves disbelievers, whether or not they expressed their disbelief openly or conformed minimally. But their number was increasing. Catholic baptisms in Paris fell by 20 percent between

of France by Prussian-led and primarily Protestant Germany in 1871 had made many Catholics newly sensitive to the forces menacing their identity as French and Catholic. Their concern was expressed monumentally in the church of Sacré-Coeur, with its vow of national expiation, and most vocally in the exhortations of the Assumptionist Fathers, who managed to be both strongly ultramontane and strongly nationalistic, as well as antirationalist.[16]

That conservative Catholics in France hated Jews is self-evident from the impact of Edouard Drumont and the condemnation of Dreyfus. Drumont, the most active French antisemite of the period, may not have been a very convinced Catholic, but his publications, above all *La France juive* (first edition, 1886), were an immense success, gaining the approval of Georges Bernanos among others. They owed their success in large part to Drumont's use of all the old stereotypes that appealed to Catholics, including the ritual murder accusation.[17] Though a small minority of Catholics defended Dreyfus, the vast majority, especially those who were antirepublican, supported the condemnation of Dreyfus and encouraged the riots of 1898 with their cries of death to the Jews.[18]

Catholics in all three countries, particularly the strong ultramontanists, may have felt ambivalent about, or openly opposed to, the rising racist thought of the period,[19] and liberal Catholics may not have approved of the Catholic campaigns against Jews,

---

1865 and 1885, attendance of males at church was minimal, and civil marriages rose to 25 percent. To a lesser extent the same trend was evident in the countryside, though many regions were still characterized by staunch adherence. See Mayeur and Rebérieux, *The Third Republic*, pp. 42, 101-108. For a more detailed survey of the trends in attitudes and practices, see Zeldin, *France 1848-1945: Anxiety and Hypocrisy* (Oxford, 1981), pp. 219-230. It is notable that, despite the decline, Catholic symbols were still very salient in the religiosity of most French people in 1961: although only 26 percent, mostly middle-class women and children, attended church regularly, 85 percent declared themselves believing Catholics.

16. Zeldin, *Anxiety and Hypocrisy*, pp. 7-9, 20, 105-106.

17. Katz, *From Prejudice to Destruction*, pp. 294-300; Mosse, *Toward the Final Solution*, pp. 155-158; Poliakov, *L'Europe suicidaire*, pp. 54-57; Eugen Weber, *Action française* (Stanford, Calif., 1962), pp. 71-72.

18. Mayeur and Rebérioux, *The Third Republic from Its Origins to the Great War*, p. 194; Bredin, *The Affair*, pp. 285-292; Weber, *Action française*, pp. 32-35, 45, 196-201.

19. Mosse, *Toward the Final Solution*, pp. 57, 145-146, 193-202, 229-231.

but there can be no doubt that many Catholics contributed heavily to the increase of hostility against Jews. Those who were royalists as well as Catholics felt particularly threatened, since the viability of their identity was threatened from many quarters. They associated Jews with all the threats they felt, and reacted xenophobically. And because their religiosity was Catholic, so also was their xenophobia. They reinvigorated all the old Catholic stereotypes about "the Jews," the incarnate symbol of disbelief. Not only that. If Catholics usually avoided the new racist fantasies, some disseminated the old medieval chimerical fantasies about Jews, and many more were receptive to them. Thus, even though national symbols had recently become salient in the religiosity of most Catholics, and even though they were in fact newly threatened by rationalism, industrialism, and liberalism, they used centuries-old stereotypes and irrational fantasies about Jews to express their fear and hostility. In this they differed considerably from Protestants.

Protestantism was unimportant for attitudes toward Jews in Austria and France but very important in Germany, and there can be no doubt that many German Protestants, following in Luther's footsteps, were hostile toward Jews. But it is difficult to generalize about their attitudes because their religiosity varied so greatly. The Lutheran attitudes to Jews ranged from the naked hostility of William I's Court Preacher, Adolf Stöcker, "the second Luther," through the strong hostility of the fiercely nationalist and highly influential historian Heinrich Treitschke, to the very moderate hostility of the famous historian of Rome, Theodor Mommsen, and the remarkable lack of hostility of Hermann Strack, professor of theology and oriental studies at Berlin, who wrote the first impressive rebuttal of the ritual murder accusation.[20] Strack deserves to be singled out for his courageous action, but his disbe-

20. Tal, *Christians and Jews in Germany*, pp. 50-56, 122-126, 136, 210, 230-234, 237, 248-259, and passim; Pulzer, *The Rise of Political Anti-Semitism*, pp. 241-243, 249-250; Craig, *Germany 1866-1945*, pp. 83-84, 152-155, 204-205; Hermann Strack, *Das Blut im Glauben und Aberglauben der Menschheit* (Berlin, 1891); *The Jew and Human Sacrifice* (New York, 1909). It should be noted that the Catholic abbot Elphège Vacandard followed suit and condemned accusations of ritual murder eleven years later: "La question du meurtre rituel chez les Juifs," in his *Etudes de critique et d'histoire religieuse*, 3d series (Paris, 1912), pp. 311-377.

lief in the ritual murder charge was not as exceptional as one might think. In general, Protestants were much less prone to believe in postbiblical miracles of all sorts. Hence, even though they were aware of the medieval chimerical fantasies about ritual murder and host profanation, thanks in part to Luther, they were much less prone to believe the fantasies that Rohling and other Catholics were presently disseminating.[21]

Protestant theology was also changing much more rapidly than that of Catholics. If many Protestants remained highly conservative politically and in theology, others exercised their rights in the priesthood of all believers to interpret their faith as their religiosity directed them—and their religiosity was changing rapidly. Many Protestant theologians welcomed the recent advances in historical and philosophical scholarship and applied the new techniques to the texts and history of Christianity in ways that challenged many traditional beliefs—though still denigrating Judaism.[22] "In the long run, the result was a watering-down of dogma and theology to a point where the Protestant religion threatened to become nothing but a bundle of ethical rules, inspired not by divine authority but by social utility."[23] As that suggests, it was much easier for Protestants than for Catholics to harmonize nationalist and Christian symbols in their religiosity. By the same token, racist beliefs about German superiority were more likely to appeal to those raised as Lutherans than to Catholics, which may help explain why, later on, Nazi propaganda appealed more to Protestants than to Catholics.[24]

The doubts liberal Protestant theologians expressed in different degrees and in different ways about traditional Christianity encouraged atheism. Protestants were apparently much more influenced by the new scientific knowledge and the metaphysical spec-

21. Some Lutherans did spread the ritual murder charge in the first half of the nineteenth century: Eleonore Sterling, *Judenhass* (Frankfurt am Main, 1969), pp. 157-159.

22. Tal, *Christians and Jews in Germany*, pp. 191-210.

23. Craig, *Germany 1865-1945*, pp. 182-183. In fact, there was more than one Protestant religion.

24. See Ian Kershaw, *Popular Opinion and Political Dissent in the Third Reich: Bavaria, 1933-1945* (Oxford, 1983); James J. Sheehan, "National Socialism and German Society," *Theory and Society* 13 (1984): 851-867; Fritz Stern, *Dreams and Delusions* (New York, 1987), pp. 162-164.

ulations then flourishing in Germany than Catholics, and also more likely to abandon Christianity entirely and explicitly. Save for Marx, the Young Hegelians whose criticisms of religion led them to vocal atheism—Ludwig Feuerbach, Max Stirner (Johann Caspar Schmidt), Bruno Bauer, and Friedrich Daumer—all came from Protestant backgrounds. Feuerbach, though baptized as a Catholic, was raised as a Protestant for the ministry; and Daumer, though converted from atheism to Catholicism when he was 58, was raised as a Protestant before becoming an atheist. The atheism of Ernst Haeckel, Willibald Hentschel, and Eugen Dühring sprang from different premises, but Dühring was raised as a Protestant, and I suspect that Haeckel and Hentschel were also, though I have not been able to verify it.[25] The same seems true of those most active in promoting racial hostility to Jews, whether they were explicitly anti-Christian or not. I was unable to ascertain the religious background of Adolf Wahrmund, Paul Förster, Theodor Fritsch, and Max Bewer, but Eugen Dühring, Wilhelm Marr, Julius Langbehn (who converted to Catholicism when he was 49), and Friedrich Lange came from Protestant families.

The attitudes of atheists varied more widely than those of any other group because atheism itself is not a belief but the absence of a particular kind of belief. Though it has sometimes sounded like it under the pens of its most determined proponents, atheism is neither a creed nor an ideology. In its mildest form, agnosticism, it was, as in the case of Pierre Bayle, only the rejection of the dogmatic authority of psychocentric religions in favor of an open-minded acknowledgment of ignorance that was still compatible with a diffuse psychocentric religiosity. Agnostics might not believe there was a god, but they could still believe in the possibility of some godlike influence, as did William James. Even moderate atheists whose religiosity was firmly physiocentric, and who therefore flatly condemned both psychocentric religions and psychocentric beliefs, did not necessarily propose a new vision of ultimate reality. Their atheistic humanism could concentrate on immediate tangible problems without facing the problem of what lay beyond. But that void beckoned those whose religiosity

25. These identifications rest on an unsatisfactory ransacking of various encyclopedias and biographical dictionaries.

abhorred a vacuum, drawing them to transcend the limits of their knowledge in search of a higher understanding.

Of course, most who no longer believed in a god did not try to formulate their own religiosity coherently. Neither preachers nor promoters of a new religiosity, they only expressed it in practice by their actions and occasional utterances.[26] But many intellectual atheists were not willing to leave the question of the foundations of their reality open. The millennial European tradition of cosmic thought, whether theological or metaphysical, encouraged them to believe that if there was no "God," then there must be some other unifying force or principle which, if understood and followed, would integrate their lives. Fully aware of their disbelief in the old gods yet unable to live with the void left by their negation of "God," they turned to the advances in rational empirical knowledge to discover who or what they were and gain a new understanding of their identity. Newton and physics beckoned some, Darwin and biology others.

Ever since the sixteenth century, Christians, stimulated by the increasing knowledge of geography and their new awareness of the physiological and cultural diversity of the earth's population, had made diverse efforts to categorize humanity into different races and order them in a hierarchy of physical and mental superiority or inferiority. That manifest diversity could still be seen as the work of God; and in a period of developing inquiry on all fronts, it was only natural to try to account for it by biblical, geographical, and biological arguments, as natural as it was to explain any other natural phenomena.[27] Indeed, when Darwin published *The Origin of the Species* in 1859, he was still a Deist, even though he had become a self-professed agnostic by the time he published *The Descent of Man* in 1871.

---

26. While such atheism may be of the greatest importance to those who believe in a god, it can be of little importance to the ungodly themselves. Indeed, their atheism may only exist in the minds of others. It is quite possible to find many people who can be categorized by others as atheists because they do not believe in "God," but who, when left to their own devices, never think about "God" at all. In that sense, what can be categorized as atheism may exist without any reference to "God," and such atheism is not parasitic on the meaning attached to the word "God"; cf. Buckley, *At the Origins of Modern Atheism*, p. 337.

27. Léon Poliakov, *The Aryan Myth* (New York, 1974), pp. 11-233.

Darwin's theory was not the announcement of a new religion, but it polarized Christians and atheists, stimulating some of the latter to ever more explicit attacks on Christian religions. It also left many people adrift. Agnostic evolutionary theories provided little guidance for individual and social action. To some extent, that gap would be filled by social Darwinists, by the proponents of eugenics who took up where Darwin had wisely left off, and later in a very different way by Bergson's "élan vital," which Bernard Shaw expressed in his own characteristic way as the "evolutionary appetite."

But that there are forces at work which use individuals for purposes far transcending the purpose of keeping these individuals alive and prosperous and respectable and safe and happy in the middle station in life, which is all any good bourgeois can reasonably require, is established by the fact that men will, in the pursuit of knowledge and of social readjustments for which they will not be a penny the better, and are indeed often many pence the worse, face poverty, infamy, exile, imprisonment, dreadful hardship and death.[28]

Although Shaw's evolutionary appetite was expressed through exceptional individuals like himself, what he described is very close to an ontologizing of what I have defined as religiosity. But neither beliefs in improved breeding nor faith in a vague mysterious force provided much practical guidance. For Shaw the clues pointed toward socialism, but for others, in whose religiosity the symbols of nationalism were very salient, the new theories of human development pointed toward a racial theory of individual identity, social organization, and human destiny.[29]

Racial theories were more attractive in Germany than in most other countries. They were hardly likely to appeal to the citizens of Mediterranean countries not only because they were firmly Catholic but also because their memory of Germanic and Islamic invasions made it hard for them to think of their countries as racially uniform. Similarly, the diverse origin of the English and French populations made it hard to take racial theories seriously.

28. Bernard Shaw, *Saint Joan* (Baltimore, 1951), preface, pp. 18-19.
29. The two could and did overlap. At the beginning of the nineteenth century, Saint-Simon combined a sociological perspective on human progress with racist beliefs, and the Nazis proclaimed themselves socialists.

In England, the Ango-Saxons had conquered the Celts, the French had conquered the Anglo-Saxons, and the monarchy had Scottish antecedents. Though the influence of racial beliefs led to debates in the late nineteenth century over whether the English owed their distinctive merits primarily to their French or German antecedents, it was difficult to think of the English as a distinct race. It was similarly difficult in France, despite the nineteenth-century debate between the Romanists, Germanists, and those who proclaimed Vercingetorix and the Celts as the ancestors of the French. But in the historical memory of Germans, Germany, despite invasions and defeats, had never been conquered and settled by people of a different origin and culture. It was therefore much easier for German speakers to think of themselves as a race. And some soon went far beyond mere speculations.

But before new physiocentric religions, whether socialistic or racial, could appear, new positive beliefs on which they could be based had to be formulated. They were developed by people who vigorously rejected psychocentric religions and religiosity not simply because those beliefs seemed rationally and empirically dubious, but because they had formulated their own physiocentric beliefs in a way that contradicted psychocentric beliefs and wanted others to share their beliefs.. Hence, even after agnosticism had become socially acceptable, proponents of the new beliefs continued to be vigorously and vocally atheistic because they were fighting to replace psychocentric religions with their own beliefs, which were developing into physiocentric religions.

It is at least arguable that the new beliefs were formulated by people who felt insecure in the world in which they found themselves and sought a new foundation. The tension in their religiosity was not, as in earlier centuries, a tension between their religiosity and the prescriptions of their religion, for they adhered to no religion. It was a tension internal to their religiosity, a conflict between what they wanted to believe about themselves and what they knew about their society. They were anxiously aware that the value they placed on themselves conflicted with what they knew about their social position or social esteem, and their self-esteem suffered.

They wanted to assert themselves, but since they had discarded all religions, they had no way of symbolizing the cosmos to support their self-image. Moreover, they differed from mere agnostics who felt generally at ease in their society and were content to pursue limited goals within it. For whatever multiplicity of reasons of psychological make-up, family history, personal experience, and general social tension, they did not trust their society as it was. It did not accord them the security or importance they needed, and consequently they were not moved by most of its symbols, except to revulsion. They therefore developed their own symbolization—or paradigm—of society, a symbolization that cohered with their symbolization of themselves and accorded them social significance, a significance that would be recognized if they could only persuade others to accept their religiosity.

Since these seekers could not, so to speak, reinvent society as a whole, could not change all knowledge about society and all the symbols for it, they focused on the elements or values in society that did harmonize with their self-image, used them as dominant symbols ("Workers of the world, unite!"), and elaborated a new positive and negative symbolization of society, or set of beliefs, around those symbols. At the same time, they put their rational empirical capacities to work to rationalize their nonrational beliefs, to demonstrate that society did indeed operate as they now believed it did. Inspired by their religiosity and the tensions within it, they developed hypotheses about human relations. Whether their new beliefs would prove influential or not would depend on their heuristic potential for research, their nonrational appeal to others, and their susceptibility to empirical invalidation.

To the extent that these thinkers merely developed a hypothesis that seemed to make sense of their experiences, they were no different from other thinkers who developed theories about some aspects of social relations. Where they differed was that they claimed to have discovered a monocausal explanation of all social relations at all times. They thus resembled Christian theologians, with one exception: they did not take the final step of claiming to have revealed the cosmic foundation of all reality, observable and unobservable. They had merely applied their physiocentric beliefs to human relations. But they had imagined a "higher" or all-embracing force—material dialectic or biological evolution— whose effects comprehended both themselves and their whole immediate environment and gave it and them new meaning. And their confidence in their vision was such that they formulated their nonrational beliefs as ideologies for social action. From there, it was but a small step in nonrational thinking to universalize their beliefs and formulate them as revealing the nature of all reality. The temptation was there for their followers, and some yielded to it and created physiocentric religions out of their ideologies.

Marx (1818-1883) was baptized at age seven. Without delving into the murky depths of psychological interpretation, it seems clear that he had problems of identity, especially in connection with the Jewish background he so spurned. His *Judenfrage* (1843-1844), written when he was in exile and just when he was beginning to formulate his communism, was a violent caricatural attack on Jews. He simply took over the Christian stereotype of Jews as usurious manipulating financiers and made "the Jew" the symbol of what he most hated.[30] His neglect of the empirical reality of Jews is striking. And so, in a very different sense, is his interpretation of history. It provided answers that, despite the vast knowledge on which they were based and the confidence with which they were proclaimed, went far beyond what could be verified. He neglected important observable phenomena right before his eyes such as religions and nationalism, dismissing them as false consciousness. He made abstract mental categories such as class, feudalism, the bourgeoisie, and the proletariat salient symbols in his religiosity and ontologized them as if they were distinct entities; and he made dialectical materialism the governing force of the human universe.

To say that does not deny the heuristic value of his insights any more than a questioning of Freud's "death instinct" necessitates a denial of his valuable insights into nonrational and irrational processes. For that reason alone it would be impossible to classify all Marx's followers as people with problems of identity. Once Marx had propounded his impressive theory, others could find it appealing for various reasons of their own. Nor should we attribute to Marx himself the development from Marxism as an ideology to the physiocentric religions prescribed by Stalin and Mao, a development we need not trace here. For my purposes

30. See Poliakov, *De Voltaire à Wagner*, pp. 432-437.

the Marxist religion is significant primarily for what it did not do. Despite the importance of Soviet Russia in the history of hostility toward Jews, and despite the fantastic accusations that brought Stalin's doctors to trial, dogmatic Communism produced little in the way of chimerical fantasies about Jews.

One reason is that the Bolshevist campaign against Christianity denied public access to Christian fantasies about Jews. Another is the role of individuals of Jewish backgrounds in the creation and spread of Marxism. A more important reason is that dogmatic Marxism was generally less conducive to irrationality than the Aryan myth—and has lasted longer—because its fundamental beliefs were initially formulated as a hypothesis or ideology by someone with great knowledge, and his basic beliefs were couched in highly abstract terms that referred to intangible entities. Hence, Marxist beliefs could be interpreted in many ways to explain apparently contradictory observable events. Moreover, the great value Marx attached to rational empirical thinking influenced even dogmatic Communists thereafter to try to adjust their beliefs, predictions, and promises to take into account what they could observe.

Even when dogmatic Marxism was implanted in Soviet Russia, where Enlightenment thought had only had a very restricted impact and Christian fantasies about Jews still had wide currency, it induced little irrationality. It did, however, produce a new kind of xenophobia in the Soviet Union. The main trouble with Jews, or many of them, was that they did not respond to the victory of the proletariat by abandoning their Judaic religiosity. Hence, like any other form of nationalism or ethnocentrism, their maintenance of their identity constituted an empirical challenge to Communist beliefs. But that challenge inspired few totally irrational reactions.

Many other explanations could be given of why Soviet Communism did not encourage chimerical fantasies about Jews. For one thing, Marxist thought did not consider Jews a class. Hence, their existence did not directly conflict with the triumph of the proletariat. They were not the major antagonists of Marxist beliefs, except insofar as they were linked with the bourgeoisie and could be seen as agents of the Western powers. They were rather people whose false consciousness, like that of the Christian bourgeoisie outside of Russia, led them to maintain their religion. But the fact that many Soviet citizens maintained their Christianity made it difficult to single out Jews as the only reactionary threat to Soviet beliefs. Hence, Communist believers were not usually antisemitic; rather, they were anti-Judaic, as they were anti-Christian.

But perhaps the fundamental explanation is that Marx and the Marxists prided themselves on their scientific attitude, took physics rather than biology as their model of rational empirical thought, insisted on the uniformity of universal natural processes, and looked optimistically to the future. Thus, when Communism did turn to biology, it was to support its promise for the future rather than to erect barriers between humans in the present. Lysenko's one-sidedly biological theory of evolution by adaptation neglected genetic variation and supported hopes for the future of humanity in a different, classless society.

Racists, however, were attracted by the model of biology with its emphasis on historical evolution, variation, and uncertainty. Arthur de Gobineau (1816-1882), who may be considered the earliest unambiguous proponent of a purely racial view of human destiny, was an almost exact contemporary of Marx. Like Marx, though he certainly lacked Marx's intellect and imagination, he was a convinced atheist who drew on the best scholarship of his day. If he had a personal problem of identity, it was because he claimed a nobility to which he was not entitled. Though Darwin's main thesis had not yet appeared when he wrote his *Essay on the Inequality of the Human Races* (1853-1855), the *Essay* was an uncompromisingly racial interpretation of history designed to legitimate the aristocracy—whose dominance was, he believed, threatened by the bourgeoisie, the mob, and miscegenation. And as with Marx, though in a very different way, the enduring identity of Jews was prominent in his thought. He was profoundly pessimistic about the future of the white Aryan race, but he accorded it pride of place and later became a close friend of Richard Wagner. Nonetheless, he praised rather than condemned Jews as a race. What he admired was their success and perseverance as a race until weakened by crossbreeding.[31]

Problems of identity are even more obvious in the frenetic ef-

31. Mosse, *Toward the Final Solution*, pp. 51-56; Poliakov, *The Aryan Myth*, pp. 233-238.

forts of Wilhelm Marr to assert himself. Though Marr by no means originated the racial view of Jews, he has some claim to be considered the first to have made it his major focus. Marr did not invent the term "antisemitism" (a superb example of a second-level symbol in nonrational thinking), but it was his use of it in 1879 that brought it to the attention of Treitschke, who ensured its wide currency. Like Marx and Gobineau, Marr was firmly atheistic throughout his life, but his self-image seems strangely incoherent. The patriarch of antisemitism married two women who were half-Jewish by origin and one who was fully Jewish, and he oscillated between belief that race—barely defined—was the fundamental clue to human history, "the new gospel,"[32] and his continuing belief in democratic socialism, equally loosely defined but anti-Communist. In the end, while still thinking of Jews as a breed apart, he abandoned the antisemitic movement of his day for the socialist radicalism he had espoused in his twenties.

One suspects that many of the devotees of racist beliefs, whether in Europe or the United States, felt their identity threatened and had severe tensions in their religiosity. We may note that Paul de Lagarde, another notable apostle of racism, was born Paul Bötticher, and that Houston Stewart Chamberlain, author of *The Foundations of the Nineteenth Century* (1900), although English by birth, settled in Germany and married one of Richard Wagner's daughters. But there can be no question of pursuing those tensions here; to do so would require a biographical knowledge well beyond my competence. The important question for my purposes is why, wherever they originated, racist beliefs were most favored in Germany, even though they may not have been that important to most Germans.[33] Gobineau was French, but he argued for the superiority of the Nordic race; and as Tocqueville suspected they would, his views had more impact on thought in Germany than in France. Lagarde was German, and Chamberlain became a German. And that is to say nothing of Wagner and his support of Ludwig Schemann, the most vigorous proponent of Gobineau's views in Germany.

32. Moshe Zimmermann, *Wilhelm Marr: The Patriarch of Anti-Semitism* (New York, 1986), p. 67 and passim.

33. The question posed by Massing, *Rehearsal for Destruction*, p. 80, who answers it by stressing economic and political factors.

Only someone well versed in the area should try to explain why racist thought appealed particularly in Germany and led to the irrationality that it did. Nevertheless, the line of argument pursued here suggests one partial answer. Although Lutheranism was a particularly German religion, Germans had been seriously divided in religion since the Reformation. And although Germany had once been effectively united politically, its integration had been declining ever since the middle of the thirteenth century; when Napoleon destroyed the facade of empire, he only revealed more clearly the reality of local autonomy and religious pluralism.

Since the Germany of the latter nineteenth century could not be seen as the flowering of a long history of religious and political integration, it seems plausible that many people would have had difficulty in symbolizing their German identity and its virtues, as indeed they notoriously did.[34] One reaction was to think of Lutheranism as a peculiarly German and superior expression of Christianity with deep roots in past German religiosity, and to try to make it the religion of the state. But that solution was opposed by Catholics, liberals, atheists, and Bismarck. When combined with historicism, however, such religious attitudes encouraged the development of the Volkish mythology, a confused set of thoroughly nonrational and romantic beliefs about the historical development of a distinctively German kind of religiosity tightly linked to the German language.[35]

What the Volkish mythology in its loose romantic form lacked, however, was a basis in transcendent beliefs that could appeal to all Germans as Germans, something comparable to that provided for nationalism in Mediterranean Europe by Catholicism, or that provided in England by Anglicanism, or even that provided in France by a long history of political integration, by Catholicism, and by the peculiarly French faith in the unlimited power of skeptical reason. To provide equivalent assurance, Volkish mythology needed to be combined with some universal transcendent beliefs.

---

34. The title of Johannes Willms's history of Germany between 1798 and 1914, *Nationalismus ohne Nation* (Dusseldorf, 1983), is exemplary.

35. For the development of Volkish thinking, see George L. Mosse, *The Crisis of German Ideology* (New York, 1964). On the desire for a German religion, see Fritz Stern, *The Politics of Cultural Despair* (Berkeley, Los Angeles, London, 1974), pp. 3-81.

Racist beliefs provided that basis. They emphasized the centrality of nonrational thinking which was so prominent a feature of the Volkish mythology, and they also claimed to be the product of rational empirical thinking, which most Germans also valued highly. They were not incompatible with the attitudes of many Protestants, some of whom tried to argue for a Nordic Jesus, and they were also or even more compatible with atheistic disbelief.

Be that as it may, there can no doubt that racial symbols became as salient as Christian symbols, if not more so, in the religiosity of many though by no means all Germans. Given the state of knowledge of the late nineteenth century, and given the fact that people could perceive gross but impressive correlations between the physical and the mental and cultural characteristics of the world's populations, it is understandable that many people, and by no means only Germans, believed that biological variation had mental consequences.[36] So long as they only asserted their racism as a nonrational belief and drew comfort from it without trying to assert that it was demonstrable empirical truth, they were not irrational. Irrationality only arose when people vigorously professed specific beliefs about particular races, asserted them as empirical propositions that conflicted with readily available knowledge, and defended them by suppressing their capacity to think rationally and empirically.

For obvious reasons, belief in the racial-cultural difference of Asiatics and Africans did not fly in the face of most people's available knowledge—except in the United States, where close observation of Africans was widely possible.[37] For Europeans attracted to beliefs about the superiority of their distinctive racial identity, the great problem was the Jews. On the one hand, the idea that Jews had manifested a distinctive identity for millennia was deeply ingrained in European thought; hence, according to racial beliefs, they had to be a race. On the other hand, Jews could be observed everywhere, and their physical, mental, and cultural similarity to those among whom they lived was obvious; hence, they were not a race.

36. Indeed, that correlation has been maintained by some scholars long after the Holocaust.

37. See George M. Fredrickson, *The Black Image in the White Mind* (New York, 1971); *The Arrogance of Race* (Middletown, Conn., 1988).

Jews thus posed to believers in the Aryan myth the same kind of problem they had posed to early Christians. Precisely because of their similarity to the believers, the fact that Jews thought and acted as they did was a direct empirical challenge to the beliefs on which both Christians and believers in the Aryan myth had based their sense of a different superior identity. And in both cases, the believers explained the contradiction away by insisting that Jews were nonetheless fundamentally different in a way that might be hard to detect empirically but could be explained by the mysterious workings of a higher power. Whatever Jews might seem, they were fundamentally different and inferior beings who had been made incapable of participating in the highest values by the forces that controlled human destiny.

Since enduring physical differences accompanied by cultural differences delimited the frontiers between races, did not a cultural difference that had proved so enduring indicate that Jews were a race, even though any obvious shared physical difference was hard to detect? A secret race, so to speak? A biological menace so hidden that, as the Nuremberg laws assumed, it could often be detected only by people's cultural ancestry?

The idea that Jews had hidden characteristics, that they were a camouflaged conspiracy, was very old. It had appeared with the first chimerical fantasy about Jewish ritual murder in 1150; it was characteristic of all the chimerical fantasies of the Middle Ages; and it had been preserved down to the nineteenth century, above all by Catholics, although Luther had played his part. For those made anxious by the unsettling and little-understood changes of a new era, belief in a conspiratorial enemy was appealing. In 1797, the Abbé Barruel published five volumes that spread his fantasy about a centuries-long conspiracy of the Freemasons to overthrow the established Catholic order. The fantasy was soon adapted first to implicate Jews and then to make them the major conspirators, thereby producing perhaps the most famous modern chimerical belief about "the Jews," the myth of the *Protocols of the Elders of Zion*.[38]

Jews were first made the center of the conspiracy in Germany, starting about 1850. Their menace was then imagined dramatically

38. See Katz, *Jews and Freemasons in Europe, 1723-1939.*

in *Biarritz*, a novel published in 1868 by Hermann Goedsche under the name of Sir John Retcliffe. One chapter depicted Jews as participating in a mysterious ritual at night in the Jewish cemetery in Prague, where they reported on the success of their efforts to undermine and control European society. By 1872, this fiction had been reworked in Russia and published as an allegedly true account of what Jews were actually doing. The fantasy then spread throughout Europe, reappearing in various forms with ever more circumstantial details and alleged eyewitnesses. And after many borrowings and forgeries, it took its final form as the *Protocols* in 1917.[39] When combined with racist beliefs, and after the staggering challenge to German identity of the defeat of 1918, it could easily lead to the chimerical fantasy of the *Dolchstuss*, the belief that Germany had been defeated because "the Jews" had stabbed them in the back, and that the Jews were the greatest single menace to Aryan identity.[40]

Except for their biological premise and the accusation of the *Dolchstuss*, the Nazi stereotypes of Jews were remarkably lacking in originality; most were simply repetitions of the old Christian xenophobic and chimerical accusations already embedded in the religiosity of many Europeans. For, as is evident from Christian syncretism, elements of religiosity from one type of religiosity or religion can easily become part of another that shares some of the same symbols. But the Nazi solution to the Jewish problem differed fundamentally from that of Christians, and the problem that remains is why the Aryan myth inspired an effort to extirpate Jews physically. Although medieval Christians had made "the Jews" the incarnate symbol of disbelief and persecuted real Jews severely, medieval authorities almost never condoned the slaughter of Jews. And whereas even the medieval mobs that slaughtered Jews usually spared those who accepted baptism, the Nazis sedulously slaughtered people who were zealously loyal to Germany and had abandoned Judaism. Why?

A part of the answer is that the Nazis were politically and technologically able to put their beliefs into action. And that raises

39. Norman Cohn, *Warrant for Genocide*, 2d ed. (New York, 1969), pp. 25-76.

40. As it did in the case of Dietrich Eckart, who so influenced Hitler: Mosse, *Toward the Final Solution*, pp. 205-206.

the troubling questions of how Hitler gained power, of who supported him, and of how many Germans wittingly supported his policy toward Jews. It is certain that not all Germans supported Hitler, and that many people from different sectors of the German population who did support him for various reasons often came to regret it.[41] It can also be argued that Hitler's attainment of power was a political abnormality made possible only by the crushing combination of the defeat of 1918, the change of regime, and the depression of 1930. And it can be argued that Hitler's antisemitism was only expressed gradually and was not what most voters noticed and approved.[42] Yet however valid those qualifications, they only carry so far.[43]

Even if Nazi propaganda by no means always harped on antisemitism, and even if many who supported Hitler disapproved of some specific anti-Jewish actions of the government, such as "Kristallnacht," it was next to impossible not to recognize that Hitler hated Jews violently—as did many others in less violent ways. And it was indisputably impossible to ignore Hitler's adherence to, and propagation of, the well-known Aryan myth. While we do not know just how many people were attracted to the Aryan myth, or how firmly they believed it, Hitler's preaching of it must have been a major part of his appeal, in no small part because what he preached and practiced was not new. Whatever the general xenophobia against Jews, whatever the constitutional, political, economic, and social stresses in Germany in the 1930s, and whatever Hitler's political genius, the extermination of Jews was possible only because racist beliefs had appealed peculiarly strongly to many Germans well before Hitler.

What Hitler did, with the active collaboration of his Nazi subordinates and the tacit support of many other Germans, was to institutionalize those physiocentric beliefs as a religion and attempt to make Germany the society of that religion. Yet granted that Hitler was able to gain sufficient support to prescribe and

41. See Stern, *Dreams and Delusions*, pp. 147-191.
42. As it has been by Ian Kershaw, *The "Hitler Myth": Image and Reality in the Third Reich* (New York, 1987).
43. The difficulties with the various intepretations are discussed in François Furet, ed., *Unanswered Questions* (New York, 1989).

implement his beliefs,[44] there remains the final question: why did his religiosity necessitate the physical extermination of Jews?

I have labeled this kind of antisemitism physiocentric antisemitism because it was an expression of physiocentric beliefs that were institutionalized briefly, but all too long, in a physiocentric religion. But there is a more compelling reason. In contrast with Christian antisemitism, Nazis were obsessed with the alleged physical characteristics of Jews; that obsession culminated in the determination to eradicate all "Jews" physically; and it was carried out regardless of any of the observable characteristics of real Jews. Whereas Christians had imagined a damnable and dangerous inferiority in the psychic characteristics of "Jews" that could have degrading physical consequences, Nazis imagined that "Jews" were damnably and dangerously inferior biologically in a way that had degrading psychic consequences. Whereas Christians believed that Jews' minds, like those of anybody else, could be— and ultimately would be—changed, the Nazis eliminated Jews bodily because they knew they could not change the biological characteristics of Jews, otherwise than by miscegenation—which would only contaminate Aryans with Jewish inferiority, indeed was already doing so. Jews therefore had to be physically eliminated.

Yet if that was what the Nazis believed, we cannot use their beliefs as our explanation of why millions of Jews were killed, since we judge Nazi ideas about themselves and about Jews to have been monstrously false and irrational. Nor are we likely to find an explanation if, as is so often done, we concentrate on Jews and the descriptive history of ideas about them. As was true of the Christians who believed chimerical fantasies about Jews and killed them, what the Nazis believed about Jews was a consequence not of what Jews really were but of what the Nazis believed or badly wanted to believe about themselves. And as was true of those Christians, Nazi irrationality was the result of the fact that they expressed their beliefs in the form of empirical assertions, confused them with empirical assertions, and were unable to defend them without inhibiting their rational empirical

44. See Raul Hilberg's magisterial description, *The Destruction of the European Jews*, 2d ed., 3 vols. (New York, 1985).

capacities. But if Nazi irrationality thus fundamentally resembled Christian irrationality, Nazism was a physiocentric religion, not a psychocentric one, and the difference was lethal.

Physiocentric religions prescribe that their beliefs explain everything important that is observably going on. As Stark and Bainbridge have stressed, they are therefore more susceptible to disproof than psychocentric religions. How susceptible depends on the nature of their beliefs. Because the basic beliefs of dogmatic Marxism were so abstract, they were not immediately susceptible to rational empirical refutation; and like Christian beliefs, they could be interpreted to adapt to changing conditions, as seems presently the case in the Soviet Union. But the more concrete and specific the basic beliefs and this-worldly predictions of a physiocentric religion, the more likely it is that its adherents will become aware at some level that what they can directly observe clashes with what their religion asserts must be going on.

Consequently, the authorities of such a religion are likely to act much more irrationally than the authorities of psychocentric religions. Because the physiocentric beliefs they prescribe focus attention so directly on what is physically and observably going on here and now, they cannot simply distort their thinking about what they consider evil realities of this world or simply disregard them and focus on another world, as adherents of so many psychocentric religions have. To protect their own beliefs and their authority over their adherents, they have to try to suppress knowledge of realities that, if observed, would directly contradict the basic beliefs of their religion. And when the contradiction is glaringly obvious, the only way to suppress that knowledge is to eliminate the realities.

The heritage of Judaism and Christianity ensured that the symbol "Jews" and the chimerical fantasies associated with it would be salient in the religiosity of those attracted to the Aryan myth. The Nazis therefore thought of Jews as a race. But the reality of Jews contradicted Nazi beliefs far more obviously than Christian beliefs. Hitler could not content himself with degrading and marginalizing the Jews, as Christians had for centuries to provide proof of their beliefs. At some level, he was aware that the very existence of Jews as Jews would always be a direct empirical invalidation of his beliefs about "Jews"—and therefore of the Nazis' belief in their own superiority as "Aryans." The contradiction was so blatant that the only way Hitler could protect his Aryan religion was to suppress knowledge of the human reality of those labeled "Jews" by exterminating them.[45]

Never has there been a more sweeping expression of religious irrationality than the "Final Solution." And Nazi awareness that rational empirical thinking about Jews would invalidate their non-rational beliefs, and that only by suppressing the reality of Jews could they preserve their beliefs, is nowhere more obvious than in Himmler's infamous speech of 4 October 1943 to the higher officers of the SS.

Our concern, our duty is to our people and our blood; it is for them we have to provide and to plan, to work and to fight, and for nothing else. . . . I also want to refer before you here, in complete frankness, to a really grave matter. . . . Each of us shuddered, and yet each one knew that he would do it again if it were ordered and if it were necessary.

I am referring to the evacuation of the Jews, the annihilation of the Jewish people. This is one of those things that are easily said. "The Jewish people is going to be annihilated," says every party member. "Sure, it's in our program, elimination of the Jews, annihilation—we'll take care of it." And then they all come trudging, 80 million worthy Germans, and each one has his decent Jew. Sure, the others are swine, but this one is an A-1 Jew. Of all those who talk this way, not one has seen it happen, not one has been through it. Most of you know what it means to see a hundred corpses lie side by side, or five hundred, or a thousand. To have stuck this out and—excepting cases of human weakness—to have kept our integrity, that is what has made us hard. In our history, this is an unwritten and never-to-be-written page of glory.[46]

45. Of course, the nineteenth-century racial antisemites only proposed that Jews be expelled, and that was also Hitler's public policy. But Hitler envisaged world domination, and here at least, he carried his thought to its logical conclusion of total elimination—and carried his subordinates along with him.

46. Lucy S. Dawidowicz, *A Holocaust Reader* (New York, 1976), pp. 131-133.

Chapter Seventeen

Religiosity and Objectivity

It is hard to be objective about what happened to Jews under Hitler. Every choice of words seems perilous and inadequate. Every description barely conceals a cry of horror; every cry of desolation seems a description. There seems no single word to denote it. The killing and suffering have been referred to by synecdoche as Auschwitz or the camps, by a religious allusion as the Holocaust, by the perpetrators' euphemism as the "Final Solution," by a metaphor as Hitler's war against the Jews, or by a biological assertion as a genocidal campaign. To symbolize what horrifies us, we have borrowed words that are redolent of values; either they express our moral revulsion at the reality, or they implicitly reverse what the perpetrators thought they were doing.

Most people now refer to that complex of events as the Holocaust, and the victory of that symbol illustrates the bonds between religion and history that pose problems of historical objectivity. It is the symbol with the richest religious evocations and the least denotative precision. Like "antisemitism," it is used in a way that contradicts its earlier meaning. Although, by focusing attention on the ovens, it seems to denote something perceptible and specific, it is a cosmization of what Jews (and others?) suffered. Far from being an unambiguous denotation of observable events, it is an expression of nonrational thinking that confuses religious beliefs and knowledge.

It is hard to avoid the confusion, for history and religion spring from the same urge. In the myths of origin of the earliest times, the recounting of history and religious expression were indistinguishable, and although Herodotus and Thucydides tried to distinguish them, they were fused again through the centuries from Augustine to Bossuet. Only for little more than a century have their practitioners been sharply distinguished in principle according to a recognized difference in methods and aims. Whereas preachers continue to explain particular human actions according to their beliefs about all existence, historians, while still ranging over the whole human past, have limited themselves increasingly to what they can infer and deduce about particular human activities from the evidence unevenly available to them—though they still seek broad explanations and write syntheses.

Writers of history still share with preachers of religion the pretension of answering our eternal question: how have we come to be here and why we are as we are? They write about any and all aspects of human existence, and they use their imagination to make sense of it all. Imagination is never lacking, even in the most dry-as-dust histories, because it is part of our humanity, inseparable from our religiosity. From infancy, the mixed blessing of memory assures us that we exist and that our family and our community have a past, however proximate.[1] We fill out that awareness with the disjointed material gleaned from the talk of our elders and our peers and from the writings and pictures of people long dead. In our childish ignorance, we join and transmute those scattered impressions and symbols to form a largely mythical idea of who we are and how we came to be here. With experience and education, our ideas become richer, and perhaps more solidly based as we rely increasingly on wider and apparently authoritative information. But that socially warranted information is not simply knowledge. It also evolved from imagination and myth and rests on socially distilled paradigms of human existence.

Though performed by individuals, historiography and the teaching of history are also social enterprises. Not only do historical research and writing require social cooperation, but many still expect the teaching of history to provide a justification of their

1. Volume 3 of *Coming to America* by Angela Steele and her Third Year English-as-a-Second-Language Students (Sequoia High School, Redwood City, Calif., 1989) is an immensely touching set of answers to those questions. I would like to thank Ana Castañeda for bringing the book to my attention.

society and its way of life that will mold the next generation into the paths of virtue. And though historians may modify the assumptions that developed with their society and are embedded in their language, they cannot help relying heavily on them. Those assumptions, which might be called their broadest paradigms of existence, mold their perceptions, link their thought about their experiences, guide their search for knowledge, and structure how they express it.

The great variety in historiography, in the questions asked and the way answers are presented, reflects the differences between societies and the differences in religiosity and historical imagination of individual historians. The differences between different generations of historians are obvious. While the nation and its political institutions may be most significant to one generation of historians, another may give priority to the sufferings of the exploited. Even historians of the same generation with rather similar religiosities have differed somewhat, and often considerably, being attracted to different subjects, approaching common subjects somewhat differently, having different styles, and providing different explanations. Even on the same subject, no historian will write the same book. So obvious are the differences in historiography that the ideal of historical objectivity has been compared with religious myths,[2] and historiography has been said to be meaningful only in hermeneutic terms.[3] How, then, can historians be objective?

I am a historian, not a philosopher. I am not competent to pronounce on truth with a capital "T," declare the meaning of the seamless past as a whole, or reveal the secrets of the universe. I have not discussed the coherence and correspondence theories of truth or all the other epistemological issues involved in speaking of objectivity. By objectivity, I mean no more than the criteria every serious professional historian tries to satisfy in practice in his or her detailed scholarship.[4] If keeping one's feet on the

2. Peter Novick, *That Noble Dream: The Objectivity Question and the American Historical Profession* (Cambridge, Eng., 1988), pp. 3-5.

3. Especially by Paul Ricoeur. See John B. Thompson, *Critical Hermeneutics* (Cambridge, Eng., 1981). For a lucid summary of Ricoeur's position, see Hayden White: *The Content of the Form* (Baltimore, 1987), pp. 49-54, 169-184.

4. One of the fascinating aspects of Novick's superb book is that, while he

ground means being pedestrian, so be it. What has concerned me is an immediate and practical historiographic problem for which philosophy, however valuable, provides no direct answer.

Like many others, I could not help asking why Hitler had wanted to exterminate Jews and had been able to kill millions of them. Explanations that rested on premises about a loving god, a chosen people, or a superior race could not satisfy me. I did not want an explanation limited by religious or ethnocentric boundaries that gratified the amour propre of any particular group. I wanted a more objective explanation, limited, so far as possible, only by the limitations of my knowledge about humanity. And there was one certainty that made some measure of objectivity seem possible and imperative.

Whatever language I used, I could not deny that something had happened because it had left so many traces—photographs of dead and emaciated bodies, testimonies of participants of all sorts, governmental documents, gold fillings, hair. Though I had not experienced it directly, and though my knowledge of its details was limited, I knew that thousands of small children had died in gas chambers, tight-packed against taller adults. If I encounter individuals who deny that anything like that happened, I can only assume their individual irrationality, their cynical political immorality, or the irrationality of their social indoctrination.

That happening affected all who were aware of it, challenging both their faith in the value of their identity and their pride in their knowledge. Jews, who were under no temptation to deny their awareness of what had happened, responded in diverse ways ranging from suicide to political redefinition, theological reflection,[5] and the search for historical understanding. Non-Jews, less

---

treats objectivity as a myth in the sense of an ideal and carefully refrains from committing himself to any precise definition of historical objectivity, his revelations about prominent historians depend for their impact on our recognition that these were manifest failures of objectivity and were recognized as such by some people at the time. What that suggests is that objectivity is not a vast corpus of certain knowledge, not some ultimate synthesis that all historians thereafter would have to accept, but rather a way that historians can think, but often do not, at the time they are addressing some problem.

5. See Amos Funkenstein, "Interprétations théologiques de l'holocauste: Un bilan," in *L'Allemagne nazie et le genocide juif*, Colloque de l'Ecole des hautes études (Paris, 1985), pp. 465-495.

affected, reacted less decisively. Most, however, were sufficiently horrified that they felt compelled to think more rationally and empirically about Jews. Their knowledge of what had happened conflicted directly with their religiosity and impelled them to modify it, and when they did, they found they also had to change their thoughts about the past.

To explain what Hitler had done, scholars found they had to rewrite sections of earlier history. Many Christian scholars were gradually forced to admit that, for centuries, Christian beliefs and the religious irrationality of Christians had caused similar, if less extensive, suffering and prepared the way for the horrors of their own day—even though that increased objectivity posed fundamental theological problems. Most historians, both Jews and non-Jews, began to write more objectively about the interactions of non-Jews and Jews through the centuries. They recognized that for generations historians had been blind to many factual aspects of Jewish and non-Jewish conduct through the ages, that what they had written about many events that had occurred centuries earlier and in lands distant from Germany was wrong. Historical objectivity generally prevailed over subjectivity. Though incomplete, the change in historiography is already extensive.

What makes objectivity possible, it seems to me, is our perception of objects whose existence we can no more deny rationally than we can deny the existence of our own bodies. The moral judgments which the killing of so many defenseless Jews suggests about ourselves or our immediate ancestors may make objectivity remarkably difficult, but that is precisely because we wish the killings had never happened but are too aware that they did to be able to dismiss them from our minds. Whatever we call them, they happened, we react to them, and how we know about them is no different in principle from how we know about any other major sequence of events that historians write about.

What occurred was, at the least, a very complex network of very different kinds of observable actions involving very many people—and very different kinds of people—in many different ways. I might denote it as the most violent social expression of twentieth-century physiocentric antisemitism. It involved governments, war, the production and transfer of material resources, and technology. Its roots lay deep in the past, and it had important consequences for the future. Millions of people of all social ranks across a wide area were directly or indirectly affected, and it had powerful moral implications for contemporaries. If we cannot be objective about those events, we cannot be objective about any other historical events, but I think we can, provided we limit what we mean by objectivity.

Our objectivity stems from our undeniable awareness of realities that impinge on us as objects, objects we did not create that do not come with names attached, although we give our perception of them names. Our thought is not just self-contemplation or solipsistic rhetoric; it is determined in large part by our physical interactions with realities beyond the boundaries of ourselves. We are aware that we perceive objects and relations between them whose existence—however we conceive and symbolize them— we cannot deny without imperiling our own or someone else's existence. And we are sure that others perceive those realities too, even though they may not perceive or conceive them in the same way. Whether or not we think in Newtonian or Einsteinian terms and however we express it, we know that things fall and that people who have fallen from great heights with nothing to impede their fall have died—whether they wanted to or not. And we are certain that people throughout history have known that. Hence the dream of Daedalus, the fall of Adam, and the reality of parachutes. Perhaps our capacity for objectivity depends in the last analysis on our sense that stone dead hath no fellow, the awareness of the finality of death that other animals apparently do not share.

Yet if pretheoretical knowledge about undeniable objects or processes is necessary for objectivity, it alone is insufficient to produce it. Only when individuals think about how they think and distinguish different ways of thinking can they conceive of thinking objectively. To think that they can think objectively, they must know what it means to think objectively; they must be able to engage in second-level thought. They must be able to think about the symbolic expression of their thoughts as objects and classify their different ways of thinking. We, of course, as beneficiaries of centuries of philosophy and more recently of psychology and cybernetics, take that ability to think about our thinking for granted, and we have developed many second-level symbols to express it. Those symbols denote at least two different kinds of thinking. We use symbols such as "ludic," "poetic," "artistic," "moral," "tragic," "cathartic," "romantic," or "aesthetic" to denote our nonrational thinking, and symbols such as "logical," "rational," "deductive," "inductive," "empirical," "analytic," "pragmatic," or "conclusive" to denote our rational empirical thinking. The kind of thinking about realities that second set of symbols denotes is what I mean by rational empirical thinking.

Needless to say, we do not think objectively all the time. Indeed, many people have never or only rarely been objective. Probably most people throughout history have never thought abstractly about how they think; they engaged in both nonrational and rational empirical thinking without being conscious of the difference. Acting and thinking practically, they used symbols equivalent to our symbols such as "want," "love," "fear," "hate," "cry," or "tremble," to direct attention to their own reactions, and they used symbols, such as "woman," "stone," "spear," "look," "water" (or names for specific instances of them), to direct attention to realities that were what they were whether they liked them or not, and to which they had to react if they were to preserve themselves. But the meanings of those symbols were so fused in their thinking that they did not recognize they could think in two different ways. Though we may distinguish between their nonrational and rational empirical thinking, they did not. But we should not feel superior, for we do the same thing, only we do it at a different level because we can generalize and think abstractly.

So long as we stay close to the ground and describe particular, universally perceptible, objects or processes such as earth, water, fire, birth, eating, growth, or death, we can be highly objective. People at other times and places may have conceived them and connected them with each other differently, but what they experienced concretely can be reexpressed in our language because we too have experienced those concrete objects or processes.[6] Hence, given sufficient evidence of artifacts and writings, histo-

6. On the debated issue of commensurability, see Kuhn, *The Structure of Scientific Revolutions*, pp. 198-204. See also the excellent discussion of that issue and various other arguments against historical objectivity in Novick, *That Noble Dream*, pp. 531-572.

rians can establish the occurrence of many of these highly perceptible events, thanks to the commonalities of human life. In the sense of establishing more and more facts of this kind, historiography can be cumulative. But, *pace* J. B. Bury, such facts are not very meaningful by themselves.

To be meaningful, a description of even the most concrete occurrence relies on a tacit explanation of its occurrence, be it only as simple as the explanation that splitting someone's skull with a sword will kill him. But at this level, the explanation is one that anyone who knows what a sword is will accept. And the same can be said for Zyklon B. For historiography to be significant, however, it must link many events together. When it does, serious problems of objectivity arise, for the explanations that underlie and integrate the description, whether tacitly or explicitly, rest not only on knowledge of simple physical causes but also on beliefs about humanity and the universe that are far from universal. The more embracing the account and the more abstract the terms used to correlate the facts, the greater the reliance on the knowledge and paradigmatic assumptions of a particular period, and on the historian's own religiosity. In other words, the broader the range of human affairs the historian seeks to describe and explain, the more religious the enterprise.

Manifestly, my hypotheses about antisemitism express my own knowledge or lack of it and my own attitude toward life, obviously so in the questions asked, the style, the formulation of the arguments, the choice of citations and illustrations, and the occasional moralizing adverb or adjective, but also in the underlying assumptions, and nowhere more so than in the value I attribute to thinking rationally and empirically. Manifestly, this book and I are the resultants of personal experience, particular historical conditions, present states of knowledge, and particular problems in historical scholarship. And if the breadth of the subjects on which I have committed myself here makes that very obvious, it is true *in parvo* of the most detailed and limited article I have written on any subject, and I think it true of any historical work. It is precisely that recognition of subjectivity, however, which makes historical objectivity possible.

I conceive of objectivity not as a characteristic of historical assertions that makes them valid for all historians hereafter but as a way of thinking at a particular time, as a process, not its product. Objective thinking, I suggest, is how we think about objects when we think rationally and empirically about how we think about them and how others think of them, including how contemporaries think about ourselves and our expressions of thought—for we are objects for them as they are for us. No history book is the objective truth or the past as it was. Historical works are objective only in the derivative sense that, at the time the authors were seeking answers to the questions they themselves had posed about past human actions, they were thinking as rationally and empirically as they could about how they were thinking—including their effort to imagine the flaws others might find in their arguments. Hence, a historical work is usually considered objective only so long as those who read it ask the same sort of questions and think more or less the same way about the same things. The objectivity of historical work resides in how the historians were thinking when they made their assertions, not in the assertions themselves. How long historical work will be considered objective will depend on whether others will be able to think more rationally and objectively about more questions in the future.

Objectivity, then, is the ability of historians to distinguish when they are thinking nonrationally about objects and when they are thinking rationally and empirically. The degree of their objectivity depends on how salient the various symbols denoting rational empirical techniques are in their religiosity (even symbols as colloquial as "Use your head!"). The more salient they are, the more they will value their capacity to think rationally and empirically, be impelled to use it, be aware that their thinking is a perpetual dialectic between their nonrational and their rational empirical thinking, and be conscious of the limitations of the latter. And the more they value their capacity for rational empirical thinking, the more they will try to ensure that their nonrational thinking stimulates rather than inhibits their use of that capacity, not only when they think about the objects they experience but also when they think about how they think. The paradox of historical objectivity is that it stems from subjectivity. Their religiosity drives historians to write history, and insofar as they think objectively, they do so because their religiosity values rational empirical thinking, which forces them to recognize their subjectivity.

The pitfalls menacing objectivity are too numerous to mention. Some are personal, some very common. Historians have only so much time and energy. They cannot stop and think about every aspect of the subject on which they write or every expression they use; they must frequently rely on assumptions and language they have not examined very closely. And because many of the unexamined symbols have no precise meaning, it is often difficult to distinguish belief from knowledge, especially about contemporary history.

When discussing recent events, historians cannot help using abstractions that are themselves recent and emotionally loaded and mean different things to different people. The imprecision of symbols such as socialism, nation, antisemitism, genocide, and the like makes it particularly difficult for historians to distinguish between their own beliefs about that kind of thought and action and what they assert to be knowledge about what their contemporaries or near contemporaries had been thinking and doing. Fortunately, however, the difficulty of being objective about recent history is proverbial, and such terms come with warning signals attached. Anyone who now writes about the history of the United States knows the perils lurking in symbols such as Negro, Black, or African-American. Historians recognize that such terms pose severe problems of objectivity because of their contemporaneity and emotional significance, and they often indicate carefully what they mean by them, as indeed they should. Yet even if they do not, most readers will be conscious of the emotional significance of the terms and likely to think critically about how they are being used. Historiography about events more distant in time and space, however, often uses symbols that lack those warning signals.

We tend to think that historians can be more objective when discussing more remote events, and in many ways that is true. No longer are historians themselves more or less directly and emotionally involved in the events they describe. They have also had time to examine the evidence more exhaustively, thereby enabling them to establish many facts that make flagrant failures of objectivity easier to recognize. Disagreements between historians therefore seem more a matter of conflicting hypotheses and new knowledge than of personal bias. But the challenge to objectivity, if better concealed, is still there; it has simply moved to a different and more abstract or fundamental level.

When formulating and colligating their facts about the more distant past, historians can avoid using recent, emotionally evocative, symbols such as communism. But they cannot help using other denotative and explanatory symbols that have existed for centuries, such as family, commerce, monarchy, justice, exploitation, poverty, piety, superstitition, barbarian, ambition, self-seeking, reason—as well as the terms that have concerned me here: religion, spirituality, Jew, Christian, Catholic, Lutheran, and the like. Since these symbols are both so old and so commonly used in the present, many do not ring warning bells to alert historians and their readers to the fact that they have meant different things to people at different times—and still mean different things to different people now, including historians.

It is here, I think, that historians face a choice crucial for their objectivity: what or whose meaning are they attributing to those terms? Are they using them with the meaning they had for people in the past, with the meaning consensually attributed to them in their own society, or with the meaning which they, as objective historians, give them? Take "the Reformation," for example. It has been used since the sixteenth century to express the religious meanings that people attributed to what they conceived of as a single, great, complex event, and historians have often treated it as an event. Since the symbol did not unambiguously denote any specific observable event, it was easy for historians to use it in ways that allowed the religious meanings evoked by the symbol to determine which actions and interactions they would consider part of that event, and even to think of the period in which those actions occurred as a separate period.

Alternatively, "the Reformation" may be used simply as a conventional label to indicate an open-ended area of research into a process about which a lot but by no means everything is known: the emergence of new religions that ended the European hegemony of the Roman Catholic religion. Provided the meaning of "religion" is specified in rational empirical terms, historians can then use the symbol objectively to refer to our partial and fragmented knowledge of a broad network of events that has no clear

boundary and no integrated explanation. Used this way, the symbol no longer denotes a precise historical phenomenon; rather, it
indicates a focus for more specific questions. There can be no
single answer to the question, "What was the Reformation and
why did it occur?"

On the basis of rational empirical research on present data, we
can assert that Luther nailed the writing known as his Ninety-
Five Theses to the door of the castle church at Wittenburg on
31 October 1517—a manifestly perceptible event even though the
dating convention is Christian. From there, after analyzing a
much vaster body of present evidence, we can use our best present knowledge about human behavior and other realities to establish that that event was related to other perceptible events at
the time and before and after it and to explain how we think they
were related. Nothing in this procedure, however, guarantees
that the outcome will be an integrated description and explanation
of everything relevant to that particular event. But, if we think
objectively, can we expect anything more?

The purpose of objective historical thinking is to discover and
communicate our answers to our questions about past events. Our
memory, however faulty, assures us that we had experiences before our present experience, and that certainty impels us to wonder what we can know about other past events. The primary task
of professional historians is to determine that reasonably unambiguously denoted events that some contemporaries could have
perceived directly happened; to establish as many of the empirical
characteristics of those happenings as possible; and to explain so
far as they can why or how they occurred. To perform that task,
historians analyze perceptible data in the present—for example,
a manuscript, a sunken galleon, a history book—whose existence
is explicable only as a result of events in the more or less remote
past. For, in the last analysis, historical knowledge is the result
of people seeking cooperatively to explain rationally and empirically what they perceive in the present by what must have happened in the past.

But though the knowledge thus laboriously acquired about
some past events may be so dense as to make them seem as real
to us as our yesterdays, it is not a reproduction *of* them; it is only
assertions *about* them. The reality of those events, like our yes-

terdays, now exists only in their consequences, including our thoughts about them. Unless historians espouse some prior overarching explanation of all human action—and how much easier it is to write history if you claim to know beforehand what makes everything tick—historical thinking can only produce a diversity of relevant and interlaced, but imperfectly correlated, answers. So long as we restrict ourselves to trying rationally and empirically to answer questions about reasonably unambiguously denoted events, we are forced to recognize the limits of our knowledge. The further we go from descriptions and explanations of simple perceptible events to descriptions and explanations of more complex or less directly perceptible events, the more uncoordinated and tentative our answers become. Fortunately or unfortunately for historians, their work will never be complete. They will always have ample room to revise their accounts on the basis of new evidence, new hypotheses about human behavior, and changes in religiosity. But as they do, they should strive to prevent their religiosity from inhibiting their capacity to think rationally and empirically.

So far as this book has an overriding thesis, it is that historians should make more explicit than they often do what rational empirical meaning they attribute to the symbols they use to colligate their facts, thereby diminishing the confusion between their own explanation of what happened and what those they study thought was happening. As I argued in chapter 3, I think that to ask whether historians should describe and explain events according to the knowledge and assumptions of the period studied or whether they should do it in their own terms presents a false dilemma. Historians cannot help describing and connecting what they think occurred in their own way. They may try with considerable success to describe how some people in the past thought, even directly by quotation, but they do so according to their own understanding; even a quotation is not a reproduction of the consciousness partially expressed in that writing. It is the historian who decides which and whose expressed thoughts and actions should be described, who understands and connects them in his or her own way, and who describes and explains them so that they will be comprehensible to a present audience. When historians present descriptions of past thoughts as explanations of those people's actions, they camouflage the extent to which they have infused that explanation with their own knowledge and assumptions. Historians cannot help answering their own questions and explaining what happened in the past in their own way.

Most of this book has been devoted to making a virtue of that necessity, to arguing that historians should do consciously what they can't help doing unconsciously. If they distinguish clearly between what people in the past thought they were doing and what they themselves think those people did, they will be more conscious of how they themselves are thinking. They may therefore be better able to recognize when they are thinking rationally and empirically and when they are expressing their nonrational understanding of the value of their lives. But it is one thing to advocate in general terms standards of practice with which many historians may agree, quite another to implement them.

I have argued that a major cause of confusion is the ambiguity lurking in the denotative and explanatory symbols that historians use to categorize, or generalize about, people, thoughts, and actions, symbols such as "Jew," "Christianity," "antisemitism," and, above all, "religion." Confusion is least likely to occur when historians are dealing with very limited subjects and answering precise questions about concrete actions of the type anyone then and now could observe, for example, where was a person on a given day. Here, even though the search for an answer may depend on nonrational considerations such as a nationalistic interest in Napoleon's whereabouts, the answer the historian asserts rests solidly on a universal kind of knowledge of physical interactions. But the broader the question asked, the greater the possibility of confusion, for the explanation no longer rests on that universal kind of knowledge.

In an article establishing Napoleon's whereabouts on a particular day, abstract terms such as society, state, war, commerce, or enemies might appear as background explanations of why Napoleon went where he did, but the answer to the question of where he was on that day is unlikely to depend on them. The moment, however, that historians attack broader questions—for example, why did Napoleon attack Russia or who started World War I—the validity of their answers depends heavily on the meanings they attribute to such abstract terms—which were also

used by the historical actors. Even more obviously, when historians write a history of a whole area and period, such as a history
of Europe from 1517 to 1559 or a history of Germany from 1866
to 1945, what binds the facts they include together and accounts
for their silences is their general ideas about what is important
in life. They rely heavily on knowledge and paradigmatic assumptions that are far from universal. But that fact can be concealed by ambiguous language.

When a synthesis or answer to a broad question is presented
in the form of a chronological narrative, traditional assumptions
can be woven into the fabric by the use of unglossed symbols so
that they are almost imperceptible—and the reader may be un-
wittingly influenced to share the author's adherence to traditional
values. When the synthesis is divided under topical rubrics that
indicate different kinds of human activity and the relative weight
and kind of treatment the author thinks each deserves, the underlying assumptions are more obvious. And in some syntheses,
some of the controlling assumptions are indicated explicitly: "Essentially the central axis round which I have tried to organize the
history of the century is the triumph of capitalism in the historically specific forms of bourgeois society in its liberal version."[7]

In this case, the use of carefully chosen, more or less technical,
terms or jargon clearly indicates a particular way of conceiving
human activity. That admirable honesty reminds readers that
what they are reading about the past is not something transcen-
dentally conveyed from the past; it is a partial description and
explanation of a whole period controlled by that historian's assumptions about what is most important in the human condition
and by use of knowledge not available to the historical actors.
Yet, although that kind of honesty makes it easier to distinguish
between what the actors thought and what the historian thinks,
and between the historian's religiosity and his or her rational empirical knowledge, the lines are still hard to draw. Though some
controlling assumptions have been made explicit, nonrational beliefs, rational hypotheses, and objective knowledge interact so si-
multaneously at this level of symbolic generality that it is hard to

---

7. Eric J. Hobsbawm, *The Age of Empire, 1875-1914* (New York, 1989), pp.
8-9.

distinguish their respective influences and easy for the historian to mistake his or her beliefs for knowledge about past realities.[8]

The great danger is illicit reification. By that I mean the tendency to think that the nonrational meanings evoked by a symbol are a rational empirical description of a reality independent of the historian's thought that is denoted by that symbol, for example, the attribution of characteristics and qualities nonrationally associated with "Jew" to the human reality denoted as Jews. Illicit reifications may be either nonrational or irrational, xenophobic or chimerical, depending on whether or not they rest on a kernel of truth. When Christians asserted that the Jews were responsible for the killing of Christ, they engaged in nonrational illicit reification because they attributed to all Jews what was true only of some Jews. When they accused Jews of ritual murder, they engaged in irrational illicit reification that had no kernel of truth, for no one had ever observed Jews committing ritual murder.

It is, of course, very difficult not to engage in nonrational illicit reification about groups about which we know little. When thinking of "Judaism" and "Jews," most non-Jews in the past, including historians as great as Gibbon, Michelet, and Trevelyan, and even Mommsen, unreflectingly expressed their xenophobia by nonrational illicit reifications that supported their sense of identity. Yet if we can recognize where they stumbled, it is very difficult for us to recognize when we engage in illicit reifications ourselves. Desiring the continuity of our own identity, we are prone to project our beliefs and imperfect knowledge into the past as well as the present and future. We may no longer do so as blatantly as those whom Herbert Butterfield excoriated as "Whig historians," but we do so in less evident ways. When Butterfield turned to the relation between Christianity and history, he himself engaged in a subtle form of Whig history.[9] Indeed, it seems we only recognize our own failings when our awareness of events

8. I therefore agree broadly with Hayden White's rhetorical analysis of historical narrative: *Metahistory* (Baltimore, 1987); *The Content of the Form*. But, since he pays so little attention to how we acquire and communicate the knowledge about past events that narratives use, there is the implication that narrative is the only important way of communicating historical knowledge to those who seek knowledge, and here I would disagree.

9. Herbert Butterfield, *The Whig Interpretation of History* (New York, 1951); cf. *Christianity and History* (Glasgow, 1949).

we had not anticipated impels us to doubts about our faith, our knowledge, or both.

Of course, people always use old symbols in somewhat different senses and invent new ones to deal with new problems. The general notions that symbols evoke change gradually for each generation and each individual, usually in ways of which they are little aware. Changes in the meaning of historical terms may be made more consciously by scholars engaged in dispassionate analysis of the realities embraced by them, but that is typically very gradual and has only a limited influence on common usage. It seems that rapid and self-conscious revolutions in the meaning of habitual symbols only occur when we are highly elated or seriously disturbed by unexpected events we cannot deny. When that does occur, however, scholars should seize the opportunity and analyze the challenged beliefs and concepts as objectively as they presently can.

The rapid change in the meaning of "Jew" or "antisemitism" for many non-Jews after 1945 owed more to Hitler than to scholarship before 1945. It was a result of the strong emotional reactions to the monstrosity that had just happened. Awareness of those events forced many historians, among others, to question what they had previously believed and thought they had known about Jews and antisemitism and to modify the meanings they attributed to those symbols. To improve understanding of the recent horror, some historians then began to examine the implications of the new meanings for the writing of earlier history. Those who did, however, could not avoid writing about religion according to their conception of it. Whether or not they recognized it, the events were a challenge to reexamine as objectively as possible the meanings attributed to "religion" and related terms—as some Christians immediately recognized.

For Christians, the pressing question was whether belief in the divinity of Jesus of Nazareth was a major cause of the hatred of Jews manifest at Auschwitz. But, in order to distinguish the historical consequences of genuinely religious thought and conduct from the consequences of other kinds of thinking and action, they first had to decide what Christianity was. They cut the Gordian knot by using their faith to distinguish Christian anti-Judaism from antisemitism—even though their increased objectivity forced them to modify their religiosity by reformulating centuries-old Christian doctrine. For other historians, however, those whose rational empirical thinking was not circumscribed by nonrational beliefs about Jesus of Nazareth, the challenge to see if they could think more objectively about religious phenomena remained.

I have tried to respond to the challenge posed by Hitler's implementation of antisemitism to think objectively about religion, but my response is certainly inadequate. And not only because of the inhumanity involved. The challenge goes to the heart of historiography because historical and religious thinking are so similar. Moreover, "religion" has richer nonrational connotations than any other symbol historians use, yet they cannot help writing about "religious" phenomena. For those and other reasons such as personal belief, it is probably harder for historians to think objectively about religious phenomena than about anything else— which may be why they have so often bracketed the problem.

I have argued that historians should not avoid the problem, that they should not use the language of the believers in religions to describe and explain past religious thought and conduct, while carefully refraining from indicating how they themselves would rationally and empirically describe and explain that thought and conduct. I have argued that, although historians must describe as best they can what believers in religion then believed, they should also make explicit what they themselves now mean when they symbolize thought and action as "religion" or "religious" and how they themselves explain that kind of activity—so far as they can.

I have proposed that historians should make three fundamental distinctions: between religion and religiosity, between nonrational and rational empirical thinking, and between irrational thinking and either rational empirical or nonrational thinking.[10] These are distinctions not between things or particular beliefs but between processes by which individuals and societies act and react to their environment. Whether or not they are adequate for other purposes, I think they apply effectively at the level of human conduct

---

10. I consider irrational thinking to be the expression neither of nonrational nor of rational empirical thinking but a symptom of their rupture. It is the thinking that results when interaction between those two modes stops and they can no longer be integrated.

historians must deal with and provide categories that may advance historical research on religion and antisemitism.

Of all the implications of my arguments, the one most likely to trouble many people is that the future of religion—or at least of any particular religion—is uncertain. I have argued that, if historians examine religious phenomena rationally and empirically without using prescribed religious beliefs as premises, they may find it necessary to distinguish between religions as a form of society and religiosity as a property of individuals, between what religions have prescribed and what individuals have actually believed. And if one makes that distinction, although religiosity emerges as an enduring property of human beings with the potential for maintaining old religions and creating new ones, the future of any particular religion seems as uncertain as the future of any particular society.

That rational empirical proposition is not an ethical criticism of those who have prescribed or adhered to religions. I have not denied the value of religions for their members or their importance for human progress. Whether I believe what their adherents believed or believe is beside the point. No one has ever believed all the beliefs of the different religions, for they manifestly conflict. But one does not have to believe to recognize that religions—like the arts and often in close conjunction with them—have distilled and preserved awareness of what many individuals under various conditions have felt to be their most important insights about their existence. Whatever the damage sometimes done by the enforcement of their prescriptions, religions have provided a treasury for thinking about the quandaries of existence that has enabled untold millions to face their uncertainties and to act.

Yet if there is a Kantian category of understanding for historians, it is that human beings existed and acted in the past, and that how they acted has always changed. To deny that is to reduce human beings to a few rudimentary drives, such as the instinct for survival, and to disregard all the more specific characteristics and actions that have brought us to where we are now—and now threaten the species. The historian's domain is those changing specifics, including the diversity of religious beliefs and their manifest modifications and discontinuities. Though religions may provide comforting beliefs about eternity to help people through their present, and though their social stabilization of prescribed beliefs may make them seem eternal, they are not. Historians must recognize their great historical significance, high stability, and value for their adherents, but they can neither think objectively of religions as unchanging nor write objective history according to any prescribed religious belief.

The future of religion thus seems uncertain, but nonrational thinking and religiosity will endure as long as humanity. Though any particular religiosity will die with the individual, individuals will always have their distinctive religiosities that provide their understanding of their existence and enable them to act, whether their religiosity be integrated or fragmented, and however it may differ from those before, around, and after them. That is as true of historians as of anyone else. Though those of one generation may be quite similar in religiosity, they will still differ somewhat, often considerably, being attracted to different subjects and approaching common subjects somewhat differently. They may be able to think objectively, but they cannot help thinking religiously.

Another implication arising from my distinctions is unsettling. It is that, in the foreseeable future, there will be many individuals who think almost entirely subjectively about other people, and some who think irrationally. Indeed, the probability of irrationality is increased by the solid institutionalization of rational empiricism in Western civilization—in universities, research institutes, journals, and the like. More individuals are likely to become uneasily aware of a conflict between beliefs they badly want to maintain and what they could know if they were able or willing to use their capacity for rational empirical thinking. They may therefore defend themselves from self-doubt by inhibiting their use of that capacity, and they will be encouraged to do so by political expressions, often cynical, of visceral thinking. More optimistically, however, it could be argued that the value placed on rational empiricism and its institutionalization, diffusion, and material fruits may limit the impact of individual irrationality on others, thereby reducing the likelihood of social irrationality.

I have defined antisemitism by the extreme irrationality that distinguishes it from other kinds of hostility toward Jews. That enabled me to distinguish Christian anti-Judaism from antisemitism without relying on theological premises. From that it also follows that belief in the divinity of Jesus of Nazareth does not necessarily produce antisemitism. Moreover, when the distinction between religions and religiosities is applied to Christianity, it highlights the diversity of Christian religiosities and religions and makes it meaningless and morally lazy to ask whether Christianity was responsible for Auschwitz. Nonetheless, I have not absolved all Christians and Christian religions.

The ground for antisemitism was prepared by the prevalence of Christian xenophobic beliefs about Jews; chimerical antisemitic beliefs emerged in the twelfth century; and they became socially significant in the thirteenth. Those irrational fantasies were created by northern Catholic Christians who sought to repress doubts about their Christian beliefs; they were ecclesiastically supported; and they came to be widely believed in Catholic Christendom. Christianity was not the cause of antisemitism, but antisemitism was created by certain Christians and expressed by multitudes of Catholics and, later, Protestants.

Christian nonrational beliefs about the life, death, and continuing presence of Jesus of Nazareth inspired nonrational beliefs about Jews. When Christians illicitly reified their nonrational beliefs about "Christ," doubts arose, such as doubts about Christ's real presence in the bread and wine of the mass. To defend their faith, some Christians reacted irrationally and experienced miracles. But in their midst were real Jews, the incarnation of disbelief, and to defend themselves against that stimulus to doubt, some Christians engaged in irrational illicit reification. They not only attributed characteristics observed in some Jews to all Jews, they also, like Hitler, attributed characteristics and conduct to all Jews that anyone should have been able to observe but that no one in fact had ever observed—and that many Christians at the time did not believe had been observed.

The institutionalization of those irrational fantasies by psychocentric Christian religions made them part of European culture and encouraged the killing, isolation, and expulsions of Jews. Much later, when the Nazis created a new physiocentric religion premised on illicit reification of their self-image, they could protect their faith in themselves only by illicit reification of other peoples. And because Christian beliefs and irrational fantasies about Jews permeated their culture, they took them over and made Jews the target of extreme illicit reification: they thought of "Jews" as viruses. That belief so conflicted with the reality of Jews that the Nazis' faith in themselves could be defended only by destroying whomever they thought of as a "Jew," and they killed as many as they could. Thus, at first thousands, and finally millions of Jews died because many Christians and Nazis treated Jews as if they were really what the symbol "Jew" meant in Christian and Nazi nonrational thinking. They died because so many Christians and Nazis inhibited their ability to think rationally about observable realities that existed independently of their thinking about them.

If there is any lesson to be drawn from our understanding of the irrational inhumanity with which Christians and Nazis treated Jews, it is that any religion or any religiosity, whether psychocentric or physiocentric, that condones, encourages, or demands the inhibition of our capacities for rational empirical thinking represses awareness of our common humanity and threatens humanity itself. To think that material realities such as bread, wine, pork, cows, or flags are in reality what they evoke symbolically in nonrational thinking is dangerous enough; to treat human beings that way is deadly. Millions of human beings died because other human beings inhibited their rational empirical capacities to the point that they could no longer recognize in the defenseless victims they symbolized as "Jews" the readily perceptible human characteristics they shared.

Index

Abraham, 37, 52

Action française (Weber), 327n

Adorno, T. W. et al., 316: *Authoritarian Personality, The,* 316n

Afterlife, 92–93, 98–99, 102n

Africans, 340

Agnosticism, 333–334

Ahlstrom, Sydney E., 43

Albert, Phyllis Cohen: *Modernization of French Jewry: Consistory and Community in the Nineteenth Century,* 323n

Allport, Gordon, 81; *Nature of Prejudice, The,* 81n

Ambiguities: in belief, knowledge, 50–52, 156n, 360–362. *See also* Language, common usage

Ambrose, Saint, 289

Anglicans, 8, 182, 185, 312–313

Ankersmit, F. R.: *Knowing and Telling History,* 67n

Annan, Noel: *Leslie Stephen: The Godless Victorian,* 313n

Anselm, Saint, 291n

Anti-Christianity, 222

Anti-Judaism: antisemitism and, 23–41, 275–305, 341–346, 366–368

Antisemitism: anti-Judaism and, 23–41, 275–305, 341–346, 366–368; appearance of term, 71; as concept, 64; defined, 275, 366–367; explaining (formation, history/religious, Christian roots of), 7–17, 18–41, 67–68, 146, 275–368; outside Christianity source of, 30, 31; physiocentric, 318–346; re-

thinking problem of, 15–17. *See also* Aryanism; Hitler; Nazism

Apologetics, 34

Aquinas, Thomas, 126, 152, 170, 196, 239n, 251n, 261, 288

Arendt, Hannah, 10, 24, 34, 205n, 276; *Origins of Totalitarianism, The,* 10n, 24n

Arkel, Dirk van: *Antisemitism in Austria,* 325n

Artificial intelligence, 152

Aryanism, 10, 19–20, 43, 121–122, 223, 224, 225, 231, 336, 341–346

Assertions (assumptions), 3, 47, 63, 92–99 passim, 104, 135, 143–146, 147, 221–222, 355, 358, 361

Atheism: Darwin and, 331–332; history of, 223, 309–311; increases in, 329–334; symbols of, 334–335

Attribution (theory, process), 81–82, 229, 261n

Augustine of Hippo, 143, 194, 196–198, 226, 287, 289; *City of God,* 294; *Confessions,* 194, 196

Aurelius, Marcus, 196

Auschwitz. *See* Hitler

Austria, 322–323, 325, 328

Austro-Hungarian Empire, 217, 322–326

Authorities (religious), 137–139, 175n, 185, 258, 282. *See also* Popes

Autobiography of Malcolm X, 244n

Averroes, 229n

Awe (concept of), 69, 74, 75, 78, 83, 84, 115–116, 117

Axioms, 89

Designer: U.C. Press Staff
Compositor: Auto-Graphics, Inc.
Printer: Edwards Bros., Inc.
Binder: Edwards Bros., Inc.
Text: 11/13 Caledonia
Display: Caledonia